A Field Guide to the Poetry of Theodore Roethke

A FIELD GUIDE TO THE POETRY OF THEODORE ROETHKE

Edited by WILLIAM BARILLAS

Foreword by EDWARD HIRSCH

SWALLOW PRESS / OHIO UNIVERSITY PRESS
ATHENS

Swallow Press
An imprint of Ohio University Press, Athens, Ohio 45701
ohioswallow.com

Printed in the United States of America
Swallow Press / Ohio University Press books are printed on acid-free paper ∞ ™

31 30 29 28 27 26 25 24 23 22 21 5 4 3 2 1

Library of Congress Cataloging-in-Publication Data

Names: Barillas, William David, editor. | Hirsch, Edward, writer of foreword.
Title: A field guide to the poetry of Theodore Roethke / edited by William Barillas ; foreword by Edward Hirsch.
Description: Athens : Swallow Press/Ohio University Press, [2021] | Includes bibliographical references and index.
Identifiers: LCCN 2020036861 (print) | LCCN 2020036862 (ebook) | ISBN 9780804012317 (paperback ; acid-free paper) | ISBN 9780804041164 (pdf)
Subjects: LCSH: Roethke, Theodore, 1908-1963--Criticism and interpretation.
Classification: LCC PS3535.O39 Z628 2021 (print) | LCC PS3535.O39 (ebook) | DDC 811/.52--dc23
LC record available at https://lccn.loc.gov/2020036861
LC ebook record available at https://lccn.loc.gov/2020036862

Para María,

el amor de mi vida

I believe that, as time passes, and as factions perish and seas move and all the rest that dies and dies forever is forgotten, some of Roethke's poems will remain among all our priceless things. And it is only the true criticism, the honorable effort of our very best intellectual attention, that can clarify for us what there is of immortal and mountainously enduring in Roethke's art.

—James Wright

Contents

Contents

Foreword

Theodore Roethke moved among the mysteries. He celebrated and moralized the American landscape, schooled his spirit in the greenhouse and the marshland, and transformed himself into a major Romantic poet. His work, which began in Michigan, ended up embracing all North America. He was a mid-century American poet, a key figure in the so-called Middle Generation, who worked himself free of the straitjacket of American poetry in the forties and fifties. He worked against the grain. It is a marvel how he managed to inherit and extend the Romantic tradition of W. B. Yeats, Wallace Stevens, and Hart Crane, and belongs to that visionary company.

Roethke is much more than the few key anthology pieces by which he is mostly known. His large, multitudinous body of work, while never out of print, has somehow gotten lost in the past decades. *A Field Guide to the Poetry of Theodore Roethke*, expertly edited by William Barillas, should help rectify that odd neglect. It puts his work in perspective. We think of a field guide as a manual to help us identify things in their natural environments and, by association, that's precisely what this collection does for Roethke's poetry, which is itself so indebted to the natural world. It helps us to identify and recognize Roethke's work in its native habitat.

As a poet, Roethke worked by pressurizing sound—his language was often ahead of his thought and he loved to be carried away. Always, he courted the strange, the uncanny, the irrational. He constructed himself poem by poem, sequence by sequence, book by book. Each essay in this book carefully helps to illuminate the work of a poet who threw himself into the natural world, who stood up for the most vulnerable creatures alive, and wandered the fair fields. This guidebook leads us down the different pathways of his imagination. It enables us to see him whole.

Edward Hirsch

Preface

This book, as its title suggests, was created as a companion to the poetry of American poet Theodore Roethke (1908–1963). Forty-four essays about representative poems, sequenced in the order of the poems' appearance in Roethke's *Collected Poems,* provide brief explications that illuminate Roethke's poetics, themes, and biographical, historical, cultural, and literary contexts.[1] The essays need not be read in sequence; they may be consulted as one leafs through field guides to birds, mammals, flowers, trees, or rocks, seeking a clear picture of a particular subject. Consultation, rather than continuity, is the principle at play. In addition to formalist close reading, contributors employ a number of critical approaches, including ecocriticism (Aaron Moe, for example, on "The Pike," and Bernard Quetchenbach on "The Far Field"), feminist criticism (Marcia Noe and Laura Duncan on "Frau Bauman, Frau Schmidt, and Frau Schwartze"), and reader-response (Carrie Duke on "Transplanting" and Jeff Vande Zande on "Otto"). Many of the authors have previously published scholarly articles on Roethke, and seven have published books on the poet: Peter Balakian, Don Bogen, Neal Bowers, Norman Chaney, William Heyen, Walter Kalaidjian, and Jay Parini. In the small world of Roethke scholarship, they are the stars, and their contributions to this book provide welcome postscripts to their earlier work.

Essays in this book are organized into sections focused on Roethke's individual volumes. Roethke published seven books of poetry during his lifetime: *Open House* (1941), *The Lost Son and Other Poems* (1948), *Praise to the End!* (1951), *The Waking* (1953), *Words for the Wind* (1958), and *I Am! Says the Lamb* (children's poems; 1961). At the time of his death in 1963, he was preparing *The Far Field* (1964). Only that final, posthumous volume and the first two are full-length collections of new poetry written for adults. *Praise to the End!* collects and extends the Lost Son sequence begun in *The Lost Son*, and both *The Waking* and *Words for the Wind* are volumes of collected and new poems. *The Collected Poems of Theodore Roethke* appeared in hardcover in 1966, featuring all of the poems from the previous books, along with a section of "Previously Uncollected Poems." The 1975 paperback edition of *The Collected Poems* has slightly different pagination. Because it is the version still in print, the present book cites it in all cases.

Roethke's poetry evolved over time, advancing through a series of stylistic phases. The formalism and metaphysical abstraction that characterize much of his first book gave way to the wildly original psychic autobiography of the free verse "greenhouse poems" and Lost Son sequence, followed by the heightened formalism, some of it strongly influenced by Yeats, of his midcareer work. His later poetry continued shifting between free verse and poetry in meter and rhyme, while adding a new approach, a long, descriptive, and meditative line inspired by Whitman and Eliot. Although some critics have charged Roethke with inconsistency not only in style but also in quality, with some suggesting that his later work is too derivative of earlier poets, the scholars in this book make a case for Roethke's poetry as a complete and unified body of work that acquired new qualities and values as his career progressed. The poet's range and progression lend themselves to, and even necessitate, the wide variety of theoretical approaches taken in the present volume. That the essays shift from one perspective to another reflects the complexity and multivalence of the poetry. Contributors are exploring a poetic landscape with features as varied as the actual territories of Roethke's life, from the Michigan of his youth to the Pacific Northwest of his last years, both of which provided imagery and themes for some of his greatest poems. The essays are by authors with divergent perspectives, concerns, and styles, a diversity that underscores this book's contribution to Roethke studies.

NOTE

1. Most of the essays in this book have as their subject a single poem. Three diverge from that pattern, as discussed below.

Michael Hinds's essay deals with both "Cuttings" and "Cuttings (*later*)," the first two poems in Roethke's second book, *The Lost Son and Other Poems* (1948). The two exist symbiotically, as if the second poem is a revision of the first, or a commentary on it.

Adam Putz focuses on "The Dance," the first part of "Four for Sir John Davies," which functions differently from Roethke's other long poems with numbered parts. While "The Lost Son," for example, is quite unified as a single poem, "Four for Sir John Davies" consists of four poems, as suggested by its title. The four are only marginally more integrated than the separate poems in Roethke's sequences, such as "North American Sequence." They have been previously approached by scholars both individually and as a single long poem.

Joseph T. Thomas Jr.'s essay draws wider conclusions about Roethke's poetry for children by focusing on three poems about a pair of anthropomorphic turtles, Myrtle and her cousin. The "Myrtle" poems, as Thomas points out, constitute Roethke's only grouping of poems for children.

Acknowledgments

I wish to thank the contributors for their excellent work as well as their patience during the editing process. Corresponding and collaborating with them has been a distinct pleasure.

My gratitude also extends to the staff at Ohio University Press, some of whom also had a hand in the publication of my 2006 book, *The Midwestern Pastoral: Place and Landscape in Literature of the American Heartland.* Tyler Balli, Ricky Huard, and Beth Pratt have been my correspondents and advocates throughout the process.

Philip A. Greasley provided vigorous, thorough critiques of the preface and introduction in draft, for which Luke Brekke, María Ghiggia, Marcia Noe, Peter Brock Olson, and Rod Phillips also shared helpful insights and suggestions. Anonymous readers for Ohio University Press assisted in the final polishing of the manuscript, and John Morris did outstanding work as copyeditor.

The cover art is a detail from *Autumnal,* a wood engraving by Wisconsin artist Tony Drehfal. Marked at once by clarity and a sense of nature's dark mysteries in the upper Midwest, Drehfal's rendering of oak branches calls to mind Roethke's early poem "The Coming of the Cold," as well as a line from "The Longing": "A leaf, I would love the leaves, delighting in the redolent disorder of this mortal life" (*Collected Poems,* 182).

Poet Edward Hirsch's foreword establishes the tone and spirit of this book. My gratitude for this gift, as well as for Dr. Hirsch's poetry and lifelong advocacy for poetry, runs deep.

Three essays in this book have seen previous publication, including two by William Barillas: "Meter in 'My Papa's Waltz'" appeared in *The Explicator* 73, no. 1 (January–March 2015): 9–12; "'Once More, the Round': Roethke's Last Word" appeared in *MidAmerica* 43 (2016): 14–28. "The Visitant" by Camille Paglia was one of three explications of poems by Roethke in *Break, Blow, Burn: Camille Paglia Reads Forty-three of the World's Best Poems,* copyright © 2005 by Camille Paglia. Used by permission of Pantheon Books, an imprint of the Knopf Doubleday Publishing Group, a division of Penguin Random House LLC. All rights reserved.

A Field Guide to the Poetry of Theodore Roethke

House, Field, Stones, and Stars

An Introduction

WILLIAM BARILLAS

> A house for wisdom; a field for revelation.
> Speak to the stones, and the stars answer.
>
> —Theodore Roethke, "Unfold! Unfold!"

THERE IS in American literature a tradition of wisdom writing: poetry that speaks to eternity in the present moment, and sacredness in our places on earth. It constitutes a secular scripture, with Emerson, Whitman, and Dickinson as its chief prophets and a number of later poets as their apostles, or at least as occasional mystics contributing verses to the book of time. Some of this writing corresponds to what translator Stephen Mitchell calls "poems of fulfillment," created by men and women who seek to inhabit the center of things, "which is called God in Jewish, Christian, and Moslem cultures, and Tao, Self, or Buddha in the great Eastern traditions": "Sitting or dancing, all of these poets have found themselves inside the circle—some of them a step within the circumference, some far in, some at dead center. Looking out from the center, you can talk about the circumference. But really, there is no circumference. Everyone, everything, is joyfully included" (*Enlightened Heart,* v). This mystical, participatory spirit is strongly evident in poets who respond to the natural world. Robinson Jeffers, James Wright, Mary Oliver, Jim Harrison, Pattiann Rogers, and others follow Emerson in expressing "an original relation to the universe" in "poetry . . . of insight" that results from being "[e]mbosomed for a season in nature" (7). As ecocritic Bernard Quetchenbach says of Robert Bly, Gary Snyder, and Wendell Berry, such poets "communicate what is essentially a privately held faith in the 'meaning' of the natural world . . . through contemporary poetry, a vehicle designed more for introspection and individual experience than for public and shared values" (xi).

Among mid-twentieth-century American poets, Theodore Roethke epitomizes this spiritual tradition. Jay Parini, one of Roethke's best readers, identifies him as "the central American Romantic poet of [his] generation . . . the celebrant of a uniquely American nature, a Romantic [in] the Emersonian tradition" (15) whose "poetry is secular religion" (36–37). Roethke's biographer Allan Seager elaborates: "He was a religious man, but he was not concerned with sin . . . nor was he much interested in being his brother's keeper. . . . Rather, he was troubled about the nature of God, not necessarily a Christian God, his own relation to Him, and his relationship to what he believed to be God's primary creation, nature" (225). For Roethke, all of nature is conscious and endowed with spirit or soul, particularly plants and animals, who figure in his poems as companions and spirit guides. He emphasizes this faith in his essay "On Identity": "If the dead can come to our aid in a quest for identity, so can the living—and I mean *all* living things. . . . This is not so much a naïve as a primitive attitude: animist, maybe. Why not? Everything that lives is holy: I call upon these holy forms of life" (*On Poetry and Craft,* 40).

Roethke's totems include flowers grown by his florist father, memorably evoked in the famous "greenhouse poems" that begin his second book, *The Lost Son and Other Poems.* Orchids, chrysanthemums, azaleas, carnations, tulips, roses, and many other flowers bloom there, remembered by Roethke as mysterious beings resembling small animals or children. His life force and theirs are one and same, reaching downward into the soil and upward to the sun. Thinking about being lifted by his father above the roses "in the wide six-hundred-foot greenhouse," Roethke recalls an early experience of transcendence, "how those flowerheads seemed to flow toward me, to beckon me, only a child, out of myself" (*Collected Poems,* 197). That mystical fellow feeling also attends general references to birds, fish, and other animals, as well as appearances of particular species, in Roethke's poems. Roethke wrote many poems titled after their animal subjects, including "The Bat," "The Swan," "Snake," "Slug," "The Pike," and "The Meadow Mouse." He emphasizes the singular and the *small,* a word that Roethke employs more often than any other adjective.[1] Whereas nineteenth-century poets and painters found the sublime in mountains, storms, waterfalls, and other grand spectacles, Roethke "woo[s] the fearful small" (*Collected Poems,* 142), elements of nature that he also calls "lovely diminutives" (60) and, in the title of one poem, "The Minimal." The fish most frequently appearing in Roethke's poetry is the minnow; other characteristic images include pebbles, sticks, moss, and invertebrates like the "lowly worm" that "climbs up a winding stair" in his great villanelle "The Waking" (104). The worm's ascent symbolizes the unification of body and spirit, space and time, the present moment and eternity. Likewise, Roethke confesses in "On Identity" that "in calling upon the snail, I am calling, in a sense, upon God" (*On Poetry and Craft*, 40).

As a way to frame the essays collected in this volume, this introduction centers on Roethke's poetry as spiritual expression, considering the circumstances of its inspiration, production, and legacy among readers, scholars, and subsequent poets. I first establish the autobiographical basis of Roethke's work in a brief biographical sketch. Then I turn to the nature and evolution of Roethke's poetry as seen in each of his books, summarizing themes and stylistic changes and noting key poems and poetic sequences. While providing an interpretive time line of Roethke's publishing history, I comment on certain poems covered in this volume, emphasizing their significance to the books in which they appear and to Roethke's career in general. In some cases I refer to contributors by name and touch on their critical perspectives. My next topic, Roethke's influence on later poets and his elevation into the canon of twentieth-century American literature, leads into a review of one of the main critical debates over Roethke's work: whether his late poetry continued to develop in quality and insight or weakened and became derivative. The discussion then shifts to the fortunes of scholarly production on Roethke—especially the publication of books, which began in the 1960s, accelerated in the 1970s, peaked in the 1980s, declined in the 1990s, and stopped entirely thereafter. After identifying signs of renewed interest in the new century, this introduction concludes by indicating possible directions for future Roethke studies.

Roethke's mysticism was rooted in his personal origins and experience, particularly the circumstances of his childhood, a central subject of the poems that established his place in literary history. He was born and grew up in Saginaw, Michigan, a former lumber town then becoming a center for light industry and agricultural processing. His German-born parents, Otto and Helen Roethke, operated a florist business, one of the largest in the Midwest, consisting of twenty-five acres, with about a quarter of that area under glass. "[I]t had its own ice-house," Roethke wrote, with more than a little pride,

> a small game preserve, and the last stand of virgin timber in the Saginaw Valley (mostly walnut and oak—not pine). . . .
>
> As a child I heard Europeans, Dutchmen and Belgians, say repeatedly it was the most beautiful greenhouse in America. My father specialized in roses and orchids particularly. (qtd. in Seager, 12–13)

While Otto directly appears in only seven poems ("Premonition," "Old Florist," "My Papa's Waltz," "The Lost Son," "Where Knock Is Open Wide," "The Rose," and "Otto"), his presence is felt in all of Roethke's work. Otto grew flowers; Theodore Roethke wrote about them, or more generally about the vital essence they represent. Capable of both delicacy and harshness, Otto modeled for his son an approach to art, one that accepts that "[h]e who loves the small can be both saint and boor," as Roethke wrote in his tribute poem "Otto":

> A florist does not woo the beautiful:
> He potted plants as if he hated them.
> What root of his ever denied its stem?
> When flowers grew, their bloom extended him.
>
> (*Collected Poems,* 216)

The Freudian cast of so much of Roethke's work is unmistakable here: the father is the root, and the son—the poet—is the stem. As much as the great Romantic and modernist poets, Otto Roethke figured as both competition and inspiration for his son. "One dares to stand up to a great style, to compete with papa," Roethke wrote in his essay "How to Write Like Somebody Else" (*On Poetry and Craft,* 62). The immediate reference here is to major influences like Yeats, Hopkins, Eliot, and Auden, and to lesser-known figures who left a powerful impression on Roethke's early work, Elinor Wylie and Léonie Adams. Roethke imitated Adams in one poem, because, as he wrote, "I loved her so much, her poetry, that I just *had* to become, for a brief moment, a part of her world. For it *is* her world, and I had filled myself with it, and I *had* to create something that would honor her in her own terms" (*On Poetry and Craft,* 59). He could have said much the same of his poetry in regard to his father's work as a florist.

The relation between Roethke's work, his spirituality, and the figure of his father was shaped, tragically, by Otto's death of cancer when the future poet was fourteen. The family was already reeling from the recent suicide of Otto's brother Carl, who had lived next door and had kept the Roethke company books. Seager tells us that on the day of Otto's funeral, Roethke "took his father's place at the head of the table and he sat there from that day on": "Once the numbness of shock had worn away, it must have seemed to Ted that the stays and props of his whole life were broken. In the space of three months, the greenhouse was gone, his uncle was gone, his father was gone. The stage where he had played out his childhood was no longer his. . . . [W]hat he lost when the dirt fell in in his father's grave was going to take him the rest of his life to learn" (43). Roethke lost what he perceived to be the unified selfhood of his childhood, which was inseparable from the greenhouses and his father's commanding presence. As the title poem of his second book has it, he felt himself to be "The Lost Son," forever separated from the boy he had been, peering out his bedroom window over "those fields of glass," as he calls the greenhouses in "Otto." He remained in some sense that

> sleepless child
> Watching the waking of my father's world.—
> O world so far away! O my lost world!
>
> (*Collected Poems,* 217)

By elegizing the greenhouse world, Roethke sought to transform his grief, reconstructing the greenhouses by means of the imagination.

Roethke discovered his calling in college and, like many later American poets, sustained it in an academic career. He earned his bachelor's and master's degrees at the University of Michigan, where he also briefly studied law. Subsequent legal studies at Harvard confirmed his unsuitability for the bar, so as the Great Depression worsened in 1931, he accepted a job teaching English at Lafayette College in Easton, Pennsylvania, where he taught for four years. He thereafter taught part of a semester (fall 1935) at Michigan State University, followed by seven years at Penn State (1936–1943), four years at Bennington College (1943–1947), and the remainder of his career—and his life—at the University of Washington (1947–1963). By all accounts an inspiring if unorthodox instructor, Roethke pioneered the teaching of creative writing, in his case poetry, in the college setting. His best-known students included poets Tess Gallagher, Richard Hugo, Carolyn Kizer, David Wagoner, James Wright, and Duane Niatum, and composer William Bolcom, who has set several of Roethke's poems to music. Despite the demands on his time and energy posed by his work as a professor, Roethke wrote continually, maintaining voluminous journals and crafting the poetry that would earn him the Pulitzer Prize, the National Book Award, and many other honors.

As for Roethke's personal life, the crucial fact was his mental illness, knowledge of which bears significantly on the reading and analysis of his poetry. Roethke suffered from bipolar disorder complicated by alcoholism, with severe attacks of mania that required sedation and extended hospital stays. His working methods may have precipitated those episodes; Seager suggests that Roethke partly brought them on himself in a search for mystical insight and poetic expression. The attacks also related to unresolved grief and irrational guilt over his father's premature death, and a deep insecurity about his calling as a poet and his very self-worth:

> His father's death was the most important thing that ever happened to him. . . . The love and fear he felt for Otto Roethke were the deepest emotions he ever had and his complex feelings for nature were tied to his father, almost as if Otto working Ted in the greenhouse and taking him fishing and for long walks in the woods, had created the woods, the lakes, and the carnations. . . .
>
> . . . If, when Ted received praise or awards, he suffered privately because he did not think he deserved them, the suffering may have come from a fear that his father would have disapproved. . . .
>
> . . . If he were to justify himself before his father, he would have had to re-create the world of woods and greenhouse his father had made for him (if only to show he could do it, to make himself equal). (104–5)

In public—as a professor, as a writer meeting editors, readers, and other writers, seeking publication, book sales, prizes, speaking invitations, and critical acclaim—Roethke dealt with his anxieties by assuming the persona of a "tough guy," aficionado of professional boxing and purported friend to gangsters.[2] In his poetry, he portrayed himself as "the Lost Son," a troubled, grief-stricken seeker after identity, transcendence, and oneness with the natural world. Roethke's poetry, according to Karl Malkoff, "alternates between extreme joy at the miracle of his existence, and unendurable anxiety at the thought of its tenuousness." From first book to last, Roethke's poetry constitutes what Malkoff calls a "spiritual autobiography" (220), or, as Neal Bowers describes it, an "extraordinary unity . . . a journal, the record of a man's attempt to discover his identity and his place in existence" (2).

In 1955, fourteen years after the publication of his first book, *Open House,* Roethke wrote, "It took me ten years to complete one little book, and now some of the things in it seem to creak. Still, I like about ten pieces in it" (*On Poetry and Craft,* 29). His self-assessment is accurate. Most of the poems in the volume (many of which first appeared in prestigious publications like *Poetry, The Atlantic,* and *The New Yorker*) are apprentice pieces, metaphysical musings striving to evince a wisdom and wit beyond the poet's actual reach at the time. Even when virtuosic, they are derivative of the poets Roethke was reading. Walter Kalaidjian has listed them for us: "John Donne and William Blake . . . Léonie Adams, Louise Bogan, Emily Dickinson, Rolfe Humphries, Stanley Kunitz, and Elinor Wylie." (Humphries and Kunitz became friends and mentors to Roethke, and Bogan, briefly, his lover.) "Moreover," Kalaidjian continues, "the whole book is dominated by the kind of formal craft and metaphysical irony then prized by American New Criticism" (30). Such is the case with the book's title poem, adroitly explicated in the present volume by Brandon Rushton. "Open House," as Kalaidjian observes, "satisfied New Criticism's criterion of formal craft in the 1940s." At the same time, the poem "anticipates the unfolding drama of the self in quest of identity, a key theme that profoundly shapes the poet's entire career," clearly a departure "from modernist doctrines of impersonality" (33). Confessional poetry is anticipated here, the work of twentieth-century Americans who took as their main subject their own lives and emotional suffering, among them Robert Lowell, John Berryman, Anne Sexton, and Sylvia Plath. "Open House," however, offers neither narrative nor imagery beyond metaphysical conceits: "I'm naked to the bone," Roethke declares, "With nakedness my shield" (*Collected Poems,* 3). That insistence on revelation and truth-telling would become a hallmark of Roethke's mature verse.

A few poems in *Open House* figure significantly in Roethke's oeuvre both for their own merits and for the ways in which they anticipate his mature work. Marked by vivid imagery, grounding in place, and use of sound devices and rhythm to convey bodily experience, a handful are treated here: the landscape poems "The Light Comes Brighter," "Interlude," "Highway: Michigan," and "Night Journey," the last a textbook favorite. Poet and anthologist William Heyen contributes a creative piece, addressed to Roethke, on "To My Sister," one of the autobiographical poems in *Open House.* Like "The Premonition" and "On the Road to Woodlawn," which allude to his father's life and death, "To My Sister" focuses on the poet's family and early life in Saginaw. Roethke's

Lost Son persona tentatively emerges in these poems, among the best in this initial collection.

By wide consensus, Roethke's second book, *The Lost Son and Other Poems* (1948), is his greatest work. One of the words most often used to describe *The Lost Son* is "breakthrough." Kenneth Burke, who befriended Roethke at Bennington College when he was working on the poems, and who wrote the first extended analysis of his work (1950's "The Vegetal Radicalism of Theodore Roethke"), later described the production of this book as a "sudden, exceptionally beautiful breakthrough" ("Cult of the Breakthrough," 25). More recently, Edward Hirsch has asserted that "the greatest single moment in [Roethke's] writing life was the breakthrough from the abstract strictures of his early manner into the textured free verse of his second collection" (xviii). *The Lost Son* is the volume around which the rest of Roethke's work must be read. Here his influences have been integrated and absorbed—the Romantic nature mysticism of Wordsworth and Whitman, the modernist precision and clarity of William Carlos Williams (another friend and mentor during Roethke's Bennington period), the rhythm and wordplay of Mother Goose, Freudian and Jungian psychological theory—in a surprising and original way. An archetypal exploration of the unconscious mind, expressed in striking, palpable language, *The Lost Son* is one of the most influential and critically acclaimed volumes of twentieth-century American poetry.

Roethke organized the book into four sections, the first of which presents what have become known as the "greenhouse poems." Peter Balakian aptly describes these as advancing "a creation myth" that follows "a torturous journey in which the poet moves from darkness to light, charting . . . the development of his consciousness . . . moving from the loamy, procreant earth to the light on top of the greenhouse" (49). Organic growth in these poems parallels the development of a child's mind and the creative process entailed in poetry, which Roethke later described as "shot through with appeals to the unconsciousness, to the fears and desires that go far back into our childhood, into the imagination of the race" (*On Poetry and Craft,* 70). Kalaidjian points to "Roethke's stylistic use of hyphenation, irregular strong-stress rhythms, and colloquial diction" as key to this effect, with many monosyllabic words of Anglo-Saxon or Germanic origin, and phrasing connoting sexuality and birth. The reader perceives Otto's greenhouses, the loamy soil, the roots and shoots, and the work that went into producing the luminous beauty of his father's flowers, through a child's eyes as well as through the filter of memory and contemplation. In the fourteen greenhouse poems, nine of which are explicated here, Roethke presents nature not as sweetly pastoral but as strange, eerily conscious, and at times frightening. Beginning, as he put it in his essay "Open Letter," "in the mire; as if man is no more than a shape writing from the old rock," Roethke launches into the journey of all his subsequent poetry by means of regression and descent: "I believe to go forward as a spiritual man it is necessary first to go back. Any history of the psyche (or allegorical journey) is bound to be a succession of experiences, similar yet dissimilar. There is a perpetual slipping-back, then a going-forward; but there is *some* 'progress'" (*On Poetry and Craft,* 51).

The second and third sections of *The Lost Son* feature a variety of short lyrics, with those in the former group largely set indoors, in the social world: at a cinema in "Double Feature," for example, and in the Heinz Company plant in Saginaw where he worked as a teenager in "Pickle Belt." The poem "Dolor," taken up in these pages by Luke Brekke, evokes the dehumanizing office spaces Roethke knew from his life in academia. He also recalls himself at about age five, roughhousing in the kitchen with his father, in "My Papa's Waltz." Familiar from anthologies and textbooks, this popular favorite suggests oedipal struggle as well as affection and joy shared by the Prussian perfectionist father and his young son. "My Papa's Waltz" is a marvel of narrative concision that employs connotatively rich word choice and, as I demonstrate in my essay on the poem, metrical subtleties to signal the physicality of the dance and the poet's complicated feelings about his father. The short lyrics in part 3 continue the archetypal approach introduced in the greenhouse poems, whereby Roethke simultaneously looks out to the natural world and into his own mind. In "Night Crow," explicated here by Sarah Kathryn Moore, he recalls how the sight of a "clumsy crow / Flap[ping] from a wasted tree" provoked a vision of a

> tremendous bird
> . . . .
> Deep in the brain, far back.
>
> (*Collected Poems,* 47)

The book's fourth and final sequence begins with the book's title poem, a symbolic narrative of a spiritual and psychological crisis taking place partly in Saginaw, past and present, but mainly in the poet's mind. The action in "The

Lost Son" recalls Roethke's first major manic episode, which occurred in East Lansing, Michigan, in 1935. The thrust of the poem, however, and that of the subsequent poems in the sequence, is mythological. As Jay Parini points out, the "images of the greenhouse, the father-florist, and the open field come directly from his personal experience. Yet these personal images take on greater meaning when framed by a mythic pattern," in particular, "the initiatory journey, a rite of passage" (85). The protagonist in "The Lost Son" endures an archetypal dark night of the soul, descending into a landscape of fear and disintegration in which the death of Roethke's father is unmentioned but inferred. The familiar spirit guides, small animals and other elements of nature, appear unable or unwilling to answer the speaker's supplication:

> Snail, snail, glister me forward,
> Bird, soft-sigh me home,
> Worm, be with me.
> This is my hard time.
>
> (*Collected Poems,* 50)

While detailed discussion of "The Lost Son" in this book will be left to Borja Aguiló Obrador, it should be noted that this important poem establishes the pattern for the entire Lost Son sequence, also represented here in Jeffrey Clapp's explication of "A Field of Light." The pattern is one of private references rather than a collective or traditional set of symbolic images: a descent into the unconscious mind and a psychic crisis, followed by movement upward to the light. Images of morning in the greenhouses indicate a return to consensual reality in the last two sections of "The Lost Son." In "A Field of Light," creatures and plants announce that return, "lovely diminutives" of nature offering at last a sense of hope and reciprocity:

> I could watch! I could watch!
> I saw the separateness of all things!
> My heart lifted up with the great grasses;
> The weeds believed me, and the nesting birds.
> . . . .
> The worms were delighted as wrens.
> And I walked, I walked through the light air;
> I moved with the morning.
>
> (*Collected Poems,* 60)

The Lost Son poems begin, as Roethke says in "Open Letter," in "the marsh, the mire, the Void," but achieve conciliation and reintegration with the world: "in spite of all the muck and welter, the dark, the *dreck* of these poems, I count myself among the happy poets" (*On Poetry and Craft*, 52).

Roethke's next book, *Praise to the End!* (1951), consists of an extended Lost Son sequence, beginning with six new poems in part 1, followed by the four poems from the last part of *The Lost Son and Other Poems* and then three more new poems in part 2. The new poems continue Roethke's experimentation with "language that appeals more to the intuition than to the intellect . . . deliberately confounding our analytical minds with unanswerable questions" (Bowers, 104). They delve into the unconscious mind with startling, sometimes nonsensical passages, inspired according to Roethke by "German and English folk literature, particularly Mother Goose; Elizabethan and Jacobean drama, especially the songs and rants; the Bible; Blake and Traherne; Dürer" (*On Poetry and Craft*, 52–53). Two poems in part 1, "Where Knock Is Open Wide" and "I Need, I Need," are partly spoken from Roethke's perspective as a child. The first, considered here by celebrated contemporary poet David Wojahn, touches on the suicide of Roethke's Uncle Carl as well as Otto's skills as a florist and as an outdoorsman. In his essay on "Give Way, Ye Gates," Pulitzer Prize–winning poet Peter Balakian discusses that poem's role in the Lost Son sequence, or as Balakian prefers to call it, the Praise to the End! sequence. Roethke concluded the sequence with a fourteenth poem, "O, Thou Opening, O" from *The Waking* (1953), which can be said to have completed the most radical, innovative period of Roethke's career.

The Waking, which won the Pulitzer Prize for Poetry, offered new poems that document Roethke's transition from experimentalism to a renewed focus on traditional meter and rhyme. The former impulse is expressed in poems like "The Visitant," the subject of an explication, reprinted here, from Camille Paglia's book *Break, Blow, Burn;* "A Light Breather," with its familiar representation of the "spirit" in images of a blossom, a minnow, and a snail; and "Elegy for Jane," one of Roethke's most famous poems, a lament for a student of his who died in a horse-riding accident. After that poem, discussed in these pages by David Radavich, and "Old Lady's Winter Words," two poems mark Roethke's turn to formalism: "Four for Sir John Davies" and "The Waking." The first is a group of four semi-independent love poems in iambic pentameter that speak to poetry, as Jenijoy La Belle puts it, as "a combination of the individual creative choices of the artist and of the inherited traditions of linguistic and poetic forms" (108). Adam Putz here treats the first poem, "The Dance," with its signal line: "I take this cadence from a man named Yeats" (*Collected Poems,* 101). Finally, the title poem of *The Waking* articulates the essence of Roethke's vision of life as a quest for unity with the mysterious order of nature, knowable only through intuition and experience. In his essay for this volume, Frank J. Kearful provides new insights into "The Waking," probably the best-loved villanelle in American literature and a prime example of Roethke's mastery of traditional poetic form.

That mastery is on full display in the new poems in *Words for the Wind: The Collected Verse of Theodore Roethke* (1958), especially the reverent, grateful, and sometimes humorous love poems. Written following his marriage in 1953 to former student Beatrice O'Connell, these verses treat consummate love as a transformation of self, both physical and spiritual. They place Roethke's prosodic skills on full display, as with the sensitive—and frequent—use of slant rhyme (tongue / song, for example, from "She") and consonance, assonance, and alliteration (from the same stanza, "She makes space lonely with a lovely song. / She lilts a low soft language, and I hear / Down long sea-chambers of the inner ear") (*Collected Poems,* 124). The love poems are represented here by "Words for the Wind," explicated by Andrew David King, and "I Knew a Woman," parsed by distinguished poet, novelist, biographer, and critic Jay Parini, author of the much-cited study *Theodore Roethke: An American Romantic* (1979).

The free-verse poems in *Words for the Wind* provide thematic and formal continuity between Roethke's earlier and subsequent work, with their treatment of animals and landscapes both actual and symbolic. In his essay on "First Meditation," written for this book, Don Bogen demonstrates how this first of five "Meditations of an Old Woman" presages the "North American Sequence" in Roethke's next and final book, the posthumously published *The Far Field.* Based on Roethke's mother, the speaker in these poems tells of journeys across North America and "into the waste lonely places / Behind the eye; the lost acres at the edge of smoky cities" (*Collected Poems,* 153). The greenhouses are remembered, and a new empathy emerges, a concern for people alienated from others, from themselves, and from nature in the modern industrial world. In the "Fourth Meditation," for example, the Old Woman cries,

> How I wish them awake!
> May the high flower of the hay climb into their hearts;
> May they lean into light and live.
>
> (*Collected Poems,* 163)

Roethke begins in these poems to relate the individual's spiritual quest to social (dis)order and the destruction of the natural environment.

During his last years, Roethke published *I Am! Says the Lamb* (1961), his book of children's poetry, discussed here by Joseph T. Thomas Jr. in his essay on "Myrtle" and two related poems. He also labored over his last poems and their arrangement in what would become *The Far Field.* Roethke seems to have had a presentiment of his impending death at age fifty-five. "As the fabric of his body begins to give way," Seager writes, "the best part of his mind, his poetry . . . strives toward a mystical union with his Father. . . . [T]he last poems seem prophetic; they read like last poems" (251). He continued to write love poems inspired by his wife Beatrice; transcendentalist nature poems about landscapes, plants, and animals; and poems about the journey through darkness, despair, and disintegration in search of reconciliation: "A fallen man, I climb out of my fear" (*Collected Poems,* 231). "[T]here is no real departure in subject matter," Parini notes; "the myth of the lost son, with its personal symbology, is once again rehearsed. It is also extended. The long journey out of the self is, Roethke would have us believe, accomplished" (161). Both in loose, confident free verse and in some of his best poems in rhyme and meter, Roethke glances back one last time at childhood and his psychological and spiritual struggles, and turns forward to "rehearse" himself for the "stand at the stretch in the face of death" like "a blind man, lifting a curtain, [who] knows it is morning" (*Collected Poems,* 189).

The first section of *The Far Field* (1964) consists of "North American Sequence," six long meditations in free verse in which Roethke both celebrates the physical world and tries "to transcend this sensual emptiness" (*Collected Poems,* 181). Influenced by Whitman and the T. S. Eliot of *Four Quartets,* these poems employ long, descriptive lines that catalogue images of the Michigan of his youth—the greenhouses, fields, the Tittabawasee River, highways to the north—as well as the American West, and the Pacific Northwest of his later years, with its rocky ocean coasts. This "Journey to the Interior," as the title of one of the poems has it, takes the poet to the heart of the continent and out of his fears and doubts. He sets forth on a "long journey out of the self" in which there "are many detours, washed-out interrupted raw places" (*Collected Poems,* 187), but also places where Roethke says he "learned not to fear infinity, / The far field, the windy cliffs of forever" (194). The continued power of this sequence and, in this time of global environmental crisis, its urgent relevance commend the inclusion in this volume of essays on all six poems: "The Longing," "Meditation at Oyster River," "Journey to the Interior," "The Long Waters," "The Far Field," and "The Rose."

Essays in this book on other poems from *The Far Field,* both formalist and free verse, bring new insights to bear on Roethke's subjects and themes. These include Roethke's father in "Otto"; kinship with animals in "The Meadow Mouse" and "The Pike"; spiritual crisis and mystical perception in "The Abyss" and "In a Dark Time," one of Roethke's most compelling, durable poems; physical ailment and acceptance of death in "Infirmity"; and the poet's arrival at closure, completeness, and joy in "The Tree, the Bird" and "Once More, the Round." These last poems nod to Taoism and Buddhism, as in "The Abyss" when the speaker's "thought flies to the place by the bo-tree," the site of Gautama Buddha's enlightenment (*Collected Poems,* 214), and the moment remembered in "The Tree, The Bird," when he felt himself to be "a finger pointing at the moon" (240). The image comes from the Shurangama Sutra, an ancient Buddhist text, in which the finger stands for religious teaching that may point the way to truth but must not be confused with the truth itself, the ineffable but constant reality represented by the moon shining in the night sky.

That lesson concurs with Roethke's fundamentally Romantic mysticism, his belief in the primacy of individual experience over religious doctrine. As Emerson urged the Harvard Divinity School class of 1838, "Let me admonish you, first of all, to go alone; to refuse the good models, even those which are sacred to the imagination of men, and dare to love God without mediator or veil" (88–89). At the end of "The Rose" from "North American Sequence," Roethke remembers his father's greenhouses and "how those flowerheads seemed to flow toward me, to beckon me, only a child, out of myself." He concludes by asking, "What need for heaven, then, / With that man, and those roses?" (*Collected Poems,* 197). The quest for a firsthand glimpse of eternity on Earth, whether in a greenhouse or a "far field," or facing "the windy cliffs of forever," remains a consistent motif in Roethke's poetry from *Open House* to *The Far Field.* In his last poem, "Once More, the Round," the quest reaches its apotheosis in a moment accordant with Buddhist teachings about interdependence. Accompanied by nature's small beings, the speaker's "true self runs toward a Hill" where "everything comes to One, / As we dance on, dance on, dance on" (243).

When Roethke died in 1963 his reputation and influence were at a height. *The Far Field* received strong reviews and won the National Book Award. Many poets who emerged during the late 1950s and early 1960s found Roethke uniquely inspiring, including his friend and former student James Wright, who made a breakthrough of his own from formalism to free verse in his third book, *The Branch Will Not Break,* published the year Roethke died. Wright's new poems, like those of Robert Bly and other so-called Deep Image poets of the period, drew extensively from European and Latin American poets like Rilke, García Lorca, and Neruda. They also owe much to Roethke in their imagery, sense of place, and leaps of spiritual imagination—qualities highly valued by many young poets of the time.[3] Galway Kinnell spoke for many when describing himself as a young man in the early 1950s, looking for contemporary American poetry with which he could identify:

> I didn't find any living poets whose work I greatly admired until I ran across Theodore Roethke's poems. . . . [T]hey touched my own experience. I found it hard to understand the poems of John Berryman and John Crowe Ransom and R. P. Blackmur, people like that. Their poems seemed far fetched and ornate and intellectual and learned and polite, and not really like anything that I really wanted to do. Roethke's poetry seemed direct and forthright and full of real things. He was the only person I had encountered who seemed to relate to Whitman. (211–12)

Roethke has since been a poet's poet, praised in print by poets as different as Delmore Schwartz, William Stafford, Richard Wilbur, Richard Hugo, James Dickey, Gerald Stern, Donald Hall, Charles Wright, David Young, Jim Harrison, Seamus Heaney, Martha Collins, Robert Hass, David St. John, Edward Hirsch, Marianne Boruch, Joy Harjo, Mark Doty, and Sherman Alexie. Others have gone so far as to write poems about Roethke, including Stanley Kunitz, John Berryman, John Ciardi, Robert Lowell, Stanley Moss, Carolyn Kizer, David Wagoner, Richard Murphy, John Montague, Michael McClure, Keki Daruwalla, Duane Niatum, William Heyen, Charles Martin, Tess Gallagher, James Tate, Thomas Lynch, Laura Kasischke, and Elaine Feeney.[4] Peter Balakian, winner of the 2016 Pulitzer Prize for Poetry, calls Roethke "our first contemporary" (1), writing that Roethke "pioneered our first important postmodernist poems," having developed "a relationship between an idea of the transcendent, a modern notion of the natural world, and a concept of the contemporary human self" by which he "forged our first contemporary confessional persona" (12–13). It is difficult to imagine Sylvia Plath, Ted Hughes, and many other poets having developed as they did without the experimentalism, psychological daring, and fecund earthiness of Roethke's work. He was a pivotal figure in twentieth-century poetry, a member, along with Lorine Niedecker, Elizabeth Bishop, Robert Hayden, Robert Lowell, and others, of what scholars call the Middle Generation. Their work, according to Eric Haralson, "constitutes *the* center of twentieth-century American poetry—the bull's-eye, pulsing heart, eye of the storm (choose your metaphor)" (1). Like that of Lowell and the others, Roethke's work represented a transition from the high modernist cult of "impersonality" fostered by T. S. Eliot and Ezra Pound (and insisted upon by the New Critics of the 1940s and 1950s) to the autobiographical, frequently place-centered and visionary free verse of the 1960s and 1970s.

Roethke is also a well-read, much-loved poet, and his work appears in most college anthologies of twentieth-century American literature and many high school textbooks. Generations of students have read his best-known poems, including "Night Journey," "Big Wind," "The Waking," "Elegy for Jane," "In a Dark Time," and especially "My Papa's Waltz." *The Collected Poems of Theodore Roethke,* first published in hardcover in 1965, remains in print in paperback and can be found in most well-stocked bookstores and libraries. Given the limited, if constant, readership for poetry, Roethke's enduring presence in American literature and acknowledgment as an important poet—his place in the literary canon—are notable. To put it simply, Roethke is here to stay.

The history of scholarship on Roethke's work is another matter, roughly describable as a rise followed by a fall and perhaps the beginning of another rise. The late 1960s saw the first books, starting with Arnold Stein's edited collection *Theodore Roethke: Essays on the Poetry* in 1965 and Karl Malkoff's monograph *Theodore Roethke: An Introduction to the Poetry* in 1966, a refinement of his dissertation from the previous year, the first on the poet. While acknowledging Roethke as an innovative and "important poet, perhaps a major one" (225), Malkoff questions his tendency to write "almost exclusively about himself and his own personal concerns" (224), the aphoristic aspect of his style, and what he sees as the poetry's occasional "derivative qualities." He allows, however, that when Roethke "was at his best he could use anybody or anything and make them peculiarly his own" (222–23), but the comments quoted above from Malkoff's last chapter introduce a persistent critical refrain: that Roethke's best poems had appeared in *The Lost Son* and *Praise to the End!* and that his later work owed too much to his predecessors, especially Yeats, Eliot, and Whitman.[5] Harold Bloom puts a subtler, donnish spin on the argument in *The Anxiety of Influence* (1973). In the last chapter he quotes lines from "The Dying Man," Roethke's poem about and after Yeats, and lines from "First Meditation," and describes them as unsuccessful attempts at *apophrades.*[6] Bloom defines the term as the "grand and final revisionary moment" of "triumph" when especially gifted late-career poets make a reader "believe, for startled moments, that they are being *imitated by their ancestors*":

> Roethke hoped [the passage from "The Dying Man"] was late Roethke, but alas it is the Yeats of *The Tower* and *The Winding Stair.* Roethke hoped [the passage from "First Meditation"] was late Roethke, but alas it is the Eliot of the *Quartets.* . . . There is late Roethke that is the Stevens of *Transport to Summer,* and late Roethke that is the Whitman of *Lilacs,* but sorrowfully there is very little late Roethke that is late Roethke, for in Roethke the *apophrades* came as devastation, and took away his strength, which nevertheless had been realized, which had become something of his own. Of *apophrades* in its positive, revisionary sense, he gives us no instance; there are no passages in Yeats or Eliot, in Stevens or Whitman, that can strike us as having been written by Roethke.

Among poets of the time, Bloom gives the nod to John Ashbery as having achieved *apophrades,* in his case by supposedly making "us," in at least one case, "return . . . to Stevens, somewhat uneasily to discover that at moments Stevens sounds rather too much like Ashbery, an accomplishment I might not have thought possible" (141–43).[7]

Bloom's preference for Ashbery exemplifies one persistent intellectual agenda in recent poetry criticism. The more theoretical, aestheticist critics tend to champion abstruse, "difficult" free verse like Ashbery's that focuses on the nature of language and its relation to reality. In a 1976 profile in *The New York Times,* Richard Kostelanetz describes Ashbery's poetry as "subtle, allusive, indefinite, perhaps obscure . . . not familiar, not declarative, not rhymed, not sentimental, not accessible," all adjectives describing the kind of poetry favored by the theoretical crowd. By contrast, Roethke's work is subtle in a different way, more referential than allusive, tangible, more multivalent than obscure, deeply familiar with person and place, declarative, sometimes rhymed and sometimes not but always musical, willing to risk sentimentality but never mawkish, rarely "easy" to understand but seeking to *be* understood. Roethke appeals to a wider readership than Ashbery and to poets and critics who prize poetry attuned to rhythms of the body, the natural world, and life as lived in particular places.[8]

Some critics have challenged the views advanced by Bloom and others on the quality of Roethke's late work and its relation to literary tradition. Jenijoy La Belle is of particular importance in this regard. In her book *The Echoing Wood of Theodore Roethke* (1976), La Belle argues that Roethke's "sense of tradition encompassed not only a conscious historical attitude, but a psychological state, and his act of imitation was not a mechanical process, but a basic component" of his poetics (166). As a *man* Roethke was jealous of and competitive toward other poets, living and dead, but as a *poet* he engaged his influences in conversation, both assenting to and dissenting from their forms and philosophies. He was speaking with, rather than over, poets such as Whitman, Yeats, and Eliot, his primary antecedents. His dialogue with Whitman comes in seeming response to the ending of "Song of Myself":

> If you want me again look for me under your bootsoles.
>
> You will hardly know who I am or what I mean
> But I shall be good health to you nevertheless.
>
> (88)

Roethke's direct reply comes in "The Abyss," where he says, "Be with me, Whitman, maker of catalogues: / For the world invades me again" (*Collected Poems*, 212). Such invocations of other poets express Roethke's sense of "his literary tradition not as a series of periods but as a community of selected individual talents, somehow in touch with one another even as he was in touch with them" (La Belle, 165).

His conversation with Eliot in the late poems is more pointed. Although he echoes Eliot's *Four Quartets* in "North American Sequence," Roethke espouses a very different metaphysics. La Belle contrasts the two poets by describing Eliot as "pervasively religious, even theological, in interests, and thus he must move from the physical world and the imagery of that world to a spiritual world in which abstract concepts replace images from nature. . . . Roethke is never so willing to desert the natural world: these same questions are answered not by leaving the woods and the waters but by penetrating more deeply into their interiors"

(156–57). He directly asserts as much in the final stanza of "The Longing," where he replies to Eliot's statement in *Four Quartets* that

> Home is where one starts from. . . .
> . . . .
>
> Old men ought to be explorers
> Here and there does not matter.
>
> (189)

After evoking the near-extinction wreaked upon the American bison by Anglo-Americans as a synecdoche for the environmental and, by implication, the cultural destructiveness of conquest, Roethke asks, "Old men should be explorers? / I'll be an Indian" (*Collected Poems,* 183). As I have elaborated upon elsewhere, Roethke here rejects Eliot's Eurocentric, Christian vision for "an autochthonous spirituality of place" in the Emersonian tradition (*Midwestern Pastoral,* 133). He finds himself most at home in landscapes both real and symbolic, in the company of fellow beings, as in "Once More, the Round," which finds him

> ador[ing his] life
> With the Bird, the abiding Leaf,
> With the Fish, the questing Snail.

That poem also finds him "danc[ing] with William Blake" (*Collected Poems,* 243), a motif recalling "The Dance" from "Four for Sir John Davies," in which he exclaims "I'll sing and whistle romping with the bears" before confessing "I take this cadence from a man named Yeats; / I take it and I give it back again" (101). Roethke ultimately displays less of Bloom's "anxiety of influence" than an artistic desire to join the living and the dead in reciprocal dance and song. As Kalaidjian stresses in his succinct retort to the critical dismissal of Roethke as "a derivative talent," the emphasis placed by Bloom and his followers on "Roethke's failure to displace the aesthetics of High Modernism ignores both the powerful transformations his work accomplished within that tradition and the influential directions he pioneered for a later generation of Postmodern poets" (64).[9]

The heyday of Roethke scholarship was the 1970s and 1980s, when production of scholarly articles peaked and most of the books on his work were published. Including essay collections, bibliographies, and a concordance, ten books on Roethke appeared in the 1970s. Distinguished monographs ranged from Richard Allen Blessing's *Theodore Roethke's Dynamic Vision* (1974) to Jay Parini's *Theodore Roethke: An American Romantic* (1979). Eleven books found their way to bookshelves in the 1980s, from the decade's first monograph, Norman Chaney's *Theodore Roethke: The Poetics of Wonder* (1981), to the last, Peter Balakian's *Theodore Roethke's Far Fields: The Evolution of His Poetry* (1989). Thereafter, scholarship on Roethke fell into a precipitous decline. The 1990s saw only four books on Roethke, two of them published in India and not widely available in North America or Europe.[10] The most recent full-length study published in the Western world, Don Bogen's *Theodore Roethke and the Writing Process,* came out in 1991; Robert Kusch's *My Toughest Mentor: Theodore Roethke and William Carlos Williams (1940–1948)*, from 1999, is the last book published about Roethke, until now. Dissertations on Roethke similarly declined, with fifty being accepted between 1965 and 1990, but only four since 1991.

Scholarly articles in journals and edited volumes also started to appear much less frequently after 1990, with the MLA database indicating that the number of articles fell from 242 between 1965 and 1990 to 74 between 1991 and 2015. The numbers represent a 70 percent drop, a steeper decline than occurred with any other major mid-twentieth-century American poet, in a period when the amount of writing on Lowell, Berryman, and Sexton remained relatively consistent and that on Plath and Bishop proliferated. During the nineties and the first years of the new millennium, Roethke became a "lost son" in literary scholarship.

This situation did not go unnoticed. Poet David Young lamented in 1995 that "[o]ne hears Roethke's name very seldom these days. He seems to be undergoing the kind of innocuous neglect that follows writers who have, in their lifetime and immediately after, been recognized as major figures. The trough that seems to follow such fame may be inevitable, but we think it is time to begin rescuing Roethke from his gradual obliteration in the fitful memory of American letters" (7). In her 2008 keynote address at the Roethke centennial event at the University of Michigan, Camille Paglia declared herself "horrified to discover a dribbling out of scholarly books about Roethke over the last twenty years. . . . An American literary criticism that neglects Theodore Roethke has sunk into irrelevance and folly" ("Dance of the Senses" 245).

Scholarly production surely dropped, in part, because the first generation of Roethke scholars had created such a robust secondary bibliography; so much had been said, and perhaps it was time for a breather. Besides, young academics had other interests. Much of the focus had shifted to poets of color—African American, Latinx, Native American, and Asian American—poets with working-class backgrounds and identities, and women poets. The new attention to previously neglected or oppressed voices has been both just and justified. But more interest in some poets does not necessitate less in others, and new generations of readers read the same poetry with new eyes and ears. They may rediscover writing from the past, rehabilitating it and identifying heretofore unnoticed beauty and new meanings.[11]

Recent signs of reappraisal and reappreciation of Roethke's life and work suggest that rediscovery may be underway. Copper Canyon Press published an expanded edition of Roethke's selected prose in 2001, changing the title from *On the Poet and His Craft* to *On Poetry and Craft* for gender inclusivity. In 2004, the American Library Association designated his childhood home in Saginaw a National Literary Landmark. The property is maintained as a museum by the Friends of Theodore Roethke foundation, which sponsors cultural events on the site. The year 2005 saw the publication of Roethke's *Selected Poems,* edited by Edward Hirsch, whose marvelous introduction provides an important reassessment of Roethke's life and work. The 2008 centennial of Roethke's birth was marked by observations in Saginaw, Ann Arbor, State College, and Seattle. In 2012, the U.S. Post Office issued a Roethke stamp, part of a commemorative series featuring ten twentieth-century American poets. All along, prizes and events named after Roethke have kept his name in circulation: the Theodore Roethke Memorial Poetry Prize, awarded by Saginaw Valley State University and running concurrently with their triennial Roethke Arts and Poetry Festival; the annual Theodore Roethke Poetry Prize, from the journal *Poetry Northwest;* and the annual Theodore Roethke Memorial Poetry Reading at the University of Washington in Seattle.

Roethke scholarship has not increased dramatically, but critics are treating the poetry in novel ways that bode well for the future.[12] Scholars working in the interdisciplinary field of ecocriticism have been especially engaged. Emotional, aesthetic, and spiritual dimensions of the human relationship to nature in Roethke's poetry have always been obvious to readers and critics. "There is no poetry anywhere," James Dickey once wrote, "that is so valuably conscious of the human body as Roethke's; no poetry that can place the body in an environment—wind, seascape, greenhouse, forest, desert, mountainside, among animals or insects or stones—so vividly and evocatively, waking unheard exchanges between the place and human responsiveness at its most creative" ("Greatest," 220). Ecocritics, however, go further into the social, historical, geographical, biological, and ethical implications of Roethke's work. In his foundational 1978 essay "Literature and Ecology: An Experiment in Ecocriticism," in which the word "ecocriticism" first appeared, William Rueckert employs scientific terminology to rephrase Roethke's journey through darkness and light, suffering and joy, earth and air, starting a section of his essay with the heading "Entropy and Negentropy in Theodore Roethke's 'Greenhouse,' 'Lost Son,' and 'North American Sequence.'" His comments place Roethke at the center of the ecocritical project: "Was there ever a greater ecological, evolutionary poet of the self than Roethke . . . one so close to his evolutionary predecessors that he experiences an interchange of being with them and never demeans them with personification and seldom with metaphor[?] Kenneth Burke's brilliant phrase—vegetal radicalism—still takes us to the ecological centers of Roethke, self-absorbed, self-obsessed as he was" (119).

Three contributors to this book—Bernard Quetchenbach, Trenton Hickman, and me—published signal works in the ecocritical turn in writing about Roethke that occurred during the first decade of this century. Quetchenbach devotes a chapter of *Back from the Far Field: American Nature Poetry in the Late Twentieth Century* (2000) to Roethke and Jeffers, contrasting the two while making a case for each as the most significant nature poets of their respective generations. In his 2006 essay "Theodore Roethke and the Poetics of Place," Hickman demonstrates how Roethke "elaborat[ed] a mode of American poetry that makes human experience accountable to natural and physical landscape, and that externalizes such experience as one node of the biological 'web' to which it belongs" (183). My 2006 book *The Midwestern Pastoral: Place and Landscape in Literature of the American Heartland* features a chapter on Roethke as a bioregional poet who "draws significantly from midwestern landscape and cultural archetypes" in ways that challenge narrowly utilitarian views of nature (106).[13]

Ecocritical analysis of Roethke's work has been more recently advanced by Christian Knoeller, author of *Reimagining Environmental History: Ecological Memory in the Wake of Landscape Change* (2017), in a chapter that emphasizes the "North American Sequence" as the "consummation" of "Roethke's vision of environmental history and a spiritual relation to the natural world" (130). Knoeller argues that in "the twenty-first century, we read Roethke at a time when environmental decline has been greatly exacerbated by climate change. . . . We need more than ever to recognize what must be seen as sacrosanct, inviolable, and fundamentally a part of us. This vision underlies the enduring significance of Roethke's work" (11). Quite in opposition to the mistaken view of Roethke's poetry as private and insular, ecocritics like Knoeller demonstrate its relevance to the environmental crises of our time, from habitat loss and mass extinction to pollution and global warming, suggesting how a poet so affected by a greenhouse may inspire us as our planet faces a very different sort of greenhouse effect.

A Roethke renaissance, however, will require the publication of books, especially monographs, devoted to his life and work. A full-length ecocritical study is overdue, as is a book on Roethke and philosophy, with interpretations of his work in light of existentialism, phenomenology, and other philosophical perspectives. A survey of his affinity with and influence on Native American poets is indicated,[14] as is a reading of Roethke from a feminist perspective, which could illuminate his close study of poetry by women, the figure of woman in his love poems, and the appearance of female speakers in his later poetry. Roethke's Irish connections merit extended treatment, considering his deep engagement with the work of Yeats and his influence on Richard Murphy, John Montague, Seamus Heaney, Elaine Feeney, and other poets. There has long been a need for a critical biography, one that directly quotes Roethke's work and draws on the Roethke archives at the University of Washington, Allan Seager's unpublished interviews and other materials held by the Bancroft Library, and sources published after Seager's *The Glass House* appeared in 1968. Such a volume ought to feature photographs spanning Roethke's life and perhaps a selection of manuscript pages. An updated review of scholarship, building on Randall Stiffler's 1986 study *Theodore Roethke: The Poet and His Critics,* would benefit both critics and students, as would a searchable, online concordance and an updated bibliography of primary and secondary sources. As for Roethke's writing, a newly typeset edition of his collected poems would be very welcome, preferably with the same pagination as the current paperback. A volume of collected works might feature previously uncollected poetry and prose, in addition to *The Collected Poems* and *On Poetry and Craft: Selected Prose of Theodore Roethke* in their entirety.

The present collection will hopefully spur such scholarly efforts, the "true criticism" anticipated by James Wright in the epigraph to this book, a quotation from a letter Wright wrote shortly after Roethke's death.[15] In that letter Wright calls for a criticism predicated less upon intellectual pride than mindfulness and care: "To cherish [Roethke's] work, his art, by demanding that it respond to our most severe and attentive questionings by revealing suddenly, as it were, the precious stones that vein it . . . is to love the art as the poet himself loved it" (295). Contributors to this volume clearly love the art, as demonstrated by their close reading and contextualization of Roethke's writing. Like the many poets who have attested to Roethke's influence, these critics have looked for Roethke under their bootsoles, to invoke Whitman once again. Also invited along that path are students and general readers, who may take with them Roethke's *Collected Poems* and the poet's own hopes for his work: "I think of myself as a poet of love, a poet of praise. And I wish to be read aloud" (*On Poetry and Craft,* 33).

NOTES

1. Lane, 460. In his "Table of Word Frequency," Lane notes 92 uses of the word "small." The word "light" has 150 appearances, but that includes uses of the word as a noun as well as an adjective. The next substantial words after "small" in the table are "love" with 85 uses, "long" (both adjective and verb) with 84, "water" with 80, "bird" with 74, and "dark" with 70. A great degree of Roethke's thematic content is contained in these words ("light," "small," "love," "long," "water," "bird," and "dark").

2. According to Seager, Roethke's "tough guy" persona was rooted in adolescence, when he needed to thwart bullies. It solidified during college in Prohibition-era Ann Arbor, when gangsters like Capone were iconic figures in popular culture:

> As big as he was, broad, thick, unhandsome, he looked tough. He began to wear what became his permanent costume, the double-breasted suit. . . . His talk became profane, full of coarse[,] vigorous, idiomatic phrases, often dirty, often very funny. . . .
>
> . . . [He began] to suspect that poetry, having no voice in the community where he lived, was antisocial. . . . Poetry was akin to crime. Strange and unwelcome in middle-class America, the poet was a criminal. And since he was, he had better act like one. . . .
>
> . . . Hints, suspicions, inklings, his father's death, all these persuaded him to assume his tough mask. And from this time on, it is hard to penetrate, to catch any glimpse of the essential tenderness behind it. (Seager, 56, 60)

During mental crises, Roethke's "tough guy" persona and thoughts about gangsters became full-on paranoiac delusions. In ordinary moments, they manifested simply in untoward behavior and speech. James Dickey portrays this side of Roethke in his essay "The Greatest American Poet: Roethke," originally published in *The Atlantic* in 1968 and reprinted in the collection *Sorties* (1971). Since Dickey was even more of a fabulist than his subject, one should view with skepticism his portrait of Roethke and his assumptions about the production of Seager's biography. His account of time spent with Roethke, however, has the ring of truth, corroborated as it is by Seager and other sources, and he makes a number of insightful comments.

3. On Roethke's influence on Bly, Wright, and other poets of the 1960s identified as "Deep Image poets," see Harry Williams.

4. See, for example, "A Garland for Theodore Roethke," a collection of tribute poems in *The Michigan Quarterly Review* 6, no. 4 (Fall 1967): 252–75, available free online.

5. Essays in Stein's collection by poets Stephen Spender, William Meredith, and W. D. Snodgrass express much the same reservations as Malkoff. Their criticism of the poetry seems to reflect mixed feelings about Roethke as a person as well as their readings of the work.

6. *Apophrades* is the last of Bloom's six "revisionary ratios," techniques used by poets, according to Bloom, as they struggle with the accomplishments of their great predecessors, seeking to achieve poetic originality and immortality.

7. Randall Stiffler provides a wry riposte to Bloom's assessment of Roethke, stating that "[n]o one has yet refuted Harold Bloom's conclusion by locating 'passages' of Theodore Roethke in the works of the poets he mentions" (184).

8. Ashbery has garnered much more critical attention than Roethke since 1976: Google Scholar provides over thirteen thousand results on Ashbery in that period of time, but fewer than six thousand on Roethke.

Oddly enough, Ashbery shared a major influence with Roethke: W. H. Auden, Roethke's friend and mentor and best man at his wedding. As Patrick Gill points out in his essay for this volume on the poem "Lull," Roethke, early in his career, admired Auden to the point of occasional emulation and abject jealousy. Ashbery, for his part, always considered Auden the first and most enduring influence on his own poetry. Auden awarded Ashbery's first book the Yale Younger Poets Prize for 1956, though he later said he never understood the poems.

9. Literary critics publishing in prestigious mass market venues continue to parrot Bloom's dismissal of Roethke's later work. One such critic is Clive James, in a review of *Break, Blow, Burn: Camille Paglia Reads Forty-three of the World's Best Poems* (2005) appearing in *The New York Times Sunday Book Review* for March 27, 2005. "[M]ost of [Roethke's] longer poems," James asserts, "prove to be helpless echoes of bigger names. Ambition undid him, as it has undone many another American poet infected by the national delusion that the arts can have a major league." A fellow traveler of James is Adam Kirsch. Conflating Roethke and James Wright as men and poets, Kirsch claims that they "paid a high aesthetic price for their belief that earnestness could make a poem live. . . . To justify their calling they had to insist that poetry had more to do with authenticity than with artistry" (89). Nothing in their articles suggests that either James or Kirsch have read any Roethke scholarship, but they seem quite familiar with Bloom's elevation of *The Lost Son* and *Praise to the End!* and disparagement of *The Waking, Words for the Wind,* and *The Far Field.* Kirsch exactly reiterates Bloom's opinion in *The Anxiety of Influence.* Although "Roethke manage[d] to invent an entirely new kind of nature poetry, in which the earth is not reassuringly earthy but teeming and alien," Kirsch writes, "[w]hat is most disappointing in Roethke's late work is the way he fell back into emulation of the established modernist idols, especially Yeats and the Eliot of 'Four Quartets'" (90, 91).

10. Singh; Padma.

11. Roethke's German American ethnicity offers another opportunity for critical inquiry. His poetry may be studied as that of a second-generation immigrant, one who grew up in a family and community steeped in German language and folkways. That

fact is evident in Roethke's portrayal of his family and their employees, his preference for Anglo-Saxon rather than Latinate diction, and the appearance of German words in his poetry and prose.

It should also be noted that Roethke was eight when the United States entered World War I, old enough to have lasting memories of the anti-German hysteria of the period. Harassment was acute in the upper Midwest, including Roethke's home state of Michigan, with its large German immigrant population. There were physical assaults on individuals and mob attacks against German American businesses and institutions. German-language schools and newspapers, like Saginaw's *Post-Zeitung*, shut down, and people stopped speaking German in public. Local zealots removed German books from libraries, burning them in some cases, as in Spring Lake and Zeeland, two Michigan towns. Place names were changed. Berlin, Michigan, for example, became Marne, after the 1914 battle in France. In Saginaw, Germania Avenue was renamed Federal Avenue, and the Germania Society became the Lincoln Club, switched to English, and closed their German library. See James Cooke Mills, 2:440.

Roethke's parents would have noted these developments with alarm. They likely heard about the six professors summarily fired from the German Department at the University of Michigan, and worse, the lynching of Robert Prager, a German immigrant miner, in Illinois. The xenophobia and assimilationism attending World War I likely played a role in Roethke's inability as an adult to speak or read German, even though he "studied German for an hour every school day from the age of five to the age of fourteen" (Seager, 20).

12. Important twenty-first-century Roethke scholarship includes the chapter "Hello, Thingy Spirit" in Sharpe; and Bearss and Primeau, eds., "Being a Collection of Essays on Theodore Roethke," special issue, *Midwestern Miscellany* 36 (Spring/Fall 2008), from the Society for the Study of Midwestern Literature. The issue, which features a wide range of essays, and a few poems, about Roethke, is freely accessible online at the Society's website. Sharpe's chapter and four essays from the special issue also appear in the large selection of secondary material, old and new, collected in the Gale series *Poetry Criticism,* vol. 205 (2018), pp. 69–209.

Another important essay is Camille Paglia's "Dance of the Senses: Natural Vision and Psychotic Mysticism in Theodore Roethke's Poetry," delivered as the keynote address of the Roethke centennial celebrations held at the University of Michigan in October 2008. It appeared in the *Michigan Quarterly Review* and was reprinted in her book *Provocations*. Paglia also included explications of Roethke's "Cuttings," "Root Cellar," and "The Visitant" in *Break, Blow, Burn,* mentioned above in note 9.

13. The decade's ecocritical reframing of Roethke was capped by an entry on Roethke in *Modern American Environmentalists: A Biographical Encyclopedia*, edited by George A. Cevasco and Richard P. Harmon. Entry author Rebecca Onion asserts that although "Roethke would not have identified himself as an environmentalist . . . his sympathies and structures of thought were always environmentalist, in the purest of senses" (421). She identifies Roethke's concern for vulnerable, small organisms, "his intense sympathy for the members of the biotic community that are the least spectacular," as "the most indelible aspect of [his] poetic environmentalism" (424). Roethke's poetry, Onion

concludes, "with its fine-tuned sensitivity toward the natural world, has no doubt influenced the environmental ethic of countless readers" (426).

14. Kenneth Lincoln parallels Roethke with Native traditions and trends in *Sing with the Heart of a Bear.* Sherman Alexie, Duane Niatum, and Joy Harjo, Native poets mentioned earlier in this introduction, have all testified to Roethke's compatibility with Native perspectives or their own individual experiences.

15. In his journals, James Dickey defined the opposite of Wright's "true criticism": "Contemporary criticism of poetry: far too much is made of far too little. The critic is attempting to be more ingenious and talented than the poem, and stands on his head to be original: that is, to *invent* an originality for the poems that can come to them only through him" (*Sorties,* 6).

Open House (1941)

1

"Open House"

Prying and Potential in an Early Poem

BRANDON RUSHTON

THEODORE ROETHKE'S *Open House* (1941) is the end result of an arduous journey. The publication of the poet's first book marked the culmination of a ten-year endeavor, a decade-long literary apprenticeship characterized by meticulous attention paid to the forms, styles, and successes of his predecessors. For Roethke, a poet concerned with literary reputation and fame, the ultimate goal of his first book was not to reshape contemporary literature or to discover a new direction for American poetry—it was to gain admission to the world of American letters. A sensitive thirty-three-year-old still reeling from his first major psychological breakdown in 1935, Roethke longed for acceptance by the literary community. Having always perceived himself as the deficient son of a stern, Prussian father, he projected the need to please his Papa onto the poets he looked up to and admired. His feelings of inadequacy were also due to his having been brought up in the Midwest, which he saw as an intellectually isolated region. In the period leading up to the publication of his first book, Roethke was on the outside looking in. He modeled his poetry after the poetry of his mentors so they might extend him an invitation. Writing, to that end, would eventually reveal the limitations of his early work, much of which presented him as a poet of contradiction: one then dedicated to probing the depths of his psyche without ever bringing himself to do so, exploring the self only insofar as that exploration was expressed in a way consistent with the work of already established poets.

"Open House," the title poem of Roethke's first book, embodies that paradox. A poem comprised of three sestets, written in tight iambic trimeter, and following an *ababcc* rhyme scheme, it asks readers to wrestle with the book's promise of openness while not offering any revelation; it compresses abstract notions of pain and suffering into highly crafted, abstract verse. This formalist, intellectual approach was meant to impress his mentors Stanley Kunitz, Louise Bogan, W. H. Auden, and Léonie Adams, poets already comfortable inside the house of American letters. By adhering to the prosody and philosophies of its predecessors, "Open House" represents the poet's desperation to join the poetry establishment. Roethke's willingness to let his early work be shaped by others originates in his incessant impulse to please, to flatter. He eagerly applied the advice and suggestions of others so that the poem and the book it introduces might create a space for himself, so that his mentors of the day might say he'd made it, that he belonged, and that he was welcome. "Open House" isn't the self-announcement of his own arrival; it is the ticket he hoped would grant him admittance.

Roethke's need for admittance directed his life during the years he produced *Open House.* In fact, it wasn't only upon the metaphorical door of the house of American letters that he knocked. In an interview with Robert Boyers for *Salmagundi,* Stanley Kunitz recalled the first time he met Roethke. In the mid-1930s, when Kunitz was living in a cottage in New Hope, Pennsylvania, Roethke knocked on his door one evening with a copy of Kunitz's first book, *Intellectual Things* (1930), in his hand. Roethke was quick to recite Kunitz's poems from memory, hoping to impress Kunitz enough that he might be willing to read Roethke's own poems, ones he'd brought with him that evening. Kunitz remembered, in that interview, Roethke's early limitations: "One of Roethke's problems in the beginning was that he was so impressionable. There was a good deal of Eliot in those early poems . . . obvious echoes. An even stronger influence was his friend Louise Bogan. The other women who influenced his work, but to a lesser degree, were Elinor Wylie and Léonie Adams. Sometimes I'd find my own lines coming back to me—that was a delicate matter" (78). Roethke's habit of lifting lines and appropriating them for his own use unsettled Kunitz. The impulse to lift must be attributed to Roethke's own misguided understanding of flattery. In his mind, absorbing the poetic style of those he looked up to was not enough. He had to absorb their content, recreate it, and send it back to them in a carefully coordinated effort to gain access to the literary establishment. Kunitz saw through the impressionability of his friend, interpreting it as a potential inhibition to Roethke's artistic growth. Kunitz, being the true mentor and friend Roethke thought he was, sought to push him past that tendency. Kunitz recalled, "I wanted him to pry open his interior world. In those early years of our association I tried to liberate him into his own identity" (78). Despite Kunitz's attempt to push Roethke toward finding his own identity, however, it would still take him years to develop it.

"Open House," then, must be viewed in regards to Roethke's impulse to please and as a poem less dedicated to defining the self than to reassuring it. Timid and cautious, he was wary of moving forward without the nod of approval from those reading and considering his work. In this way, Roethke's early poem is somewhat collaborative, as he had relinquished some of the creative control to his mentors. As the introductory poem to his oeuvre, "Open House" presents readers a self-conscious Roethke sulking in fears of inadequacy. For example, the final two lines of the poem read, "Rage warps my clearest cry / To witless agony" (17–18). Here, Roethke concludes this highly formal poem by questioning aloud whether his rage-based rhythm has rendered his objectives obsolete, clouding them in an air of foolishness. Considering his self-consciousness about both form and content, it's no wonder that he sought feedback from Louise Bogan. In an earlier version sent to her, the final two lines read:

> Rage warps my lyric cry
> To witless agony.
>
> (qtd. in Bogan, 102)

Bogan was not sold on the concept of the "lyric cry," thinking it could be interpreted as too easy. She encouraged him to find a word more aligned with the poem's content rather than its form. She wrote to Roethke with thoughts on the direction in which she'd take the poem: "A fine sounding word meaning *apparent* would, to my mind, bring the intensity of the last stanza to a practically unbearable point of crisis, and that, my dear, is as you know, the great triumph of a short lyric: that it can be brought up, at the end, into a sound that tears the heart in twain" (102). Bogan's letter reveals just how pointed the feedback for Roethke had to be. She leaves very little room for him to choose wrong. She intentionally provides a synonym of the word she is hoping will replace "lyric."

Well aware of the poem's strict iambic trimeter, she suggests "apparent" so that it throws off his syllabic pattern and directs him closer to the two-syllable word "clearest." Bogan leads Roethke just enough so that he doesn't make a mistake. When he revised the ending, replacing "lyric" with "clearest" and thus producing the couplet in the "Open House" that readers are familiar with, he might even have believed that the choice had been his alone.

The paradoxes of Roethke's person and poems are many. Considering that, "Open House" becomes the quintessential intersection of the two. Roethke begins his poetry career by undercutting himself, giving readers a fuller understanding of his inferiority complex. In the second line of his poem he states, "I have no need for tongue" (2), a statement that Randall Stiffler believes "actually advances a negative attitude toward language" (16). The poet's main tool is his voice, his ability to speak. In *A Necessary Order: Theodore Roethke and the Writing Process* (1991), Don Bogen argues that Roethke believed the "raw emotional power of the secrets themselves" was enough to establish a sense of persuasiveness—that Roethke felt language itself was not strong enough to translate the pain and agony he was alluding to. Despite that, Bogen still believes the "poem begins with a denial of its own reason for existence" (11). This isn't a mistake, though; it is a part of Roethke's careful coordination. He knew he was creating a poem of paradox, as evidenced by its appearance in the May 1936 issue of *Scribner's Magazine* under an earlier title, "Strange Distortion." Bogen believes Roethke's "reasons for eventually rejecting [the original title were] clear: the title ["Strange Distortion"] would have made the paradox obvious and diminished the movement and surprise in the poem" (12). That, coupled with the fact that Kunitz suggested he title his first book *Open House,* made Roethke consider how he could introduce himself—as a more complicated poet—to the world.

Considering the ways in which Roethke wrote to impress his mentors Bogan and Kunitz, the difficulty of this early poem becomes clearer. The paradoxes are a defense mechanism meant to protect the truths these raw emotions represent. The "anguish self-revealed" is anything but. Although he purports to have "no disguise," the speaker is *all* disguise. More than influence and feedback, Roethke's mentors unintentionally provided him with a way to protect himself. If he imitated their tendency to abstraction he might be able to refrain from exposing his true self to others. They unintentionally encouraged his timidity. It would take him years to discard the concept that "the deed will speak the truth" (14), a line that Stiffler believes runs counter to the ideal of poetry, advancing "the antipoetic sentiment that actions speak louder than words." For Stiffler, the first poem in Roethke's first book runs counter to what such a poem should aim to accomplish: "[I]nstead of being an introduction to his book that invites the reader to follow, Roethke's inaugural poem shuts the door on language" (16). Roethke's first book, then, is a product of his feeling like he had been left out in the cold. Roethke had been on the outside for so long that his first book, along with his inaugural poem, functioned as a formal vendetta. Just as the world had closed its door on Roethke, he decided to close the door of himself to the world.

Despite its retaliatory intent, Roethke's inaugural poem crafts a sense of stability. It showcases his carefully coordinated efforts to strike balance. As closed as "Open House" is in form and content, Roethke understood the poem had to serve as his poetic crowbar. It had to open the door. It had to get him inside. In that sense, Roethke allowed his poem to reflect the hurt he felt only insofar as the translation of that hurt wouldn't jeopardize his access to the house. He knew he was writing to please poets; if he were to have success he couldn't repel his mentors or the literary movements of the day. In *Understanding Theodore Roethke* (1987), Walter Kalaidjian notes how *Open House* was "dominated by the kind of formal craft and metaphysical irony then prized by American New Criticism" (30). In this way, it's important to consider how Roethke was writing to please that audience: by composing poems in a way that was consistent with the critical preference for formalism. As Kalaidjian says, in the poems of *Open House* "Roethke's tightly organized closed-form lyrics . . . satisfied New Criticism's criterion of formal craft in the 1940s" (33–34). Roethke was aware of the popular approaches of his era and wrote "Open House" with the intent to fulfill them. Deeply envious of established poets, Roethke could feign resistance up until the point that it might damage his chance to take his place among them.

This need for acceptance, however, would not leave the poet's personal or professional life after the publication of his first book. Despite the positive reception of that book and the pleasure it gave his mentors, Roethke still believed acceptance eluded him, and that belief was a driving factor in his poetry and in his life. Richard Hugo, who studied under Roethke six years after the publication of *Open House,* testified to the elder poet's insecurity. Remembering Roethke in the time when he was working on the poems that would make up *The Lost Son and Other Poems* (1948), Hugo reflected on the way he thought Roethke carried his need for acceptance, physically, within his person. In Hugo's mind, Roethke always appeared out of place: "His addiction to bourgeois values, his compulsive need to be loved by all, but most of all the rich, was of course the obverse of the way he felt about himself. In his mind I believe he was always poor and unwashed, and he showed it when he walked" (50).

Hugo's observation emphasizes how Roethke's commitment to truth was both ontological and corporeal. For Roethke, it was important to minimize the division between his body and his body of work. In this way, "Open House" is the poet's instruction to himself, a pact to present that self honestly "[i]n language strict and pure" (line 15). Thus Roethke begins to open the door for the possibilities of his next book, *The Lost Son and Other Poems,* tearing away the pleasantries and calling for revelation, a stripping "naked to the bone" (line 9). Roethke always felt more at home among the underrepresented and undesired; these feelings directly led to the shift in his second book, toward the minute and microscopic topics of the greenhouse poems.

"Open House" is quintessential in its representations of Roethke's contradictions. At the beginning of his career, he was already practicing what he would eventually come to call his "steady storm of correspondences" (*Collected Poems,* 231), his interest in the paradoxes that make up poems and people. "Open House" reveals Roethke's homelessness, his feelings of being perpetually out of place. This inaugural poem is his methodic attempt to remedy those feelings. If he imitated the formal styles of the day, he might create a place for himself inside the house of American letters. That said, the poem also highlights the lack of confidence he had in his aims. If the poem didn't accomplish its task of prying open the door, if it didn't get him inside, he could fall back on the reassurance he gives himself in his poem: "My heart keeps open house" (3). In his mind, Roethke saw himself outside of the house. He was willing to shape his poetry after that of his mentors so that they might admit him. "Open House" shows readers the lengths Roethke was willing to go to feel included, much like that evening on Kunitz's porch, knocking on the door and waiting to be let in.

2

"To My Sister"

WILLIAM HEYEN

O MY Ted (presumptuous of me, I with no rights in this matter but now about forty years older than you were when you wrote your June in this way) remember the words the lines the *sounds* as you *sounded* your anxieties we have the transcript of your "original manuscript" as you call it in *Selected Letters* as you sent it to a friend the poem was in a mag you were honing it for *Open House* you heard yourself at first saying but then crossed out "Remember too the loins from whence you sprung the limbs" & "Rejoice in narrow thighs" & "the buds of breasts" & "And spill no precious blood"[1] so that we see/hear you clarifying toward your finished / more decorous eleven lines in your first book

so here you are & who knows what-all is moiling in you during a time you hunger for publication so you can land a good job & as you anguish within a poetry scene wherein all these thighs & buds of breasts & hymenic blood are unchaste but what in any case is definitely here is the fact that what is said *is* how it is said that if you keep talking keep fathoming & sounding stars & tears & trains the poem will come to revelation the faith that your Genius—that which is of the soul (Emerson says "the soul is light"),[2] that which is not cunning but guileless, that which is tyrannical & will *out,* that which is of the transpiercing eternal, is instinctual & evanescent & dangerous, which detests the respectable & conservative, that which is fluid & infused & intuitional & as you know even seeks so-called vulgarity, & receives, & makes its own luck, that which by abandonment comes to integrate, that which disrupts & is impulsive & irrational—what's all this stuff about her needing to preserve her hate, anyway, except good sounds at the end?—& inspired by hungry ghosts, that which is unconscious & is the madness of Emily's "divinest sense"[3]—that faith that your Genius & not an iambic tetrameter or pentameter argument will enable you to have your say as Saint Walt said to Horace Traubel that he'd had his say & therefore could die happy, or at least content in Camden as he poked among his papers to remember sisters & brothers for whom his *Leaves* was his advice & prayer as "To My Sister" at your beginnings became a prayer . . .

so with "To My Sister" you must have had what you say in a notebook, the feeling "that one is on the edge of many things" yes you worked these edges & got them down to eleven lines & maybe a couple-three of your first blurts scared you how could you ferchrissakes even think about even with Emerson's plea for wildness by way of the "flower of the mind"[4] as opposed I suppose to the machine of the intellect O your sister June's closed thighs & budding breasts so you cut what during a more rational revision didn't compute & your *Open House* poem bespeaks a more conventional older brother advising her to "[d]efer the vice of flesh" & you unmention your mother's loins & your mind taboos itself against even vaguest suggestions of incest or whatever all is going on before your scratches & deletions of some pretty scary stuff

but "To My Sister" in finished form still retains your flow, does not creak as do some of your other crafted first book poems, eschews the formalities & diction ("from whence") & the semicolon & colon empiricism that usually inhabits the closed house of poetry—this poem comes to trust, is foreshadowing (with "Premonition") the organic the "vegetal radicalism" (Kenneth Burke) of the later breakthroughs that here were just intimations in you but you knew you knew your own bedeviling Power that you'd more & more come to need & trust but here you're halfway to your devil spoken in an early notebook entry "A poem that is the shape of the psyche itself; in times of great stress, that's what I tried to write"[5] & meanwhile the beauty of this measured free-flowing lyrical consolidation for now that marks your faith along the way to what Selden Rodman wrote of *The Lost Son* that your "verse communicates nothing except to the reader who is willing to surrender himself to the music of suggestive incantation"[6] my Ted I remember

bundling in your Saginaw bed in your childhood home to which you returned after various unravelings to try to balance & center yourself again I couldn't sleep I probed attic to cellar & opened cabinets & saw still your sister's clothes & medicines & I wondered what she when she was young was supposed to preserve her heart her hate for had something happened or maybe might happen that her protective older brother couldn't protect her even as he tells her to remember their shared past but it's best that forever your poem of course resists our probing our settlements & sureties, its generative force is its emotional caring your heart we hear gone wild within form from & for your summer-month muse here your sister we'll let this poem preserve its/your mysteries within its music that you came to trust Amen

NOTES

1. Roethke, *Selected Letters,* 11.
2. Ralph Waldo Emerson, "Self-Reliance," in *Essays and Lectures,* 270.
3. Emily Dickinson, poem 620 ("Much Madness is divinest Sense"), in *The Poems of Emily Dickinson,* 278.
4. Emerson, "The Poet" (1844), in *Essays and Lectures,* 459. Emerson is citing the second-century Chaldean Oracles.
5. Roethke, *Straw for the Fire,* 174.
6. Cited in Seager, 197–98.

3

"Beneath an Undivided Sky"

Environmental Disorder and Human Passivity in "Interlude"

KRISTIN M. DISTEL

SINCE ITS initial publication, there has been a considerable amount of criticism on Theodore Roethke's *Open House* (1941), much of which has valued this first volume almost exclusively for the ways in which it helped Roethke advance toward the characteristic style of *The Lost Son and Other Poems* (1948) and later, even more experimental collections.[1] As his writing evolved, Roethke came to question the volume's success. He noted in a personal essay, "It took me about ten years to complete one little book, and now some of the things in it seem to creak. Still, I like about ten pieces in it" (*On Poetry and Craft,* 29). In a 1949 letter to fellow poet John Ciardi, Roethke explained that while he himself felt "Interlude" (*Collected Poems,* 6) was a strong poem, he suggested its inclusion in Ciardi's forthcoming anthology *Mid-Century American Poets* (1950) "just for the hell of it" (*Selected Letters,* 158). This equivocation belies the great care with which Roethke wrote early poems such as "Interlude" and compiled *Open House.*[2] I would argue that "Interlude," a poem infrequently discussed in Roethke scholarship, is a valuable example of the poet's ability to examine the effects of environmental forces on the human psyche. As Jay Parini notes, "[t]he main themes" of *Open House* are "the need to establish a firm sense of self and the discovery of a correspondence between internal and external realities" (38). Indeed, "Interlude" takes as its theme the conflict between the internal and the external, between the speaker's fear and a looming thunderstorm. In this sense, "Interlude" is an important poem, worthy of further examination. Specifically, the destructive power of nature and the way in which it suppresses human action in this poem warrant analysis. The role of nature as both cause and mediator of chaos, a theme observable in much of Roethke's work, is also of note. What makes "Interlude" a distinctive poem, though, is the speaker's marked passivity and immobility: he is powerless to act in the face of nature's arresting, robust strength.

In his analysis of the book, Don Bogen remarks, "If we look at *Open House* in the light of Auden's idea that a good poet 'can be recognized by his tense awareness of both chaos and order,' Roethke's first volume clearly tends more toward order than chaos" (28). This conflict between "chaos and order" is specifically apparent in "Interlude," beginning with the opening lines: "The element of air was out of hand. / The rush of wind ripped off the tender leaves" (1–2). Roethke's use of iambic pentameter and elegiac stanzas, as well as the poem's reliance on rhyme, provide a means by which to examine the passivity of the speaker in the face of natural forces. Human anxiety and passivity in contrast to the forcefulness of nature, the poem's form and meter, human submission to nature's potency, physicality (or lack thereof), and the untamable nature of the environment are all essential to an understanding of "Interlude."

With few exceptions, "Interlude" employs elegiac stanzas: iambic pentameter lines rhyming *abab*. Roethke deviates from strict iambic pentameter in four of the poem's twelve lines (4, 7, 9, and 10). The poem's first three lines describe environmental chaos: the violent wind, the "confusion on the land" (3), and other aspects of atmospheric disorder. By adhering to strict iambic pentameter in the first three lines, Roethke suggests that chaos (expressed in the trochaic substitution in the fourth foot of line 4 and the anapest that concludes line 7) is normative, rather than unanticipated. The poem's final stanza supports this concept of environmental disorder as a standard of normality; that is, in the final quatrain, the speaker explains that the anticipated storm never actually occurs. In that stanza, two of the four lines deviate from strict iambic pentameter. Line 9 features a spondee ("full dark") and four iambs. Line 10 contains two pyrrhic feet (the final two syllables of "motionless" and the words "in the") and a spondee ("long grass"). These marked variations from iambic pentameter reinforce the poem's theme of environmental chaos and unpredictability. The meter becomes irregular at the same moments at which the speaker is particularly awed by the capriciousness of nature. Since each of these nonstandard lines reveals that the storm did not materialize, their variations from iambic pentameter imply that atmospheric quiescence is both problematic and rare. That is, by deviating from its standard meter, the poem reinforces its thematic preoccupations with chaos, the fickleness of nature, and the inability of humans to effect change or sometimes simply to act. These metrical variations coincide with the speaker's marked helplessness against the potential force of the storm.

The poem's premise, then, suggests and perhaps demands human passivity. The speaker's action, or lack thereof, is dependent upon the environment; indeed, even the poem's title underscores this concept: an "interlude" is a short moment between events. During an interlude, an audience (or speaker) waits for something to begin again; it is a pause, a period spent in anticipation. In this sense, the title of this poem is perfectly apt, as the speaker is largely inert throughout the poem's twelve lines; the speaker simply waits, and though there are strong winds and the "unnatural night" strongly suggests a storm, the anticipated rain never falls. Beginning with the title, the poem features very little movement; the speaker is inactive, perhaps even submissive to nature's power, even though that power is never fully realized or observed:

> We waited for the first rain in the eaves.
>
> The chaos grew as hour by hour the light
> Decreased beneath an undivided sky.
>
> (4–6)

By the tenth line, even the wind has stilled, stripping the poem of its most violent and notable action. Peter Balakian compares the aforementioned lines to a creation account: "Although the supernatural light of creation ignites the inner light of imagination, the storm's failure to climax leaves the poet, in a sense, betrayed, suspended between expectation and stasis. . . . The unconsummated event in nature undercuts any possibility of transcendent experience for the poet" (27). In contrast to a typically Edenic interpretation, Norman Chaney has explained that for Roethke, nature supplants the typical notion of God (or humans) as creator. Chaney notes that "[m]an is not a creator in any ontological sense, and there are mysteries of growth within the realm of nature in relation to which he is no more than an astonished witness," and that "Roethke as a poet characteristically designated [the] other as nature" (27, 83). If nature in Roethke's poem does indeed take on the features and the fickle power of a deity, it is logical that the speaker would be fearfully reverent in the presence of the environment.

The speaker is physically inactive, as evidenced by Roethke's use of verbs such as "waited" and "had hoped." These verbs stand in contrast to the otherwise concrete diction of the poem. The information readers glean about the speaker comes through the speaker's telling passivity and careful observations of natural surroundings. The speaker, of whom Roethke provides few specific descriptions, stands in deference to the environment and seems stripped of agency in the face of dominant ecological forces. However, readers can presume a great deal about Roethke's intention and the poem's purpose by considering the type of information the lines omit—namely, descriptions of deliberate physical action. The speaker's actions are largely involuntary; throughout the twelve-line poem, the speaker does not make purposeful movements. Roethke writes, "Our pupils widened with unnatural night, / But still the road and dusty field kept dry" (7–8). The dilating of the pupils is of course an involuntary reaction to stimuli. The speaker has not willed the pupils to widen; it is a simple reflex, a physiological response to nature. The poem's penultimate line also reveals the speaker's unintentional physical activity: "The veins within our hands betrayed our fear" (13). Again, the speaker has not willed this response; in fact, the only deliberate "action" is trying to hide the sentiment of fear. The speaker seems to believe that this act of physicality—the clenching of the veins—is an act of disloyalty. Since Roethke has opted not to describe the collective first-person speaker in active terms, the reader's focus is logically drawn to the poem's visceral portrayal of nature and weather.

Whether nature is violent or stable, environmental forces astonish the speaker. As the poem progresses, the atmospheric conditions change; the speaker, however, ostensibly remains the same. Jenijoy La Belle (*Echoing Wood,* 11) astutely compares the looming (though ultimately nonexistent) thunderstorm in "Interlude" to T. S. Eliot's "dry sterile thunder without rain" (*Collected Poems,* 66). La Belle also states, "Just as weather vanes show the condition of the atmosphere, so the veins in the hands show the condition of the man. The storm, instead of producing rain, produces chaos" (*Echoing Wood,* 11). In considering La Belle's analysis, it is appropriate to return to a discussion of the poem's opening stanza. The poem's first line, "The element of air was out of hand," immediately endeavors to categorize and bring stability to nature; the speaker attempts to establish order by identifying the strong winds as "the element of air," one of the four elements of nature in ancient Greek philosophy, along with fire, earth, and water. The first line also suggests a cautious connection between the environment and the body. That is, the phrase "out of hand" implies that there should be an interdependent relationship between nature and humankind, though the environment is not subject to human control. With "[t]he element of air" being "out of hand," we see that an immediate sense of chaos, perhaps even disaster, is the foundational motif of "Interlude." The speaker waits for an ecological disturbance and seems powerless to act or move while observing the imposing atmosphere.

George Wolff has claimed that the "best poems in *Open House* are ones that present a natural description laden with implications of another order of experience" (*Theodore Roethke,* 24). "Interlude" meets Wolff's criteria, particularly in the sense that its theme is the intersection between humans and untamable nature. However, "Interlude" is also notable in terms of the speaker's marked stillness in the face of ultimately nonthreatening environmental forces. In *Open House,* as Richard Allen Blessing notes in *Theodore Roethke's Dynamic Vision* (1974), Roethke "tries to compress the great emotions—rage, anguish, love—into the tightest forms imaginable" (43), a tendency that is apparent in Roethke's use of elegiac stanzas, his diction, and the understated descriptions of the speaker. In this sense, "Interlude" distinguishes itself somewhat from the rest of the collection; it contradicts the tone established by the title poem of *Open House,* which, as Blessing notes, features emotions that "all reveal themselves in action, in the poet's every deed and gesture," with the "inner life translat[ing] itself clearly into *pure act*" (43, emphasis added). In contrast to the title poem, the speaker of "Interlude" is submissive, nearly motionless. For its unique treatment of the relationship between humans and their physical surroundings, "Interlude" merits a place in the ongoing discussion of Roethke's oeuvre.

NOTES

1. I refer here to Walter B. Kalaidjian's *Understanding Theodore Roethke,* Lynn Ross-Bryant's *Theodore Roethke: Poetry of the Earth . . . Poet of the Spirit . . . ,* and other commentary that, though thoughtful and well-researched, may not have given sufficient credit to *Open House* as an independent volume. In a 1965 article in *The New Republic,* even Roethke's friend Stanley Kunitz noted that the collection was largely imitative.

2. At the time of its publication, *Open House* received considerable commendation. Critics, though, tend to see the collection as rather derivative. Jay Parini notes, "The book fails on many counts, and only a few of the lyrics suggest that Roethke was a potentially important poet" (38). Eventually, even Roethke himself came to see the limitations of *Open House,* stating, "My first book was much too wary, much too gingerly in its approach to experience; rather dry in tone and constricted in rhythm" (*Selected Letters,* 114). Despite the book's shortcomings, it is still worthy of consideration, particularly as the genesis of Roethke's oeuvre.

4

"Sharper on the Ear"

"The Light Comes Brighter" and the Subtle Phenomena of Place

ROD PHILLIPS

IN 1940, Theodore Roethke was asked to submit ten poems to a volume, soon to be published by the University of Michigan Press, titled *New Michigan Verse.* The poems, nine of which were soon to be published in Roethke's 1941 first collection *Open House,* represent a fine sampling of the poet's early work, including "'Long Live the Weeds,'" "Highway: Michigan," "The Heron," and the subject of this essay, "The Light Comes Brighter" (*Collected Poems,* 10). Roethke was pleased, as any poet at the beginning of his or her career would be, by having his work selected along with that of other writers representing the state's best new poetry.[1] But Roethke also had one misgiving about his inclusion in the Michigan anthology: he did not want to be pigeonholed as a "regional poet" (Seager, 133).

It is a dilemma faced by many writers, before and after Roethke: how to write about one's own home region, lovingly and accurately, without being limited *by* that region, reduced to second-class status and damned by the faint praise of being called one of the state's best poets. As William Barillas points out in his study *The Midwestern Pastoral: Place and Landscape in Literature of the American Heartland* (2006), Roethke was thoroughly grounded in the natural world and in matters of place, and the wealth of creative inspiration provided by his deep roots in the Midwest was immeasurable (105–7). But in a publishing world dominated (then, as now) by Eastern elites, the challenge of transcending the label of "regional poet" must have loomed large in his consciousness in the early years of his career. Roethke's poem "The Light Comes Brighter" provides an excellent example of the ways in which the poet was able to avoid the stigma attached to regionalism by moving beyond the simplistic use of local color details, such as plant life, geographical features, and place-names, choosing instead to focus on the more subtle and elusive phenomena of place that allow the reader to connect more fully with the poet's language.

"The Light Comes Brighter," first published in the March 1938 issue of *The Atlantic Monthly* before its inclusion in Roethke's first collection, *Open House* (1941), is a poem detailing the changing of the seasons, from winter to spring, in Roethke's native Michigan. Like several other poems in *Open House,* including "Slow Season," the triptych "The Coming of the Cold," and "Vernal Sentiment," the poem draws its subject from a decidedly regional occurrence: the changing of the seasons. All three are brilliant in their own right, with "Slow Season" and "The Coming of the Cold" providing stark, earthy depictions of Michigan's descent into autumn, and "Vernal Sentiment" offering a whimsical and enthusiastic embrace of the returning spring. Both in imagery and in theme, however, these three poems offer a fairly standard approach to their respective topics. The "season's wreckage" of an orchard's rotting fruit, and the walker trudging "ankle-deep in leaves" in the two autumnal poems, lead readers to an elegiac view of nature during the changing season (*Collected Poems,* 13, 11). Likewise, with its emergent crocuses "in the usual places," courting teenagers "with last year's fatuous faces," and another "similar litter" of newborn kittens, "Vernal Sentiment" revels in the predictable yet still wondrous advance of spring (23).

In "The Light Comes Brighter," however, Roethke's treatment of the changing season is much more nuanced and complex, relying on the description of a number of subtle sensory observations of seasonal phenomena to portray the change from winter to spring both in the natural world and within the human mind. Consisting of five quatrains of rhymed iambic pentameter, the poem describes a series of observations of a solitary walker near a river's edge during the frozen month of March. The first of these comes in the poem's first line: "The light comes brighter from the east," describing the almost indiscernible change in the angle and quality of sunlight as the Michigan days begin to lengthen towards the spring solstice. In addition to these changes in the quality of the light, the speaker also notes that sound travels readily on the cold clear air of March, allowing the "restive" calling of nearby crows to be perceived more clearly, "sharper on the ear" (the word "restive" first signaling the theme of expectation that will be carried throughout the poem) (2). The sound of a sudden "cannon crack" presages the coming breakup of river ice just now beginning to shift from its winter-long location (4). As Peter Balakian notes in *Theodore Roethke's Far Fields* (1989), many of the nature-based poems in *Open House* focus on "nature's in-between times" (27) during which the natural world "embodies a fecundity of spirit which is the poet's hope" (26). Certainly, that is the case with "The Light Comes Brighter"; from its very first lines, the poem depicts a winter landscape pregnant with the changes spring will bring with it.

The second quatrain depicts a "winter-sealed" landscape just starting to show subtle signs of yielding to spring as "[t]he sun cuts deep into a heavy drift" (5). River ice, forced by currents to pile up and buckle around bridge-heads, "begins to shift" (7), spilling over the river's banks into nearby fields. The rhyming of "drift" and "shift" at the end of the stanza's first and third lines emphasizes the slow seasonal metamorphosis unfolding. This is not the powerful and bridge-shaking "sudden sucking roar" of the breakup of ice on Michigan's Tittabawasee River, later described by Roethke in "Meditation at Oyster River" (*Collected Poems,* 185), from the "North American Sequence" in *The Far Field* (1964); the nascent breakup of ice depicted in "The Light Comes Brighter" is not a dramatic event but a slowly unfolding process.

The gradual thaw begins to gain momentum in the third stanza, as the poem's speaker articulates changes to the landscape both seen and unseen. As snow melts from their branches, "trees assume familiar shapes" (9) and water dripping from them "escapes / In rivulets." These actions above ground are mirrored by other unseen phenomena, underground, as "cold roots stir below" (11–12). Coming as it does at the midpoint of the poem, the pivotal image of the thawing roots slowly returning to life, unseen but intuited by the speaker, prepares the reader for the transition from the description of the external changes taking place in the natural world to other changes taking place within the human mind as spring approaches.

"Soon," the speaker predicts at the beginning of the fourth stanza, "field and wood will wear an April look" (13). The poem's focus moves from the observable phenomena of the present moment to predictions of the coming spring, predictions based on cyclical patterns provided by years of observation. The cawing of winter crows and the sounds of cracking river ice will soon be gone, "for green is breaking now," and in their place the song of the spring migrant "ovenbird will match the vocal brook" (15).[2] Roethke's choice of the ovenbird as a symbol of the coming spring is emblematic of his deep engagement with the Michigan landscape and his use of subtle and elusive phenomena to describe it. The ovenbird is a small, drab, ground-nesting warbler, a bird much more often heard than actually seen, and one that is often mistaken for the wood thrush. A dozen better-known species of Michigan birds might have been chosen in its place to represent the coming of spring—the robin, the red-winged blackbird, the eastern bluebird—but none of these would have matched the ovenbird as an image of the unseen in nature.

In the final quatrain, the focus of the poem shifts from the outer world to the "hidden scene" of the "leafy mind," dormant in some sense and "tightly furled" during the long winter. The changes wrought by the coming of spring will be reflected here as well, Roethke's speaker assures us, as the mind transforms "its private substance into green / and young shoots spread upon our inner world" (17–20). The poet's final lines on one hand acknowledge the Cartesian divide between the human mind (the "private substance" of "our inner world") and the natural world, while on the other hand they attempt to deny that such a divide exists; the subtle external clues of the seasonal transformation of the Michigan landscape the poet observes are no more and no less a signal of the coming spring than the unfurling of the "leafy mind" of the observer (18).

NOTES

1. Among other poets included in the anthology, edited by Carl Edwin Burklund, were A. J. M. Smith and John Malcolm Brinnin.

2. The ovenbird, *Seiurus aurcapillus,* is a "common breeding warbler in forests throughout Michigan" (Brewer, 434). As Roethke suggests in the poem, its annual spring migration brings it to the state each April.

5

Smart Like Auden?

"Lull" and "September 1, 1939"

PATRICK GILL

THEODORE ROETHKE'S "Lull" (*Collected Poems,* 29), first published in the February 12, 1940, issue of *The New Republic,* is amended by a subtitle, a simple date given in parentheses: "(November 1939)." This may seem a negligible detail in a relatively minor poem, but it offers two more or less explicit references of a kind not commonly associated with Roethke's poetry. The first is to a concrete historical context. Generally speaking, while "centrally preoccupied with the self" (Brown, 1239) and predominantly known for poetry displaying a "private sensibility" (Barillas, *Midwestern Pastoral,* 105), Roethke prefers the absolute, the universal, to the concrete and pragmatic in his titles. But in the subtitle of "Lull" we have an open reference to a moment in time that lends the date a troublesome significance: here, we are given to understand, is a poem reflecting on the beginning of the Second World War. The second reference is to the work of W. H. Auden, his poem "September 1, 1939" in particular. By means of this reference Roethke positions "Lull" in relation to Auden's poem, and it is a relation not of parodic mockery but of assenting emulation. After all, Roethke was full of admiration for Auden, even before their very first encounter in 1941, when they "hit it off at once and . . . remained friends" (Seager, 115). So impressed was he by the Englishman's person, intellect, and poetic talent that in the same year "Lull" was written, Roethke amended a letter to Louise Bogan with an addendum stating, "Oh, why am I not smart like Auden?" (*Selected Letters,* 81).

In Roethke criticism the case is clear: "Lull" is a minor Roethke poem because it is imitative in nature. It merits little critical response simply because it is "too close to Auden" (Parini, 47). The following observations will revisit the discussion about the resemblance of "Lull" to Auden's poetry, placing particular emphasis on those aspects of the poem that are unmistakably rooted in Roethke's own outlook rather than that of his admired friend, namely a predominant interest in capturing complex emotional states on the level not of society or civilization but of an individual who may also serve as a universal figure.

In order to consider which aspects of "Lull" are reminiscent of Auden, it is necessary to highlight certain features of "September 1, 1939." Although Auden would later disown it, calling it "trash" and saying he was "ashamed to have written" it (qtd. in Skelton, 41), the poem offers a useful adumbration of the style and tone of Auden's poetry of the 1930s because it is such an extreme example of the Yorkshireman's work of that period. "September 1, 1939" presents a politically engaged poet's reflections on hearing the news of the outbreak of the Second World War, in a total of nine eleven-line stanzas. It is written in lines featuring three stresses, similar to those used by Roethke in "Lull." While such lines are not uncommon in Roethke's earlier writing, they tend to be taken up by polysyllabic Latinate words, while the later verse prefers shorter and simpler vocabulary in such short lines (see Blessing, 177). The uncharacteristic formality of the language on display is another feature of Auden's poetry: he liked to employ in his poetry the vocabulary of intellectual concepts, ideologies, and debates of his day, being "determined to engage with the actualities of his time" (Emig, 1). Thus "September 1, 1939" features such diction as "psychopathic," "enlightenment" (95), "Collective Man," "[i]mperialism," "conservative," and "ethical" (96). Roethke's "Lull" has a few phrases that sound quite similar, as for instance

> Intricate phobias grow
> From each malignant wish
> To spoil collective life.
>
> (4–6)

While both poems are characterized to some degree by this technical, impersonal vocabulary, they both also feature examples of everyday language. Auden's poem begins "I sit in one of the dives / On Fifty-second street" (95), while in Roethke's poem "[t]he newsmen suck their thumbs" (14) in a highly quotidian gesture.

It is easy to see, then, why critics think of these poems as very similar: they were written one after the other, they have metrical similarities, and they share a propensity for Latinate vocabulary laced with Germanic everyday words. Most importantly, they are concerned with the same subject matter: the outbreak of the Second World War and the effect that news has on the poem's speaker and on the civilian population at large. It is, of course, fairly obvious that the one poem must have had an influence on the composition of the other. On the point of influence, Roethke has a number of interesting things to say. In his essay "How to Write Like Somebody Else" he writes, "[i]mitation, conscious imitation, is one of the great methods, perhaps *the* method, of learning to write" (*On Poetry and Craft,* 61). But what is contained in that statement, besides an explicit admission to imitative acts, is the implicit verdict that the objective of "learning to write" is the development of a voice of one's own rather than the fulfillment of a purely imitative remit. In light of this opinion, then, imitation—far from being an end in and of itself—becomes part of the maturing process of a poet. Seen from this perspective, Roethke's imitation of Auden's "September 1, 1939" can give us an interesting glimpse of the essential, ineradicable properties of Roethke's poetry at this point in the poet's career.

In terms of sheer word count, Auden's poem is not only significantly longer than Roethke's, it is also (and this is often forgotten because of some eminently quotable lines that occur at the end) substantially concerned with the political and intellectual history of Germany "[f]rom Luther" to "what occurred at Linz" (95), an allusion to the establishment of Nazi concentration camps in the late 1930s. While four of its stanzas are thus concerned with intellectual and cultural history as well as political events and psychoanalytical insights into a dictator's and an entire nation's corrupted soul, only five are set in or make reference to the speaker's immediate and concrete surroundings: stanza 1 sets the scene in a New York bar, stanza 5 briefly references that setting, stanza 7 contemplates the reactions of the civilian population to news of the outbreak of war in Europe, and stanzas 8 and 9 deliberate on the efficacy of poetry in the face of geopolitical disaster. Simply put, this makes Auden's poem a narrative world-historical treatise with an addendum on the role of the poet in society.

Contrasted with these qualities of Auden's poem, Roethke's "Lull" turns out to be an entirely different type of poem altogether. Its mere twenty-one lines are subdivided into two unequal portions of seven and fourteen lines respectively. Given its relative brevity, its emphasis is clearly not on providing historical and intellectual background to the events then unfolding in Europe. Instead, it focuses on the individual. In this, it foregrounds the person of the speaker, as does "September 1, 1939." The palpable difference between the roles and portrayals of the speakers in both these poems, however, is that Auden's persona remains detached from the anonymous mass of the "dense commuters" (96), whereas "Lull" gives us a complex mixture of separation and unity between persona and people. While the emotions evoked may easily be imagined as affecting the speaker of "Lull," their description is introduced not by possessive pronouns but by the definite article, so as to make them applicable to all humanity: "the anxious heart" (3), "[t]he mind" (15), "the wish to love" (21). So while "each man stands apart" (7), and that statement is emphasized by its position just before the break between the two stanzas, there is a spirit of universality very much inclusive of the persona.

Its subtitle aside, "Lull" offers no concrete indication of the exact conflict at its heart, no explicit reference to historical events, place-names, or proper names. Whereas Auden's poem gains an encyclopedic quality through the sheer density of its references, Roethke could be speaking to us about any number of armed conflicts. The most concrete references to contemporary life made in "Lull" are found in lines 10–14, with "generals" (11) sitting on their "well-upholstered bums" (10) and "newsmen suck[ing] their thumbs" (14).

Finally, Roethke's poem offers no hint of the call to action that constitutes the final two stanzas of Auden's "September 1, 1939." In its recognition of "the will to love" (21), Roethke's poem posits that there is a quintessential benevolence to be found, not just in his persona but in humanity. That is the reassurance he can give us and the closure his poem can provide. In fact, whereas Auden's persona analyzes and argues in rational terms, rejecting "[t]he romantic lie in the brain" (97), Roethke's "Lull" posits that "[r]eason embraces death" (19). While our naturally benevolent human instincts and emotions find war unacceptable, rational arguments are being made in favor of war, leading to Roethke's telling "rejection of the sophistications of the civilized" (Sullivan, 14). In his efforts to overcome division and achieve an essential unity, "Roethke was a Romantic" (Parini, 3). Where Auden sees a disparity between the "man-in-the-street" and "the Just," who can meet the global threat by "[s]how[ing] an affirming flame" (97), Roethke places his faith in the universal "wish to love" (21), as the closing line of his poem has it.

"Lull," then, while influenced by "September 1, 1939," expresses a philosophical perspective typical of Roethke rather than Auden. The claim that Roethke's poem "reads like a very rough draft" of Auden's (Parini, 47) may be easy to agree with given the obvious similarity between the poems. However, once the reader has processed this first impression of its undeniable similarity to "September 1, 1939," Roethke's "Lull" merits further reading for the subtle but telling ways in which it differs from Auden's political poetry of the 1930s and provides an illuminating window into the development of Roethke's poetic voice.

6

Ironic Quest in "Highway: Michigan"

RONALD PRIMEAU

THEODORE ROETHKE'S poem "Highway: Michigan" (*Collected Poems,* 31) first appeared in *The New Republic* in 1940, anticipating by nearly two decades the many American road narratives that would follow the success of Jack Kerouac's novel *On the Road* (1957). Roethke was working simultaneously in two competing traditions he knew well: one epitomized by the expansiveness and optimism of Walt Whitman's "Song of the Open Road" (1856) and the other skeptical of restless wandering and in tune with Ralph Waldo Emerson's proclamation that "[t]raveling is a fool's paradise" (278). As is typical in a poem by Roethke, a lot is compacted into twenty lines in "Highway: Michigan." In four five-line stanzas in iambic tetrameter, the poet describes autoworkers on their frenzied commute home after a shift in an automobile factory. This description expresses in compressed form an expansiveness of theme, as the American road quest, sociopolitical analysis of American labor, and insightful psychology merge into the fast lane. By means of verbal and situational irony, achieved through word choice, juxtaposition, understatement, paradox, and synecdoche, Roethke critiques the mythic freedom of the American literary road quest, portraying instead the destructive power of technology and workers' entrapment by industry.

Each stanza in the poem adds its own ironies while heightening the sense of tension and danger. The opening stanza establishes a neutral tone of ironic distance and a nervous atmosphere suggesting the general state of mind in the

Machine Age. "Here from the field's edge we survey / The progress of the jaded" (1–2): from this first sentence forward, the speaker comes across like a lecturer showing images on a screen or leading students on a field trip to view traffic patterns and the behavior of drivers. The poem's first foot ("Here from") is a trochee, an initial substitution that immediately breaks the iambic pattern to follow, signaling the speaker's air of objectivity and anticipating the poem's subsequent disruptions. From the outset we view the action from a field, probably in or near the city of Saginaw, Roethke's hometown.[1] This "edge" or transitional zone between pavement and the pastoral "field" communicates tension, an "edginess" prefiguring the disastrous crash to come. The effect is enhanced by a trochaic substitution in the third foot of line 1, which puts the stress on the word "edge" and its connotations.

A distanced, empirical tone is also created by the clause "we survey," both in its use of the first-person plural voice (associated with scientific discourse) and in the implications of inquiry, analysis, and appraisal conveyed by the verb "survey." Ironic duality enters with the direct object "progress," which refers both to the forward movement of the vehicles and to the cult of economic and technological development stemming from the Enlightenment. The drivers have been "jaded," made cynical by their alienated industrial labor. They may be moving forward in space, but that movement does not constitute freedom and autonomy. As William Barillas points out in his commentary on the poem, the clause "traffic from the town / Rides by" (3–4) is a synecdoche that "endows the cars, collectively 'traffic,' with agency and control" (*Midwestern Pastoral,* 112). The workers are less driving than being driven by their cars; they have been subordinated to an industrial system that operates for its own ends.

In stanza 2, the desire for freedom begins to exact its price. Dangerous darting in and out of lanes seeking to pass other cars underscores a frantic hope for release, increasing the dramatic tension in the poem. In line 10, the poem's midpoint, the speaker states that the drivers "toy with death and traffic fines." Here Roethke inverts the expected sequence. Less important traffic fines should precede the more ominous threat of death, were the pattern not disrupted by the drivers' false sense of security and power behind the wheel. The word order of "death and traffic fines" creates ironic juxtaposition and understatement suggesting that danger has become normal, even trivial (something to be toyed with), in the Machine Age. In broaching the subject of traffic fatalities by means of a concluding irony, line 10 also foreshadows the poem's grim ending.

Stanza 3 opens with the proclamation that "[a]cceleration is their need" (11), asserted ironically, as if speed were a biological necessity like air, water, or food, or an emotional one like love, rather than a desire induced by consumer culture and a built environment that makes driving an unavoidable part of life. The drivers' spirits and bodies are caught up in a "mania" (12), a pivotal subject of the poem since everything happens in a rush. "The modern obsession with mechanically derived speed," writes ethicist Michael Northcott, "is such that it eviscerates moral deliberation over its ecological or human costs":

> Speed produces an altered state of consciousness . . . [a] form of ecstasy [that] generates detachment from the violent effects of the ownership and use of devices which confer speed on the millions who have been killed and seriously injured by them, and from the systemic effects on the ecology of the earth. . . . Speed involves a kind of moral perversion which is indicated in the extent to which danger to life and limb from fast cars forms part of the appeal of cars and other such devices to some of those who use them. (220–21)

Roethke expresses much the same concern in "Highway: Michigan" about the "mania [that] keeps [the drivers] on the move / Until the toughest nerves are frayed" (12–13). The unique power of his expression, however, lies less in its consistency with academic analysis than in its poetic and rhetorical qualities. These include the double irony that concludes stanza 3, a paradox intensified by situational irony: the drivers "are the prisoners of speed / Who flee in what their hands have made" (14–15). The sentence complicates the idiomatic expression "prisoners of their own device" by linking speed with confinement rather than escape, then reducing the drivers to their hands, a synecdoche for their entire selves, bodies and spirits which are captive to the automobiles they themselves have manufactured. The popular association of automobile travel with freedom and autonomy is thus revealed to be a false myth, one that dehumanizes the workers and subordinates them to the industrial system.

Stanza 4 presents the crash that had to come, and its arrival is brutal, first in the ironically understated description of the moment "two cars meet" and then in the savagery of "steel rip[ping] through conflicting steel" (16–17). As the poem concludes, the perspective pulls back, returning the readers and speaker to the edge of the field observing the scene of the crash and listening to "the siren's blast" (18). Not unexpectedly because of earlier foreshadowing, one driver escapes the prison of speed, but only because the crash has "pinned" him "beneath the seat" (19). At least one critic reads the poem's last sentence as suggesting that the driver survives the accident. "In Roethke's infernal vision of mechanized modernity," writes Walter Kalaidjian, "near death by machine marks modern man's doom" (24). But irony is so pervasive in "Highway: Michigan" that we are compelled to read the last two lines as indicating the driver's death. That he or she is "pinned beneath the seat" suggests fatal, crushing injury; there is no hint of rescue by onlookers or first responders. The synecdoche created by the last noun in the poem implies as much: the driver escapes not the car but "the machine" (20), meaning the entire industrial complex. The only way to do that is to die—the poem's final, devastating irony.

Meter and rhyme do not draw attention to themselves in "Highway: Michigan," allowing a natural quality to the speech while enhancing the poem's ironically dispassionate tone. The poem's iambic tetrameter is subtle, with many softly stressed syllables such as the words "from" in line 3 and "lines" in line 8. The poem's rhyme scheme is also unobtrusive. Each stanza features two end-rhyming pairs: the first and fourth lines, and the third and fifth. The separation between the rhyming sounds of the first and fourth lines mutes the poem's music. Slant rhymes in the first and second stanzas (town/own and on/won) contribute to the prosaic, dispassionate tone in the first half of the poem. They also set up the perfect rhymes that follow, which by contrast ring more clearly, causing the ironies they accompany to strike the reader with greater emotional force. Frederick Philip Lenz links such use of sound devices in "Highway: Michigan" to a "feeling of unbalance mirroring the alienation and repression of workers" and a foreshadowing of "the inevitable destruction depicted in the closing lines of the poem" (98). The poem's music is not joyful but relentless and bleak, providing a pattern that contains and advances the speaker's deterministic outlook.

"Highway: Michigan" marks a turn toward pessimistic responses to car culture in American literature, expressed in texts that focus on adverse effects of automobiles, the automotive industry, and roads. Between Roethke's poem in 1940 and the wave of postwar American road quests appeared Karl Shapiro's poem "Auto Wreck" (1941) and Henry Miller's dystopian travelogue *The Air-Conditioned Nightmare* (1945). Many poets followed in challenging the myth of freedom associated with the automobile, among them William Stafford in "Traveling through the Dark" (1962); Louis Simpson in "Walt Whitman at Bear Mountain" (1964), in which the speaker asks, "Where are you, Walt? / The Open

Road goes to the used-car lot" (64); Philip Levine in "Coming Home: Detroit, 1968" (1972); and Joyce Carol Oates in "F—" (1978). The failed journey of disinherited questers is also captured by Jim Harrison in his novel *A Good Day to Die* (1973) and Robert Fanning in *American Prophet: Poems* (2009), in which Fanning revisits Whitman's bardic yawp only to find that it has given way to a failure of communication. The automobile, as sociologist Dennis Soron argues, serves "as both a badge of individual empowerment and as a condensed symbol of many troubling aspects of our collective life that we seem impotent to change," including "social atomization, time poverty, stress, tragic injuries and fatalities, deteriorating public health, ecological destruction, social exclusion and the evisceration of public space" (181). For many writers, the negative aspects of cars have come to outweigh associations with freedom and adventure.

Roethke's abiding interest in roads and cars is a matter of record. His biographer Allan Seager relates the details of Roethke's plans, outlined in his last notebooks, for a sequence of poems describing journeys by automobile across North America to places related to the abuse and defeat of Native American tribes (279). Roethke's "North American Sequence" poems, collected in *The Far Field* (1964), do not follow that plan but include passages that suggest it, such as the winter drive that ends with the car stalled in a snowdrift, in the first stanza of "The Far Field." In the journey motif of "North American Sequence," Roethke is much more positive about the quest. Nonetheless, he still emphasizes alienation, stress, and danger when it comes to automobiles, themes underlined by the ironies that drive "Highway: Michigan."

NOTE

1. At one point Roethke titled the poem "Dixie Highway: Michigan," which more specifically identified the setting. The Dixie Highway was a system of paved roads, developed and linked between 1915 and 1927, that ran as far north as Sault Ste. Marie in Michigan's Upper Peninsula and as far south as Miami, Florida. The eastern section of the Dixie Highway passed through the Michigan industrial cities of Saginaw, Flint, Pontiac, and Detroit. To this day, the name "Dixie Highway" identifies sections of the former route in Michigan and elsewhere in the United States. A road running from downtown Saginaw south to Flint, for example, is still named Dixie Highway, as is another running from near Holly, Michigan to Clarkston. Roethke was almost certainly inspired to write this poem by viewing traffic on Dixie Highway in or near Saginaw. A draft titled "Dixie Highway: Michigan" is found in Box/Folder 20/34 of the Theodore Roethke Papers in Special Collections of the University of Washington Libraries.

7

Movement through Space, Sound, and Time in "Night Journey"

MARCEL INHOFF

THEODORE ROETHKE'S "Night Journey" (*Collected Poems,* 32) brings closure to his first collection, *Open House* (1941), by using images, rhythm, and literary allusions to describe the visual and physical experience of train travel and to augment Roethke's poetic palette. Ready to leave behind the cautious formalism and philosophical abstraction that characterize much of *Open House,* Roethke could now move ahead toward the spiritual exploration of his later poetic career, in which the archetypal journey begun in "Night Journey" becomes a central theme and motif. As Peter Balakian puts it, "Roethke no doubt made 'Night Journey' the final poem in the collection not only because he considered it one of his best poems to date, but also because it summed up some of his largest concerns and foreshadowed things to come" (29).

"Night Journey" employs a formal arrangement that helps the reader imagine felt experience through images and rhythms, including the "clickety-clack trimeter," which, as Jay Parini points out, "suggests the rhythmical sway of the train" (47). The poem's short verse lines and metrical precision also convey a sense of the sleeping car as an enclosed space and of the poet as a willing captive of the technological sublimity of the train in motion. Its power and speed seem to increase as the poem presses on in the present tense, sentences shorten, and their rhyme schemes become more regular.

Despite the lack of stanza breaks, each of the poem's six sentences constitutes an internal stanza with its own rhyme scheme, but one that picks up rhymes from previous sentence-stanzas and incorporates them into new rhyme schemes. For starters, lines 1 to 5 form a cinquain rhyming *abbca* (west, earth, berth, night, rest), framed by "west" and "rest" but with "night" remaining unrhymed. Lines 6–10 form an *abcdab* sestet (lace, trees, mist, sight, place, knees) that remains rhymeless for four lines, as if the train were picking up speed, but concludes with an enclosing *ab* couplet, "place, knees," that provides rhymes to match "lace, trees." The train's incessant forward motion is acoustically suggested by these changing rhyme schemes. But Roethke also uses his rhymes to create literary allusions. Note, for example, how in the second sentence-stanza "night," unrhymed in the first sentence-stanza, paradoxically becomes "sight," reminding us of visionary mystical texts like John of the Cross's "Dark Night of the Soul," or, of particular significance to Roethke, T. S. Eliot's "East Coker": "O dark dark dark. They all go into the dark" (*Collected Poems,* 185). In the fourth sentence-stanza, a quatrain rhyming *abcb* like a ballad stanza (swing, bright, ravines, sight), "night" and "sight" become "bright / light," as in a miraculous vision or a near-death experience. The alliteration that encloses the stanza (swing / sight) instead of rhyme adds its own vibrancy to the symbolic mystique that pervades the sentence. In the final sentence-stanza, "night" will return, or at least half of it, in the penultimate line, "I stay up half the night" (26). But "love" will have the last word in another ballad stanza rhyme scheme, *abcb* (stone, shove, night, love). The entire twenty-seven-line poem is a continuously echoing night journey.

The reader participates vicariously in this journey, while the poem's speaker, as a passenger in a railway sleeping car, gives his body over to the physical sensations of train travel as he watches the landscape go by. Each line presents another moment, another sensory experience, even as the assertions "I stare" (4), "I feel" (12), "I wake" (15), "I watch" (16), and "I . . . see" (26–27) frame the poem's sequential imagery. The first sentence emphasizes physical experience as the "train bears west" (1) while others "take their rest" (5). There is no such rest for the speaker, as the train's "rhythm rocks the earth" (2) and he is jolted into alertness. This heightened attention then leads to visual experience: "I stare into the night" (4). Throughout the poem's journey bodily reactions and fleeting visual moments join forces. For the passenger and the responsive reader, the journey is felt as well as seen.

In the second sentence-stanza (lines 6–11), a sestet with one rhyme missing, visual imagery conveys a physical sense of the train's velocity and a temporal sense of the speaker's glimpses of each place. Roethke evokes the visual experience of a traveler looking out a train window and seeing landscape as if it were moving and the train stationary. Three scenes pass in quick paratactic succession:

> Bridges of iron lace,
> A suddenness of trees,
> A lap of mountain mist
> All cross my line of sight,

followed by "a bleak wasted place, / And a lake below my knees." One of the poem's most memorable phrases, "a suddenness of trees," subordinates what is seen to how it is seen: quickly approaching and just as quickly left behind. Similarly, there's a "suddenness" in the poem, as well; the stanza becomes metrically hyperactive and visually inventive, as when trochaic substitution launches "Bridges of iron lace" (6). "Then a bleak wasted place" (10), which brings to mind T. S. Eliot's *The Waste Land,* slows things down by diverging from normative iambic trimeter with four strong stresses: "*Then* a *bleak, wast*ed *place.*" Drawn-out assonance also weighs down "wasted place," which rhymes stunningly with "iron lace," before consonance does the same with "bleak / lake." As multiple sound patterns connect, overlap, and reinforce each other throughout the poem, so do Roethke's spiritual themes and environmental concerns. The "wasted place" also anticipates later poems by Roethke such as "Moss-Gathering," with its memory of having "disturbed some rhythm, old and of vast importance, / By pulling off flesh from the living planet" (*Collected Poems,* 38) and "The Longing," in which "slag-heaps fume at the edge of the raw cities" (*Collected Poems,* 181).

The third sentence (lines 12–15), a quatrain rhyming *abab,* returns to the physical experience evoked at the poem's outset:

> Full on my neck I feel
> The straining at a curve;
> My muscles move with steel,
> I wake in every nerve.

This awakening is expressed, for the first time in the poem, in four lines describing the speaker's centripetal sensation as the train takes a curve. At the end of this kinetic third sentence, "I wake in every nerve" not only parallels but also thematically advances "I stare into the night" from the first sentence. It does not refer to a sleeper waking, as the speaker is already awake, but to becoming alert, as defined by *The American Heritage Dictionary:* "To be brought into a state of awareness or alertness." The same meaning applies to Roethke's "The Waking" and to "Song," in which he wonders, "Do the dead wake in their own way?" (*Collected Poems,* 251). Roethke breaks with the one-image-per-line density of prior sentences, and renders only two dominant sensations by using the kinetic energy of his syntax to provide density. Significantly, "I wake in every nerve" is the first time the speaker offers the reader a kind of summary of his observations and experience. Seeing the "bleak wasted place" and other features of the American landscape jolts him into personal awareness with environmental implications.

As if to emphasize the speaker's alertness, the fourth sentence (lines 16–19), an *abcb* ballad stanza, offers an active assertion:

> I watch a beacon swing
> From dark to blazing bright;
> We thunder through ravines
> And gullies washed with light.

The first three of the poem's six sentences alternate physical, visual, and then physical imagery, while the poem's fourth, fifth, and sixth sentences all feature references to both senses. There is another notable change: it is now "I watch" (16) after the more passive "I stare" (4) and "[a]ll cross my line of sight" (9). The perception of the nighttime landscape becomes more than a collection of impressions or a lonely act of looking out a train window "while others take their rest." In the clause "[w]e thunder through ravines," "we," rather than only an "I," are traveling together. The other passengers may sleep, but the speaker's interaction with the landscape has made him aware that he is part of a community.

The train thunders, but there are also multiple visual cues to the importance of light in darkness. The beacon that swings "from dark to blazing bright" (17) compels the reader to consider the material basis of the speaker's perception. Does the light swing back and forth behind an object that recurrently obscures it? Does it turn itself off and on? Given the train's speed, the speaker's observation of whatever is occurring is necessarily brief, but Roethke's description makes it an almost slow-motion moment. There is also a contrast between the beacon and the second source of light, the "gullies washed with light" (19). We yet don't know that a storm is coming, presaged by the train's thundering, but halfway through the sentence-stanza Roethke switches from a slow-motion observation to the quick one-two punch of the train passing through ravines and by gullies, ditches cut into the earth by repeated downpours. Neither "swing" nor "ravines" is rhymed anywhere in the poem, which creates a sense of suspense that is only relieved when the "light" finally connects with "bright," bringing closure to a sentence that started with three apparently unrhymed end words—unrhymed, that is within the sentence-stanza. After all, "bright" and "light" do rhyme with "night" and "sight" earlier in the poem.

A sense of acceleration pervades the second half of the poem (lines 13–27). Tactile and visual sensations collaborate in each sentence, along with images of movement accompanied by words like "blazing" and "thunder" (17–18). Furthermore, four successive lines (22–25) are impelled by the verbs "rush," "rattles," "shake," "jerk," and "shove." Roethke structures the second half of "Night Journey" roughly along the classical lines of a five-act drama: sentence four offers rising action, sentence five leads into the climax, and the final sentence provides the denouement. The description that opens the fourth sentence-stanza sustains the action that concluded the previous sentence:

> Beyond the mountain pass
> Mist deepens on the pane;
> We rush into a rain
> That rattles double glass.

The sentence parallels the preceding one: both contain an observation, and both evoke a physical impression as well as the communal "we" of passengers and crew, attendants, and the unseen driver of the train. The main structural difference is in the rhyme scheme. After the suspension created by the fourth sentence's alternation of unrhymed and rhymed lines, the self-contained, completed *abba* rhyme scheme signals a change. Indeed, we have reached the poem's climax. The train not only passes through a mountain pass; it also weathers a storm that rattles the train windows, creating a physical sensation with a pun on "pane"/"pain." This marks an intrusion of the weather outside into the passenger car: the rattling glass can be felt inside.[1] The glass, as a divider between inside and outside, detaches slightly from its frame (thus "rattling"), and a certain permeability is suggested. Previous physical sensations were all created by the train itself, whether it was the train's "rhythm," centripetal "straining," or thundering "through ravines." The poem records not simply an external journey of the poet but allegorically an internal one, psychological and perhaps spiritual, that reaches its goal not without rattling pain.

The final sentence emphasizes physical sensation: "Wheels shake the roadbed stone, / The pistons jerk and shove," followed by "I stay up half the night / To see the land I love" (24–27), which provides the climactic moment of this physically exhausting train ride through the night. The transition between the jerking pistons and "I stay up half the night" appears to be abrupt, but only superficially. Indeed, reading these four lines together—

> We rush into a rain
> That rattles double glass.
> Wheels shake the roadbed stone,
> The pistons jerk and shove.
>
> (22–25)

—reveals a transition from the rain outside to the physical intrusion into the train via the rattling glass and back outside again, as the train intrudes on the world by disturbing "the roadbed stone." The poem's two-line finale ends its own journey by creating a thematic link, only implicit before, between looking and love. Significantly, we encounter the "-ight" rhyme again, which first surfaced at the end of line 4 as "night," a part of the poem's symbolic allusions to metaphysical darkness. It then turned into its opposite, into "sight," "bright," and "light." Now that the rhyme returns as "night," the meaning of the word has changed. An almost metaphysical darkness has turned into one that is merely the period between sundown and sunrise. The phrase "half the night" (26) is unlike "all night," "until morning," or similar expressions in that it does not refer to the whole period of darkness. "Half the night" suggests literally staying up part of the night and then sleeping, which undercuts the pathos of the final line. Rather than nationalist sentiment, the final line of "Night Journey" should be read as personal. Throughout the poem, Roethke has alluded to darkness in a mystical sense while looking at a landscape that is both symbolically charged and painstakingly, unromantically described. When the speaker looks out the train window at the changing landscape, that act itself is love, much as in "Lull," only a few pages before "Night Journey," Roethke describes "frightened eyes" out of which "stares the wish to love" (*Collected Poems,* 29). But there is more to that final line than this. For a reader in the early 1940s, "the land I love" carried a political connotation, specifically alluding to Irving Berlin's song "God Bless America" (1918), which was popularized by singer Kate Smith in Berlin's 1938 revision.[2] Notably, that revision contains the line "guide her through the night," which connects Roethke's final line to the central rhyme of the poem. Indeed, Roethke often expressed personal, ecocritical, and political concerns in his poems, often towards the end. This is true of "The Longing," for example, from the "North American Sequence," which concludes

> Old men should be explorers?
> I'll be an Indian.
> Ogalala?
> Iroquois.
>
> (*Collected Poems*, 183)

There is a subtle shift in those lines, a denial of simplistic, impersonal patriotism. Moreover, as Frank Kearful points out in his essay on "North American Sequence," it is a political statement, as "Roethke's allying himself with the Iroquois may be read as a consciously defiant gesture" (255). The same impulse towards irony and defiance, decades earlier, marks the evocation of love, landscape, and personal recovery in "Night Journey."

"Night Journey," a memorable poem in its own right, acquires added significance when considered in relation to what came both before and after in Roethke's poetry. It shows that Roethke had learned to use rhyme and meter to reinforce and enrich meaning, imagery, and tone. Thematically, it embodies the poet's concern with landscape, evident in the second section of *Open House* and in the two poems preceding "Night Journey," and later more fully explored in *The Lost Son and Other Poems* and the posthumous *The Far Field*. The "North American Sequence," which opens that last book, consists of six poems that explore the subject of "seeing the land I love." The archetypal quest introduced in "Night Journey" became a central concern for Roethke, who asserts in "The Waking" that he "learn[s] by going where [he has] to go" (*Collected Poems*, 104). Likewise, the motifs of darkness, light, and vision appear in many of Roethke's later poems, including major works like "The Lost Son" and "In a Dark Time." In its symbolism, diction, poetic form, and especially its imagery, "Night Journey" remains one of Roethke's best poems and a signal accomplishment in the early phase of his career.

NOTES

1. This is not modern-day "double glass," as we understand it—a compound material. Modern double-glass windows were not released as a product until 1944, although patents had been filed earlier. These are likely just two panes in a frame, which explains the "rattling" and the speaker's feeling of vulnerability in the train car.

2. The political aspect is enhanced by the disputes around the songs that led Woody Guthrie to compose "This Land Is Your Land" (1940), a critical reply to "God Bless America," which became even more familiar in 1940 as the campaign song for both the Democratic and Republican presidential candidates. That "Night Journey" first appeared in the June 8, 1940, issue of *The New Yorker* lends credence to my suggestion that the poem's final line is, like Guthrie's song written the same year, a retort to Berlin and Smith.

The Lost Son and Other Poems (1948)

8

"Cuttings" and "Cuttings (*later*)"

Roethke's Minute Carnivals

MICHAEL HINDS

THE READER of Theodore Roethke can hardly ignore how "Cuttings" and "Cuttings (*later*)" (*Collected Poems,* 35) are mapped into the very beginning of *The Lost Son* (1948), the book that is commonly granted as representing the poet's breakthrough into poetic maturity. In any long view of Roethke's development, these first of the "greenhouse poems" are where he announces the themes and modes that would persist throughout his career. In the "Cuttings" poems, new growth is made to happen, sprouting from the productive culling of existing material. The poems are also declarations of artistic purpose for Roethke, indications of the course that his poetry will take. This assumption of poetic authority is founded on Roethke's discovery of psychosexual themes and tropes that allow him to generate powerful correspondences between external nature and his own mind and body. In effect, he grows massively powerful metaphors out of his singular self, something that makes these poems so enthralling, with all of the pleasure and terror that implies.

Critics have always recognized this unity of purpose in the "Cuttings" poems, stressing their achievement of a newly singular poetics based on what Kenneth Burke saw as "the imagistic figuring of a human situation" ("Vegetal Radicalism," 68). Seamus Heaney's reading of the poems, especially "Cuttings (*later*)," adds a spiritual dimension, regarding them as Genesis texts: "Now the free, nervous notation of natural process issues in a state of unity with cosmic energies and in quiet intimations of order and delight. They are acts of faith made in some state of grace" ("Canticles," 191–92). Whatever their framing, these poems convey the sense that we are at the start of a brilliant career, the place where discussion of Roethke begins. There is room for trouble in paradise, however, and this essay will query the presentation of the "Cuttings" poems as beginnings. To write of them only as points of origin is to risk overstressing their narrative significance at the expense of their internal dynamics; that is, emphasizing the poet's historical progress overwrites their particular drama, turning the poems into stepping-stones when they demand our pause. Although it is tempting to read the poems as necessarily sequential, given that their titles map them onto the same timeline, we should not necessarily read "Cuttings (*later*)" as correcting "Cuttings," viewing one as a false start and the other as wholly achieved. That each poem is powerfully conclusive in itself, with Roethke demonstrating his peculiar originality in an exemplary way, is well illustrated by how Camille Paglia's close reading of "Cuttings" in *Break, Blow, Burn* (2006) makes no reference at all to "Cuttings (*later*)."

This essay will also stress how the originality of these poems is a complex phenomenon, recognizing how critics like Jenijoy La Belle have insisted that Roethke is a poet of extraordinary sensitivity to the work of others: "Roethke's sensibility is not 'isolated,' but is continually referring the reader to a heritage of poetry that at once defines the cultural ambience in which the work must be understood and aids the poet in moving beyond 'solitary experience' to the creation of transpersonal experience" (*Echoing Wood,* 4). While "Cuttings" and "Cuttings (*later*)" are poems about writing in which Roethke realizes the potential of his art, they are only allusions to a life force that language can describe but not command. He discovers authority through the emergence of his shoot-pen in "Cuttings (*later*)," watching it "lean to beginnings," but also recognizes that his kind of creativity is just another form of expression in a nature that is extravagantly gifted with such activity. This is further confirmed by the intertextual hyperactivity of both poems, how they infinitely generate possibilities for reading across traditions and categories, moving beyond their author's control.

"Cuttings" uses the third-person voice to represent the motions of plant growth, and a remarkably tactile and physically present language, both of which create a peculiar friction between the objective experience being described and the subjective mind trying to describe it. This also adds to the oddness of the poems' prosody and form; Roethke's weird word music has been well demonstrated by the micro-reading of Walter Kalaidjian: "employing assonance, consonance, onomatopoeia, and spondaic stress patterns, he recreates the alien textures of the glasshouse landscape." Yet this is not a landscape; it is nature in miniature, and what Roethke suggests is not a spectator's omniscience, but rather something much more intimate. Kalaidjian also identifies Roethke's creation of compound phrases in the greenhouse poems as alienating warpings: "by hyphenating nouns and modifiers into unexpected surrealistic juxtapositions ('sticks-in-a-drowse,' 'slug-soft,' 'thorn-bitten,' 'snuff-laden,' 'stem-fur,' 'monkey-tails,' 'adder-mouthed'), Roethke jars one's conventional experience of nature" (41). These fusions, however, are also peculiarly *realistic* in their very strangeness, causing the peculiar shock of something never before encountered; it is the realism of imagination moving into an environment that is ordinarily beyond perception.

The peculiar liberation of this writing precisely comes from its immersion in the microscopic, an apt demonstration of what Gaston Bachelard identified in the miniaturism of botanical writing: as the reader enters a miniature world, "images begin to abound, then grow, then escape" (154), and the "miniature deploys to the dimensions of a universe" (157). Roethke's bizarre images escape back into themselves, resisting his (and our) control; this contrasts vitally with a poem like Robert Frost's "Design," a terrifying poem constructed by minute elements of a natural scene warped into a theological system. Frost locates terror in the power of the creator of nature, the one who brings things together into significant tableaux. Roethke does not allow for such a discovery; nature in the "Cuttings" world is not so choreographed.

For all the structural devices that articulate the poems, the individual words within them seem remarkably independent, each a miniature organism with its own texture and substance. The vigor of Roethke's work comes as much from the highly individual words that he chooses as from the way he arranges them into an ensemble; every part is as dynamic as the whole. These words themselves are cuttings, and they are not just providing the occasion for an assertion of the poet's selfhood or synthetic powers; they are what allow that self contingently to declare itself (and only after considerable struggle). This self does not necessarily arise to dominance; rather, it learns its place. The words are predominantly Anglo-Saxon, and as such brandish their histories rather bellicosely, but these are intermittently cut with Latinate dactyls communicating problematic nuance: "tendrilous," "intricate," "delicate." Whatever their derivation, each word seems contrived to demand attention, as the poems build an acute sensitivity to etymology in the reader. The words are self-reliant cells, only uncertainly interdependent. Getting from one to the other is hard, even absurdly difficult: these are short poems, but strangely porous ones, in which the pressure of the unexplained is never diminished. These gaps make it a fundamentally erotic poetry, not least because of the way in which language is mysteriously enlivened by desire. As such, the remarkable pelt textures that Roethke generates fulfill Roland Barthes's description of language in *A Lover's Discourse* (1977) as an independent body between self and other: "Language is a skin: I rub my language against the other" (73).

Both poems conclude with images of emergence and urgency, phallic happenings that are also readable as forms of birth or breakthrough. "Cuttings" evokes the poking-through of a "pale tendrilous horn" (8), whereas "Cuttings (*later*)" culminates in a "[s]lippery" wetness (10). In "Cuttings" these motions remain objectively mysterious or secretive; in "Cuttings (*later*)" the first-person voice announces itself as peculiarly alert to what is happening in plant and soil. The consciousness of "Cuttings" has discovered self-consciousness, and has learned to speak subjectively. This can be read as an allegory of psychosexual becoming, neatly captured by Paglia in relation to "Cuttings": "It's as if sex and consciousness were simultaneously awakening" (*Break, Blow, Burn,* 147). Paglia also offers the more specifically Freudian explanation that represents the struggle of the plant stalks as directly analogous to Roethke's efforts to overcome the shadow of his father, "the earthly realm's omnipotent master gardener" whose "Prussian drive for order, efficiency, and perfection cowed his shy, sickly son, who came to identify with the manipulated plants" (146). In Paglia's reading, "[i]f the damp 'sheath' can be understood as a prepuce ('poke' is sexual slang), then the horn is the nascent phallic power of a timid boy craving freedom from overbearing authority" (147). It is a compelling explanation, hard to refute; and yet it seems to take us away from the compelling mysteries of the poem, steering instead towards its utter rewriting as an exemplification of a textbook type of masculinity.

It also needs to be argued that the language used to describe sexual stirring is redolent of disgust, albeit curious disgust. The phallus that presents itself is evidently forceful, but it also generates the revulsion that might be experienced upon seeing a dog or cat licking itself with particular ardor. The mysteries of sex can appear nasty to the beholder, and Roethke communicates this with peculiar intensity. This is not the hubristic priapism of Philip Roth or the terrified impotence of Eliot; these are not poems about masturbation, but actualizations of it.[1] They resemble the inevitable functionalism of sex that can be found in Beckett, where desire remorselessly makes a man quail and pale. Rosemary Sullivan's reading of "Cuttings (*later*)" is particularly sensitive to this, referring to how "creation is a humiliation" in this experience, "terrifying . . . in its sheer tenacity" (27).

The problem with the "Cuttings" poems, their peculiar quality, is how they encourage such allegorization, as if their sheer literal force is almost counterproductive. The power of their micro-realizations seems to demand that we produce an equally powerful explanation for them. The temptation is to read them as if they were *The Waste Land,* with an unacknowledged subtitle of "The Demonstration of an Idea." Indeed, the intertextual pressure of Eliot on Roethke (or perhaps more precisely, the reader of Roethke) is particularly noticeable; throughout the greenhouse poems and farther fields, we can hear Eliot's adaptation of Ezekiel:

> What are the roots that clutch, what branches grow
> Out of this stony rubbish? Son of man,
> You cannot say, or guess, for you know only
> A heap of broken images.
>
> (*Collected Poems,* 53)

Bernard W. Quetchenbach writes about Eliot's presence in Roethke in the familiar terms of the anxiety of influence, in which Roethke's psychological progress towards poetic selfhood is described by his struggle to adopt (and overcome) poetic father figures: "Roethke recasts Eliot's language in a more personal context and with a more internalized effect. This reflects both Eliot's dominance of the literary generations that succeed him and the conflicting desires of middle-generation and contemporary poets to escape from the shadow of the Great Moderns while at the same time recapturing the inventiveness and significance of these predecessors. Roethke's poems 'break through' to his own life, but that life includes his exposure to literary influences, especially to the towering figures of the early twentieth century" (48). Quetchenbach is surely right, but it can sound as if writing a poem is only an exercise in acquiescing in tyranny and as if Roethke's only option is to write in search of his own domination. In both of the "Cuttings" poems, however, Roethke discovers minute realities that are compelling for their resistance to overdetermination by big ideas. Breakthroughs *do* happen in the "Cuttings" poems: artistic, poetic, psychological—and that is just a beginning of a potentially long list. But on the other hand, perhaps such breakthroughs are routine, momentary rather than momentous. Cuttings germinate every day. When the lyrical "I" sprouts in "Cuttings (*later*)," it is with the immediate thrill of doing what everything else does in nature. Things break through there irrepressibly; the poet's dilemma is whether he can emerge with the same facility, because for him, language is in the way.

Roots are roots, and the literal force of that idea generates the remarkable intelligence of Roethke's attention to nature in these poems. He has no need either to pose or answer Eliot's question. In "Cuttings (*later*)," Roethke performs a counterinquiry, one that debunks the saintly effort and suffering that Eliot demands. Sainthood is humiliated in Roethke's imagining by the "resurrection of dry sticks" (1) and by his rhetorical question about the cuttings, "What saint strained so much[?]" (3). The magic of the resurrection process in the cultivation of cuttings is biological rather than theological (Barillas, *Midwestern Pastoral,* 117), so rather than an anxious deference to Eliot, we witness instead a dismissal of the spiritual qualms that informed his vision. Roethke recasts the sublime-deprived thirstscapes of "The Hollow Men" as bristling worlds-in-waiting, minute carnivals of appetite.

This counter-Eliotic reading is only the beginning of the allusive and intertextual possibilities at play here. Paglia remarks on the negotiation of Blake's "World in a Grain of Sand" in "Cuttings" as well as Roethke's debt to Wordsworth. The root system of "Cuttings (*later*)" also traces back to the revolutionary agitations of Shelley's *Prometheus Unbound* (1820), where Mother Earth awakens to a reborn subjectivity that is felt in every particle of nature:

> I hear, I feel;
> Thy lips are on me, and their touch runs down
> Even to the adamantine central gloom.
>
> (247)

Roethke's emphasis on what the self can "hear" and "feel" also derives from another example of Shelley-inspired hearing, that of "the deep heart's core" by Yeats in "The Lake Isle of Innisfree" (35). If Shelley is audible in Yeats, then so too is Whitman, another vital part of the intertextual confluence in the "Cuttings" poems; the natural energies being imagined in all of these poets find complex expression in the discovery of the subjective voice, an "I" that sprouts just as anything else does in nature. Poets are not isolated, but are always participating in the complex hypercreativity of nature; growing chaotically and rhizomatically, their poems are not just the product of a single root, but rather are part of a network of strands. These poems speak to modernism just as confidently as they do to the Romantics; Roethke's debt to Baudelaire, D. H. Lawrence, and William Carlos Williams is particularly clear in their vibrant physicality, in which language is morphing radically to model the integrity of material things.[2]

Trenton Hickman has described Roethke's influence on subsequent poets as founded in "an ethical commitment to the earth itself, eschewing an easy anthropocentrism in favor of a more complicated communion with the natural world." For Hickman, Roethke "offered . . . a precedent for paying close attention to nature and physical place as poetic subjects in their own right. . . . [T]he verse of many other American poets, such as Richard Hugo, Robert Bly, James Wright, and James Dickey, and even that of the Irish poet Seamus Heaney, bears Roethke's imprint" (183). Heaney seized on what he saw as the self-determination of Roethke, how the poems stressed his sense of poetic and spiritual mission: "An awareness of his own poetic process, and a trust in the possibility of his poetry, that is what a poet should attempt to preserve; and whatever else Theodore Roethke may have lacked, he did possess and nourish this faith in his own creative instincts" ("Canticles," 190). Heaney saw Roethke as a prototype for the modern poet as priest *cum* nature wrangler, a notably masculine figure (and a notably anthropocentric one, despite what Hickman argues). In "Digging," published in *Death of a Naturalist* (1966), Heaney famously achieves a sure sense of identity between his own work and that of his father:

> Between my finger and my thumb
> The squat pen rests.
> I'll dig with it.
>
> (14)

The work of the poem is continuous with other forms of working with nature and is legitimized accordingly.

For Roethke, however, such continuity between occupations was not so readily discovered; as Paglia states, Roethke "came to identify with the manipulated plants" rather than with the gardener (*Break, Blow, Burn,* 146). The "Cuttings" poems demand a properly botanical reading, one that recognizes their inhuman inspiration; reading them as parts of a progress (either psychological or poetic) takes us away from their real pleasure and disturbance. The life of these poems is in their perverse vocabularies and how they hearken to the lure of the underneath. So while the "Cuttings" poems are often read for the surface that they crawl towards, their singularity resides in the skins and grains they grow out of. It is difficult to think of poems that are like "Cuttings" and "Cuttings (*later*)" because there are none, so unusual is their odd jostle of words, their determination to sound *other.* Roethke writes with a cellular sensitivity and an apt terror of the life force in nature. Even if we might want to explain that terror, it is hard to avoid the sense that all we have done is provide an inadequate fiction for what is infinitely intimate and compelling. The poems might be read as breaking through to the sublime or as describing the overcoming of a domineering father, yet the furry weirdness of individual words remains inscrutable to a large degree. The "Cuttings" poems resemble the unforgettable scene in David Lynch's 1986 film *Blue Velvet,* in which the camera goes underground to reveal a violently inhuman and menacing domain, the kind of hypernatural place that drives you into building the containment structure of a metanarrative. Although Freudian readings of *Blue Velvet* are commonplace,[3] they do not redeem us from the terror of the underneath that Lynch made visible. We can similarly allegorize and narrativize the "Cuttings" poems to dispel their strangeness, but this relies on embracing them as representations of ideas rather than of things.

The rough magic of the poems lies in their thrilled engagement with what lies below. They express not only a subterranean homesick blues, where father-and-mother fear will encode your story, but something more thoroughly soiled and enthralling. The critical word may well be *fear,* which is what Roethke identified in both minute experience ("The Small") and "infinity" ("The Far Field"). This fear is a primitive phenomenon, a motive for living that connects all phenomena; the brute motions of the "Cuttings" poems are an exemplary biopoetry that humbles human-centered experience and introduces it to a more complex ecology. John Felsteiner writes that in Roethke "[s]ome mystery draws him down into a world that clasps his turbulent inner world too" (217), and that downward momentum is most manifest in the poet's reverence for "every kind of lowlife" (218).

The "Cuttings" poems, therefore, are not only of interest as directions for the formation of a self, either literary or psychological. They are subversive poems that barely contain the revolutionary violence they discover, and the integrity of their minute details implies a firm resistance to explanation in terms of the Romantic sublime. Roethke discovers simultaneous beauty and ugliness in just this way, returning us to the massive potential of miniature grossness, the coarse material that can never entirely be broken through. Art is work, life is work, all part of the same struggle, and every discovery is also a humiliation. What might be a birth might also be just another seed spill; an end is as good as a beginning.

NOTES

1. A comment that William Carlos Williams critically visited upon another poem, "Visitation": "It's too God damned like masturbation. I don't like it" (qtd. in Kusch, 32).

2. Williams made his admiration for the poems very clear: "Specifically, by all means, keep both the poems 'Cuttings' in the group, they are both among your best and each, at the same time, has its own excellence" (qtd. in Kusch, 32). In their correspondence about *The Lost Son*, Williams wrote also that Roethke reminded him of Baudelaire for his "unflinching stare at corruption and disease" (qtd. in Mariani, 559).

3. See, for example, "Netherworlds and the Unconscious: Oedipus and *Blue Velvet*," chapter 9 of Mulvey, 137–54.

9

All the Small, Unlovely Things

"Root Cellar"

JOHN ROHRKEMPER

THEODORE ROETHKE'S first volume of poetry is titled *Open House,* but there is something cramped and tentative about many of the poems in that volume. In his second volume, *The Lost Son and Other Poems* (1948), Roethke found his true and revealing poetic voice, and he seemed to discover that authentic voice in the first section of the volume, the greenhouse poems. It is appropriate that "Root Cellar" (*Collected Poems,* 36) comes early in the greenhouse sequence, for the poem deals with the beginnings of things. Roethke's root cellar is not a storage room to preserve potatoes, onions, and other root vegetables (one meaning for the term), but the unromantic, unbeautiful place where a florist keeps bulbs out of the light, at a constant cool temperature, to delay their sprouting into flowering plants until an opportune time for their sale. It is an unappealing place, "dank as a ditch" (1), where shoots loll "obscenely from mildewed crates" (4), where "[l]eaf-mold, manure, lime" are "piled against slippery planks" (9).

And yet it also is a place bursting with life where "[e]ven the dirt kept breathing a small breath" (11). It is a place of small, unlovely things, but, if one follows the arc of the greenhouse cycle, in this damp and malodorous ditch starts a process that will culminate, as Roethke says in "Carnations," the last poem of the cycle, in a "windless perpetual morning," the "clear autumnal weather of eternity" (*Collected Poems,* 41).[1] While all of the greenhouse poems are about becoming, in all its uncertainty and glory, "Root Cellar" describes the first inchoate stirrings of life in the greenhouse world.

In a sense, the greenhouse poems chronicle Roethke's youth, the time of his life when the family greenhouse and its grounds were his entire world, which seemed Edenic to him. Many years later he recalled that "it took up twenty-five acres within the city of Saginaw with a quarter million feet under glass. . . . It had its own ice-house, a small game preserve, and the last stand of virgin timber in the Saginaw valley" (*Selected Letters,* 253*)*. While he worked on the poems he claimed he wanted to show "the full erotic and even religious significance . . . in a big greenhouse: a kind of man-made Avalon, Eden, or paradise" (*Selected Letters,* 113). And undeniably, Roethke wishes to show the parallels between a boy's development and the development of flowers from roots to full showy blossom. The way that parallel development has been understood by readers has been shaped by the time in which the poems were written and appeared, and also by the poet's own experiences at that time. By the mid-twentieth century the psychological thinking of the previous half-century informed analysis in many disciplines, but particularly in literary studies. Furthermore, Roethke had been in intensive therapy for nearly a decade. Thus, it isn't surprising that early critics tended to read these poems as an allegory for a boy's coming of age that emphasized the psychosexual elements of the poem. Karl Malkoff, for instance, asserts that the poem's "shoots that dangle and droop, 'lolling obscenely,' like snakes, clearly qualify as Freudian symbols" (48), and further that the poem "is filled with images of darkness, of boxes; the cellar itself is a symbol of the womb" (51). In this kind of reading, critics have tended to see "Root Cellar" as an expression of a boy's fear, confusion, and guilt as he becomes aware of and begins to explore his own sexuality.

Clearly, the critics were seeing what Roethke put there, his imagery often adapting the tropes of psychoanalysis. This psychoanalytic approach has much to tell us about Roethke's poetry and "Root Cellar" in particular. But, during the period in which he was working on the greenhouse poems, Roethke noted in his journal that a poet is "someone who is never satisfied with saying one thing at a time" (*Straw for the Fire,* 166). So while it is appropriate that Malkoff and others viewed these poems through the lens of psychoanalytic theory, in recent years ecocritics such as William Barillas have tended to read the greenhouse poems, and much of Roethke's oeuvre, as examinations of the natural world and our relation to it. Such a shift in the intellectual atmosphere during the last fifty years has led to significantly different readings of the poems. The psychological critics found in the forces of nature a map paralleling a child's psychological development, while the ecocritics are more interested in the *relationship* between different forms of natural development, human and vegetative. Certainly Roethke's poems offer much straw for the fire for both psychoanalytic and ecocritical criticism.

Yet another way to understand "Root Cellar" and the other greenhouse poems is to consider the poem as an examination of the nature of creativity, of the creative process, and of the creative artist's psyche. Roethke felt that his creativity was intricately tied to the demons of his own mental illness. "Root Cellar" is often linked with the proximate poems "Forcing House" and "Weed Puller," for the way they all portray "the terrifying and procreative powers of the subhuman world" (Balakian, 33). For Roethke, such procreative energy is terrifying because it suggests not only a boy's aversion to and desire for the faintly grasped world of sexuality, but also the mature poet's realization that his creativity, the procreative energy of his imagination, might arise from the terrifying energy of his illness. He had experienced the full fury of his illness in November 1935, when he experienced his first breakdown while teaching at Michigan State and working on the poems that would comprise his first book, *Open House* (1942). During the subsequent thirteen years before the publication of *The Lost Son and Other Poems,* which included the greenhouse poems, Roethke suffered repeated bouts of emotional instability and several traumatic breakdowns. Therapists who treated him during and subsequent to these years diagnosed him variously as "manic-depressive neurotic," "manic-depressive psychotic," and "paranoid schizophrenic" (Seager, 101). In today's terminology he might be diagnosed as having suffered from bipolar disorder. While his illness took a tremendous toll on him physically and mentally, Roethke seems to have believed that it was an important engine of his creativity. I have argued elsewhere that after many years of being buffeted by the illness he appeared to invite for the sake of his poetry, he found a way to use memory rather than his pathology to stimulate his creative energy (Rohrkemper). But as he composed "Root Cellar" and the rest of the greenhouse poems, he was just beginning to wrestle with the relationship of his illness to his art.

Roethke, or at least the "I" of the poem's persona, is present in many of the greenhouse poems, but "Root Cellar" is "I-less": it does not employ the first-person voice, as if the self has not yet been formed. This is the world of preconsciousness, before the self has emerged, before the artist has emerged. It is a site of potential energy still waiting to be released or expressed. Roethke finds a music for that energy in the poem's language. Like most of the other poems of the cycle, the poem's language is lushly sensual. Nearly every line is a riot of alliteration, assonance, and consonance.

Excising the alliterative, assonant, and consonant words from each line and reconstituting them to stand alone makes clear the poem's dependence on sound devices. One can get the basic gist, the essential feel of the poem, from just these words:

> sleep, cellar; dank, ditch
> bulbs, broke boxes; chinks, dark
> shoots, drooped
> lolling, obscenely, mildewed; obscenely, from
> long, yellow, evil, like tropical
> congress, stinks
> roots, ripe
> pulpy; stems silo
> leaf-mold, lime, slippery planks; slippery planks
> nothing, up
> kept, breath; breathing, breath

This is not the mellifluous harmony of end rhyme, but a coarser, harsher kind of music in which, for example, "bulbs broke out of boxes," and "[s]hoots dangled and drooped, / Lolling obscenely from mildewed crates" (2–4) The first example above, with its explosive *b* sounds, bursts with procreative energy; the second is effused with liquid *l* sounds that suggest the dankness and vaguely unsettling aspect of this procreative place. This combination might suggest Roethke's own unease as he considered the terrifying and possibly destructive source of his own creativity. The use of alliteration, assonance, and consonance creates an earthy lushness, heard in the repetition of *r* and long *i* sounds near the middle of the poem: "Roots ripe as old bait, / Pulpy stems, rank, silo-rich" (7–8). If any music, even this rough music, at first seems at odds with the poem's unlovely subject matter, we should remember that in fact this dreary unlovely place is rich and fecund, bursting with life and nurturing the beauty that will blossom into the carnations, chrysanthemums, sweet-peas, and roses of later poems in the sequence.

The penultimate line of "Root Cellar" is the plainest, with only a subtle assonance in "nothing" and "up." But this slight variation in the pattern signals a summary moment, a contemplative moment for the poem. Although the poem is not a sonnet, it has a structure akin to sonnets, particularly in its final two lines, which suggest a sonnet-ending couplet. After the previous descriptive catalogue—"a congress of stinks"—here is the meaning of the root cellar: "Nothing would give up life: / Even the dirt kept breathing a small breath" (10–11). And there is something particularly beautiful about the way his last two lines echo the poem's first: "Nothing would sleep in that cellar, dank as a ditch" (1). If the poem begins with restless life as insomnia, as a living burial, it quietly and calmly ends in "breath," a promise of more life to come. In this poem Roethke moves from the fearful ugliness of the cellar to the beginnings of the beauty that it nurtures. Possibly he saw in that process his own journey from the ravages of mental illness to the beauty of poetic creation. As he wrote in his journal, at about the time he composed the poem, "Deep in their roots, all flowers keep the light" (*Straw for the Fire,* 40).

Late in his life, in the essay "On Identity," Roethke enumerated his four principal themes: "(1) The multiplicity, the chaos of modern life; (2) The way, the means of establishing a personal identity, a self in the face of that chaos; (3) The nature of creation, that faculty for producing order out of disorder in the arts, particularly in poetry; and (4) The nature of God himself" (*On Poetry and Craft,* 35). Neal Bowers has written that the shoots and bulbs of "Root Cellar" "become a metaphor for the spirit groping toward the light of true perception, struggling to ascend from its own black cellar" (83). Roethke's list of his themes is an apt expression of "the spirit groping toward the light." He may not have achieved the ultimate theme in "Root Cellar," but he certainly explored the first three. In "Root Cellar" Roethke parallels the chaos of modern life with the seeming chaos of nature, but he also suggests in this and the other greenhouse poems that the establishment of order is the function of both nature and the creative artist. He found in some of his earliest experiences as a boy in the greenhouse a powerful metaphor for his own creativity.

NOTE

1. "Carnations" concludes part 1, the greenhouse sequence, in *The Lost Son and Other Poems* (1948). Roethke added the poem "Frau Bauman, Frau Schmidt, and Frau Schwartze" at the end in *The Waking: Poems, 1933–1953* (1953); that poem also occupies the final spot in part 1 in the 1975 edition of *The Collected Poems of Theodore Roethke,* which remains in print.

10

Locating the Poet in "Weed Puller"

LYN COFFIN

I LIKE it first as a wash of sounds (*Collected Poems,* 37). I like that it uses a whole bunch of negative words: "concrete," "hacking" "black hairy roots," "lewd monkey-tails" (1–3). Clearly something is going on, but it is not ugliness for the sake of ugliness. The ugliness serves something that is not quite a "meaning."

I like that although this is an intensely personal poem, there are only two *me's,* both delayed. It's not until the eleventh line that we get "blooming above me," and then in line 14 we get an initial, capital M in "me": "Me down in that fetor of weeds."

And I start thinking about prepositions, the locating words. The poem is full of them: all the flowers are "above" (11) and he is "down" (14). He is "[c]rawling on all fours" (15).

Thinking about "four," I begin counting. Counting syllables, words, lines, I discover the poem goes from an eleven-syllable line, "Digging into the soft rubble underneath," immediately to a three-syllable line, "Webs and weeds" (4–5). That makes me feel better somehow. The author is thinking about varying lines.

Sixteen lines gives me a small *aha* moment. Sixteen lines is a "stretched sonnet." I feel good, feel educated, because I know about sonnets—fourteen lines, high school Shakespeare—and I know about stretched sonnets: George Meredith, "Modern Love."

So then I start looking for rhyme. And I can't find a one. Well, I do find a sort of reverse slant rhyme. I note "lovely and inviolate" (13) and appreciate the roundness of that. But there's no real "form" here, or none that I can find. Irregular line lengths, no rhyme: it's all wildly irregular. Like weeds. Aha!

There is one word in the poem I don't know. Smilax. It sounds terrible. Chopping a "smile" with an "ax." I look it up and discover that it's a weed. No surprise there. But I also find advertisements for "smilax wedding garlands," so I take the wedding garland ad and do some erasing (I'm an erasure poem fanatic) and it comes out pretty good. I especially like the line "The body itself is a vine extending outwards."

When I get back to "Weed Puller," I start to think about the verb-ness of it, all the -ing verbs, those present participles. There are a lot of them! "Hacking" and "hanging" and "digging" (2–4) and "yanking" and "dripping" and "tugging" (7–9) and "blooming" (11) and "[c]rawling" (15). All that active present-ness really plunges us, the readers, into the sprawling aliveness of the world of the poem, the world of being in the weeds. And I start to distinguish between the verbs having to do with the speaker's actions, which are aggressive—hacking, digging, yanking, tugging (maybe not crawling)—and the vegetative ones, which are passive: hanging, dripping, blooming.

And thinking about verbs leads me to thinking about nouns, all the Anglo-Saxon, one-syllable, gritty nouns in the poem: roots, webs, weeds, grubs, snails, sticks . . .

Wait. What logic is this? I back up. The "soft rubble" (4) into which he's digging contains webs and weeds and grubs and snails and . . . sharp sticks. That "sharp" pokes up at you out of the line, rather like the stick itself.

But this is a list. Brachylogia, I think, remembering college rhetoric. But of course it isn't, because brachylogia is where you have just the nouns without the conjunctions. Brachylogia comes later in the poem—"Lilies, pale-pink cyclamen, roses"—whereas this rubble list is an example of polysyndeton.

I've gone astray again. Never mind.

There are two places in the poem that strike me as out of keeping with the rest of it. The first is the adjective "lewd" (3). Compare that with the other adjectives: "concrete," "hairy" (1–2), "soft" (4), "green" (8), "pale-pink" (12; speaking of brachylogia). "Lewd" is something different. "Lewd" is not descriptive but evaluative. It's pejorative. It goes with "perverse." And then comes the cry, the ejaculation.

I look up "ejaculation." Some dictionaries define it first as a short cry, and then the semen. Others reverse that.

Anyway, the short, exclamatory utterance here is "The indignity of it!" So what the speaker objects to is the feeling of shame that his activity costs him. This goes perfectly with "[c]rawling on all fours." How different the poem would be if it ended there. "Crawling on all fours" (15) is undignified. Weed pulling, with its requirement that one crawl under concrete benches and so on, would correlate perfectly with where the poet seems to be going. We would have a poem that could be encapsulated in the thematic statement "Weed pulling is an unattractive and undignified activity, and I don't like doing it."

Then we get "Alive" (16). We're still okay. Most of the things in the poem are alive. The poet is one with the monkey-tails, the smilax, as well as the lilies, the roses. He is alive.

But now all those prepositions come, as it were, into full bloom. The poet, we think, has already located himself under and below, looking up. But now we get the full equation.

We thought the poem was about life: perverse life, life that expresses itself in icky weeds and lovely flowers, is really about death. Death is only given one word, but what a word it is.

So much ugliness in life: grubs and snails and sharp sticks. So much beauty: lilies, pale-pink (not just pink, but "pale" pink) cyclamen, roses. And yet, if you'll pardon the expression, what it all comes down to is—

We are among weeds, looking up at flowers, "[a]live in a slippery grave" (16).

For an ending, there is nothing quite like it. Unless maybe Hawthorne's Wakefield being told "step into your grave" (71).

I put the poem down.

I'm going to go out and walk the fields and look down at the flowers.

I am going to pretend a field can be inviolate.

Roethke was brave.

I am not.

11

"Orchids"

Undomesticating the Greenhouse

BROOKE HORVATH

IS IT possible for a poem to release meaning as a hothouse orchid its scent—that is, hardly at all?[1] Probably not, for being made of words, poems cannot escape signifying *something*. They can, however (and often do), frustrate our desire for straightforward, predictable communication. They can likewise remind us that all meanings are human creations, including everything we think we know about the rest of creation. One such poem is Theodore Roethke's "Orchids" (*Collected Poems,* 37), which, refusing to deliver whatever it is one expects from a "flower poem," instead troubles its subject in an attempt to help us see these orchids as though for the first time and in a manner evocative of awe.

Orchids arrive as a subject with more cultural baggage than I can readily unpack. Used by florists chiefly in prom corsages and wedding bouquets, orchids, in the "language of flowers," have traditionally symbolized ecstasy (Scoble and Field, 17) as well as "love, luxury, beauty and strength" ("Orchid Flower Meaning"). In Greek mythology, Orchis, feckless son of a nymph and a satyr, was metamorphosed into his namesake flower for the attempted rape of a priestess, and many readers of Roethke in 1948 (when the volume containing "Orchids" appeared) might have been aware of Rex Stout's popular detective Nero Wolfe, who cultivated orchids while ratiocinating. Perhaps most surprisingly, "orchid" derives from the Greek *órkhis* (όρχις), meaning "testicle." Now, although such lore is interesting, these are precisely the associations Roethke wishes to negate, for what they have in common is appropriation: the erasure of the orchid as orchid, the orchid *qua* orchid overwritten by cultural meanings and uses.

I suggest Roethke was alert to such appropriation even as he participated in it, insisting as he did that his "greenhouse poems," of which "Orchids" is one, represented "a quest for identity," with the greenhouse his "symbol for the whole of life" (*On Poetry and Craft*, 40, 51). Many of Roethke's critics have understandably followed this lead, unpacking the poems' autobiographical connections, psychological implications, mythic ambition, and spiritual raison d'être. Jarold Ramsey, for instance, sees the greenhouse poems as an attempt "to recover something of the unity of Self" Roethke recalled having felt in childhood (36), and George Wolff sees the poems' speaker "struggl[ing] to find or make an identity" ("Syntactical," 287). Similarly, Karl Malkoff asserts that Roethke felt his "ultimate responsibility" was "to his own inner self" (47) in poems rife with "Freudian possibilities" (48).

Closer to the point I wish to make is Walter B. Kalaidjian, who describes the greenhouse poems as "primal witnessing" (40); John D. Boyd, who suggests that the poems' tone of "hushed, breathless mystery" stems from an effort to evoke a "vegetative world [that] partakes of a life force partly its own" (411); and Jay Parini, who concludes his brief discussion of "Orchids" by asserting that, before it is anything else, it is "a poem about orchids" (75)—a shrewder observation than it may at first seem to be. Still, a question remains: why is this short poem, which critics are quick to see as one among others rooting about in the loam of a lost childhood, so damn creepy? "Eerie" is the word both Boyd (412) and Ramsey (36) use when discussing the greenhouse poems, and regarding "Orchids" specifically, Boyd notes the poem's "rising tide of wonder and strangeness" (420) and Ramsey, a feeling of "hallucinated wonder" that is "strange and sinister" (42).

The effectiveness of "Orchids" results in part from what Wolff terms "syntactical distortion" ("Syntactical," 282).[2] It is, however, Roethke's metaphors that are largely responsible for the poem's phantasmagoric unease. Continuing the snake imagery of "Root Cellar" and "Weed Puller," "Orchids" gets no further than its second line before the flowers' labella (their "lips," in casual orchid parlance) transmogrify into the mouths of adders. If space permitted, a quick look at other orchid poems or the effusions of orchid enthusiasts would reveal how startlingly unusual such language is.[3] Because "adder" designates a category that includes many venomous snakes, and because these adders, "soft and deceptive"

(4), overhang the path "close to the face" (3), the perhaps anticipated treatment of orchids is immediately, alarmingly destabilized—even if one knows that North American adders are harmless.[4] For those with a botanical background, "[a]dder-mouthed" (2) should recall "adder's mouth," a wild orchid not typically grown in greenhouses, and possibly "adder's tongue," which, depending upon where one lives, names either a type of fern or a wild lily. Calling wildflowers into this poem about cultivated orchids efficiently measures the distance between wild nature out beyond the "whitewashed glass" (10) of the hothouse and that more malleable nature inside: an acknowledgment, as William Barillas observes of Roethke's "The Lost Son," that the poet, like the florist, is routinely busy about the task of shaping a recalcitrant nature (*Midwestern Pastoral,* 128).

In the fifth line, the orchids metamorphose again, the poem's constantly evolving metaphoric language reminding us that plants are literally continuous shape-shifters. "Limp and damp," which begins line 5, seems to carry forward the unpleasant snake comparison, but the ophidian/orchidian metaphor abruptly gives way to "delicate as a young bird's tongue"—moving us from one to another faunal category while troubling our sense of how both to read these lines and to see these shifty orchids. Line 6—"Their fluttery fledgling lips"—would seem to extend the image just offered, but "their" cannot grammatically refer to the singular bird of the previous line; instead, "their" takes the reader back to "they" of line 1—the orchids (plural in the poem's title). The semicolon punctuating line 5 may have prepared the careful reader for this return to the metaphors' shared tenor, but the slippage is easy to fall victim to and thereby further destabilizes any meaning the reader has been working to formulate, while raising, at least momentarily, the question of what sort of birds possess lips, "fluttery" (6) or otherwise, and thereby conjuring a second manifestation of an ever more suffusing strangeness. Line 6 has apparently simply returned us to the orchids, but, as noted, the poem encourages the reader to extent the bird metaphor. "Flutter" has among its definitions the rapid flapping of wings, and these "fluttery" lips are "fledgling lips," which here must evoke a just-fledged bird (while anticipating the infants of line 14). However, as in a dream, these fluttery lips "[m]ove slowly" (7)—an oddity insofar as "flutter" typically indicates rapid, excited motion. In short, the first stanza offers increasingly surreal, problematic metaphors that are themselves troubled by syntactical uncertainty.

The second stanza makes clear that it is now night, the preternatural orchids lit by the light of a "faint moon" (10) as the air cools and "their musky smell comes even stronger" (12).[5] "Their" must, of course, refer again to the orchids, though we have here another instance of attenuated pronoun reference; indeed, remove its title and "Orchids" becomes a riddle poem akin to Emily Dickinson's poem 383 ("I like to see it lap the miles"; *Poems* 176). As the poem threatens to lose its referent amid its loose sentence structure and shifting metaphors,[6] the orchids transform again, now into "[s]o many devouring infants!" (14)—a phrase that, in context, may well strike the sentimental reader as appalled misopedia. Moreover, these infants possess "[s]oft luminescent fingers," "[l]ips neither dead nor alive," and "[l]oose ghostly mouths" (15–17). "Luminescent" transforms both halves of the metaphor into the tenor of a new metaphor—infants and orchids now compared to some other, possibly deep-sea life form—even as the poet locates these bioluminescent flower infants somewhere between life and death in "mossy cradles" (13): a confusion of metaphors that distressingly conflates cradles and graves, living plants and dead children.[7] The poem concludes with the ominous one-word line "Breathing" (18), which leaves the infantile orchids hovering "soft and deceptive" (4) in the pale moonlight like the adders they once were or the ghosts they now are.

The cumulative effect of Roethke's metaphors and destabilizing syntax is, first, to remove the poem from traditional floral associations and poetic uses—whether Herrick's maiden-gathered rosebuds, Wordsworth's daffodils "[c]ontinuous as the stars that shine," Blake's lily that "shall in love delight," or Dickinson's flower children that "peep, and prance" come the morn.[8] Unsettling bemusement is the second, more consequential effect achieved by this riddling distortion of a flower otherwise sweetly familiar to prom dates and brides. But why attempt such an end? "Defamiliarization"—a term coined by the Russian Formalist Victor Shklovsky in 1917—provides an answer, for according to Shklovsky, the purpose of art is "to make the stone *stony,*" a task achievable by "impart[ing] the sensation of things as they are perceived and not as they are known." Toward this end, an author adept at "making strange"[9] shakes readers free of habitual ways of seeing by increasing "the difficulty and length of perception" (12). The means of defamiliarization are several and include a device central to "Orchids": the refusal to call familiar objects by their given names or to use the "accepted names" of their parts. The effect—Roethke's third effect—is, Shklovsky concludes, to see something as though "for the first time" (13): not "to make us perceive meaning, but to create a special perception of the object," the text *"a 'vision' of the object,"* not *"a means for knowing it"* (18, Shklovsky's emphasis).

That defamiliarization describes the effect of "Orchids" seems clear. But more, I would suggest, is at issue here than helping us see orchids as though "for the first time." In *The Social Creation of Nature* (1992), Neil Evernden argues that our current environmental crises turn in part on the ways nature has been conceptualized, ways that "extinguish wild otherness" (116). A "new conversation" (102) is needed, he insists, one that escapes the "conceptual domestication of nature" by "peeling back the culturally given" (123) and recapturing the child's way of encountering the world before more mature ways of knowing intervene. Only by so doing, Evernden believes, citing theologian Rudolph Otto, do we stand the chance of experiencing awe, for "the experience of radical otherness is at the base of all astonishment or awe, all 'numinous' experience" (117). To be open to such life-enhancing astonishment, Evernden adds, requires forgoing the imposition of any order "that makes the world seem comprehensible" (119) and, echoing Shklovsky, "entail[s] a challenge to our habitual language" (132). Freed of "conceptual domestication," "Orchids" provides, as its fourth effect, just such a deep ecological vision of astonishing otherness.

Imaginatively seen through the eyes (if not exactly the words) of a child, "Orchids" boldly attempts its rehabilitative seeing in that locus of domesticated nature par excellence: a greenhouse. However, although none of the other greenhouse poems stands so nakedly open to the possibility of wonderment, even here appropriation cannot be avoided, which may explain the poem's disturbing portentousness, its discovery, in the words of poet Marianne Boruch, of "something terrifying in flowers . . . scary and immensely odd" ("Conversation," 109). Snakes swaying close to one's face before metamorphosing into hallucinated birds that themselves transform into "devouring infants" with glowing fingers and spectral mouths respiring in the musky, moon-washed dark: if this is not the return of the repressed, it is most certainly blowback. Terror, after all, is one petal of awe.

NOTES

1. The three most common orchid varieties offered by florists are *Cymbidium*, *Phalaenopsis*, and *Dendrobium*. Each comes in a variety of colors, and all are virtually scentless.

2. Wolff's brief analysis focuses primarily on Roethke's use of absolute constructions as the poem moves from the "conventional syntax" of stanza one into the "disordering of grammar" in stanza two ("Syntactical," 283–84).

3. The interested reader might compare "Orchids" with other orchid poems collected in Sarah Maguire's *Flora Poetica* (2001) or, more dramatically, with the many orchid poems on offer online at PoetrySoup.

4. The adder with which Roethke would have been most familiar with would be the eastern hog-nosed or deaf adder of Michigan's Saginaw Valley, where he grew up.

5. Since greenhouse orchids have virtually no scent, this line must be an exercise in metonymy, the "musky smell" arising rather from the flowers' "mossy cradles" (12–13).

6. A third long-distance "their" occurs in line 13, a faulty comparative in line 12.

7. The equation of "mossy" with death is reinforced in the next greenhouse poem, "Moss-Gathering," wherein moss is used "for lining cemetery baskets" (*Collected Poems,* 38).

8. Robert Herrick, "To the Virgins, to Make Much of Time" (72); William Wordsworth, "I Wandered Lonely as a Cloud" (207); William Blake, "The Lilly" (*Complete Poetry and Prose,* 25); Emily Dickinson, poem 127 ("As children bid the Guest 'Good night'"; *The Poems of Emily Dickinson,* 65).

9. "Making strange" is the literal meaning of Shklovsky's *ostraneniye,* rendered in English as "defamiliarization."

12

"Moss-Gathering" and Roethke's Romantic Child of Nature

MARC MALANDRA

"MOSS-GATHERING" (*Collected Poems,* 38) unfolds in the virginal woods that thrive not far from the glass, metal, and wood structures of the greenhouses that serve as Theodore Roethke's metaphorical lost Eden, an environment that is itself rendered in an almost prelapsarian majesty. These woods, being outside the greenhouse literally, and metaphorically inside what Jay Parini has called Roethke's "secret planet" (3), reveal an environment in which the consequences are more global, and potentially more urgent, than the greenhouse proper. This poem's uncultivated, natural environment functions as the perfect soil for a poet of Roethke's uniquely modernized Romanticism.

Roethke's "Moss-Gathering" carefully unearths the symbiotic relation between a personal human history and "organic," natural history. It is very likely that the woods that provided the moss are the same patches of virgin forest, Roethke family property, that eventually became part of what is now Roethke Park in Saginaw, Michigan. "It was a universe," Roethke once said of the family's greenhouses and affiliated lands, "several worlds, which, even as a child, one worried about, and struggled to keep alive" (*On Poetry and Craft,* 22). These burgeoning forests, so intricately linked to the Roethke family's horticultural enterprises, become through "Moss-Gathering" the site for Roethke's confrontation with the natural world outside the fluctuating boundaries of the greenhouses and within his own psychological and spiritual lost paradise.

As one of the strongest poems in this horticultural matrix, "Moss-Gathering" elevates this youthful excursion through the primeval forest into a meditation on humanity's relation to the non-human, though tangibly vital, world:

> To loosen with all ten fingers held wide and limber
> And lift a patch, dark-green, the kind for lining cemetery baskets,
> Thick and cushiony, like an old-fashioned doormat.
>
> (1–3)

The spondaic thrust of "dark-green" not only provides the verdant palette from which most of the greenhouse poems are painted, but also foreshadows the somber purpose to which this moss will be put, namely as part of a memorial to the deceased. The poet's language becomes "[t]hick" and "cushiony" (3) itself as he continues to describe the organic cushion of "sticks," "roots," and "berries" (4–5) that adhere to his prize object. The experience of thrusting his hands into all of this fecundity is the titular activity of the poem, expressed in the deductive main clause that concludes the poem's first sentence: "That was moss-gathering" (6).

The moss will return to the earth in the guise of an ornamental appendage to a cemetery, a decorative basket in a garden of human bones. The "carpets / Of green," the "spongy yellowish moss" (7–8) it is the youth's duty to collect, leave him feeling that he has been unkind ("mean") to the environment that has sustained his romantic wanderings (9). Duty requires the speaker to collect moss in order to further the family business, but such economic motivations have grown stale. This sensitive poet-in-the-making fears he has violated ("broken") the "natural order of things" (10), a self-accusation that particularly stings his conscience. This romantic's greatest anxiety is that he has perhaps

> Disturbed some rhythm, old and of vast importance,
> By pulling off flesh from the living planet;
> As if [he] had committed against the whole scheme of life, a desecration.
>
> (11–13)

Of all the poems in the greenhouse mode, this one displays the greatest evidence of biocentrism—the view that all organisms, including humans, are part of a larger biotic web whose interests must govern the human interest—and is arguably the strongest environmentalist text as such. Once the speaker establishes the unique, solitary nature of the enterprise, he realizes that a larger issue is involved, namely his relation to the "living planet" (12). There is an ironic parallelism between the moss-gatherer and the subjects to be memorialized by means of the cemetery baskets: something "always went out of" him (7), much as life had recently departed from the dead to be posthumously honored by the cemetery baskets. As the speaker thrusts his hands into the "marshes" (8) he reenacts on a different scale the descent into earth the cemetery baskets will venerate, and the subsequent decay of both flesh and flower. No longer an agent acting on a passive landscape, Roethke records remorse over violence toward another "living" entity whose integrity, whose very "flesh" (12) has been violated. The speaker's guilt is framed within an environment in which the encroachment of people is marked by the very "logging roads" (9) he must travel to commit his acts of sacrilege against the earth. Here the greater part of sympathy is transferred not to the human dead, but to the desecrated earth: the moss has been transformed from the product of a *desecration* to a human *decoration.*

In "Moss-Gathering," the Roethkean persona finds himself in an ethical bind, harvesting the swamplands in order to honor the recently deceased while inadvertently participating in their destruction. As William Barillas has noted, there is a history of environmental degradation that took place in the Saginaw Valley due largely to the lumber industry, a legacy with which Roethke was keenly aware (*Midwestern Pastoral,* 110). The speaker in "Moss-Gathering," echoing the ecological sensitivity of his creator, feels the urge to confess the harm he may have done to the wild land that has provided him with so much material and spiritual inspiration.

Raymond Benoit's recovery of one of Roethke's undergraduate essays, "Moss-Picking," clarifies both the poem's origins and its link with Roethke's Romantic, archetypal self-imagining. "You will feel a close harmony between external nature and your inner self," Roethke pronounces in the essay (48), charting the environmentally sensitive course the writer would follow throughout his poetic career. "Nature seems to regard the moss-picker kindly." Invoking an act of Romantic reverie worthy of Wordsworth or Whitman, Roethke recounts that the "idyllic labour" of moss-picking is likely to make one "quite sleepy." He urges his reader not to resist this urge, but rather to succumb to it, knowing that if you do you will "feel . . . that you are a true child of nature—that she has accepted you and taken you into her arms" (49). With Roethke's Romanticism much in evidence in the essay, as it is in the poem, the ability to appreciate the nonhuman world as more than an extension of his own psyche in "Moss-Gathering" reveals a deeper understanding of the intrinsic value of the natural world in its own right.

Roethke's youthful impressions center more on his own "idyllic labour" and the ease with which it is accomplished than the more critical issue of nature's potential destruction that is the ethical crux of the poem (49). Whereas moss-picking, according to the young Roethke, is a "primitive process that requires no particular skill at all" (48), "Moss-Gathering" calls for a moral obligation to a "living planet" whose interests the poetic speaker's conscience can no longer ignore.

Such an affinity to the organic, nonhuman world is not unusual for this poet. The notebooks are scattered with phrases revealing a person who perceived himself to be able to "change into vegetables," who claims at another point, "I can project myself easier into a flower than into a person" (*Straw for the Fire,* 84). Walter B. Kalaidjian suggests that "[t]he sudden erosion of identity is the precondition for oneness with nature" (43–44). What one finds in "Moss-Gathering" is not so much a loss of identity as a willingness to expand one's personal identity to include aspects of the self that are most organic, most analogous to the life of trees and plants. Roethke's identification with plant life parallels that of George Perkins Marsh, the man often considered the first American ecologist, who once wrote that most people "would find it hard to make out as good a claim to *personality* as a respectable oak" (qtd. in Lowenthal, 19). A psychic and spiritual attachment to his father Otto's greenhouses and nearby woods and swamplands magnified the young Roethke's appreciation of the natural world, a world that "Moss-Gathering" renders as vibrantly alive.

In affinity with the Romantic writers who, as Kenneth Burke, Kalaidjian, Parini, and others have convincingly shown, largely inspired Roethke's poetics, and as "Moss-Gathering" illuminates, Roethke was a writer constantly in touch with his own childhood. His ability to transform landscape into lyric arises from a quasi-Romantic conviction that any attempt at a poetic reconstruction of the self involves a root-seeking appreciation of the environs of one's youth. As a forebear of such poets as James Wright, Richard Hugo, David Wagoner, and Gary Snyder, Roethke infused a renewed sense of the importance of the inner and outer worlds of nature in American poetry not seen since Emerson, Thoreau, and Whitman, an organic intervention that was initially accomplished by acquiring environmental sensitivity within the seemingly limitless boundaries of his father's greenhouse world. "Moss-Gathering" establishes the important connection between Theodore Roethke's horticultural heritage and a larger commitment to the natural environment to which his modernized Romanticism pays homage.

13

The Storm of the Mind vs. Family and Machine in "Big Wind"

RUSSELL BRICKEY

"BIG WIND" (*Collected Poems,* 39) is a somewhat surprising entry in Roethke's overall canon. Its brief but dramatic narrative structure, play on violent imagery, and overarching use of the pathetic fallacy to describe the resiliency of human industry, and thus humanity itself, seem out of place among Roethke's love poems, imagistic greenhouse poems, and many long, meditative poems about the natural world and its relationship to the mind. Likewise, the poem is deceptively complex given that its story—about the Roethke family saving their harvest of greenhouse roses during a windstorm—is relatively straightforward. On a literal level, the poem is a story of heroics and human genius in the midst of savage nature; on a symbolic level, "Big Wind" is a portrait of the Roethke family nursery, which represents the taproot of emotional life, juxtaposed with the turbulent weather of the Great Lakes, which in turn personifies upheavals in the human psyche. Further hermeneutic complexity appears when we take into account the biographical background of the poem, the ornamentation of nautical imagery, and Roethke's clever use of line length, word choice, shape, and sound to craft "Big Wind" into a simulacrum of storm violence.

Biographical approaches take into account Roethke's numerous bouts with mental illness and institutional recuperation (Kalaidjian, 2–3; Seager, 90–109, 245–57). In these readings, "Big Wind" renders psychological upheaval through a constellation of symbols—the storm (emotion), the greenhouses behind the family house (the world), help from one's fellows (humanity), and the roses (life's vulnerability) within the greenhouse (the fragile house of the psyche)—that represents the phases of the speaker's journey—his "miniature epic" (Barillas, *Midwestern Pastoral,* 121)—as he perseveres and triumphs, miraculously, through the communal strength of his family. This constellation also reflects how Roethke's use of greenhouse plant life (nature, in other words, directed by human industry) almost always describes the poet's conflicted emotional life in Michigan. As Roethke himself writes about the beautiful rotting stink of greenhouses in his essay "An American Poet Introduces Himself and His Poems," "What the greenhouses themselves were to me I try to indicate in my second book, *The Lost Son and Other Poems.* . . . They were to me, I realize now, both heaven and hell, a kind of tropics created in the savage climate of Michigan, where austere German Americans turned their love of order and their terrifying efficiency into something truly beautiful. It was a universe, several worlds, which, even as a child, one worried about, and struggled to keep alive, as in the poem 'Big Wind'" (*On Poetry and Craft* 22). This is a poem of violent encounters between "heaven" (nature, beauty, growth, flora, and family) and "hell" ("order," "terrifying efficiency," austerity, and the "savage climate" of home), symbolized by the action of the storm threatening the greenhouse. Just as storm fronts are created by system-wide differences in barometric pressure, encounters between emotional highs and lows generate emotional upheaval which threatens the delicate housing of the psyche, and yet these same conflicts provoke the heroic, innovative salvation which allows the mind to sail through the tempestuous dark to the calm light. The forces of renewal and destruction intertwine and overlap—much as greenhouse vines might—into "several worlds" that stay with the speaker from childhood on. Another way to state this: storm and greenhouse symbolize conflicting forces in the speaker's psyche, which has grown since birth; the storm signifies forces, both human and natural, that work to destroy the interlocking worlds of the mind; saving the greenhouse signifies the psychological triumph over the dangerous weather of the psychological landscape; and these adventures are associated with childhood and home, particularly when viewed as part of a process within *The Lost Son and Other Poems.*

With this in mind, it is significant to note that "Big Wind" is based upon an actual incident from Roethke's youth when a winter windstorm blew the Tittabawasee River away from the intake pipes that supplied his hometown of Saginaw, Michigan, and the Roethke family's greenhouses with water. To save their crop of roses, the family ingeniously flooded the heating pipes, which normally sported steam heat, with superheated liquid fertilizer, thus keeping the roses warm. The young poet worked alongside the adults that night, and ostensibly received the approbation of his famously hard-to-please father, Otto (Seager 150; Wolff, *Theodore Roethke,* 39–40; Barillas, *Midwestern Pastoral,* 120). These biographical aspects are hard to overlook and overshadow most readings of the poem.

Likewise, "Big Wind" responds to the character of the Great Lakes, which border Michigan on three sides. Saginaw's proximity to Lake Huron probably accounts for the nautical themes and controlling metaphor of the storm. The greenhouse is portrayed as a ship weathering a tempest, "[l]unging" and "lashing" through "[w]ind driving water" (2–3). The family and workers in this conceit are sailors who work "the rusty boilers" (9) as if in the engine room of a steamship, and stuff broken windows with burlap as if patching a great sail of a galleon. The speaker says of the greenhouse that "she rode it out" (using a pronoun generally reserved for ships) even as she "hove into the teeth of it" (21, 23) as if bravely sailing into a gale—an apparently deliberate use of the pathetic fallacy (the notion that inanimate objects have animate or human attributes), furthering the notion that the greenhouses represent life, particularly that of the speaker. Finally, the images suggest a satisfying, familiar denouement when "[s]he sailed until the calm morning, / Carrying her full cargo of roses" (32–33). Overall, the conceit represents the stoutness and ingenuity of the Roethke family, and by extension of the entire human family, when faced with forces beyond their control, both natural and economic.

Roethke's constellation of nature, family, and commercial enterprise is a paradox, however, when viewed within the traditional scope of nature poetry. As a neo-Romantic poem, "Big Wind" runs counter to its own traditions: American Transcendentalism and British Romanticism both privilege nature as a healing and rejuvenating force, most often counteracting the dehumanizing aspects of industry and society. Yet here nature is both an overwhelmingly destructive force and a vulnerable living presence, and human industry is the stalwart counterpoint to either. Roethke has reformed Romantic nature into a synergistic marriage of nature and commerce, producing new (un)natural entities of combined biology and technology. William Barillas writes in *The Midwestern Pastoral* that "Big Wind" "reconciles, if temporarily, technology and agriculture, utility and aesthetic values in midwestern pastoral ideology" (121), reshaping the concept of machine-versus-nature conflict. As Louis Martz points out, "'Big Wind' throws a special emphasis upon the physical properties of the greenhouse, its 'manure-machine,' its 'steam-plant,' its 'rusty boiler,' its 'cypress window-frames' . . . to stress the element of deliberate art in the creation of these flowers" ("A Greenhouse Eden," 26). Roethke's "deliberate art" celebrates nature and machine as if they are symbiotic beings. Roethke's union of nature and technology, Barillas argues, reverses Leo Marx's famous metaphor for American pastoralism in *The Machine in the Garden,* in which the machine is the dominant presence. Now, in this brief adventure story, the communal triumph of family/machine "symbolizes the possibility of appropriate technology that would sustain rather than destroy nature and human lives" (*Midwestern Pastoral,* 121). In doing so, Barillas concludes, the speaker not only saves the family fortune, he also achieves a sense of place in the Saginaw Valley. Moreover, the roses, which represent nature, are safeguarded by human effort, the greenhouses and the family, to create a new nature which encompasses both worlds which were once disparate. As is typical of the *Lost Son* poems, Roethke looks deeply into the relationships between all elements of human industry—because even nature is predicated upon the works of days and hands—and finds the hierarchy of "several worlds" intertwining.

All of this is encapsulated brilliantly in a driving, linear narrative that emphasizes heroic action against overwhelming odds, in this case the time-honored theme of humanity versus animate but menacing elements. Like a miniature epic, "Big Wind" launches with a rhetorical question posed directly to the reader, "Where were the greenhouses going . . . ?"; as with any quest narrative, the adroit narrative hook begins *in medias res,* in the midst of the action, to draw its audience in as if the narrative is being spoken aloud. This is an adventure story, after all, not unlike many nautical journeys from *The Odyssey* to Yann Martel's *The Life of Pi.* As such, the poem's oratorical quality should not be overlooked, and, in fact, Roethke writes of his poems in the essay "Open Letter," "*Listen* to them, for they are written to be heard" (*On Poetry and Craft,* 50).

At the same time, "Big Wind" is also an example of concrete poetry, and utilizes techniques that are most apparent when examined on the page. The short lines and vertical orientation of the single long stanza represent the oblong construction of a greenhouse; at the same time, the unevenness of the right margin suggests an object, perhaps the poem itself, tattering or flapping in the wind. Word count per line is artful: two lines have three words; fourteen lines have four words; eight lines have five words; three lines have six words; two lines have seven words; and one line has eight words. It is interesting to note that the majority of smaller-word-count lines (three to five words) occur in the first two-thirds of the poem (lines 1–22) and the longer lines occur in the final third (lines 23–33). This distribution creates a visual and linguistic crescendo corresponding to the mounting drama of the narrative. As Walter Kalaidjian has observed, the "energetic images rely on participial verbs to evoke nature's dynamic imagery" (49). Thirteen of these participles are the initial words of their lines, and are either paired vertically ("Creaking" and "Cracking" in lines 17 and 18; "Ploughing" and "Bucking" in lines 25 and 26; "Flailing" and "Flinging" in lines 28 and 29) or in close proximity to each other ("Lunging" and "lashing" in line 2 and "driving" in line 3; "Pumping" in line 8 and "Watching" in line 10; "Whistling" in line 31 and "Carrying" in line 33), creating a studied interplay of language and image. Beginning so many lines with an active verb in the present participle invests the poem with the sense of ongoing action and propels its reading.

Roethke also peppers the stanza with assonant and alliterative relationships ("greenhouses going" in line 1; "manure-machine" in line 6; "Waver over to red" in line 11; "seams" in line 12 and "steam" in line 13; "worst wind was" in line 16; "rode," "old rose-house," "hove," and "broke over the whole of her" in lines 21–27, which play with the long "O" sound). Finally, it is hard not see the four initial verbs in lines 28 to 31 as a synecdoche of the struggle and eventual triumph of the poem. Each initial word—"Flailing . . . Flinging . . . Finally . . . Whistling"—represents a stage of the journey, from thrashing in the wind, to throwing the canvas over the broken windows, and then, finally, to whistling happily as the family sails into the calm morning. Such attention to the sonic and visual qualities using a more or less sprung rhythm (composed of a regular number of stressed syllables interspersed with an unpredictable number of unstressed syllables) creates an onomatopoeic expression of the narrative's turmoil. Kalaidjian names this aspect of the poem a deliberate play "to register the discordant tones of natural chaos" (49). Notice, however, that the last two lines soothe this discordance with sibilance ("She sailed"), assonance, alliteration, and consonance ("calm morning" / "cargo of roses"), and a limit on percussive sounds (32–33). Precision of this sort creates a gentle, sonorous conclusion which corresponds to the metaphoric renewals of dawn light, calm seas, and safe passage which end the poem.

Thus "Big Wind" is a poem of triumph. Despite the frequent allusions in his poetry to family and psychological dysfunction, Roethke writes that "in spite of all the muck and welter, the dark, the *dreck* of these poems" in *The Lost Son,* "I count myself among the happy poets" (*On Poetry and Craft,* 52). One could debate this self-analysis, but comparisons to other Roethke poems illustrate the resolution that "Big Wind" offers to a number of themes in *The Lost Son and Other Poems* and elsewhere in his canon. George Wolff observes in his book *Theodore Roethke* that the greenhouse poems are arranged "in a sequence from birth to death," starting with the two "Cuttings" poems which deal with uprooting and rebirth; followed by poems about unstoppable biological growth amidst decay ("Root Cellar" to "Orchids"); followed by five poems ("Moss Gathering" to "Child on Top of a Greenhouse") about "the very chancy attainment of maturity"; and ending "with two views of death ("Flower Dump" and "Carnations") (34). "Big Wind," which in Wolff's designation fits into a theme of maturation, is found within this sequence as the penultimate stage, a precondition for final rest, yet also a moment when personhood is attained through action. Also, the entire notion of a "Lost Son" is important once Otto's premature death from cancer, when Theodore was only fourteen, is taken into consideration: all the greenhouse poems are about survival on some level, death on others. "Big Wind" suggests that death is not an absolute certainty, even under dire circumstances, and that life, both flora and fauna, can endure through heroic ingenuity and stalwart community.

14

"Long Days under the Sloped Glass"

Greenhouse Memories in "Transplanting"

CARRIE DUKE

IN A review of Theodore Roethke's *The Lost Son and Other Poems* (1948), Robert Fitzgerald wrote that "children . . . rare farmers and greenhouse keepers" are closer to the earth than almost anyone else (qtd. in Seager, 158). As a third-generation "greenhouse keeper," I share with Roethke the personal experience of developing a close relationship to the natural world through growing up in and around the greenhouses of my grandfather and mother. Fitzgerald's observation that children and greenhouse growers establish a special bond with the earth is particularly poignant for those who have lived their childhood in greenhouses. I recognize the almost mythic quality of Roethke's flowers because I, too, grew up watching how integral plant life is to human life. As Roethke's poetry so powerfully demonstrates, being a child and being in greenhouses fosters a distinctive awareness of plants that transcends their utilitarian purposes.

In *The Midwestern Pastoral: Place and Landscape in Literature of the American Heartland* (2006), William Barillas notes that Roethke continues the Transcendentalist "critique of utilitarian progressivism: the dominant notion that industrial advancement equals human progress, that the subordination of nature and the individual to technology and the market economy is inevitable, and even to be desired" (111). Roethke's criticism of technological and economic growth demonstrates an intriguing paradox found in the greenhouse business between the love of plants and the use of plants for money. Despite Roethke's family's interest in accruing wealth, Roethke acknowledged that "a good many of [his father, Otto's specialty roses and orchids] were never put on sale at all" (qtd. in Seager, 13). Even though Otto worked hard to make his greenhouses financially successful, he enjoyed some plants for reasons other than pecuniary value. Otto may have refrained from overtly displaying his love of flowers, but he expressed it in subtle ways. Otto's "love was revealed rather in the choice of career itself and the artistry he had with little touches like the harmony of color between sweet peas and carnations" (Seager, 15). Just as Otto's love appeared concealed beneath his exterior show of professionalism, there often exists a dichotomy between a grower's need to make money and a grower's love of plants. My mother has commented on this dichotomy in greenhouse work by noting that "[n]o one works this hard for material compensation" (Pence, 2). For many growers, including my family, the desire to work in greenhouses stemmed more from the love of plants than the desire for profit.

Roethke's poem "Transplanting" (*Collected Poems,* 40) plays with this dichotomy by examining how a grower exerts power over plants in order to produce a salable item, but then the poem develops a profound understanding of plant life which complicates this assumed power structure. This reading of "Transplanting" provides more than just an interpretation of the human relationship to plant life; the poem enables readers to trace a history of greenhouse work, which has become so mechanized that the essential connection between plants and humans is being lost to the same utilitarian progressivism that Roethke critiqued in the 1940s.

Transplanting seedlings, as Roethke knew (and as my mother and I practiced before the sale of her greenhouses in 2012), requires the dexterous use of the growers' hands to pull and separate tiny plants from the seed flats in order to place them in new containers where they can grow and bloom. The poem begins with an almost absent speaker "[w]atching hands transplanting" (1). The importance of hands should not be underestimated in the close relationship between growers and the plants they work with, especially now when large corporations are making it almost impossible for small greenhouse growers to maintain that relationship. Today's greenhouse owners, including my family, have been pressured through market demands and corporate plant patents to ship in fully grown flowers ready for sale. Most of these flowers and vegetables are seeded and transplanted by machines and drenched in chemicals so that they can be shipped hundreds of miles in compact, convenient containers. This whole process negates the relationship of small-town greenhouse growers to the plants they could bond with by touching and holding them in their hands.

Roethke recognizes how a celebration of human hands stands in opposition to industrial modernization in "The Longing" when he writes, "I would delight in my hands, the branch singing" (*Collected Poems,* 182). Although Roethke likely could not foresee a time when machines would take plants away from growers' hands, poems like "Transplanting" recognize how indispensable the sensual process of touching and feeling flowers is to understanding plant life. The speaker watches the grower's hands quickly work in a multitude of intricate ways, and while dominating the placement of plants, the working hands also protect the developing plant life:

> Turning and tamping,
> Lifting the young plants with two fingers,
> Sifting in a palm-full of fresh loam . . .
> . . . .
> Then plumping in the bunched roots.
>
> (2–6)

The process of planting the seedlings may seem simple enough, but before mechanized planters and individualized plastic cells, growers like my mother had to disentangle, delicately but swiftly, the roots of hundreds upon hundreds of tiny plants. It is an intricate process basic in the interrelationship between human and floral life.

Many aspects of "Transplanting" remind us of the essential harmony and even unity that exist between plants and humanity. The poem is separated into two stanzas, but upon closer inspection we realize that the entire poem is, in fact, one long compound-complex sentence. The process of a person planting and a plant growing may have inherent differences, but the practice is inextricably bound and unified. The speaker's repetition of the word "one" portrays this sense of unity. Initially, the speaker only appears to be describing the grower's method of planting with the phrases "One swift movement" (5) and "All in one" (8). But the use of "one" in the second phrase connotes a holistic quality to the reciprocal relationship between the planter and the plant; they are, in a sense, "all in one." Our lives are often as dependent upon the plants we grow for both spiritual and physical needs as cultivated plants are on us for nurturance.

The planting method described by the speaker in "Transplanting" not only reminds readers of the unity between humans and plants; the description also provides us with exact imagery of the physical process by which growers tend their flowers. The speaker describes the grower as transplanting the seedlings with a "swift movement" (5) and then "[q]uick on the wooden bench" (9). The words "swift" and "quick" make me feel as if Roethke had been watching my mother transplanting, but then again most greenhouse growers from my mother's generation, as well as previous generations, had to plant as rapidly as possible. They were dealing with hundreds and thousands of seedlings all maturing at the same time, all destined to die if left too long in the seed flats. The hands that the speaker watches exert the power to lift, plump, tamp, and twist the delicate seedlings in the first stanza, but these actions are still a part of a larger and encompassing process of plant growth that will come from "the long days under the sloped glass" (13).

I know from experience that the greenhouse grower who plants in this way intimately participates in the process of growth. So much of Roethke's poetry expresses an interest in process rather than results, and his greenhouse poems accurately reveal how humans can be closely connected to the development of plants. Michael O'Sullivan describes this process as the "visceral moment where all that is described is some sort of change, where the means rather than the end of growth is emphasized" (24). While greenhouse growers want their flowers to mature properly for sale, a relationship develops between them and each plant they touch, water, clean, and caress. I remember my mother referring to all the hundreds and thousands of her flowers and vegetables as her "babies." This was not the depersonalized world of product management and profit margins; this was a world where plant life could assert its own meaning, much like O'Sullivan's assessment of Roethke's biosphere, where he "dares the natural objects to state their own case, their own means of being" (29).

The last stanza of "Transplanting" opens up the possibility of watching plants assert their own meaning. The speaker describes the small seedlings as they begin to grow:

> The young horns winding and unwinding,
> Creaking their thin spines,
> . . . .
> Breaking into nakedness.
>
> (15–18)

The seemingly omnipotent grower leaves the second stanza for a fuller expression of the singularity and strange independence of plant growth. O'Sullivan notes that even while Roethke personifies plant life, that life retains an alterity that resists "human language" (30). The growth of the new transplant is something we can only begin to understand in human terms, and Roethke's plants exist incongruently with our anthropocentric understanding of the world. We see young tendrils both "winding and unwinding" with the flexibility of early shoots, yet we seem to hear the "[c]reaking [of] their thin spines" (16). The underleaves are breaking into a nakedness that is natural for plants while the blossoms are extending and extending again. In an effort to allow plant life to exert its own meaning, language seems to break down so that it no longer indicates what we think it should. Are the tendrils winding or unwinding? Are the young plants flexible or brittle? Is the bare existence of plant life naked or natural? To the untrained or inexperienced eye, plants may appear to be all the same, a mass of homogenous insensate life, but for those who work closely with flowers, as have my family and I, our relationship with each plant acknowledges the inherent differences. Perhaps one plant will exhibit an unusual variegation, or another will branch uncharacteristically. Even though growers exercise a modicum of control over life in the greenhouse, we also recognize the aspects of nature we cannot control.

Despite this difference, this "separateness of all things" (*Collected Poems,* 60) as Roethke states it in "A Field of Light," there exists an effort at some type of communication, a reaching across the biosphere for understanding as we see in the last lines of "Transplanting": "The whole flower extending outward, / Stretching and reaching" (21–22). The word "reaching" suggests that the plant's efforts to extend are purposeful, even conscious. Identifying this imagined consciousness in "Cuttings" and "Cuttings (*later*)," Barillas writes that Roethke "closely observes the process, accelerating movement so that the cuttings seem as active and conscious as [his] herons, snakes, and other animals" (*Midwestern Pastoral,* 116). Roethke would not be alone if he sensed a communicative awareness not just between humans and plants, but also within the plant community. My mother and I have often shared our experiences of entering a greenhouse at night and feeling that we have entered a world of the *other*—where we do not quite belong. Instead of the anthropocentric view of plants serving humans, the nighttime greenhouse inverts this dynamic, so that one feels an uncanny sense of a process for which our language is inadequate. This experience is now being backed up by scientific evidence that confirms plants do communicate with biochemical messages, and "Transplanting" suggests imaginative ways in which we might understand this new world (McGowan, par. 4).

The first stanza of "Transplanting" begins by asserting a dynamic where the human planter is in control of the plants. After all, human hands have the ability to turn, tamp, lift, and plump, but the relationship between the grower and plants may be more complex. In my experience, it requires an incredible gentleness to transplant seedlings quickly by hand. Seedlings may be only an inch tall, sometimes smaller, with their roots tightly tangled together. Although it may seem violent to rip a plant from one space of growth and plunge it into another, a practiced grower can perform the process with a dexterity that does not injure the plant. The seedlings transplanted by my mother always grew better than those planted by inexperienced part-time employees.

This utilitarian process of transplanting was once closely aligned with the grower's careful and intuitive understanding of plant life, but now the mechanized process of plant production is increasingly imposing boundaries between plants and people. Not only have machines taken over the planting process, large corporate greenhouse production creates flowers and vegetables permeated with chemicals, and as more and more people buy their plants from big-box stores they will continue to be exposed to pesticides and growth regulators. Even when shoppers believe they are reconnecting with nature through their flower purchases, they actually might be poisoned by their attempt to reconnect with nature. I have personally witnessed what economic growth (in the form of big-box stores and corporate behemoths) has done to small greenhouse businesses in the Midwest. One after another, these greenhouses have had to close their doors, and a way of life, where growers develop an intimate understanding of the plants they grow, is gradually disappearing from our culture.

While reading Roethke's greenhouse poems, all the sights, sounds, and smells of growing up in the greenhouse business return to my memory. But more than anything, Roethke's words create nostalgia for the feeling of being closely connected to developing plant life. I can still recall gazing in amazement at the incredible glowing pink of a petunia blossom, or stopping a moment to soak in the myriad of colors blending into harmonious flowerbeds on bench after bench of potted plants in May. My memories remind me that my childhood experience, of watching all the various forms of plant growth in greenhouses, is a life that modern progress has almost extinguished. I cannot read Roethke's beautiful, yet haunting stanzas without remembering the loss of this "old-fashioned" way of life. Although my grandfather's and my mother's greenhouses are gone now, Roethke's poetry brings them back to me with the awe and magic of a child's vision of "long days under the sloped glass" (13).

15

"Frau Bauman, Frau Schmidt, and Frau Schwartze" and the Sleeping Beauty Tale

MARCIA NOE and LAURA DUNCAN

ROETHKE'S ELEGIAC "Frau Bauman, Frau Schmidt, and Frau Schwartze" (*Collected Poems,* 42) has enjoyed relatively little sustained critical discussion. Most of the scholars who have written about this poem have either debated its inclusion in the greenhouse sequence or noted its Yeatsian influence.[1] Another element of Roethke criticism has drawn parallels between the three eponymous greenhouse workers and mythic figures such as the Fates.[2] However, we believe a strong connection can also be made between these "ancient ladies" (1) and the fairy godmothers of the Sleeping Beauty tale, a connection illuminated and supported by the poem's biographical context, textual history, prosody, and patterns of imagery. Reading this poem through the lens of the Sleeping Beauty tale stresses Roethke's appreciation and gratitude, not only for the nurturing role these women played in his life but, more importantly, for their gift of feminine sensibility, which enriched his creative powers and helped to shape his poetics.

The connections between "Frau Bauman, Frau Schmidt, and Frau Schwartze" and the Sleeping Beauty tale can best be understood within the context of poem's mythic dimensions. From this perspective, the word "ancient" that describes the ladies in the first line can be seen to denote much more than their chronological age. In the second stanza, after the ladies are compared to nurses, birds, and witches, the word "ancient" is used again when they are called "ancient leathery crones" (32). The archetypal connotations of "witches" and "crones," as well as the adjective "ancient," thus direct us to view the Fraus not only as the real-life greenhouse workers of Roethke's childhood—Frau Bauman, Frau Zeiler, and Frau Schwartze—who inspired this poem, but also as mythic figures (Seager, 11, 16).

The lengthy description of the Fraus' winding, straightening, tucking, tying, sifting, and sprinkling the plants, as well as "teas[ing] out the seed that the cold kept asleep," emphasizes their role as creators and nurturers (23). Peter Balakian describes the ladies as "agents of cosmic process . . . full of maternal earthiness and supernatural force" (60); Richard Allen Blessing says that they "have the power to transform their energy creatively into the life around them" (80). Thus, they conform to Ralph Mills Jr.'s description of the typical female figure in Roethke's early poems: "a creature of spiritual and mythological proportions" (*Theodore Roethke,* 36). The significance of these ladies is further enhanced by their function as both childhood memory and sustaining presence in the adult speaker's life; as Blessing points out, they are "'Gone' and 'still hover[ing]' simultaneously" (80). Moreover, they are, as Jenijoy La Belle says in *The Echoing Wood of Theodore Roethke,* "part real, part imaginary" (142).

Placing the poem in its biographical context can also help the reader understand the Sleeping Beauty connection, focusing specifically on the reason that these three elderly greenhouse employees played such a key role in the life of their boss's young son. The poet was born in Saginaw, Michigan, to German American florists, Otto and Helen Huebner Roethke, whose rather detached parenting style was a far cry from that practiced by many parents today. Roethke biographer Allan Seager comments that "[e]xcept for their angers, the Roethkes do not seem to have been emotionally demonstrative. His mother did not lavish the treasures of her affection on him so much as that she brought him up, as she would have said, 'in the way he should go'" (33). Seager also reprints an essay Roethke wrote in college, concluding that "Ted seems to have remembered his father as a stern, short-tempered man whose love he doubted" (26). Moreover, in the 1975 Anchor Books edition of *Collected Poems,* "Frau Bauman, Frau Schmidt, and Frau Schwartze" is located on the page that faces "My Papa's Waltz," a poem in which the child-speaker is handled roughly by an inebriated father while his disapproving mother looks on.[3] Thus, a plausible inference, based on this biographical and textual evidence, is that as a child Roethke sought the loving nurturance he failed to receive from his parents in the ministrations of the Fraus, who

picked me up, a spindly kid,
Pinching and poking my thin ribs
Till I lay in their laps, laughing,
Weak as a whiffet.

(26–29)

Scholars who emphasize the mythic parallels to the Fraus liken them to the Fates—Clotho, Lachesis, and Atropos—who spin, measure, and cut the thread of each individual's life. Balakian further articulates their multivalence, stating that "[t]hey are simultaneously nurturers of life in the greenhouse and muses who embody the poet's realization of the creative process" (60). Blessing adds that they "give the poet himself a symbolic birth" and delineates their tripartite significance: "through the Fraus who were, through the Fraus mythologized, and through the Fraus who remain as a felt presence, he has made a poetic representation of the living extension of the past into the ever-moving present" (81–82).

While we agree with scholars who see the Fraus as archetypal figures such as earth mothers, muses, magical witches, and Fates, we find an equally strong and illuminating parallel in the fairy godmothers of the Sleeping Beauty tale.[4] Karen Rowe observes that writers of fairy tales have traditionally claimed to have heard them from "nurses . . . old crones . . . and wise women" (62); clearly, Roethke's Fraus are all three. Joan Gould links the mythology of the Fates to the Sleeping Beauty tale when she argues that the spinner in Sleeping Beauty is an appropriation of Clotho, the spinner sister among the Fates (103), who spins the thread of life, and equates the spinning of thread with fertility, another link to the greenhouse Fraus, who tend the plants, "keeping creation at ease" (20).

The language of the poem's second stanza makes this connection with feminine creativity and the Sleeping Beauty tale more salient. Although the story has a number of variants, in one of the best-known versions, "The Sleeping Beauty in the Wood," a beautiful young princess pricks her finger on a spindle, a motif echoed in the speaker's characterization of himself as "a spindly kid" (26). Although the spindle in the Sleeping Beauty tale functions as a plot device, the instrument of a curse placed on the princess in her cradle by an angry fairy who was not invited to her christening, spindles traditionally have strong ties to wise women, tale-spinning, and feminine nurturing, as seen in the Fates' mythological functions. In Roethke's poem, the boy is spindly not only in being thin and weak, but also in being *like a spindle:* he is the instrument by which the Fraus figuratively spin a thread of thought to be woven into poems such as the present verse.

Rowe also links the female craft of spinning to truth telling and the "female acts of birthing, nursing, [and] prophesying" (63). Kay Stone concurs, noting that "[f]eminists have favored the weaving and spinning image for its connection with traditional female occupations and its optimistic images of connecting and creating positive patterns" (233). Significantly, the word "text" derives from the Latin verb for "to weave": *texere;* throughout human history, women have been not merely spinners and weavers who have produced textiles but wise women who have spun and woven texts/tales from which people have drawn insight, strength, and guidance, perhaps best exemplified by the goddess Procne, who, unable to tell of her rape by Tereus because he tore out her tongue, wove the story into a tapestry; and Arachne, who wove a more beautiful storytelling tapestry than Athena and consequently suffered the wrath of that goddess. Thus, the three Fraus, who "tied and tucked" (11) and "sewed up the air with a stem" (22) can be seen to be three modern examples in a long line of creative female tale weavers who derive from ancient times, beginning with Procne and Arachne and extending through Scheherazade and the Wife of Bath to the many vibrant women storytellers of today.

The "thorn-bitten wrists" (34) of the Fraus offer another link to the Sleeping Beauty tale, for during the hundred years that the princess slumbers, along with the other inhabitants of the castle, a thick facade of briars and brambles grows up around the building, presenting a thorny challenge to anyone who contemplates entering it. A third and more significant connection to the tale is found in the last line of the poem. Here the image of the fairy godmothers hovering over the baby princess's cradle as they offer their gifts is evoked when the speaker feels the Fraus' "snuff-laden breath blowing lightly over me in my first sleep" (35). Blessing's reading is insightful here, characterizing the Fraus as "witches capable of collapsing time so that the cold sleep of the adult is at one with the first sleep from which he wakened into life" (82).

This allusion to birth suggests the christening party of the Sleeping Beauty tale, to which several fairies (the number ranges from three to eighteen, depending on the variant of the tale under discussion) are invited to serve as godmothers. The fairy godmothers bring a number of gifts to the baby princess; among them, again depending on the variant under discussion, are song, wit, beauty, grace, dance, and music, all suggestive of female creativity. Balakian stresses the power of the Fraus to endow the speaker with such gifts when he asserts that "they become the agents of Roethke's own poetic gift"; they provide the connection between "the deep relationship between poetic process and cosmic creation" (60–61).

When "Frau Bauman, Frau Schmidt, and Frau Schwartze" is read through the lens of the Sleeping Beauty tale with a focus on Roethke's prosody, the uniquely feminine sensibility that the Fraus engender is underscored, one that exemplifies the embodied poetics of *l'écriture feminine* espoused by theorists such as Hélène Cixous, who argue for a uniquely female form of expression, derived from female sexuality and characterized by fragmentation, indirection, fluidity, nonlinearity, repetition, and other departures from traditionally masculine writing (Cixous, 256–58). This feminine quality is readily apparent in "Frau Bauman, Frau Schmidt, and Frau Schwartze," as well as in a number of Roethke's other poems. Here, as in his other free-verse poems, he eschews traditional metrics that specify a set number of feet to a line and a set number of stresses to each foot, replacing it with a metrics that Rosemary Sullivan likens to Gerard Manley Hopkins's sprung rhythm, in which lines are scanned according to the number of stresses per line rather than the number and placement of stresses per metric foot (31). In the absence of a set rhyme scheme, he substitutes alliteration, assonance, and consonance, which create a softer, more subtle but still musical prosody.

Charlotte I. Lee notes that diminished line length and unstressed line endings are also feminine characteristics of Roethke's prosody, observing that "[o]f the more than two hundred poems which Theodore Roethke published, a fair proportion of them are for or to or about women" (23) and noting that the "sound patterning . . . supports and helps unify the content" (24). We can see this feminine sensibility in evidence in the middle section of "Frau Bauman, Frau Schmidt, and Frau Schwartze":

> Quicker than birds, they dipped
> Up and sifted the dirt;
> They sprinkled and shook;
> They stood astride pipes,
> Their skirts billowing out wide into tents,
> Their hands twinkling with wet.
>
> (13–18)

Here we see two elements of Roethke's prosody that Lee identifies as feminine: the diminished line length and the use of alliteration and assonance in place of a traditional rhyme scheme. In this section of the poem, a series of short "i" and short "e" sounds ("quicker," "dipped," "sifted," "sprinkled," "billowing," "twinkling," "tents," "wet"), along with repeated initial sibilants ("sifted, "sprinkled," "shook," "stood," "skirts"), creates a soft musicality that complements the feminine and subtly sexual content of the poem that is suggested by lines like "They stood astride pipes, / Their skirts billowing out wide into tents" (16–17).

Moreover, a third element that Lee identifies as characteristic of Roethke's prosody, the feminine line ending, is present throughout the poem. Eight of the poem's lines have final unstressed syllables: "ladies," ladders," "smilax," "climbing," "straighten," needle," "laughing," and "whiffet." These endings appear in clusters of two and three that alternate with the more conventionally stressed masculine endings to further enhance, along with the enjambed lines, the poem's gentle, elegiac tone:

> Gone the three ancient ladies
> Who creaked on the greenhouse ladders,
> Reaching up white strings
> To wind, to wind
> The sweet-pea tendrils, the smilax.
>
> (1–5)

The concrete sensory imagery of "Frau Bauman, Frau Schmidt, and Frau Schwartze" further establishes the poem's feminine sensibility. Kenneth Burke points out that in such poems Roethke "goes as far as is humanly possible in quest of a speech wholly devoid of abstractions" ("Vegetal Radicalism," 73), and Karl Malkoff observes that the greenhouse poems present experience "not as subject to intellectual analysis, but directly in terms of sensory perception," noting their tactile, auditory, visual, olfactory, and gustatory imagery (47). Imagery of this kind is plentiful in this poem: the Fraus creak on the greenhouse ladders, with billowing, tent-like skirts and twinkling wet hands. The auditory and tactile imagery of the first stanza continues in the second, as they pinch and poke the speaker until he lies laughing in their laps. As Lee observes about another Roethke poem, "Old Lady's Winter Words," the "tactile and thermal imagery" is "so strongly female in its candor and in the details . . . that it shows remarkable insight into the feminine mind" (24).

The preponderance of flower imagery early in the poem recalls Burke's assertion that Roethke's flowers become "Woman in the Absolute" ("Vegetal Radicalism," 108). Earlier in his essay, in discussing the range of meaning in Roethke's flower imagery, he links Roethke's flowers to "children in general, or girls specifically" (85). In "Frau Bauman, Frau Schmidt, and Frau Schwartze," the Fraus are subtly likened to the flowers they tend; as they wind the sweet-pea tendrils, smilax, nasturtiums, climbing roses, carnations, and chrysanthemums, the reader's attention is directed to "the stiff / Stems, jointed like corn" (9–10), an image that alludes as much to the elderly Fraus' limbs and fingers as it does to the plants that they "tied and tucked" (11).

The final lines of the poem employ an unappealing yet arresting set of visual, olfactory, and tactile images, as the speaker recalls the Fraus' leathery skin, sweat-stiffened bandanas, thorn-bitten wrists, and snuff-laden breath. These deeply female but superficially unfeminine fairy godmother figures are no less bountiful than their counterparts in the Sleeping Beauty tale. Like the prince who kisses Sleeping Beauty into consciousness, they have awakened in Roethke a feminine sensibility, endowing his work with added complexity and emotional resonance.

NOTES

1. Among the scholars who have discussed Roethke's relationship to Yeats are Louis L. Martz (in his essay "A Greenhouse Eden"), Jenijoy La Belle, Jay Parini, and Karl Malkoff.

2. Among the scholars who have discussed parallels between the three greenhouse workers and the Fates are Rosemary Sullivan, Peter Balakian, Louis L. Martz (in "A Greenhouse Eden"), and Jenijoy La Belle.

3. "Frau Bauman, Frau Schmidt, and Frau Schwartze" was first published in *The New Yorker* in 1952; it was not included in the original greenhouse sequence that appeared in *The Lost Son and Other Poems* (1948). However, the poem appears between "Old Florist" and "Transplanting" in *The Waking* (1953) and in *Words for the Wind* (1958), as well as at the end of the greenhouse sequence in the 1975 Anchor Books edition of *Collected Poems,* with "My Papa's Waltz" on the facing page. William Barillas suggests that Roethke, upon reflection, included the poem as part of the greenhouse sequence in later collections because "[h]e seems to have decided that there was a silence, an absence that needed to be peopled. It was the strong female presence of these women that he had left out of *The Lost Son,* and that he added in the collections that followed" ("Re: More on 'Frau Bauman'").

See Stiffler for a summary of the scholarly controversy about whether the poem should be considered a part of the greenhouse sequence.

4. The story of Sleeping Beauty originated in France as "La Belle au bois dormant." First published in Charles Perrault's *Histoires ou contes du temps passé* (1697), it subsequently appeared as a chapbook in England and has been a perennial favorite of English pantomime. However, the tale has many variants throughout the world, including Sweden and Chile. In Germany, a similar story is entitled "Brunhild." The variant from Italy is called "Sun, Moon, and Talia"; Sicily has a similar version, "Sun, Pearl, and Anna." There is also an Arabic variant from Palestine called "Wadiah." For a detailed discussion of the variants of the Sleeping Beauty tale, see Opie and Opie, 81–83.

16

Meter in "My Papa's Waltz"

WILLIAM BARILLAS

SINCE THE publication in 1950 of Kenneth Burke's essay "The Vegetal Radicalism of Theodore Roethke," psychological and biographical approaches have underlain critical responses to Roethke's poetry. Later critics have problematized but not rejected Burke's Freudian analysis of "[t]he preconscious, the infantile, the regressive, [and] the sexual" in Roethke's poems, especially those dealing with plant life in his father's greenhouses (85). Even formalist analyses address the poet's preoccupation with childhood and his own mental processes. "When Roethke is at his best," Richard Allen Blessing argues, "'meaning' is a complex of forces, a musical expression growing out of the pre-conscious resonances of the language, out of the play of sound against sound, out of the energy of primitive rhythms . . . out of an intensification through repetition and variation" (222). Auditory elements complement and reinforce meaning and tone in Roethke's poems, especially those written in traditional meter and rhyme, expressing the sensory qualities of experience through the sounds of words.

A paradigmatic poem in this regard is the frequently anthologized "My Papa's Waltz" (*Collected Poems,* 43), in which Roethke remembers himself as a child, dancing with his father in the family kitchen. Discussions of this poem typically emphasize its tonal ambiguity, as certain words imply that the boy reacts with fear, as well as pleasure, to the boisterous play. Critics who note Roethke's handling of meter in "My Papa's Waltz" do so mainly in general terms.

Walter Kalaidjian, for example, only refers to the poem as "registering playful but poignant tones in stanzas of iambic trimeter" (51). Likewise, Peter Balakian contends that "[m]uch of the poem's success grows out of the tension and irony created by the somewhat violent action of the waltz set against the steady cadence of the rhymed quatrains" (62). Yet the emotional impact of "My Papa's Waltz" also depends on variations from the dominant meter, metrical substitutions that provide auditory embodiments of the dance as a sensory experience.

The poem consists of four quatrains in iambic trimeter, a metrical arrangement that parallels the three-beat rhythm of a waltz. Indeed, the stanzas are well suited to musical setting as a waltz; in rhythm as well as subject matter, the poem bears out its title. As the speaker says in the fourth line, however, "Such waltzing was not easy." Subsequent lines attribute that lack of ease to the father's clumsiness and overwhelming size and strength, images of which are enhanced by the poem's metrical irregularities.

The first stanza begins with an olfactory image of liquor on the father's breath. Dancing puts the pair in such proximity that the smell of whiskey, hyperbolically, "[c]ould make a small boy dizzy." The word "dizzy" adds an extra unstressed syllable to line 2, which throws the line off balance and creates a rhythmic parallel to the boy's vertigo. The recurrence of the same variation (in metrical terms a feminine ending) in line 4 reinforces that parallel, while accentuating that line's assertion about the difficulty of the dance. "Rhythmically," Roethke held, "it's the spring and rush of the child I am after" (*On Poetry and Craft,* 53). He captures that "spring and rush" from the first stanza of "My Papa's Waltz" onwards, representing through meter the boy's reactions to, and impressions of, roughhousing with his father.

The poem's second stanza begins with the strong iambics of line 5, which suggest an increased vigor and consistency in the father's steps. The momentum of the dance causes pans to slide off a shelf and the mother to frown in disapproval, effects emphasized by two metrical variations. The first is the initial inversion in line 6, consisting of the words "Slid from." The falling rhythm of that trochee enhances the image of pans sliding and falling to the floor. Then, the final unstressed syllable in "countenance" means that line 7 ends with a pyrrhic, a foot of two unstressed syllables. This rhythmic flattening suits the mother's silent yet visible annoyance, combined with the formality of "countenance" as the longest word in the poem, the only one with more than two syllables, and the one a child is least likely to know. A kind of rhythmic variation also occurs with "unfrown," predicate verb to "countenance" in the stanza's second independent clause. "Unfrown" is the only iamb among the eleven two-syllable words in the poem, with "Papa's," "whiskey," "waltzing," and the rest all being trochees. These rhythmic anomalies intensify the mother's dismay, combined with the strangeness of "unfrown" as a neologism and its role in the double negative "could not unfrown itself."

If the second stanza is the most visual, the third is the most tactile in its imagery. It begins iambically, with the staccato, monosyllabic words of line 9 emphasizing the father's strength and the tactile pressure of "the hand that held" the boy's wrist. The metrical variation that appeared in the first stanza recurs here: line 10 is iambic with a feminine ending. Line 12, however, strays entirely from the iambic pattern, as the speaker recalls how his "right ear scraped a buckle" every time his father lost the waltz rhythm. It scans as an anapest followed by two trochees, a variation that rhythmically embodies not only the father's missed steps, referred to in line 11, but also the pain the boy feels when his ear comes into contact with the buckle on his father's belt.

The fourth and final stanza begins with the father trying to get back into step by tapping a waltz rhythm with his palm on the boy's head. Metrical variations in lines 13 and 14 display this effort. Line 13 consists of two anapests, a return to rising rhythm and the six-syllable line. Line 14 begins with an anapest ("[w]ith a palm") but then follows with two iambs ("caked hard by dirt"), showing that the father has gotten back into step, just as the poem reverts to iambic meter. Lines 15 and 16, the last two of the poem, are emphatically iambic, with soft syllables alternating with strong stresses as the speaker remembers how his father "waltzed me off to bed / Still clinging to [his] shirt." The rhythm here suggests grace and affection, a tone consistent with the connotations of "waltzed" and "clinging." While the "waltzing was not easy," with metrical stumbling to match the father's awkwardness, the speaker concludes his recollection with a sense of joy and security, rather than pain and fear.

"We must keep in mind," Roethke asserts in his prose, "that rhythm is the entire movement, the flow, the recurrence of stress and unstress that is related to the rhythms of the blood, the rhythms of nature. It involves certainly stress, time, pitch, the texture of words, the total meaning of the poem" (*On Poetry and Craft,* 69). That relation of poetic rhythm to "blood," the flow of bodily experience, operates in "My Papa's Waltz," in which patterns of sound support movement, tone, and theme. "In his great poems," Blessing writes, "Roethke's 'meaning'—never mind the ostensible subject—is always a celebration of the dance of being, the energy of life. To meet his own standards for genius he had to create a revelation of that dance for his audience, and he had to use every resource of the language to bring it off. To satisfy himself, he had to make the experience, not talk about it" (5). The verbal resources that "make" or embody the experience in "My Papa's Waltz" include the poem's artfully subtle and suggestive prosody, which imaginatively puts the reader in the boy's place as he dances with his beloved yet intimidating "Papa."

17

Syntax and Diction in "Dolor"

LUKE BREKKE

MOST POETS have only a handful of ideas; the best, it seems, have fewer. Exclude Whitman's vision of true democracy or his tally of the human body and its labors from *Leaves of Grass,* and that hefty book which sang of so much becomes rather quiet. Eliminate Wallace Stevens's investigations of the confluence of world and imagination, and his snowman melts, his jar evaporates. The poetic achievement of Theodore Roethke, similarly, draws from few sources: the greenhouse as an embodiment of "Great Nature" is one, and human deference to that force, another. As Jay Parini points out, "Roethke's poetry seems divided into periods marked by radical changes of style; but there are no real shifts of intention" (15). That intention, which stays constant throughout Roethke's career, is essentially Romantic: it aims to reveal, to praise, or to summon the vitality and potent force of nature as it relates to the emotionally alive and responsive individual. Roethke takes for granted a connection between self and the wider environment.

In his poem "Dolor" (*Collected Poems,* 44), which originally appeared in *The Lost Son and Other Poems,* the search for this connection occurs in an environment strikingly different from that in most of Roethke's work; in "Dolor" we're not in the greenhouse, but in an office. That difference has preoccupied the little criticism that the poem has received. The chief interest in "Dolor" has been its anomaly, preventing critics from giving proper attention to the poem's aesthetic qualities; its formal achievement has been glossed over in favor of its thematic novelty. Even so, what has been said about the poem's theme also privileges departures, and proper attention has not been given to the thematic elements that are in keeping with Roethke's other work.

"Dolor" is a thirteen-line poem composed of two sentences. These two sentences begin similarly: "I have known" and "I have seen" (1, 9). This loose anaphora provides the poem's most basic structure: each sentence opens up a catalogue that reveals the speaker's environment and explores his relationship to it. As Jenijoy La Belle has pointed out, Roethke's phrasing echoes Eliot's Prufrock—"And I have known the eyes already . . . I have seen the moment of my greatness flicker" (*Collected Poems,* 5, 6)—and calls to mind the "modern desolation and devitalization" that Prufrock embodies (*Echoing Wood,* 37). Roethke's speaker, like Prufrock, "has known," "has seen" the isolating, destructive effects of a life passed in the confines of a modern institution. For Roethke's speaker, the specific institution—asylum, university, or otherwise—is left unclear. What is clear, however, is that the usual connection between the emotionally active self and his environment has been altered. Those responsive centers of the natural world which Roethke accesses in other poems have been transformed, reft of their original character in order to serve questionable ends: trees have been whittled down to pencils or pulped down to paper; the lively, slippery mud has been shaped and fired and now communicates—in an inert form—the "unalterable pathos of basin and pitcher" (6). Within this environment, the individual faces a similar loss of identity and danger of stasis, the "[e]ndless duplication of lives" (8).

Roethke's speaker's emotional life is commensurate with his environment. He knows the "inexorable sadness of pencils . . . the misery of manilla folders" (1, 3), the emotional pallor of what's around him. The first sentence, extending over eight lines, reinforces this relationship. Each emotion attributed to the speaker—"sadness," "dolor," "misery," "desolation," and "pathos"—is syntactically modified and defined by what surrounds it. Most often, as in the two examples above, this modification occurs through a prepositional phrase, "dolor *of pad and paper*" . . . "pathos *of basin and pitcher*" (2, 6, emphasis added), that attaches an emotion to a specific object or set of objects. In another case, the preposition locates the emotion in a series of physical spaces: "Desolation in immaculate public places, / Lonely reception room, lavatory, switchboard" (4–5). The effect is that the speaker, the "I" of the first line, quickly recedes, overwhelmed by the isolating environment and displaced by the powerful emotions it engenders.

While Roethke's syntax embodies the basic relationship between self and environment, another feature of his language is simultaneously informing our reading: his diction. In a poem that deploys diction effectively, the poet is sensitive to a number of complex, interdependent values. When Roethke speaks of the "unalterable pathos of basin and pitcher," for instance, he is choosing *pathos* over *hurt, basin* over *sink, pitcher* and not *jug.* Part of the effect of these choices is sonic: *pathos, basin,* and *pitcher* are all self-contained trochees, and within the music of the line they establish a strong falling rhythm: the un*al*ter*a*ble *pa*thos of *ba*sin and *pit*cher. That falling rhythm is present at the end of all but two of the poem's lines (2, 10), which sonically reinforces the speaker's desperation, his *falling* spirits, the metrical stress (energy) dissipating before the line ends. That is one effect of Roethke's choices. Another effect is also present, an effect that results from the etymological origins of these words. *Pathos, basin,* and *pitcher* are all Latinate; they come into English through the Romance language family. As a general rule, Latinate words are more likely to be polysyllabic than their Germanic counterparts; they also tend to carry with them a trace of refinement. *Sink,* when compared to *basin,* sounds utterly commonplace, almost crude, while *basin* brings to mind something more akin to a font: still a place where one might wash, but a different kind of washing, an ablution. The difference, of course, is one of connotation, and it is a difference that results from the word's Latinate origin. *Basin* came into English through the Old French *bacin* sometime around 1200, at a point in history when the ruling class in England was French and spoke French, and the Anglo-Saxon (Germanic) peasants still spoke Old English. More than eight hundred years later, we still hear *basin* with a peasant's ear.

As English speakers, we register the nuanced differences that result from a word's origins intuitively, whether or not we are aware of the history that has accumulated those differences. Roethke's choices in diction lead us to understand the poem differently, which is to say they are choices that affect tone. In the opening lines, Latinate diction dominates the poem ("inexorable," "misery," "mucilage," "desolation," "immaculate," "reception," "lavatory," "duplication"). Roethke's use of high diction over simpler, more concrete language creates several tonal effects. Early in the poem, he bumps Latinate diction up against the Germanic to create a striking incongruity between the speaker's grand emotions and the objects around him: the "dolor of pad and paper-weight," "the misery of manilla folders" (2–3). A similar quality emerges from the first line's "inexorable sadness of pencils," which relies less on the Latinate and Germanic interplay but achieves a similar effect through the homely "pencils." These juxtapositions generate bathos, which "evokes the absurdity of life in the white-collar world" (Balakian, 63), and they embed a degree of self-aware irony that resists melodrama, which the poem risks.

But the poem is not comic, and by the end of the first sentence, Roethke's diction begins creating other effects. In some instances, Roethke imitates the euphemistic decorum of the institution: "Lonely reception room, lavatory" (5). These lines communicate the speaker's suffering, his loneliness, through the impersonality of the language: we sense that polite society would rather not know his emotional pain, much as they prefer the word *lavatory* to *toilet,* or *reception* to *waiting room.* It is a subtlety of the diction, which communicates that particular kind of pain, informing us just how pathological impersonality becomes in the institutional setting.

The end of the first sentence is the end of an octave, and Roethke brings us to a sonnet-like threshold. For the first time since the poem's opening word, Roethke mentions not just places or objects that correlate to the poem's grand emotions, but the people who endure them. The "[e]ndless duplication" is not only of memos or agendas, but "of *lives*" (8, emphasis added). In every other phrase, the object of the preposition has been a physical object; here, in the eighth line, it finally refers to people, and the sinister cost of displacing individuals is revealed. By delaying direct mention of the "human element" and by allowing the "lives" of the working individuals only the same grammatical weight as inanimate objects, Roethke makes his argument clear: in this setting, people are one more material.

The poem's final movement extends over five lines in which a single sentence, again, structures our understanding. The poem's first sentence accumulated significance through repetition; the subject and predicate were completed by a series of direct objects delivered in a relatively monotonous form. In this way, the syntax was imitative, embodying the repetitive monotony of the institutional setting it described. The second sentence, however, is far more active and follows the movement of the dangerously alive dust:

> And I have seen dust from the walls of institutions,
> Finer than flour, alive, more dangerous than silica,
> Sift, almost invisible, through long afternoons of tedium,
> Dropping a fine film on nails and delicate eyebrows,
> Glazing the pale hair, the duplicate grey standard faces.
>
> (9–13)

This sentence accumulates its meaning incrementally, the grammatical units frequently interrupted and delayed by modifiers, an effect which builds intensity by delaying closure. The "dust" the speaker sees is modified four times ("from the walls" . . . "finer than" . . . "alive" . . . "more dangerous") before we are given the verb "sift" that accompanies it. Likewise, the participial phrases which elaborate on this action ("Dropping" . . . "Sifting" . . .) are delayed by two more modifying phrases ("almost invisible, through long afternoons of tedium"). All of these interruptions intensify our appetite for closure: the syntax tells us we are moving toward something, so when we arrive at the concluding phrase, "the duplicate grey standard faces" (a phrase emphasized by the near repetition of "duplicate" and "duplication"), we feel behind it all the weight the sentence has been accumulating.

Even in this setting, which is so different from the "greenhouse Eden" that most of the poems in *The Lost Son* spring from, Roethke is still working with his usual materials. The original, organic forms of the plants and stones which populate his other poems, those numinous roots and tendrils which serve as models of seeking out sustenance, are still present in "Dolor," but they have been stripped of their character, of their ability to grow and reach out. Roethke's vision, though, has been witness to transformations that exceed human ends. He tells us in a later poem that "[m]ist alters the rock" (*Collected Poems,* 166), articulating how the slow processes of nature occur over timelines we cannot comprehend. The dust that falls at the end of "Dolor" is suggestive of this same slow transformation, suggestive of the same cycle of disintegration and transformation that Roethke celebrates in poems like "Root Cellar" or the "Flower Dump." Just as new growth is not surprising so much in its novelty as in the common miracle of its return, what may be most compelling about "Dolor" is not how it differs from the poet's body of work, but how it finds other means of articulating his same essential vision.

18

Imagery and Abstraction in "Night Crow"

SARAH KATHRYN MOORE

OF LITTLE poems, Roethke wrote, "a thing may be small but it need not be a cameo; it may be a cinder in the shoe or the mind's eye or a pain in the neck" (*Straw for the Fire,* 171). "Night Crow" (*Collected Poems,* 47), from *The Lost Son and Other Poems,* is just such a "cinder in the mind's eye": a very short, unsettling lyric that makes us aware of what it means to see clearly even while hindering that same lucid vision. The sophisticated interplay of abstract and concrete language in "Night Crow" begins with vision itself, subsequently moving inward and outward in parallel to end with an image that is paradoxically both formlessly abstract and situated deeply and intimately in the body.

In his essays, Roethke says little about imagery in general. In terms of craft, he gives more weight to rhythm and meter, and in fact explicitly notes that if a poet has "slick imagery" but "can't make the words move, he is nothing" (*Straw for the Fire,* 168). But the tidbits he does give on imagery are telling. For example: "The eye, of course, is not enough. But the outer eye serves the inner" (*Straw for the Fire,* 166). "Night Crow" begins with a concrete image perceived by the outer, physical eye, but by the end of the poem, the poet's (and reader's) vision has turned inward. This inward turn occurs both literally, toward the deepest recesses of the unseeable interior of one's own body, and metaphorically, into the depthless abyss of the unknown inner self.

The poem begins with a simple image, grounded in objective, tangible reality: a "clumsy crow" flies away from a "wasted tree" (1–2). It hardly matters whether Roethke literally observed this or simply imagined it; in either case, the image is grounded in the tangible act of "seeing" with physical eyes and body. This first image gives rise to a second image, initially described as a "shape in the mind" (3), in which an enormous bird flies into a fathomless darkness. The introduction of this second image ("a shape in the mind rose up") is both transitional, moving us from the first half of the poem to the second, and liminal, in that it is both concrete and abstract. "A shape in the mind" is in one sense a concrete, sensory impression; a "shape" can only be perceived through vision or through touch. This shape "rose up," suggesting it has heft and movement. Yet the phrase is also abstract, almost oddly so, in that it is intentionally vague, impossible to pin to any specific physical reality, and in that it occurs "in the mind," on a plane radically apart from and opposed to physical, tangible reality. Of course, this "shape in the mind" is immediately revealed as the poem's second image: a huge bird flying away into a depthless blackness. Nonetheless, the extreme abstraction of both "shape" and "mind" stands in palpable (and somewhat disorienting) opposition to the concreteness of the poem's initial image.

This second bird is an enormous mind-bird, the dream-world counterpart to its "clumsy" and utterly common equivalent in the real world, the crow. The movement from concreteness to abstraction is visible here both in the transition from a specific, observed "crow" to a more general "bird" as well as in the transition of the setting, from the quotidian physical world to the "gulfs of dream" (4). In addition, the mind-bird is flying "[f]urther and further away / Into a moonless black" (6–7). Like "a shape in the mind," the former is a liminal image, both concrete (in that it describes something that literally can be seen or perceived by the senses) and abstract (in that the bird gets hazier, more indistinct, and eventually merges with formless, absolute darkness). In the poem's striking last line we discover that the "moonless black" into which the bird is flying is "[d]eep in the brain, far back" (8). Here is the crux of the work. In one sense, the poem has moved linearly along the continuum of concreteness to abstraction, from the physical crow in the real world, through a still-sensory, quasi-abstract/quasi-concrete image of the supernatural "tremendous bird," to an absolutely abstract, formless, shapeless "moonless black" deep in the recesses of the brain. In another sense, however, the poem is circular, moving from a place of embodied reality—literally seeing a crow—through the fantastical, metaphysical "gulfs of dream" but then back to a place of intimate, even shocking embodiment, "deep in the brain." The paradoxical progression of this poem, simultaneously linear and circular, mirrors the liminal images at the poem's center, which are simultaneously concrete and abstract.

In fact, the poem can be read as embodying the dynamic experience of moving from what can be literally seen toward what metaphorically can be "seen" in the mystical sense of a supernatural vision.[1] This reading is supported by Roethke himself: "The body of imagery, possibly, thins out or purifies itself or the mind moves into a more abstract mode, closer to wisdom, in talent of a high order" (*Straw for the Fire,* 245). "Night Crow" is a perfect example of this "purification" in action. The poem begins in the concrete, sensory world, moves through a liminal image of "concrete abstraction," and ends with a powerful descent into abstraction that is, paradoxically, grounded profoundly in the body. The interplay between abstract and concrete language is what makes this small poem so stunning. It is significant, too, that Roethke describes this abstracting process as occurring in or to the "body" of imagery, since images are, by definition, perceived, experienced, and reacted to by the body. No matter how abstract (or "pure") images become, Roethke here tacitly acknowledges the role of the body in perception. Despite the "purification" in this poem of a quotidian image into a more abstract, archetypal one, "Night Crow" begins in the body—that is, in vision, sight, and the eyes—and ends in the body, "deep in the brain."

This poem, then, embodies liminality, moving fluidly between concreteness and abstraction.[2] In addition, "Night Crow" seems to have been a liminal poem for Roethke himself. Allan Seager notes that "Night Crow" was the only poem Roethke published in 1944; in 1945 he published none at all (144). In 1946 Roethke started on the "greenhouse poems," the sequence of fourteen lyrics that opens *The Lost Son and Other Poems.* The greenhouse poems are widely considered Roethke's poetic breakthrough, sophisticated work expertly interweaving the literal and the symbolic.[3] In many ways, then, "Night Crow" is a pivotal poem, written during a fallow time leading up to the greenhouse sequence. The poem may, in fact, represent Roethke's attempt to explain as well as enact what he hopes to achieve in his future work: poems that function simultaneously and successfully on literal and symbolic levels.[4]

"Perhaps the poet's path is closer to the mystic than we think," Roethke says: "his thought becomes more imageless" (*Straw for the Fire,* 245). Although "Night Crow" is far from "imageless," it does embody an abstracting process that Roethke apparently saw as characteristic of superior verse. "Night Crow" simultaneously describes and demonstrates Roethke's developing understanding of how images function at once on the literal and symbolic planes, prefiguring (and inspiring) the "Deep Image" poets of the 1960s and beyond: Robert Bly, James Wright, William Stafford, Galway Kinnell, and others. This poem gives readers lucid, practical insight into the ways Roethke conceived of imagery, embodiment, and abstraction. "Night Crow" is a carefully constructed puzzle box of a poem: concrete yet abstract, accessible yet confounding, firmly grounded in tangible reality yet mystically removed from it.

NOTES

1. In his foundational essay "The Vegetal Radicalism of Theodore Roethke" (1950), Kenneth Burke notes that this poem can be seen "as a particularized embodiment of a general principle, an anecdote of *one* image standing for the way of all such images, which are somehow felt twice, once positivistically, and once symbolically" (84). Indeed, "Night Crow" can productively be viewed as an *ars poetica* in which Roethke both describes and demonstrates the "abstracting process" through which concrete, real-world images are dynamically transformed into mytho-poetic symbols with Jungian weight and import. Karl Malkoff among others has emphasized Roethke's indebtedness to Jungian archetypes (58–60).

2. There is something vertiginous about this liminality; Rosemary Sullivan notes that in this poem "the psyche within the external world exists as one cylinder within the other, both infinitely extensive" (34).

3. In his 1946 Guggenheim Fellowship application, Roethke described the project that would become the greenhouse sequence as having "symbolical values. . . . They are not mere description, but have at least two levels of reference" (qtd. in Seager, 148).

4. That this poem posits a doctrine of "correspondences" between the poet's psyche and the external world has been frequently noted but rarely explored in depth; see, for example, La Belle, *The Echoing Wood of Theodore Roethke* (41) and Ross-Bryant (37).

19

"The Lost Son"

An Emotional Journey through the Landscapes of Loss

BORJA AGUILÓ OBRADOR

> A poem that is the shape of the psyche itself; in times of great stress, that's what I tried to write.
>
> —Theodore Roethke (*Straw for the Fire,* 84)

THE GENESIS and evolution of Theodore Roethke's poetic world is intimately related to the traumatic death of his father Otto during his early adolescence. Up to that point, the boy's emotional relationship to his father had been mainly characterized by stern discipline, which reflected Otto Roethke's Prussian origins. A mixture of reverential fear and utter submission helped to articulate the image of a godlike tyrant who would often torment his son with unappeasable demands (Seager, 23–24). Nevertheless, the "transcendental" dimension of this paternal figure cannot be fully understood without considering Otto Roethke's significant role as mediator between the young poet and the beloved phenomenological realm of his childhood: the family's greenhouses. As chief horticulturalist of the William Roethke Floral Company, Otto was responsible for maintaining the largest set of greenhouses in Michigan. His premature death not only put an emphatic end to the father-son bond but also signaled the crumbling down of a whole personal world for the young poet. By means of a mythical reimagination of the past, Theodore Roethke's poetry answers to the need to negotiate an irreparable emotional loss.

"The Lost Son" (*Collected Poems,* 50–55) stands as Roethke's most elaborate poetic representation of this inner struggle. By means of an economy of psychic loss and gain, this poem addresses the ultimately unresolvable trauma of his father's death. To what extent are we who we are because of what we have lost and can never recover but in fleeting moments of imaginative joy? Is it our pain that characterizes us, or is it perchance what negates who we truly are? "The Lost Son" constitutes an imaginative exploration of the very limits of subjectivity in the context of memory and loss. Roethke resorted to a mythical frame of death and rebirth as a way to transcend his own pain and sense of abandonment and thus to integrate them into a more universal quest for a meaningful identity. This new self was to be achieved through a series of rites of passage that would test and purify the hero throughout his journey. In his general commentary on the long poetic narratives of Roethke's Lost Son sequence (which includes poems in *The Lost Son and Other Poems, Praise to the End!,* and *The Waking*), Jay Parini points to Mircea Eliade's anthropological work on ancient rites of passage as providing the basis for a better understanding of the poet's self-imagining (82). Yet what is the psychological truth behind Roethke's symbolism in the specific case of "The Lost Son"? For Parini, the poem recreates the initiatory rites of primal peoples, which involved a symbolic "slaying of the child in the initiate, a severance from the parents, an assertion of manhood. This is painful, and 'The Lost Son' registers this pain" (86). An assertion of subjectivity ("manhood") in the face of utter abandonment ("severance from the parents"), "The Lost Son" attests to our tragic incompleteness and mortality as human beings.

The poem begins in a moment of crisis experienced in the Michigan cemetery where Roethke's father was buried: "At Woodlawn I heard the dead cry: / I was lulled by the slamming of iron" (1.1–2). This first image is somewhat reminiscent of Christ's desperate cry on Golgotha, but it mainly emphasizes the influence the dead exert on the living. Roethke associates the protagonist's crisis of identity with a traumatic event, the actual death of Otto Roethke, which is never directly mentioned. The poet's indirect style attempts to recreate the dynamics of a dream in the way it displaces personal meaning onto a more objective scenario. From a psychological point of view, the son's traumatic loss will "return" in the form of guilt, autoerotic isolation, and mania. The unsettling lullaby of slamming iron presented in this opening is a clear example of displacement and mania. It compulsively reminds the speaker of the impossibility of being reunited with the lost object of grief, the father. The hopelessness of this particular "song of the dead" results in hallucinatory imagery that verges on nightmare.

The son's cries for help are not answered. His creative powers have been diminished because of remorse and negation: "Nothing nibbled my line, / Not even the minnows came" (1.14–15). The poet fishing in an old wound is itself a metaphor for the act of writing the poem. This old wound that never heals is the very loss that the poem tries to negotiate. Haunted by a kind of cosmic absence, the son resumes his pleas and is again discouraged by the meaninglessness of the replies: "You will find no comfort here, / In the kingdom of bang and blab" (1.32–33). The existential consolation for the death of the father becomes an impossible wish in the disrupting "kingdom of bang and blab." This psychic state, which on one level takes the shape of a childhood fantasy, points towards the "emptiness" of the linguistic signifier. According to modern linguistic theory, the relationship between the signifier and the content it represents, the signified, is a convention, thus contradicting the Christian interpretation, which would render it ultimately divine. In the context of the poem, the loss of this transcendental imprint in language also corresponds to the loss of the father. For this reason, the son's "empty" words are at this moment of intense doubt unable to heal the painful wound caused by death and separation.

The last four stanzas of "The Flight" take the shape of infantile nursery songs, which are enacted as a kind of mantra or protection spell. For Lynn Ross-Bryant, "the result is almost an incantation to hold off the powers of darkness" (48). This is explained by the "terrifying" quality of the fishing and hunting, that is, by the revelation of their meaninglessness, which produces a regressive "flight" into childhood.

While the second section, "The Pit," questions the limits between the "I" and the "non-I" through the phobic image of slime, the third section, "The Gibber," refers back to the nonsensical "kingdom of bang and blab" (1.33). Rather than following a musical pattern of progression, the speaker makes clear that he listens again to "something / [he] had heard before" (3.3–4), indicating a compulsive and obsessive repetition of trauma.

In this psychic realm, both parents and gods have deserted the divine child to his fate. The speaker becomes increasingly paralyzed at the same time that he is beset by a castrating anguish: "Fear was my father, Father Fear. / His look drained the stones" (3.16–17). In a reenactment of old fears, the speaker's identity is dismembered into a series of contradictory voices that create a nervous, psychotic dialogue. Roethke articulates the drama of identity and self-regeneration through this confusion of emotional states that displace the son's intense guilt:

> I want the old rage, the lash of primordial milk!
> Goodbye, goodbye, old stones, the time-order is going,
> I have married my hands to perpetual agitation,
> I run, I run to the whistle of money.
>
> Money money money
> Water water water
>
> (3.37–42)

The lost son is imprisoned by his own incapacity to recreate a sustainable world in the name of the (loving) father. The fact that Roethke in his "Open Letter" associates this passage with an Elizabethan rant (*On Poetry and Craft,* 50) brings to its interpretation a certain irony and theatricality that reduce the nostalgic implications of the son's stance. This passage may even be read as an exaggerated performance that transforms the mythical narration of the lost son into empty gibberish whose finality, devoid of transcendental connotations, is ultimately aimed at filling an emotional void left in the adult self. With its insistence on sexuality ("I have married my hands to perpetual agitation") and money ("I run to the whistle of money"), this passage portrays the turbulent transition from childhood to adolescence and finally to adulthood as catastrophic.

It is no surprise, then, that at the conclusion of this section the protagonist is intensely confused and starts to panic. It is as if the world of the lost son had been threatened by the sudden appearance of an indifferent realm that holds no memories of his father. These fears destabilize the poet's reality to the point of dissolution. The speaker questions repeatedly an unknown interlocutor to reassure himself of its existence, but he is not even given an answer this time. His anxiety finds its negative expression in the destructive effect of light, "[t]hese sweeps of light undo me" (3.48) being a metonymy for the castrating aspect of the father (the sun). As a consequence of this terrifying ordeal, the protagonist is forcedly cast into the fantasized space within which subject and object become indistinguishable:

> Look, look, the ditch is running white!
> I've more veins than a tree!
> Kiss me, ashes, I'm feeling through a dark swirl.
>
> (3.49–51)

As he did in the greenhouse poems, Roethke suspends boundaries between the human and the vegetal world. This passage seems to draw the feeling of anxiety and abjection associated with this fantastic union from "Cuttings (*later*)."

The fourth part, as suggested by its title ("The Return"), constitutes a regression to the world of the greenhouse and to personal myth. The narrative significance of this "coming back" seems a priori ambiguous, since, in the first stanza, the speaker is portrayed as moving towards another sort of pit (a boiler in this case). However, he is presented as a boy again, wandering about the mindscapes of his long-lost youth. This time he is not trapped and motionless, but caught within a transitional phase that inverts the psychological drama of the ending of section 3. The adult self makes one of his last efforts to remember and thus redeem the past:

> The way to the boiler was dark,
> Dark all the way,
> Over slippery cinders
> Through the long greenhouse.
>
> The roses kept breathing in the dark.
> They had many mouths to breath with.
> My knees made little winds underneath
> Where the weeds slept.
>
> (4.1–8)

"The Gibber" and "The Return" represent two sequences of the same dream structure. This is evident in how the ending of the first and the beginning of the latter are connected by a free-associative transition that turns the images of the "dark swirl" and the "ashes" (3.51) into the "dark" path "to the boiler" and the "slippery cinders" (4.1–3). The dark pit of nondifferentiation has been transfigured into a dark passage that leads the protagonist to the ambivalent site of his childhood, the greenhouse. The poem is again written in the past verbal tense, a shift from the present tense of the Elizabethan rant and the fall into the dark swirl. This transition establishes a temporal distance that displaces the negativity of previous sections, written in the present tense:

> Once I stayed all night.
> The light in the morning came slowly over the white
> Snow.

There were many kinds of cool
Air.
Then came steam.

Pipe-knock.

Scurry of warm over small plants.
Ordnung! ordnung!
Papa is coming!

(4.13–22)

In an attempt to break from the static darkness of the maternal pit or womb, the speaker remembers a significant moment from his past. This time the light of the father does not reduce the son to pieces. It comes "slowly over the white / Snow," warming and putting into motion the "many kinds of cool / Air" that had hindered the son's act of remembrance (4.14–17). In the same way that the plants are resurrected from their dormant state by the warming sunlight, the speaker is impelled to remember his father in a very vivid manner. Moreover, the auditory image of the almost musical "pipe-knock" (19) is a further reference to the symbolic stability of the nostalgic memory of the greenhouse.

As if this were not sufficiently clear for the reader, Roethke decided to make his intentions in the passage more explicit in his essay "Open Letter": "With the coming of steam, the pipes begin knocking violently, in a greenhouse. But 'Papa,' or the florist, as he approached, often would knock the pipe he was smoking on the side of the benches, or on the pipes" (*On Poetry and Craft*, 51). The coming of the morning light and the pipe-knock are two obvious signals that announce the advent of the loving father. Kenneth Burke nonetheless prefers to associate the knock with the knock on the door in Shakespeare's *Macbeth,* thus identifying it with guilt (92). This reading recovers the ambivalence of Roethke's relationship to his father—so many times projected in his early poems—exposing how the poet felt his father's agony and death as some sort of accusation.

Roethke continues his explanation in "Open Letter" with the observation that he wanted to make of "Papa" a complex symbol: "[W]ith the coming of steam and 'papa'—the papa on earth and heaven are blended—there is the sense of motion in the greenhouse, my symbol for the whole of life, a womb, a heaven-on-earth" (*On Poetry and Craft,* 51). However, "Papa" never actually arrives. The speaker has intuited his proximity but the poem only presents an ethereal figure, a ghost. The son is addressed by a mysterious voice that twice exclaims the German word *Ordnung* (4.21), a call for attention and order that exerts his father's power over him. The unexpected use of the present tense in this short passage echoes the deranged rant of "The Gibber," hinting at the traumatic significance of the experience. The poet is not just remembering but reliving the memories of his past. The paternal garden-god may be a bringer of order and stability, but he is also the frightening representative of castrating paternal law, who in the previous section took the form of "Father Fear." This double meaning also invites a double reading that emphasizes one of the two interpretations of the father figure. In "Theodore Roethke: The Inner Wilderness and the Barrier of Ideology," Jean Philippe Lecourt identifies "Papa" with a "generalized other imposing its discipline upon the world, and forcing the standards of behavior upon the son" (54). Nevertheless, the figure of the ghost does not carry a definitive meaning; it only suspends meaning.

The shift to the past tense in the last stanza of the section suggests that the moment of excitement or anguish has passed. Yet the ghost of the father is still being alluded to in the image of a "fine haze" that "moved off the leaves" (4.23). The symbolic light of the morning produces a significant change in the landscape of the greenhouse: the rose, the chrysanthemum, and the rest of the plants in the glasshouses turn towards the sun. The establishing of a secure distance between the father and the son reduces the anxiety associated with the feeling of abjection. Like the speaker in Rilke's first Duino Elegy, the lyric self can hardly bear the proximity of the divine. For this reason, the dead father is transfigured into the sun.

One might expect the poem to end at this stage, but Roethke does not seem satisfied with the narrative structure. He provides a fifth part that serves as a commentary on the previous experience in "The Return." The emotionally intense moment in his father's reimagined greenhouse is now considered in tranquility. The speaker ponders on the implications of the mysterious light that casts a spell over the organic microcosm of "weeds," "plants," and "hushed forms." The serenity that permeates part 5 suggests that the speaker has left the pressing demands of the lost son's quest behind. Within the frozen landscape of this remembered winter, the temporal flux has been stopped, arriving at an "in-between time" (5.2) when the dynamic processes of life and growth are held at a still point. In this peaceful scene, Roethke leaves behind the tormented child of the greenhouse by means of a more impersonal language that sublimates previous feelings of pain and guilt. This new self-image referred to in the poem as "mind" is "not alone" as it moves "[t]hrough the clear air, in the silence" (5.14–15). Both self ("mind") and father ("light") accompany each other, as if to symbolize a recently acquired sense of communion and reconciliation in the poem.

However, the speaker does not seem able to understand the full significance of this experience. Roethke is drawing on the conventions of the mystic's paradoxical language here. When referring to this passage in "Open Letter," he talks about "illumination": "the coming of light suggested at the end of the last passage occurs again, this time to the nearly grown man. But the illumination is only partly apprehended; he is still 'waiting'" (*On Poetry and Craft*, 51). This illumination is intimately related to the loss that the poem has tried to negotiate. The death of the father was clearly "repressed" in the first sections of the poem through metonymy and displacement and in this way was left unconscious. The momentary return of "Papa" in section 4 makes this repressed content conscious again and thus "illuminates" the darkness that threatened to engulf the lost son. Roethke is pointing towards an idea of reconciliation understood as the subject's capacity to remember the painful past through imagination and the art of poetry. The son's insistence on negating his father's death through repression had obvious consequences in the form of feelings of meaninglessness and despair. It is nostalgia for the lost past that saves the son from the darkness of the pit. Yet—and here lies Roethke's psychological truth—the repetitive questioning at the end of the poem expresses a certain doubt. This cyclical structure gives a less triumphant coda to the poem and thus points to the interminability of self-analysis.

"The Lost Son" stands as an acute imaginative study of the psyche in the context of loss and emotional pain. The poet embarks on a journey to find a nostalgic language to help him accept the death of his father. Although the protagonist's journey through memory may be retaken in the future, he is bound to be again beset by doubt and negation. Roethke is unable to integrate fully the realities of loss and death within his representation of the self because of a radical impossibility lying at the core of the act of remembrance: the certainty of physical death. Nevertheless, Roethke manages to capture the ephemeral nature of language and subjectivity and give us a glimpse of the anguished nightmares stirring in the silences that surround them. It is in this sense that "The Lost Son" may be considered as an honest poetic testimony of the interminability and contradictions of self-expression.

20

Respite for the Lost Son

"A Field of Light"

JEFFREY CLAPP

THE EXPERIENCE of Theodore Roethke's "A Field of Light" (*Collected Poems,* 59–60) is richest when the poem is read within the framework of the Lost Son sequence, in the context Roethke chose for it. There the poem follows "The Lost Son" and "The Long Alley" and precedes "The Shape of the Fire."[1] Of these four poems, "A Field of Light" is by some measure the briefest and the most straightforward: its speaker walks out, possibly in the Saginaw Valley of Roethke's youth,[2] arrives at an open area, feels a flush of pleasure, and experiences a flash of insight. The poem's directness extends to a regularity in the form of the poem, a repeated movement from invocation, through song, to a moment's equipoise, a threefold pattern that recurs in each of the poem's three sections.

Perhaps due to its straightforward character, most critics, and perhaps most readers, have moved rapidly past "A Field of Light."[3] Yet a remarkable poignancy results from the poem's deliberately demure effects, particularly when placed alongside the labor, agony, and transcendence of the poems that surround it. Unlike *the* son, *the* alley, and *the* shape of the other poems, this is only *a* field. Whereas the other three poems each have five sections, "A Field of Light" only has three. Ampler scale makes for a deeper dive: both "The Long Alley" and "The Shape of the Fire" move at length through the "pit" and "gibber" described in "The Lost Son," but nowhere in "A Field of Light" do we find the barking diction, the nonce-songs, or the lurching, lateral aphorisms Roethke employs in the other poems. Because Roethke distinguished "A Field of Light" from the other parts of the Lost Son sequence, the poem seems to invoke a pleasant way station, rather than another stage, along the exhilarating, excruciating journey of the lost son.

Roethke begins this poem with a sharp deceleration. The "lakes" in the poem's first line, lapping multiple shores, are halted by a caesura, becoming "dead water." In the next line they are merely "ponds," so still that moss can grow in them, enlivened only by "floating" leaves. Plant life does not germinate and thrust itself forward, as so often in Roethke; instead these plants are "sunk in sand." Against this frieze or tableau, an anonymous "foot" reaches out, merely to "touch" a log (1.1–4). The movement is so slight that the "eye" which "tilted" (1.6) upward at the end of the stanza might be that of frog or fish, or might be merely a knot in the floating log.

Scene set, the speaker raises his voice and breaks into a brief, "chilly" song (1.8). This is not a full-throated kind of singing; the wind the speaker mentions is "small" and the cove is the "softest" one (1.7, 9). The "[cry] for sound" (1.10) (which in Wallace Stevens might intimate a high-toned "rage for order")[4] is here linked to unremarkable transmutations in nature and in perspective: a vague "change" in leaves, a stone which is made to be, or revealed to be, a clam (11–14). Following the deliberate omission of pronouns in the poem's first line, the arrival of a first-person human presence creates the muted crescendo of the poem's first part: "I was there alone" (17). The phrase compresses the lyric form familiar from several key epithets of literary Romanticism; the poem's first part overtly exemplifies both Mill's conception of poetry as "*over*heard" speech (95) and Wordsworth's "emotion recollected in tranquility" ("Preface," 183). In many ways, then, "A Field of Light" bears out the general conclusion of Jay Parini and others, that Roethke's work, especially as represented in the Lost Son sequence, is thoroughly enmeshed in Romantic concepts, modes, and preoccupations.[5]

The second part of "A Field of Light" puts forward a question: "Angel within me, I asked, / Did I ever curse the sun?" (2.1). Amidst the watery dampness, the drone of rain in sections 1 and 2, the speaker wonders whether he has somehow deserved this melancholy atmosphere. The "cry" from one aspect of the speaker to the "angel within" modifies a similar injunction made in "The Lost Son": "Voice, come out of the silence" (*Collected Poems,* 51); it also represents a return to stillness following the jubilant crescendo of part 4 of "The Long Alley," when the speaker exuberantly bursts out,

Light airs! Light airs! A pierce of angels!
The leaves, the leaves become me!
The tendrils have me!

(*Collected Poems*, 58)

These alternations from silence to sound, from inward query to outcry, suggest how the Lost Son sequence can be read not only according to a general logic of maturation or development, but also as what Harold Bloom calls "a second birth into poetic vision" (*Theodore Roethke*, 2).[6] When, in "A Field of Light," Roethke writes "Speak and abide" (2.3), the words may represent the reply of the angel, bidding the poet to say his piece, or they may represent a renewed request from poet to the lyric angel within. In either case, "A Field of Light," as is true of the Lost Son sequence as a whole, palpably suggests a poet arriving at his own mature matter and manner. In response to the poet's summons, the voice comes forth.[7]

In the poem's second part, as in the first, a song does emerge, and again it evokes Roethke's distinctively loamy imagery. Now the stanza's prepositions produce a series of rushing changes in perspective, always moving down and within, as though toward the center of the earth. What is ultimately found there, however, is not damp and fertile, but instead bone-dry, and the speaker ponders, "Was it dust I was kissing?" (2.9). The dust descends from that which God used to form Adam, so that this song returns not only to the womb, but to the even more primordial birth of human consciousness out of mere material. The answer to Roethke's question is a "sigh" from afar (2.10), a response which conjoins the world-weary implication that to dust we will return, with Adam and Eve's primordial procreation. The stanza terminates in a muted erotic fanfare, in kissing and dancing which prepare the way for the vigorous, if encrypted, sexual transcendence of "The Shape of the Fire."

"A Field of Light" ends in sustained uplift, a filling of the field with life. Dust first turns to "dirt," and then that dirt itself "left" the speaker's "hand" (3.1) as the questions of the poem's second section find their answers. All things begin to burgeon—and to particularize—as the poet gains energy, moving from "[t]he sun glittered on a small rapids" (3.4), first to "[t]he great elm filled with birds" (3.6), and ultimately to a vivid enthusiasm in which "[t]he worms were delighted as wrens" (3.20).[8] In this passage, the poem briefly ascends to a vision of "the separateness of all things" (3.15), and to a moment of curiously temperate ecstasy: "I walked through the light air; / I moved with the morning" (3.21–22). If, when the speaker moves *through* the air, we seem to find ourselves with Emerson on Boston Common, that thought can only be sustained only a moment—the same motion is *with* the morning. In keeping with this poem's first hesitations, in which the speaker hardly disturbs his universe, the conclusion arrives in concert with, rather than surging past, this particular "cove" and this particular "field."

The best criticism of "A Field of Light" (not to mention of the Lost Son sequence, or of the oeuvre as a whole) is likely to remain Roethke's 1950 essay "Open Letter," which offers readers the crucial trope of going backward to go forward, of Roethke's method as a system of cycles: from mire, through slime, up into light, and then down again (*On Poetry and Craft,* 49ff). If the presence of this kind of progression and logic is so clear in "A Field of Light" as to begin to resist any other explication, one can also note that the shallowness of this particular mire, and the moderate cast of this particular light, features which distinguish this poem from others in Roethke's sequence and from others throughout his work. Nonetheless, "A Field of Light" is clearly linked with "The Far Field" of the "North American Sequence," another poem which appears in the penultimate position in a sequence of poems. There, too, Roethke conceives a field as a place where one "watches": "I watched and watched" in the poem of 1964 (*Collected Poems,* 193) closely paralleling "I could watch, I could watch!" (3.14) in "A Field of Light," from 1946. As in "A Field of Light," one comes in "The Far Field" "to a still, but not a deep center" (*Collected Poems,* 195). For Roethke, then, the "field" is a place at which one arrives but where one will not stay, a plane which momentarily succors, but which can only be a way station. Rather than slackening their sequences, these twin poems provide watchful pauses, respites from the work of changing and from the work of building poetry into a vision of what Roethke described as "the very movement of the mind itself" (*On Poetry and Craft,* 27).

Nothing could be less fashionable, in the world of contemporary poetics or in the contemporary world, than an abstraction like "the movement of the mind" or Roethke's further assertion, that his sense of the mind's motion could describe the progress of "all haunted and harried men" (*On Poetry and Craft,* 28). Yet there is not any less haunting or harrying. And where it seems rather doubtful that anybody will ever quite manage to take up Roethke's particular congeries of mire, we all take moments to stretch our vision across a field. The very slightness that has caused most to pause only briefly in "A Field of Light" gestures toward what is most lasting in Roethke's work.

NOTES

1. This set of four poems was then itself set within other sequences, as in *Praise to the End!* (1951).

2. The image of "pulsing lizards" in line 11 is the only reference in the poem inconsistent with a Michigan setting.

3. Kenneth Burke's early reading, which passes over the poem in a somewhat perfunctory paragraph, has set the tone for subsequent encounters ("Vegetal Radicalism," 94–95), although later critics have tried various schemes for distinguishing the motion of "A Field of Light" from the other poems in the Lost Son sequence. Ann T. Foster associates the poem with a "phase of Roethke's poetry" in which "intellectual understanding" has not yet achieved "the perception of all created things as one, reflected in and emanating from Divine Reality" (45); Rosemary Sullivan finds that in "A Field of Light" the poet now sees "potential for change" (49). These discoveries, and the poem as a whole, doubtless do form a stage in a progression. Yet my sense is that "A Field of Light" much more manifestly figures as a pause within the sequence, offering (to use Roethke's own phrase) "a light breather" (from the poem by that title; *Collected Poems,* 97) rather than moving the son forward by any crucial increment.

4. Wallace Stevens, "The Idea of Order at Key West," in *Collected Poems,* 130. For a general assessment of Stevens's "cries" versus the modes of Roethke's affirmation, see Donoghue, "Theodore Roethke," 40–41.

5. Parini's general assertion that Roethke's is a specifically American Romanticism does not much inflect his reading of the Lost Son sequence, where Parini frames Roethke's work by drawing on discussions of archetypal narratives and initiation rituals key in Joseph Campbell and Mircea Eliade (Parini, 84ff). In her essay "Theodore Roethke's 'The Lost Son': From Archetypes to Literary History," Jenijoy La Belle proposes that the origins of some of Roethke's key concepts might be as much in Blake as in the Romantic tradition as a whole, but this is certainly not apparent in "A Field of Light," which exhibits none of Blake's prophetic radicalism or the sing-song terrors of his early *Songs,* whereas both of those Blakean modes do undergird the Lost Son sequence and other Roethke poems. The connection between Roethke and Wordsworthian Romanticism, explored by James Applewhite, is most apropos for "A Field of Light."

6. Brendan Galvin sees Roethke's address to the angel as a magical prayer that summons "meaning and identity" (92).

7. Allan Seager's biography documents the extent to which *The Lost Son and Other Poems* was understood by Roethke, and by his readers, as a major breakthrough to a mature mode (154–55; 157–59).

8. Roethke's litanies of natural objects sometimes seem to descend from Whitman; this sequence, as Peter Balakian argues, strongly recalls him (89–90).

Praise to the End! (1951)

21

Homegrown Cosmologies

Animism and Elegy in "Where Knock Is Open Wide"

DAVID WOJAHN

FOR SEVERAL months now I have had by my desk a sad and consummately strange coffee-table book titled *The Lost Tribes of Tierra del Fuego* (2015). It features photos taken in the early 1920s by Martin Guisande, a German Jesuit missionary. They document the lives of three tribes, the Yamana, the Kawésqar, and, most exhaustively, the Selk'nam, the same tribes Charles Darwin encountered during his voyage on the *Beagle* about ninety years earlier. Darwin clearly had much greater regard for the sea turtles, marine iguanas, and finches he would soon encounter in the Galapagos. In respect to the native peoples of Tierra del Fuego, he was your standard-issue Victorian chauvinist: "One can hardly make oneself believe that they are fellow-creatures, and inhabitants of the same world," he opined in his journal (qtd. in Shepard). Fortunately, Gusinde suffered from no such haughtiness, and for this we can be grateful. By the time Gusinde arrived at his missionary quarters among the Selk'nam in 1918, the tribe was on the verge of extinction, its population ravaged by measles, smallpox, and the systematic ethnic cleansing undertaken by local Chilean authorities, who aimed to clear the Selk'nam lands in order to open them for mining and ranching. Gusinde knew quite well that his photographs depicting the tribes' lifeways and rituals were less a form of ethnology than of elegy. "As these people disappear, so does their uniqueness," he wrote. "The most urgent thing, right now, is to save what is left" (qtd.

in Shepard). Although the Selk'nam and their cohort tribes adapted remarkably well to the privations of their environment, many of Guisande's images are deeply melancholy: Gusinde took a number of shots of naked and sad-faced individuals lying directly atop the snow while enacting one of their various rituals. They look uncannily like the New York City homeless photographed by Jakob Riis for his muckracking classic *How the Other Half Lives* (1890).

But the photos of the Selk'nam that most astonish me document an initiation ritual undertaken as the tribe's males enter adulthood. The young men would gather in a hut to be visited by older males, each dressed as a different fearsome spirit or demon from the Selk'nam pantheon: Ulen the Trickster, the Shoort Spirits, a malevolent shaman who lives on the moon, and the son of the demon Xalpen. The Selk'nam men in their monster costumes are so bizarre as to almost defy description. The men paint themselves, often in horizontal stripes made from a paste of bone meal, mud, or red ochre. And then, since the substances with which the Selk'nam men decorate themselves can be rather sticky, they frequently cover themselves with feathers. The end results can look like a homemade Halloween costume of Big Bird from *Sesame Street.* They also sport headgear, usually huge conical hats that recall the ones worn by the accused in Goya's famous painting of an Inquisition tribunal or the contraption Hugo Ball performed in during the Dada events at the Cabaret Voltaire. People to whom I've shown Guisande's images of the Selk'nam tend to receive them with a complex admixture of emotion, reacting first with amazement at their jaw-dropping strangeness. Then the melancholy fact of the images' transience sets in, for you are seeing images of an eons-old ritual that will never be repeated again. But I have also seen friends look at the images and guiltily and uneasily chortle. You may be watching evidence of a culture die, but you can't avoid the admission that the Selk'nam costumes are pretty damn comic.

You needn't feel too un-PC about such a response, for the purpose of the Hain ritual is indeed in a certain respect comic. At the close of the ceremony, the tarted-up elders at long last speak to the initiates, telling the youngsters that they are neither devils nor demons after all. Instead, they identify themselves as the spirits of dead ancestors, who in the Selk'nam cosmology are benevolent and revered figures. The whole ceremony is revealed to be a hugely elaborate practical joke, perpetrated by dead forebears with a sense of humor. Yes, it's a puzzling kind of levity for anyone outside the Selk'nam cultural loop. But who are we to judge another culture's conception of the comic? You have admire the Selk'nam:

the elders go to immense lengths to perform this rite—or is it a hazing ritual? The Hain ceremony suggests a great imaginative complexity. After all, the men *pretend* to be their ancestors *pretending* to be demons and evil spirits. And who's to know that the young initiates aren't also in on the joke?

I suspect, dear reader, that you will find it something of a leap to move from the Selk'nam and their Hain ceremony to the poetry of Theodore Roethke. But the fact remains that Roethke's most significant and original poetry has a similarly original approach to spiritual yearning as that of the Selk'nam and their fellow tribes, and this is especially true of the work to be found in *The Lost Son and Other Poems* (1948) and *Praise to the End!* (1951), Roethke's best and most experimental books. In these collections, the approach to mystical experience is subjective, homegrown, and not without a certain oddness and eccentricity. It's this militantly makeshift approach toward the growth of the soul that causes me to draw a parallel between the Selk'nam garbed in their Ulen and Xalpan get-ups and Roethke at his best. I say "makeshift" rather than "primitive" or "unsophisticated," for it denigrates both the Selk'nam and Roethke to make such characterizations. Still, the cosmology of the Selk'nam and that of Roethke during his *The Lost Son* and *Praise to the End!* period might be broadly defined as animistic. To the animist, every element of the natural world is imbued with a spiritual essence, a soul. James Dickey, who drew considerable inspiration from Roethke, defines the latter poet's animism in this way: "there is some mindless, elemental quality in the sound of his voice, something primitive and animistic, something with the wariness and inhuman grace of the wild beast, and with it another thing that could not be and never has been animal-like. His poems are human poems in the full weight of the adjective: poems of a creature *half* into unthinking nature and unanimal enough to be uneasy there, taking thought at what the animal half discerns and feels" ("Theodore Roethke," 150). Yet this conception extends not merely to fauna but also to flora, as we see so majestically in Roethke's greenhouse poems. Inanimate objects are also seen as having souls, and, as in the case of the Selk'nam pantheon, some souls are benevolent, some less so. Deities, per se, do not exist, though some spirits, notably those of a group's ancestors, can be seen as more powerful than others. In the Hain ceremony, it is the ancestors who deliver the initiates from peril, much in the way that the father in the title poem of *The Lost Son,* moving grandly through the nocturnal greenhouse, booming his command of *Ordnung* (German for "order"), both reawakens the sleeping plant life and saves the poem's young speaker from his spiritual waywardness and terror.

"Where Knock Is Open Wide" (*Collected Poems,* 67–70), the poem which opens *Praise to the End!,* is a typical effort from Roethke's great period. As with many of Roethke's poems from the late 1940s and early '50s, such as "The Long Alley," "Give Way, Ye Gates," "The Return," and "I Need, I Need," its very title suggests a process of initiation as well as a pedigree, for Roethke borrows the title from the eighteenth-century mystical poet Christopher Smart's *Song to David.* The poem follows many of the formal and thematic patterns which Roethke hit upon in the sequences that predominate in *The Lost Son*: the five sections of the poem are largely composed of short-lined quatrains, tercets, and quintets, which give the poem a jagged and associative quality. As in so many of the *Lost Son* poems, animals and plants are invested with a sentience that can veer from cartoonish to terrifying, and the arc of the poem invokes regression as its primary tool for the poet's attempt at spiritual rebirth. "Sometimes, of course, there is a regression," Roethke stated in an essay on his poetry. "I believe that the spiritual man must go back in order to go forward. The way is circuitous, and sometimes lost, but invariably returned to" (*On Poetry and Craft,* 25). Less eloquently, Roethke set out a kind of outline for "Where Knock Is Open Wide" in a letter to Kenneth Burke:

> Put crudely
> 1) Act
> 2) Reaction to act (quiet, sense of impotence)
> 3) Song: reason for act
> reaction again
> 4) Two flashbacks related to act, then the present again.
> 5) Sublimation (The fact that there are few human symbols here
> isn't accidental.)
>
> (qtd. in Seager, 187)

The poem commences with a kind of spiritual baby talk, nursery rhyme lingo that also manages to be highly sexualized:

> A kitten can
> Bite with his feet;
> Papa and Mamma
> Have more teeth.
>
> (1.1–4)

Karl Malkoff likens the poem's opening section to the stream-of-consciousness musings of young Stephen Dedalus in the early chapters of James Joyce's *Portrait of the Artist as a Young Man* (1916), a comparison that is in several respects an apt one (72). And if we take Roethke's use of the word "act" to be synonymous with "animation," there's plenty of that. The section begins with a child's sense of wonder at the mysteries of procreation; he speaks of cows giving birth to puppies, and surely there are sexual undertones in the speaker's reference to his parents' teeth. But the imagery soon turns more troubled: there's the desolation of stanza 3's "Sing me a sleep-song, please" (1.10) and the twisted fairy-tale phrasing of stanza 4's "Once upon a tree / I came upon a time" (1.12–13). The section's movement toward disquiet is bolstered by the speaker's opaque pronoun references: Stanza 3's "His ears haven't time" (1.9) has no clear antecedent, although Roethke may be alluding to the "Papa" referenced in stanza 1. "It" in stanza 4 may refer to either the tree or the speaker's action of coming upon "a time." And what are we to make of the "mooly man / Who had a rubber hat" (1.16–17) in stanza 6? Is "mooly" a neologism created to amplify the nursery rhyme and limerick language of the section, or something more sinister? The word has had a longstanding use in Italian American slang; the term is used both to describe a fake or a charlatan and as a racial slur equivalent to the *n* word. We are in slightly more familiar Roethke territory in the section's final stanza, with its imagery of potency and renewal and the identification of the father figure with a fish, a motif that occurs in the title poem of *The Lost Son*. Part 1 ends with an assertion of possibility and rebirth—"Everything has been twice" (1.21)—which refutes Heraclitus's famed epigram about stepping into a river. But the section of the poem which follows it can rightly be seen as an enactment of spiritual frustration and "impotence."

The child's point of view again prevails in part 2, but the tone is even more troubling than in the poem's initial section. In stanza 1 the speaker can manage only a "small sing" (2.1), and the reference to the uncle being "gone for always" (2.3) more than likely alludes to the suicide of the poet's uncle, Carl Roethke, in 1923. Roethke was fourteen at the time, and the death of his beloved father Otto from cancer occurred only three months later (Seager, 42). The relationship between Otto and Carl Roethke was a fraught one. In the words of Karen Alkalay-Gut, Carl was "thought to be the cause of the downfall of the greenhouse empire and all of the financial problems of Roethke's youth" (29). The speaker in the section seems younger than Roethke was at the time of his uncle's death, but casting the speaker as a young child offers Roethke some striking descriptive possibilities. The second stanza of part 2 suggests that, as a consequence of his suicide, Carl Roethke will never be "an angel"; the petulant statement "I don't care either" (2.7-8) which immediately follows this observation effortlessly evokes the speaker's ambivalence and incomprehension about a family member dying by his own hand. The stanza's second line, "They'll jump on his belly" (2.6), suggests that Carl Roethke will suffer the torments of eternal damnation. But the detail may also be an especially inventive description of Carl Roethke's grave being filled.

In the third stanza of part 2, the imagery of the uncle's punishment in the afterlife gives way to a description of a dead cat, presumably a childhood pet. (Images of dead cats on Roethke family property also appear in the later poems "The Far Field" and "Otto.") Her "neck has kittens" (2.10) might read as a slashed or broken neck, or perhaps as the cat's body infested with maggots. Even though the speaker cannot fully mourn his uncle, he at least seems equipped to come to terms with the animal's death. In stanzas 3 and 4, the speaker suggests he will cremate the cat by making a "hole for her. / In the fire." Over her decomposing flesh he utters a kind of Kaddish: "Winkie will yellow I sang. / Her eyes went kissing away" (2.11–14). The speaker's song has turned to keening. We can't help but note how Roethke's design for a "sense of impotence" in the section figures in his name for the cat. Roethke, with his penchant for phallic symbols, surely wants to remind us that "winky" is slang for penis, and is a term more apt to be employed by a child than by an adult. According to traditional Freudian theories of psychosexual development, male children between the approximate ages of six and eight (and the probable age of Roethke's speaker) enter into the "genital" stage—a phase of acute sexual awareness. But this stage is also characterized by an intense fear of emasculation, what Freud termed "castration anxiety." Thus, the speaker's mourning ritual for his cat may also be an expression of erotic unease.

The beginning of part 3 finds the speaker in a nocturnal landscape: "I know it's an owl. He's making it darker" (3.1). Perhaps in response to the reckoning with mortality in section 2, we are offered intimations of a descent into an underworld, where the speaker feels entrapped; he has arrived at a place where "[s]ome stones are still warm" (3.3) and a "worm has a mouth" (3.7). Even seemingly benign observations, such as stanza 3's synesthetic "I hear flowers" (3.11), suggest unease. The flowers seem to be growing above the speaker in his underground realm. When the speaker in stanza 2 asks to be "fished out" from this place, he appears to allude to the father figure mentioned in the opening section of the poem, who in turn, as in many of Roethke's poems, is quickly apotheosized. The child's rescue seems imminent as the section closes. Phrased in infantile speech, "Hello happy hands" (3.14) suggests that the hands of the father are poised for a physical and spiritual rescue of the speaker. This image also prepares us for the "flashbacks related to act" that comprise section 4. The father is present once again, but in a distinctly more realistic setting.

Compared to the ominous presence of the owl that opens the poem's third section, section 4 begins with bucolic descriptions: water birds fly about the boy and his father as they embark on a fishing expedition. But such evocations are again replaced by distraught ones as the father and son land a bullhead in their boat. The speaker initially sympathizes with the fish's plight: "Don't hit him on the boat, I said" (4.7). But after the father returns the creature to the water, the fish becomes emblematic of a fallen world, a world of sexualized adulthood: "Bullheads have whiskers. / And they bite" (4.10–11). Then, without a transition, Roethke introduces us to a second narrative, one familiar to us from the greenhouse poems: Otto Roethke is once more seen as a shamanistic figure bestowing life upon the plants: "He watered the roses. / His thumb had a rainbow" (4.12–13). But, as with the earlier scene of father and son in the boat, wonderment soon gives way to dread. The father may have magical dominion over his greenhouse, but the son feels expelled from this world. "Dark" comes early; the speaker has "fallen" once again into a kind of stygian place where even "[t]he worm has moved away" (4.17). The section's penultimate stanza, with its imagery of expulsion and desolation, is perhaps the most abject in the entire poem:

> Nowhere is out. I saw the cold.
> Went to visit the wind. Where the birds die.
> How high is have?
>
> (4.19–21)

The concluding stanza of the section, like the entreaties of section 3, seems once again an address to the poet's father, uttered half-prayerfully, half-desperately. Only the omnipotent father can "[s]ing the snake to sleep" (4.23).

The poem's fifth and final section suggests that such prayers are unlikely to be answered any time soon. Roethke's intention for the section, as outlined in the letter to Burke, seems in some ways to belie the section's actual content. The process of sublimation he alludes to in the letter certainly figures here; the child's conflating of his father with a tentative and rudimentary concept of divinity is no longer possible. But for Roethke to assert to Burke that there are "few human symbols" in the poem's conclusion is puzzling and inaccurate. Indeed, the ending of "Where Knock Is Open Wide" addresses Otto Roethke's death more directly than almost any other passage in his poetry. Once again the speaker must come to terms with the loss of a beloved relative, and it is hard not to construe the opening two stanzas as taking place beside the open casket of Otto Roethke. He is "all whitey bones / And skin like paper." As he does with his descriptions concerning the death of the poet's uncle, Roethke adopts a child's perspective during this scene, a decision that allows for the dialogue between the speaker and his mother to have a resonant dramatic effect: "God's somewhere else, / I said to Mama" (5.3–6).

But the child's point of view is abandoned in the three stanzas which conclude the poem. As the poem ends, the speaker's expulsion from childhood innocence and oneness with nature is complete. More importantly, the poet's desire to conflate Otto Roethke with a benevolent divinity, an aspiration enacted in manifold ways throughout "Where Knock Is Open Wide," is now no longer possible. Yet the final lines of the poem suggest that this new understanding is a necessary prelude to the adult poet's spiritual regeneration. Divinity will emerge in some other form. "One father is enough" (5.12), the speaker states, a bittersweet assertion, surely, for it acknowledges a definitive removal from the Edenic greenhouse world that was fashioned and *ordered* by Otto Roethke. The poet's initiation into maturity is now complete, just as it is for the Selk'nam youth as they emerge from the Hain ceremony. Perhaps this is why Roethke's conclusion—"Maybe God has a house. / But not here" (5.13–14)—seems oddly ebullient, in the manner of the lines near the closing of book 12 of *Paradise Lost,* in which Adam and Eve survey the landscape into which they have been expelled, suddenly aware that "[t]he World was all before them, where to choose / Their place of rest, and Providence their guide" (Milton, 517). The speaker has become the "man of prayer," who Christopher Smart endorses in the passage from *A Song to David* which appears immediately before the line Roethke chose for his title:

> But stronger still, in earth and air,
> And in the sea, the man of pray'r;
>   And far beneath the tide;
> And in the seat of faith assign'd
> Where ask is have, where seek is find,
>   Where knock is open wide.
>
> (66)

Not long ago, while teaching Roethke in a graduate course on the middle-generation poets, I was astonished to find that only two of the fifteen students in the class had previously read his *Collected Poems.* This information came as something of a shock to me, as did an even more shocking (and saddening) comment voiced by one of the best students in the class. Roethke, she asserted, was a minor poet because his poems were "too insular and too monothematic." Ironically, this statement was made by someone who, as a millennial, belongs to a generation more insular than any previous one in history. During the break the students had taken a few minutes earlier, they all remained at the seminar table and used the time silently and almost catatonically to text or check email on their phones. I can't remember how I countered the student's contention. If I'd had my wits about me, I might have quoted the magnificent closing sections of "Where Knock Is Open Wide." Yes, Roethke is indeed something of a monothematic poet, but the poem exquisitely embodies a formal inventiveness and sense of spiritual yearning that derives, like the rituals of the Tierra del Fuego tribes, from grand and abiding obsessions and not from mere compulsion and self-imitation. No one better understood this quality in Roethke than his biographer Allan Seager. A passage from a chapter titled "Working Methods" pretty much says it all, and I wish I had been able to read it as a rejoinder to my student: "Once he had decided—and it seems to have been a hard-won decision, weighed and judged, and not at all quick or serendipitous—that these limited areas of his childhood were to be the sources of his work because he coolly saw them as having drawn to themselves the deepest emotions of his life, he did what nearly every writer of talent does: working out of absolute conviction and sincerity, he enlarged, enriched, and dignified them until they became symbols for the whole of life" (164).

22

"Give Way, Ye Gates" and Roethke's Praise to the End! Sequence

PETER BALAKIAN

NO POET after Romanticism has furthered an idea of nature as inventively as Theodore Roethke has in his Praise to the End! sequence, a long poem cycle also known as the Lost Son sequence. In asserting this, I note the achievements of E. A. Robinson, Robert Frost, Gary Snyder, Mary Oliver, and Seamus Heaney, some of the most formidable makers of a poetics of nature.

In the mid-1940s, after the publication of his first book, *Open House* (1941), Roethke discovered, in a deeply personal way, the psychological and imaginative source of his childhood in Saginaw, Michigan, where his father and uncle owned several hundred acres of greenhouses and nurseries. In this landscape and botanical environment, where as a boy Roethke worked doing greenhouse chores, and where the dramas of his childhood were played out—especially his father's untimely death when Roethke was fourteen—he discovered what would be an essential grounding and location for his imagination. During this period he also absorbed some of the experimental techniques and psychological and linguistic orientations of modernist experimenters such as James Joyce, William Faulkner, T. S. Eliot, and William Carlos Williams. He was reading the psychology of Sigmund Freud and Carl Jung, and he brought together his new sense of language and psychology with the discovery of his own personal past.

Roethke's new orientation was inseparable from his approach to nature. Nature was always the material and the world through which he would create a personal voice. For him, nature was sensual and intimately personal, botanical and spiritual, an embodiment of human consciousness, as well as the source of childhood and family. Roethke called his greenhouse a "womb, a heaven-on-earth" (*On Poetry and Craft,* 51), a "man-made Avalon, Eden, or paradise" (*Selected Letters,* 113). He mythicized the raw Michigan landscape of his childhood as a primordial place: "the marsh, the mire, the Void is always there, immediate and terrifying. It is a splendid place for schooling the spirit" (*On Poetry and Craft,* 52).

Roethke's incisive statement about his technique and poetics is helpful in approaching these poems. He wanted to create what he called a "psychic shorthand" (*On Poetry and Craft,* 53), a technique that yielded more intuitive movements, gnomic images, and fresh language, and allowed him to pursue his goal of writing a poem "the shape of the psyche itself, in times of great stress" (*Straw for the Fire,* 174):

> I believe that, in this kind of poem, the poet, in order to be true to what is most universal in himself, should not rely on allusion; should not comment or employ many judgment words; should not meditate (or maunder). He must scorn being "mysterious" or loosely oracular, but be willing to face up to genuine mystery. His language must be compelling and immediate: he must create an actuality. He must be able to telescope image and symbol, if necessary, without relying on the obvious connectives: to speak in a kind of psychic shorthand when his protagonist is under great stress. He must be able to shift his rhythms rapidly, the "tension." (*On Poetry and Craft,* 53)

I've noted earlier that I believe Roethke's breakthrough in these poems of the 1940s grew, in part, out of his creative blending of Freudian and Jungian ideas—or what I call the ontogenetic and phylogenetic idea of self. He probed his anguished, personal, Freudian self—his experience of mental breakdowns, grief, and trauma (Balakian, 3–7). But he also embraced his idea of a Jungian self—an archetypal, universal psyche that was connected to what he believed came "from a tapping of an older memory—something that dribbled out of the unconscious, as it were, the racial memory or whatever it's called" (*Selected Letters,* 130). He believed his raw Michigan wilderness gave him a sense of a place where "man is no more than a shape writhing from the old rock" (*On Poetry and Craft,* 51).

The Praise to the End! sequence grew out of the four multisectioned poems first published in *The Lost Son and Other Poems* (1948): "The Lost Son," "The Long Alley," "A Field of Light," and "The Shape of the Fire." Those poems then took their place as poems 7 through 10 in the new sequence of thirteen poems that would make up the cycle of *Praise to the End!* (1951). Roethke noted that he added one more poem to the cycle, "O Thou Opening, O," in his ensuing book *The Waking* (1953), and that poem concluded what I would call Roethke's most inventive period. About these new poems Roethke wrote: "I've tried to . . . catch the very movement of the mind itself, to trace the spiritual history of a protagonist (not 'I' personally), of all haunted and harried men" (*On Poetry and Craft,* 28). It's interesting to see Roethke stretch here in order to universalize the "I," because this was his universalist Jungian vision, but the phrase "haunted and harried men" is a poignant way of acknowledging his own mental illness and fragility, or what we might call today neurochemical disorders. To Babette Deutsch he wrote that these new poems "were written out of suffering and they are mine" (*Selected Letters,* 142).

The Praise to the End! sequence is driven by a persona, an invented self that he called the lost son. The poems enact various stages of the lost son's psychological and biological evolution, his struggles to be born, to grow, to accrue knowledge, and to achieve spiritual awakening; there are continual meanderings, recoilings, surges forward, and slippages backward. In a statement about these poems that Roethke wrote for John Ciardi's *Mid-Century American Poets* (1950), he asserted, "Each poem—there are now eight in all and there will probably be at least one more—is complete in itself; yet each in a sense is a stage in a kind of struggle out of the slime; part of a slow spiritual progress; an effort to be born, and later, to become something more" (*On Poetry and Craft,* 50). The whole Praise to the End! sequence embodies what Roethke would later refer to as a "long journey out of the self," as he put it in his later poem "Journey to the Interior" (*Collected Poems,* 187). His ideas of the "struggle out the slime" and of the human self as a "shape writhing from the rock" (*On Poetry and Craft,* 50–51) are distinctive metaphors and images that capture his Jungian and Darwinian idea of the human that is part of an evolutionary and archetypal past.

"Give Way, Ye Gates" (*Collected Poems* 75–76), the fourth poem in the cycle, is part of the lost son's struggle out of the slime. Out of an intensified language—a poetics of compression—his three- and sometimes two-beat lines create the complexly naïve voice of the lost son. From his wellspring of images of nature and organic life, Roethke generates his idea of the unconscious mind and a landscape where the neurotic personal self and the archetypal racial or species self mingle. The poem opens with a surreal, polymorphous world of the lost son immersed in nature in a primal way in which blood and skin and water merge with the vitality of the green world:

> Believe me, knot of gristle, I bleed like a tree;
> I dream of nothing but boards;
> I could love a duck.
>
> Such music in a skin!
> A bird sings in the bush of your bones.
> Tufty, the water's loose.
> Bring me a finger. This dirt's lonesome for grass.
> Are the rats dancing? The cats are.
> And you, cat after great milk and vasty fishes.
>
> (1:1–9)

Primordial water, the animal world of birds, rats and cats, and the grasses and dirt are the elemental condition of the lost son's "green" photosynthesizing "sleep" in which his birth process commences. The oracular bursts, the quick movements, the end-stopped phrases create a rhythm and movement of Roethke's "psychic short hand." In this simplified syntax he captured the naïve, elemental mind of a child, and Roethke seems to have taken T. S. Eliot's notion of "purify[ing] the dialect of the tribe" (*Collected Poems,* 204) to a new place.

This flexible mind-play of feeling and perception is a signature of the Praise to the End! sequence. Roethke believed in the liberating power of torqued rhythm and aural kinetics. In a letter to William Carlos Williams he exclaimed that these poems were written "for the ear and not the eye . . . with the mood or the action on the page, not talked-about, not the meditative, T. S. Eliot kind of thing" (*Selected Letters,* 122). And he noted that primary influences on him were "German and English folk literature, particularly Mother Goose; Elizabethan and Jacobean drama, especially the songs and rants" (*On Poetry and Craft,* 52). The kinetic energy of the nursery rhyme, punning, and wordplay are brilliantly alive in these lines:

A moon loosened from a stag's eye,
Twiced me nicely,—
In the green of my sleep.

(1.1–13)

In section 2, Roethke calls out to the mothering force: "Mother of blue and the many changes of hay" (2.1). The lost son emerges out of an elemental landscape in which the self and nature are fused and diffused, to riff on Kenneth Burke's notion about these poems. Section 2 presents a beguiling image of the body, both animal and human, emerging out of nature:

This tail hates a flat path.
I've let my nose out;
I could melt down a stone,—
How is it with the long birds?
May I look too, loved eye?

(2.2–6)

The lost son moves toward form and motion in way that is jolting and playful. Perhaps Whitman's famous line from section 32 of "Song of Myself" is a touchstone here: "I think I could turn and live with animals, they are so placid and self-contain'd" (218). At the closing of section 2 and in the opening of section 3, Roethke's biomorphic sense of life moves beyond the botanical world as the lost son courts animal life as a way of pushing the parameters of the human and exploring a more expansive idea of being:

In the high-noon of thighs,
In the springtime of stones,
We'll stretch with the great stems.
We'll be at the business of what might be
Looking toward what we are.

3

You child with a beast's heart,
Make me a bird or a bear!
I've played with the fishes

Among the unwrinkling ferns
In the wake of a ship of wind.

(2.20–24; 3.1–5)

Roethke's evocations and intersections here are radical, and not just vegetally as Kenneth Burke noted in his seminal essay on Roethke, "The Vegetal Radicalism of Theodore Roethke," but zoomorphically. The child is measured by bird, bear, fishes, a beast's heart and the pristine ferns, and finally the cosmogonic force of the wind.

Section 4, the culmination of this birth passage, recalls those early greenhouse poems "Cuttings," and "Cuttings (*later*)," opening with sexual evocations that further the primal energy. Roethke keeps cultivating his landscape of the beginning—the beginning of time, of the birth of the species, the idea of the self "writhing from the old rock" (*On Poetry and Craft,* 51). In the closing of "Give Way, Ye Gates," Roethke creates one of his most memorable elemental landscapes, a genesis time of earth and wind and water. Here, one of Roethke's favorite birds of the unconscious—the crow—which in his earlier poem "Night Crow" he likened to "[a] shape in the mind" (*Collected Poems* 47), appears again as a signifier of deep mind.

Section 4 opens:

Touch and arouse. Suck and sob. Curse and mourn.
It's a cold scrape in a low place.
The dead crow dries on a pole.
Shapes in the shade
Watch.

(4.1–5)

The lost son's ability to push forward to the light, to higher consciousness at the end of the cycle, to some illumination, must begin in this archetype of the primal self, where life emerges from nature as the unconscious is activated and becomes a wellspring for self-awareness and growth:

I hear the clap of an old wind.
The cold knows where to come.
What beats in me
I still bear.

The deep stream remembers:
Once I was a pond.
What slides away
Provides.

(4.10–17)

The "old wind," the "deep stream," "the pond" are all elemental aspects of the beginning, the wellspring from which the lost son is nurtured and emerges. Roethke's obsession with his Jungian-Darwinian vision of the human self emerging from elemental nature defines many of the poems in the Praise to the End! sequence, and certainly here these closing images embody this emergence. Wind and water define various moments of the lost son's awakening in the cycle. In "O Lull Me, Lull Me," for example, the lost son asserts that

[t]he poke of the wind's close,
But I can't go leaping alone.
For you, my pond,
Rocking with small fish,
I'm an otter with only one nose.

(*Collected Poems,* 80)

And birth rites and water are inseparable too, as in "The Shape of the Fire," when the lost son exclaims, "A low mouth laps water. Weeds, weeds, how I love you" (*Collected Poems,* 61). To underscore the psychological resonance of the closing of "Give Way, Ye Gates," it's worth recalling Roethke's essential metaphor: "that dark pond, the unconscious" (*On Poetry and Craft,* 49). The evolution of consciousness that defines the lost son's journey often brings him to light and illumination as it does in the lost son's moment of epiphany in the memorable closing of "The Lost Son":

Light traveled over the wide field;
Stayed.
The weeds stopped swinging.
The mind moved, not alone,
Through the clear air, in the silence.

(*Collected Poems,* 55)

In these poems the capacity for seeing the light is so often preceded by the wellspring of that pond of the unconscious Roethke so obsessively probed in these poems.

"Give Way, Ye Gates," the fourth poem in the fourteen-poem cycle, can be read as Roethke hoped: both autonomously and as part of a larger whole. And I want to stress how important it is to see the Praise to the End! sequence both conceptually and literally as a long poem. But, strangely, this has not been easy to do because of a decision that Roethke's publisher Doubleday made decades ago when the editors assembled Roethke's *Collected Poems* after his death in 1963. In *Praise to The End!* (1951), as I note above, Roethke published all thirteen poems in the order he wanted them to be read. Then he added one final poem, "O, Thou Opening, O," and published the full cycle of fourteen poems in his first volume of selected poems, *The Waking* (1953). He published the full cycle again in *Words for the Wind: Collected Verse* (1958). However, in the 1965 *Collected Poems* the publisher and editors present the four Lost Son poems as they first appeared in Roethke's 1948 volume *The Lost Son and Other Poems*, but chose not to reprint them in the ensuing *Praise to the End!* section, nor did they include the final poem, "O, Thou Opening, O" in that section. Thus, in the *Collected* the reader encounters only nine of the poems in the *Praise to the End!* section; there is an absence where poems 7 through 10 should be: "The Lost Son," "The Long Alley," "A Field of Light," and "The Shape of the Fire," and another absence where the stunning, final "O, Thou Opening, O" should be. Most readers, unless they have a first edition of *The Waking* or *Words for the Wind*, books that have been long out of print, have not encountered the full long poem cycle in its original, kinetic, and visual form.

The Praise to the End! sequence remains a distinctive contribution to the tradition of the long poem in American literature. Like the long poems of Walt Whitman, Hart Crane, H.D., William Carlos Williams, T. S. Eliot, or Charles Olson, Roethke's cycle has an open-ended quality that evolves in accord with the poet's unfolding consciousness. The American long poem, a lyric sequential construct—an invention of Whitman most dramatically seen in the fifty-two-section collage of "Song of Myself"—is a form with an open-endedness that implies no resolution but only continual growth. I've noted earlier, however, that in contrast with the more discursive qualities that characterize most sequential, long poems in American literature, a lyric control and conceit-like tightness define the movement of *Praise to the End!* It's clearly not projective verse or an openly enjambed poetry that moves in and out of history or social and political engagement (Balakian, 66–67).

In creating his lost son Roethke tapped into a central Western archetype that includes a host of characters, from Ishmael, Isaac, and Jacob to Oedipus, Hamlet, Huck Finn, Stephen Dedalus, and so many more in fiction and poetry and drama. Throughout the sequence, the lost son is seeking his father, Otto, the master of the greenhouse, who died when Roethke was fourteen, and he is on a quest to find self-knowledge and spiritual knowledge, which are inseparable from nature. His labyrinthine journey takes us into various traumas and joys of the life cycle: birth, separation, growth, sexual initiation, loss and grief, and finally spiritual knowledge and illumination. Ontogenetic and phylogenetic selves overlap and merge. Nature is continually in motion: primordial, elemental, sensually personal. Out of his brew of language, poetics, and transformed autobiography Roethke invented something new.

The Waking (1953)

23

"The Visitant"

CAMILLE PAGLIA

THE POET meets his Muse. She comes as a "visitant," a messenger from the spirit world (a dimension coexistent with ours in nineteenth-century spiritualism). The poem (*Collected Poems,* 96) is structured like a dream play. In the first part, a traveler tarries by a mountain lake. In the second, an apparition emerges from the mist and floats toward him. In the third, he awakes alone and desolate the next morning. One act is missing—the night encounter, left mysteriously blank.

The nine classical Muses were daughters of Zeus and Mnemosyne (Memory) who brought creative inspiration as well as energy and endurance for art making. Carl Jung interpreted the Muse as a projection or emanation of the anima—the repressed female part of a man's psyche, experienced by the artist as an outside force conveying startling new ideas. Roethke's Muse resembles the numinous "white goddess" of Celtic myth, who is identified with the moon and the willow. In this poem, with its hint of Druidic ritualism, she is conflated with High Romantic enchantresses like Coleridge's white-robed vampire Geraldine, who stalks the maiden Christabel in "the midnight wood."

With its quiet, hypnotic language and incantatory rhythms, "The Visitant" puts us too under a spell. In the very first phrase, "A cloud moved close," space contracts, as a ghostly, gathering fog makes heaven seem to touch the earth. The shifting "bulk of the wind" is felt as a subtle pressure to which the swaying tree also responds. Time is suspended; it's like the charged, prickly moment before a storm. Is the voice with its cryptic command to "stay by the slip-ooze" internal or external? (3–4). The mud zone at the lake edge recalls our biological origins in the womb or primal sea.

Nature is cordial yet inscrutable. "Dearest tree, I said, may I rest here?" (5). The weary wayfarer feels Walt Whitman's tender intimacy with nature. But the tree is mute; only a ripple makes an ambiguous "soft reply"—perhaps the lapping of a fish breaking surface (6). Rest in any case (as Emily Dickinson's naïve protagonists discover), might be impossible before extinction. To stay by the "slip-ooze" could mean stagnation and infantile regression. "Alert as a dog"—scaled down to raw animal readiness—the poet accepts his passive state of waiting, shared by a leech and a crab (7–9). Again like Whitman, he bonds with nature's humblest creatures. There are possible bodily referents: the wily leech is visceral or penile, while the shy crab, "the quiet breather," may be the poet's own rib cage as it starts to swell and settle in sleep. Psychologically, a "leech clinging to a stone" is a shadowy symbol of emotional starvation—of an insecure child's parasitic attachment to a remote, frigid parent.

"The Visitant" charts the genesis of poetry from a spontaneous moment of heightened perception and sensory awareness to the birth of rhythm in the regular breathing and lowered heart rate of sleep. In part 2, the poet is entranced or dreaming.

> Slow, slow as a fish she came,
> Slow as a fish coming forward,
> Swaying in a long wave.

With steady, measured pulses, the Muse gradually materializes from the dusk's "soft dark," liquid and luxuriously tactile (10–13, 17). Her approach is all silent, cinematic visuals as she eerily hovers "without brushing the wet stones" (16). (The swaying fish may signal his arousal.) It's a divine epiphany, resembling the descent of the moon goddess Selene to seduce Endymion, a beautiful shepherd sleeping in a mountain cave. With "the wind in her hair" (does she bring the wind or merely ride it?), Roethke's Muse has glamour in its original sense—an atmospheric sorcery (19). As "the moon beginning," she could be the auspicious new moon or the waxing crescent whose bow or blade shape is linked to pitiless goddesses (20). "Her white arms reaching towards me": will she embrace, or choke and drown, him? (14). And is his response ecstasy or terror?

Something unexplained happens in the time lapse between parts 2 and 3 (a plot device possibly borrowed from Donne's "The Flea"), forcing us to presume or speculate. The poet wakes disoriented in the "bright" dawn light: "Staring at a tree, I felt the pulse of a stone" (21–22, 25). The spell is broken: the tree that sheltered him is now unrecognizable, and he is in shock, as if stunned by a queen bee. Reabsorbed into nature, the vanished visitant (bride or succubus) has become "the mountain's downy girl" again, nymphlike and fresh as a peach (24). It's as if her virginity has been renewed—a motif found in goddess legends. (Hera annually recovered her virginity by bathing in a magic mountain spring on Crete.)

Did the rendezvous with the Muse lead to an artistic breakthrough? If so, this poem is its result and record. In the bleak postmortem, the depleted poet resembles the hapless suitors of Blake's "The Crystal Cabinet" and Keats's "La Belle Dame Sans Merci" who are bewitched and abandoned by demure femmes fatales. By the close of "The Visitant," nature gives "no answer" whatever to the poet's plaintive cries (25). But a trace of afflatus remains: "A wind stirred in a web of appleworms" (a treetop nest of caterpillars; 26). This brilliant metaphor unites sex with aesthetics: the web, mythically associated with entrapping female power, is the mazy weaving of words in poetry. All nature-loving Romantic art is "a web of appleworms," a morally ambivalent manifesto of "the Devil's party" (in Blake's phrase about Milton), issued from Eden with its tainted fruit and traumatic revelations of nakedness and mortality.

With its archetypal universals of cloud, wind, tree, and water, "The Visitant" dramatizes the taunting unpredictability of artistic inspiration, infatuating when it comes but cruel when it goes. The poet is transfigured, then dropped. Has the Muse migrated into the swaying "close willow" (27)? The poem ends with an aching sense of men's incompletion, their anguished separation from the maternal body, to which they vainly try to reconnect through the deceptive medium of sex. The uncanny is the flip side of the all too familiar. Haunted by indistinct memory, the outcast poet quests for knowledge and, through the eyes of art, briefly glimpses the elusive spirit presences of pagan nature.

24

"Elegy for Jane"

The Nature of Grief

DAVID RADAVICH

THEODORE ROETHKE'S most memorable poems are noteworthy both for their evocative imagery and for their unusual subjects. He celebrated a root cellar, a father and son dancing together at the end of a tough workday, a woman "lovely in her bones" (*Collected Poems,* 122). "Elegy for Jane" (*Collected Poems,* 98), first published in the *Kenyon Review* in 1950, is another such unusual poem, widely anthologized and much loved. In this work Roethke has wedded form with feeling perfectly; intense grief is balanced by delicate natural imagery, decorum, and restraint.

Jay Parini describes Roethke as "an American Romantic," a "successor to Frost and Stevens" who "looked to Emerson as his first master" (3, 19). In terms of genre, "Elegy for Jane" fits squarely in the long elegy tradition in English poetry, particularly as developed during the Romantic period. Yet the powerful emotional unity of this poem resulted less from immediate inspiration than from careful craft: Parini points out that "Roethke compiled the elegy from fragments scattered over many years through the notebooks," and the poet knew the student "only slightly" (138–39).

The poem's complete title, "Elegy for Jane: My Student, Thrown by a Horse," gives us a name, identifies a relationship, and provides a presumptive cause for what will turn out to be not just an accident but death. The speaker of the poem, clearly an older male, a father figure, consistently refers to Jane as "my student" (subtitle), "[m]y sparrow" (14), "my skittery pigeon" (19), announcing and claiming a linguistic right of possession. Such references could raise the specter of patriarchal domination, a male teacher regarding his female student as small, vulnerable, and in need of protection. But the claiming seems more an act of affection, an assertion of relationship and loss.

The reader of Roethke's poem doesn't find out many facts about the young protégée. She evidently sported neck curls, was small in stature, and enjoyed being in nature. Moreover, as the second stanza suggests, Jane had a propensity for depression and withdrawal or isolation, which others could not broach. But the evocative imagery in the first stanza is not so much descriptive as associative, linking the young woman imaginatively to delicate elements of nature. Jane's curls are compared to "tendrils" (1), her "quick look" to a "sidelong pickerel smile" (2), her manner of delight to a wren with a song "trembling the twigs and small branches" (6).

Yet Roethke's student is more than just a lover of nature, an ecological dilettante: she is *of* nature, fully at home there, and more importantly, nature returns her love in kind.

> The shade sang with her;
> The leaves, their whispers turned to kissing;
> And the mold sang in the bleached valley under the rose.
>
> (7–9)

This central relationship to nature embodies what Ralph J. Mills calls in Roethke's work "the context in which the individual assumes at last his rightful identity, finds love, and engages the spirit in further encounters" (*Theodore Roethke,* 17). In this first descriptive stanza, both the student as figurative wren and the vegetation around her sing to each other in what appears to be perfect, reciprocal harmony.

The second stanza, however, introduces a contrary note: "Oh, when she was sad, she cast herself down into such a pure depth, / Even a father could not find her" (10–11). Here the speaker presumes to know about the student's father's unsuccessful attempts to console his daughter, strongly implying his own paternal interest and failure. Jane's "depth" (10) is described as pure; by implication she becomes a virginal figure. The last two lines of the second stanza highlight abrasion and disruption: "Scraping her cheek against straw; / Stirring the clearest water" (12–13). The "clearest water" (13) reinforces the purity of emotional depth in the first line in this stanza, but the student's sadness is distressingly unnatural, perhaps even suicidal, and unredemptive.

In stanza 3, the speaker shifts abruptly from empathetic depiction to direct address. Jane now is personalized as "you"; she is "not here" (14), signifying not only absence but also distortion. The person "waiting like a fern" is ambiguous; it could either be Jane—wishful thinking on the speaker's part—or the teacher himself, watching. Either way, the natural beauty of the fern has become a "spiny shadow" (15). Moss, which in stanza 1 "sang" (9) with her, now "cannot console" (16) the speaker; it is "wound with the last light" (17), ominously portending death. The depth of loss the speaker feels mirrors or echoes the depth of sadness of the student at the outset of stanza 2, answering its distress. The mood is no longer one of harmony but of disharmony.

The final stanza takes three additional, startling turns. First, abandoning the indicative mode, the speaker assumes the subjunctive: "If only I could nudge you from this sleep, / My maimed darling, my skittery pigeon" (18–19). Two main objectives of the subjunctive mode in English are to convey wish fulfillment and situations contrary to fact. The speaker wishes he could revive or resurrect his student, but of course he can't; he knows and conveys that hard reality in his linguistic mode. Moreover, he indulges in a further bit of wishful thinking by imagining Jane as merely asleep rather than dead. The iteration of "my maimed darling, my skittery pigeon" (19) not only emphasizes edgy woundedness; it also asserts a double claim of possession, reinforced and strengthened since the first line of stanza 3.

At the dramatic climax of the poem, the teacher formally "speaks the words of [his] love" over the student's "damp grave" (20). The deictic import of "this damp grave" positions the speaker physically at the burial site of the beloved. Dampness is a major motif throughout this poem, starting in the very first line and continued in every stanza until this climactic utterance, casting a mist over the whole. Moreover, the teacher in this line is not simply describing or writing but actually declaring his love aloud so others might hear.

Finally, the speaker, realizing he may have overstepped social bounds, retreats to legalistic, formal language in the last two lines: "I, with no rights in this matter, / Neither father nor lover" (21–22). This statement resonates on a number of levels. For one thing, no one has been heretofore thinking of legal rights, nor of the speaker's relationship as either parental or romantic, although clearly he has entertained such thoughts. He defends himself here against possible accusations of impropriety or even prurience. But the statement also has the reversing effect of litotes, expanding the emotional impact of the speaker's love by understating it. On yet another level, Roethke's poem asserts the dignity of intense love often present in student-teacher relations, which unite two souls in a mutual passion for learning and discovery.

Beyond all the rich, damp, skittery imagery, the overall rhetoric of the poem is startlingly unified. It moves from description and memory to grief, to wish, and finally to formal declaration. The lines are unrhymed and loosely regular and, apart from the disproportionate length of the first line in the second stanza, do not call inordinate attention to themselves, arranged in what appears to be a natural cadence. The long, long line at the outset of stanza 2, pushed out even farther than the "bleached valleys" (9) at the end of stanza 1, *does* call attention, not only to itself but also to Jane's sometimes extreme social isolation, distanced from the consoling possibilities in the next three lines.

The catalogue of images which dominates the first stanza, all the evocative natural comparisons describing Jane, gives way later to a number of balanced parallels and juxtapositions: straw/water, fern/shadow, stones/moss, sleep/grave. The last three stanzas make strategic use of negatives: "Even a father could not find her" (11); "you are not here" (14); "The sides of wet stones cannot console me" (16). The "Nor" in the final line of stanza 3 is intensified at the conclusion of stanza 4: "Neither father nor lover" (22).

Like many other Roethke poems, "Elegy for Jane" is remarkable for what it does not say. There is no mention of any mother or female figure. This is a strikingly gendered poem about an older male and a younger female, a "father/daughter" configuration of powerful affect. Roethke does not shy away from the stark emotion of that encounter. After the subtitle, no mention is made of how Jane died; apart from an oblique reference to straw in stanza 2, the horse makes no further appearance. The second stanza suggests a tendency on Jane's part to depression and possibly suicidal thoughts or other self-diminishment. We know that Roethke himself "suffered from mental illness and alcoholism" (Hoffman, 469), so it is not surprising that the speaker, who closely resembles Roethke himself as grieving teacher, sympathizes both with Jane's love of nature and with her self-destructive sense of social isolation.

In Roethke's *Collected Poems*, "Elegy for Jane" is immediately preceded by a remarkable short poem called "A Light Breather," which functions as a companion to "Elegy for Jane." "A Light Breather" not only touches on many themes prominent in the elegy but utilizes almost the exact same imagery:

> The spirit moves,
> Yet stays:
> . . . .
> Turning in the light with its tendrils.
>
> (*Collected Poems,* 97)

In addition to tendrils reaching out at the end of the line in both poems, one notes the minnow playing, very similar to "a sidelong pickerel smile" (2) in "Elegy for Jane." Water is prominent in both, with the subject in "A Light Breather" moving "in and out of the current." At the end of that poem, the spirit moves inward

> like the snail,
> . . . .
> Taking and embracing its surroundings,
> . . . .
> Singing.

"The watery finger," the snail, the minnow, the tendrils in "A Light Breather" all echo the imagery most strongly evoked in "Elegy for Jane."

The twin elements of these companion poems illuminate each other, suggesting a shared mood and response to life in this period of Roethke's poetic career. They reinforce the poet's felt experience and exploration of the triangular relationship of spirit, nature, and human sensitivity. Beyond that, "A Light Breather" offers a thought-provoking gloss on "Elegy for Jane": the unfortunate yet winsome student in the elegy emerges as a specific human example of the "spirit [that also] moves" (*Collected Poems,* 97) in snails, blooms, and minnows.

Despite the obvious pain and loss articulated in "Elegy for Jane," which Karl Malkoff calls "the first, and perhaps the finest, of Roethke's elegies" (111), the poem ends with a kind of affirmation. In his 1950 essay "Open Letter," Roethke asserted about the poems in *The Lost Son* (1948) that "in spite of all the muck and welter, the dark, the *dreck* of these poems, I count myself among the happy poets" (*On Poetry and Craft,* 52). The teacher's speaking "the words of [his] love" (20) is a daring assertion rarely encountered in literature or in public. In our age of heightened awareness of sexual predation or potential abuse, this declaration is risky yet honest, even beautiful. By reining in the speaker's emotions at the conclusion in terms of law and decorum, Roethke can express them with the intensity they deserve.

As enacted in this poem, Jane emerges as a natural, gifted student whose lively mind and sensitive spirit delighted the teacher. We feel strongly the connection and the loss. Those of us who value education immediately warm to this depiction of the devoted pedagogical calling and grieve at the unfortunate negation of youthful potential, memorialized so effectively in one of Roethke's best poems.

25

Dancing "The Dance"

Roethke's Poetics of Appropriation

ADAM PUTZ

> A good deal of nonsense has been written about "influence" in modern poetry.
>
> —Theodore Roethke, "How to Write like Somebody Else" (1959)

THIS ESSAY is about appropriation, not influence. In "How to Write Like Somebody Else," Roethke characterizes influence as something "survived" (as he says he did the influence of William Butler Yeats), while the poet learns how to write through "conscious imitation" of somebody else. He thought his own poem "The Dance" (*Collected Poems,* 101), part 1 of his four-part sequence poem "Four for Sir John Davies," a product of just such a process and provides as sound a critique of Yeats's influence on its creation as any, reaching the conclusion that "conscious imitation . . . is one of the great methods, perhaps *the* method for learning to write" (*On Poetry and Craft,* 61). However, scholars have largely overlooked the parallels between contemporary theories of appropriation like Linda Hutcheon's and Roethke's assertion that the imitation of formal or thematic elements from a source text can give these elements "another, or even better life, in the new context" (*On Poetry and Craft*, 56). Roethke echoes T. S. Eliot's assertion in "Tradition and the Individual Talent" (1919) that great poets change the tradition from which they emerge even as they secure their entry to it. This change to the source tradition is complete for Eliot, who concludes that "what happens when a new work of art is created is something that happens simultaneously to all the works of art that preceded it" (5). But Roethke also anticipates Michel Foucault's assertion in "What Is an Author?" (1969) that "discourses are objects of appropriation" in excess of authorship, so that no text can claim a uniform, fixed status for all time (108). In light of these insights, "The Dance" should be seen as marking the beginning of the end of Roethke's long apprenticeship to Yeats. Likewise, the subsequent parts of "Four for Sir John Davies" offer further evidence of Roethke starting to end apprenticeships to Eliot, if not Dante as well.[1]

Because Shakespeare scholarship has focused on adaptation and appropriation, it offers useful modes of inquiry on relationships between other authors. As Jean I. Marsden has argued, a focus on "appropriations" can generate "a view of Shakespeare embedded not only in his own culture but in ours, forcing us to consider both the impact we have on the plays and the impact they have on us" (8). Marsden's approach to literary practices of appropriation points up how writers can play with a source text in order to make its formal or thematic elements their own, by using them in a creative and often coercive exercise of authority over the past for the purposes of the present. But this exercise of authority over the past is only temporary, if the contemporary purpose of the appropriation is to learn how to write by consciously imitating somebody else. As Roethke observes, "[i]nvariably the poem moves into its own life" (*On Poetry and Craft*, 60). Play is at once a necessary and a sufficient condition for an appropriation to achieve its own vitality. Therefore, a poem like "The Dance" need not amount to anything like an adaptation of, say, Yeats's "Among School Children" (1928) or its other obvious source text, *Orchestra: or, a Poem of Dancing*, by Sir John Davies (1596), for it to have its own life. It can be "derivative" and still survive.

However, Roethke's argument introduces a problem here that complicates this model of apprenticeship, precluding it from serving as a path to knowledge of the source text or tradition. Graham Holderness has observed:

> We can only know the work by reinventing it, by appropriation. But such reinvention is conceived as a violent assault on the work's original

> identity, expropriation. Yet the work has no original identity. Or rather this "identity" is alternately denied and assumed, erased and recuperated. Writing has no meaning other than what we make of it. Yet we believe that the meanings ascribed by our appropriations are different from other meanings of the work. "Different from" predicates a comparator; there can be no difference without another. But we find ourselves no longer able, with any confidence, to relocate that elusive and inscrutable stranger. (§ II)

As a result of the contradiction that Holderness has identified here, it must be said that the knowledge gained by the apprentice is not of the source text or tradition. Neither is it knowledge of a self, the poet's own or somebody else's. Rather, it is knowledge of what language can do. The poem is the sign of this potential. For Roethke, "the final triumph is what the language does, not what the poet can do, or display" (*On Poetry and Craft,* 61). This radically reasserts the importance of form as it emerges from how the poet has arranged the words and phrases of a poem to work in concert.

Roethke argues in the postscript of a letter written to Peter Viereck that "Four for Sir John Davies" returns "to the very plain style of the 16th century—Ralegh and Davies, himself, really not Willie Yeats" (*Selected Letters,* 191). But this identification of his source tradition in the poetry of the English Renaissance also begs an important question: is the reference to Yeats in "The Dance" anything more than something like polite homage? Roethke offered his own answer:

> Oh Christ, let's before the eye of God, try to wipe away the bullshit about both Willie & Tiresome Tom & say this:
>
> In both instances, I was animated in considerable part by arrogance: I thought: I can take this god damned high style of W. B. Y. or this Whitmanesque meditative thing of T. S. E. and use it for other ends, use it as well or better. Sure, a tough assignment. But while Yeats' historical lyrics seem beyond me at the moment, I'm damned if I haven't outdone him in the more personal or love lyric. Why [W. D.] Snodgrass is a damned earless ass when he sees Yeats in those love-poems: look at that fart beat in "Words for the Wind," the 4-part poem—is that a Yeats cadence? or the tone in those love lyrics (I do agree they get a little monotonous). (*Selected Letters,* 231)

Roethke suggests here that he can "do" Yeats, even do him better. Jacqueline Maki has argued, for instance, that the presence of Yeats registers beyond the explicit reference to his cadence in "The Dance." She points to the significance of Yeats's poem "Byzantium" and some of the "Crazy Jane" poems from *The Winding Stair* (1933), "Sailing to Byzantium" from *The Tower* (1928), *A Vision* (1925, 1937), *Michael Robartes and the Dancer* (1921), and *The Wanderings of Oisin* (1889). No doubt, a more exhaustive list could be put together. Maki concludes, though, that understanding just how thoroughgoing the relationship between "Four for Sir John Davies" and Yeats indicates that "Roethke did not merely imitate; he recreated" Yeats (20). But the most important of Yeats's poems for understanding "The Dance" remains "Among School Children" because its formal and thematic elements set a rhythm for Roethke to play with.

The cadence of "Among School Children" has a name—*ottava rima*—and a history that dates back to Boccaccio, if not earlier to a similar Sicilian schema, *octave*. And, as Philip Hobsbaum has recently pointed out, Yeats led the twentieth-century "revival" of interest in the form (176). The ease of conflating the speaker of "The Dance" with Roethke has led many readers to make the mistake of thinking that he himself returns Yeats's cadence to Yeats. He doesn't. Roethke employs a stanza structure in "Four for Sir John Davies" composed of an iambic pentameter quatrain and couplet that, ostensibly, follows an *ababcc* rhyme scheme:

Is that dance slowing in the mind of man a
That made him think the universe could hum? b
The great wheel turns its axle when it can; a
I need a place to sing, and dancing-room, b
And I have made a promise to my ears c
I'll sing and whistle romping with the bears. c
(1–6)

This form is not the *ottava rima* of Yeats's "Among School Children." It takes its name, the *Venus and Adonis* stanza, from Shakespeare's long poem *Venus and Adonis* (1593), which itself draws inspiration from, among other sources, Ovid's *Metamorphoses* (8 CE). The decasyllabic quatrain was also a favorite of Davies, who uses it throughout *Orchestra*. And its conceit of the dance as a metaphor for the orchestration of life into patterns, as Jay Parini has observed, helps define the practice of appropriation in Roethke's sequence (141). But the final rhymes of Roethke's stanza slant here between "hum" and "room," "ears" and "bears," as do many of the other end rhymes of this poem, suggesting that the Elizabethan influence on these poems is indeed partial, that the appropriation of at least this formal element is incomplete and yet not less identifiable for it. (To be sure, Roethke uses slant rhymes often in his rhyming poetry, notably in "The Waking" and in "The Reckoning" [*Collected Poems,* 28], three quatrains rhyming chiefly with slant rhymes: gain/pain, sum/home, add/pad, pawn/down, fare/are, secure/poor.) But Roethke distinguishes "The Dance" from his sources in other ways.

Not only do Roethke's rhymes often slant in "The Dance," there are also discreet deviations from Yeats's cadence in the poem. Roethke deploys trochees and anapests with great tact to disrupt the rhythm of the iambic pentameter. The results reinforce some conceptual breaks with Yeats:

> Is that *dance slow*ing *in* the *mind* of *man*
> That *made* him *think* the *un*iv*erse* could *hum*?
> The *great wheel turns* its *a*xle *when* it *can*;
> I *need* a *place* to *sing*, and *dan*cing-*room*,
> And *I* have *made* a *pro*mise *to* my *ears*
> I'll *sing* and *wh*istle *romp*ing *with* the *bears*.
>
> (1–6)

Roethke immediately breaks with the iambic stressing of second syllables in a metrical foot by deploying an opening anapest, thus placing his initial emphasis on the idea that the dance upon which the speaker is reflecting has lost some of its rhythm and suggesting that it has, perhaps, started to slow its pace. Moreover, this anapest allows these syllables to bump into each other, disrupting the orderly image of the dance as Davies has it to offer a glimpse of the dancers (i.e., syllables) in the dance (i.e., the poem) before order reasserts itself. Famously for Yeats, it was impossible to "know the dancer from the dance" (221). This conceit allows for the first literalism of Roethke's poem to take shape in the image of dancers stepping on each other's toes. The congestion on the dance floor is even worse in the third line, where "great," "wheel," and "turn" are each stressed. But form merges with content in the second stanza:

> For *they* are *all* my friends: I *saw* one *slide*
> *Down* a *steep hill*side *on* a *cake* of *ice*,—

Or *was* that *in* a *book*? I *think* with *pride*:
A *caged bear rare*ly *does* the *same* thing *twice*
In the *same way*: O *watch* his *bod*y *sway*!—
This *an*im*al* re*mem*ber*ing* to be *gay*.

(7–12)

The initial trochee of the second line stresses the ecstatic over the static in the image of a bear gaily sliding down a hill. That this image might have emerged for the speaker from an error, that it was simply "in a book," means the static words on a page can—perhaps, only can—come to life in this way. The conceits here of the bear sliding and the bear swaying both reinforce a theme that Roethke and Yeats share: ecstasy's embodiment of the ecstatic. The suspicion taken from Yeats is aimed at enthusiasm, however, and consequently Roethke and Yeats maintain a similar relationship with measure and meter, a relationship that remains suspicious of free verse—or, at least, verse forms that break with "static" patterns of form—to provide the ecstasy that poetry ought to embody. As if to reinforce the point as it arises here, another anapest appears in the penultimate line, as if the dancing syllables have again lost the beat and bumped into each other, again stepping on each other's metrical feet, each other's metaphorical toes. With the final line, Roethke repeats this pattern by deploying iambic pentameter with an anapestic substitution in the final foot. This repetition reinforces the other variations on Yeats's cadence.

In the third stanza, these toes are offered some sound advice: listen to the speaker's tongue. But the first of two anapests in the second line emphasizes the speaker's own ecstasy, the speaker's own leap of joy by stressing the word "leaped" over the word "blood" as iambic stressing would dictate:

I *tried* to *fling* my *sha*dow *at* the *moon*,
The *while* my blood *leaped* with a *word*less *song*.
Though *danc*ing *needs* a *mas*ter, *I* had *none*
To *teach* my *toes* to *lis*ten *to* my *tongue*.
But *what* I *learned* there, *danc*ing *all* a*lone*,
Was *not* the *joy*less *mo*tion *of* a *stone*.

(13–18)

The stanza's alliterative progression of "leaped, listen, learned" creates a sonic and semantic concatenation that "plays" its own rhythmical "theme," contributing to the ongoing musical performance.

The image of the speaker's blood leaping offers a marked conceptual contrast with Yeatsian cosmology. Blood is not merely another example of influence "survived" by Roethke, it is rejected for its association in Yeatsian cosmology with lineage, itself pegged problematically to Yeats's notions about racial purity and eugenics that characterize his politics in the mid-1930s and inform his last play, *Purgatory* (1939), just to take an example from his dramatic works. But Roethke shifts the stress away from "blood" and onto "leaped." The result is distance for Roethke from this problematic aspect of Yeats's later works. Moreover, the final couplet of the poem breaks the structure altogether by featuring only eight syllables in the penultimate line:

> I *take* this *ca*dence *from* a *man* named *Yeats*;
> I *take* it, *and* I *give* it *back* a*gain*:
> For *o*ther *tunes* and *o*ther *wan*ton *beats*
> Have *tossed* my *heart* and *fid*dled *through* my *brain*.
> Yes, *I* was *dan*cing-*mad*, and *how*
> That *came* to *be* the *bears* and *Yeats* would *know*.
>
> (19–24)

The radical enjambment here "breaks" off the performance of iambic pentameter, altering the tempo of the performance. Meanwhile, the alliterative "keys" played, "be" and "bears," echo "beats" and "brain."

The divergences from Yeats in rhyme and meter in "The Dance" reveal that Roethke was skeptical of the racial bent to Yeats's late politics. But with the same turn in the dance, Roethke also condemns those politics to playing the part of wallflower by identifying a Yeats who would know the ecstasy of that very dance. This final act of recognition redeems Yeats. It creates a separation between Yeats's late politics and the appropriated elements of his poetics that Roethke dances with for his own aesthetic and philosophical purposes in "The Dance."

NOTE

1. There is a long history of debates over Roethke's use of Yeats, Eliot, and Whitman, with some critics charging him with overreliance on his predecessors and others arguing for what Jenijoy La Belle calls "the ways [that] Roethke . . . defined and created in his poetry that cultural tradition in which he felt himself to be living and writing" (3). La Belle's 1976 book *The Echoing Wood of Theodore Roethke* is the key text supporting that view. Another significant study that discusses Roethke's self-conscious drawing on poetic tradition is *The Universal Drum: Dance Imagery in the Poetry of Eliot, Crane, Roethke, and Williams* (1979) by Audrey G. Rodgers.

26

Subduing Fear in "The Waking"

FRANK J. KEARFUL

THEODORE ROETHKE'S fourth book, *The Waking: Poems, 1933–1953* (1953), begins with selections from *Open House*, *The Lost Son and Other Poems*, and *Praise to the End!* and finishes with six "New Poems," the last of which, "The Waking" (*Collected Poems*, 104), ends "I learn by going where I have to go." His villanelle goes where it has to go, fulfilling the exigencies of the form while providing closure for the entire volume. It is as if all of Roethke's poetry thus far, the prior work selectively represented and the new poems culminating in "The Waking," had been a learning process leading to the title poem on the last printed page. The adjacent blank page and four additional blank pages can be "read" as a visual sign that Roethke's poetic evolution, far from completed, is ongoing. That process has an inner necessity which the poet "learns" by going where it leads him in the act of writing.

The set form that Roethke employed was rare in American poetry, and 1953 readers of "The Waking" would surely have been hard-pressed to name any villanelle by an American poet, other than, perhaps, Edwin Arlington Robinson's "The House on the Hill" (1896). The first American villanelle, James Whitcomb Riley's "The Best Is Good Enough" (1883), had long since passed into oblivion, along with the rest of his poetry. Ezra Pound led readers up the garden path by titling a poem "Villanelle: The Psychological Hour," which not even remotely resembles a villanelle, a form that calls for five tercets and a terminal quatrain, all unfolding in accord with a demanding rhyme scheme, A^1bA^2, abA^1, abA^2, abA^1, abA^2, abA^1A^2. (Capitalized A^1 and A^2 signal two refrain lines, with superscript numerals ^{1} and ^{2} marking their alternating separate appearances in tercets 2 through 4.) What might have been an abA^1 fifth tercet, carrying on the tercet rhyming program thus far, goes on to become a quatrain, in which both refrains have their terminal say, A^1A^2. A sense of finality, as if an algebraic formula had been worked out, has been achieved. Iambic pentameter is not obligatory—Robinson used trimeter, Riley tetrameter—but in the twentieth century it became the meter of choice for a villanelle.

The one villanelle that 1953 readers of Roethke's "The Waking" quite likely knew was Dylan Thomas's "Do not go gentle into that good night," first published in the international literary journal *Botteghe Oscure* in November 1951 and then incorporated into Thomas's *Country Sleep and Other Poems* (1952), which Roethke reviewed in the December issue of *Poetry* under the title "One Ring-Tailed Roarer to Another."[1] Roethke also contributed to *Botteghe Oscure*, he and the Welsh poet were friends and admired each other's work, and after Thomas's death in 1953 Roethke wrote a eulogy, again linking himself with Thomas, which appeared in January 1954 in *Encounter. The Princeton Encyclopedia of Poetry and Poetics* pays tribute to "Do not go gentle into that good night" for initiating a golden age of the villanelle during the 1950s, 1960s, and 1970s, and I strongly suspect that it prompted Roethke to write his own villanelle.[2] It is worth taking a brief look at how his and Thomas's interrelate, beginning with their initial tercets. Thomas wrote:

> Do not go gentle into that good night, A^1
> Old age should burn and rave at close of day; *b*
> Rage, rage against the dying of the light. A^2
>
> (Thomas, *Collected Poems*, 128)

Roethke responds:

> I wake to sleep, and take my waking slow. A^1
> I feel my fate in what I cannot fear. *b*
> I learn by going where I have to go. A^2
>
> (1–3)

Both tercets are about "going," and about how to go. One contends with the final sleep and that final "going," while the other invokes sleep but focuses on waking; one teaches an art of dying and the other proclaims an art of learning by going where life takes one. Both tercets have to do with overcoming fear. Thomas exhorts his father fearlessly to defy imminent death; Roethke subdues a fear of his own fate and thus by implication of where he will ultimately go, but his focus is on living with fear as an intrinsic property of ongoing life. Thomas's declamatory rhetoric is powerfully unequivocal; Roethke relies on paradox and ambiguity to keep fear at bay. The "rage" that Thomas urges his father to express is no longer part of Roethke's emotional repertoire, as it was in the title poem that opened *Open House*, where he declaims, "Rage warps my clearest cry / To witless agony" (*Collected Poems,* 3).

For his refrain rhymes Thomas chooses opposites, "night" and "light," probably the most familiar rhymed pair in English poetry after "breath" and "death." Between "night" and "light" Thomas stations "day," setting up a rhyming antithesis in which "day," as yet unrhymed, will be at stake. What will happen to "day"? By the same token, Roethke pairs "slow" and "go" as the antithetical frame of the tercet, with "fear" as a middle term betwixt "slow" and "go." What will happen to "fear"? One might ask the same question of dozens of poems by Roethke, including his perhaps most lauded poem, "The Lost Son": "Fear was my father, Father fear" (*Collected Poems,* 53). It comes as no surprise that Roethke's friend and biographer Allan Seager repeatedly draws attention to "fear" as a major component of his psychological makeup.[3] How it may have been interconnected with Roethke's bipolar disorder remains an open question.

In its face-off with fear, Roethke's first tercet marshals three declarative sentences, one per line ("I wake . . . " "I feel . . . " "I learn . . . ") that entail consequences ("I cannot" and "I have to"). All this sounds simple and straightforward enough, but it isn't. Beginning with "I wake to sleep," the poem's fundamental mode of thought and expression is paradox couched in ambiguity (1). How shall one take "to sleep": as an infinitive verb expressing purpose, "in order to sleep," or as a prepositional phrase, as in "I wake to the sound of music?" What seems to me crucial is whether we let "I cannot fear" stand as an indicative statement of fact, or instead understand it, as I do, performatively, as an imperative that the speaker addresses to himself. I take it not as a whistling in the dark, but as an expressed determination buttressed by internal rhyme ("wake" and "take," "I" and "my"), polyptoton[4] ("wake" and "waking," "go" and "going"), alliteration ("sleep" and "slow," "feel, fate, fear"), and assonance ("sleep," "feel, "fear").

Roethke's villanelle transforms "fear" as its initial *b* rhyme from one tercet to the next, starting with "I *hear* my being dance from *ear* to *ear*" in the second tercet (my italics). Dancing is Roethke's favorite manner of jubilantly shedding fear, but he suggests in his poem "The Dying Man" that adept walking while talking also helps: "Walking, the edge, loquacious, unafraid" (*Collected Poems,* 149). Tercet 3 of "The Waking" intimates that the poet has learned to shun would-be leaps into some heavenly transcendent high in favor of terra firma and judicious walking, presumably without disturbing the dead buried below: "God bless the ground! I shall walk softly there" (8). Earlier in life, Roethke seems to have relished the effects of his manic "highs." Seager reports: "After he had married he told his wife that [his] first [manic] episode had been self-induced 'to reach a new level of reality'" (101). By the mid-1950s, however, "[h]is long studies of the mystics seem to have taught him the fatuity of flying from one extreme to the other" (224). "The Waking" marks a grounded turning point in going where he has to go.

The *b* off-rhyme "there" is picked up in tercet 4 by "stair" in an exemplum of humble (from Latin *humus* = ground) but artful climbing: "The lowly worm climbs up a winding stair," which echoes the opening line of William Butler Yeats's "A Dialogue of Self and Soul," from *The Winding Stair and Other Poems* (1933): "*My Soul.* I summon to the winding ancient stair; / Set all your mind upon the steep ascent" (238). Yeats himself echoes George Herbert's "Jordan (1)"—"Is all good structure in a winding stair?" (50)—which in turn echoes Sir Francis Bacon's disillusioned, pithy observation in his essay "Of Great Place": "All Rising to *Great Place,* is by a winding Staire" (36). Roethke deflates Yeats's rhetoric and gives a more positive twist to the winding stair than either Herbert or Bacon accords it. The "lowly worm" will morph into a fallen man who heroically rises in Roethke's "In a Dark Time": "A fallen man, I climb out of my fear" (*Collected Poems,* 231).

The subterranean "winding stair" leads upward, in the fifth tercet, to "the lively air" (14), into which the evolving "fear" rhyme dissolves. This final tercet radically alters the momentum of "The Waking," which until now has taken its going slow, stopped along the way by a contingent of periods, exclamation marks, and question marks. Enjambment, wholly absent before, speeds the final tercet along:

> Great Nature has another thing to do
> To you and me; so take the lively air,
> And, lovely, learn by going where to go.
>
> (13–14)[5]

What has been reflective poetry of statement abounding in paradox and ambiguity gives way to a lyrical apostrophe to a beloved, as "The Waking" now proffers itself as the aubade that its title forecast, a waking poem in which lovers who have slept the night together awake at dawn as the sun rises, or as Roethke put it in tercet 4, when "Light takes the Tree" (10).[6] Glossed simply, the sun rising shines upon a tree, but "takes" has erotic overtones and the capitalization of "Tree" suggests personification, perhaps reminding one of Daphne, who, on the point of being "taken" by pursuing Apollo, god of light and the sun, was turned into a tree. The personification "Great Nature" (13) brings to mind Edmund Spenser's Dame Nature in *The Faerie Queene* and other nature goddesses ultimately stemming from the Great Mother goddess. The implied first thing that Great Nature has in mind, if we take account of "The Waking" as an aubade, is a fulfillment of the sexual impulse with which she endowed the lovers.

But an aubade is less about what happened at night than about going where one has to go the morning after, when the sun rises, birds sing, the air is fresh, and nature wakes.[7] Whereas Thomas's father is urged to rage against the dying of the light, aubade lovers lament the dawning of the light and the "going" it entails. Shakespeare adapts the aubade and its lovers' plight for tragic purposes, when dawn breaks after Romeo and Juliet have spent their one and only night together *(Romeo and Juliet* 3.5.1–36). Their dialogue at dawn is a sustained riff on the aubade theme of the male going when and where he has to go, which Juliet at first questions, "Wilt thou be gone?" Romeo insists, "I must be gone and live, or stay and die." She twists and turns his reasoning into "Therefore stay yet, thou need'st not to be gone." He does not give in, and assures her, "I have more care to stay than will to go." Juliet's distraught, lengthy reply begins "It is, it is, hie hence, be gone, away!" and ends "O now be gone, more light and light it grows." Romeo terminates their aubade dialogue in a "grows / woes" rhyming couplet which echoes the "goes" theme they have rung changes on (159–61). Just how great their woes will grow Romeo learns only by going where he has to go. By contrast, Roethke's beloved need not protest, or mourn, or try to be brave: presumably she goes with him. Yeats also gives aubade conventions a twist in his revision of Romeo and Juliet's dialogue in his dialogue poem "Parting," from *The Winding Stair and Other Poems,* beginning "Dear I must be gone." "She" has, however, the last word: "I offer to love's play / My dark declivities" (278), a good alternative to dark woes, I should think. The woman does all the talking in John Donne's "Break of Day" and ridicules the standard male excuse for going, that a man's got to do what a man's got to do. Bending gender conventions, the male speaker in Richard Wilbur's "A Late Aubade" tries to persuade a female who would be up and going to enjoy brunch in bed:

> If you *must* go
>
> Wait for a while, then slip downstairs
> And bring us up some chilled white wine,
> And some blue cheese, and crackers, and some fine
> Ruddy-skinned pears.
>
> (229)

In the two most famous aubades in English, Donne's "The Sun Rising" and "The Good Morrow," neither party wants to get out of bed. In both it is the sun that is told to go places.

Roethke puts his own twist on the aubade by urging his beloved to go with him and "take the lively air" (14). "Great Nature has another thing to do / To you and me" (13–14) suggests that what they have experienced was no one-night stand, which unfortunately is all that Romeo and Juliet are granted. Great Nature herself, who brought them together, now bids them enter her domain to enjoy her lively and life-giving air. Such a reading of "The Waking" as, among other things, a love poem ties in with Roethke's having fallen in love with Beatrice O'Connell in December 1952 and their marrying in January 1953. Seager records—I paraphrase and condense his account of their whirlwind courtship (205–9)—that when Roethke was on his way to give a poetry reading in New York on December 4, 1952, a young woman crossing the street beside him, heading the same way, asked, "Remember me?" He replied "Hi puss," and asked where he could get in touch with her (Seager, 205). He in effect thus responded to his own question "Of those so close beside me, which are you?" at the outset of tercet 3 of "The Waking" (7). Testing to see if he remembered her name (Beatrice O'Connell had taken classes with him during his teaching stint at Bennington College, 1943–47), she said she was in the phone book. Two nights later he took her out, and she told him she had been in love with him ever since Bennington, but had despaired given their age difference. Roethke, forty-four to her twenty-six, replied, "It's not too late now" (Seager, 206). They saw each other every day and married on January 3, 1953, with W. H. Auden as best man and Louise Bogan as matron of honor. Auden offered his villa at Forio d'Ischia, Italy, for their honeymoon, and the newlyweds spent March to May there, taking the lively air, and remained in Europe some three months longer. "The Waking," perhaps as much a covert epithalamium[8] as a heterodox aubade, heralds the spate of sixteen love poems, largely inspired by his Beatrice, that Roethke brought together in his next volume, *Words for the Wind* (1958).

The happy ending of the poem considered as an aubade is not, however, the ending of the poem as a villanelle engaged in subduing fear. Imbued with the lively air of tercet 5, the quatrain begins with a jaunty paradox followed by an ambiguous addendum: "This shaking keeps me steady. I should know" (16). Still ebullient, Roethke the celebratory poet/lover and nature poet can afford to be flippant: "What, me shaking? It's just a way of keeping steady. If anyone knows that based on experience, I do." Any such flippancy aside, there is much trembling as well as shaking in Roethke's poetry, and neither is necessarily a sign of uncontrollable fear. In the sixteen-line coming-of-spring passage in section 3 of "Meditation at Oyster River," they join forces, beginning "I shift on my rock, and I think: / Of the first trembling of a Michigan brook in April," and culminating "And the whole river begins to move forward, its bridges shaking" (*Collected Poems,* 185), water going where it has to go. The passage symbolically enacts a psychic rebirth of the self, of spirit working, and of fear subdued by movement. In Roethke's poetry, viewed psychologically, the chief obstacle to individuation is fear, which poem after poem seeks to subdue.[9] Shaking directly countered fear in the opening strophe of "The Lost Son" ("I shook the softening chalk of my bones"), which recalls the colloquial phrase "to give oneself a shake," denoting to pull oneself together (*Collected Poems,* 50). We can "shake off our fears," or, in sync with Roethke's love of dancing, we can "shake, rattle, and roll." Yet more to the point, "This shaking" puts the utterance in the implicit present time of the writing of the poem, as if the poet were now directly addressing the reader and bearing witness to his shaking "now," perhaps of the very hand with which he is writing the poem. Fear has not been wholly banished and likely never will be, but it is being mastered in the act of writing, of writing this villanelle, which is in turn a means of keeping the poet "steady."[10]

One sign of the steadiness thus attained at this closing stage of the villanelle is the universalizing, sagacious discourse that Roethke employs in line 2 of the quatrain, "What falls away is always. And is near" (17). What is salient for my interpretation of the poem is the return of the *b* rhyme instigated at the outset by "fear," which was progressively transformed in the tercets to "lively air" (14).

If one includes fear among those things that "fall away" yet persist, as a rhyme it remains "near." The villanelle's rhyming program, coming toward an end, thus offers a wise reminder. Roethke learns how to subdue fear not by proclaiming its utter annihilation, but by learning as he goes to live with it, turning it to account in his writing, which keeps him steady. In biographical terms, the "slow / go" antithesis, with "fear" initially lodged between them, can be taken as an analogue of Roethke's recurrent bipolar disorder, "go" indicative of the manic phase, "slow" of the depressive. "The Waking" does not disable the polarity, but it suggests the poet's manner of riding it out and of writing it out in his paradoxical, ambiguous, artful villanelle.

There are many more ways than mine of reading "The Waking," and any interpretation of it, including mine, is bound to be reductive. In an effort to do "The Waking" partial justice, I have briefly discussed it as the title poem and closing poem of *The Waking*; as a midcareer poem in Roethke's poetic evolution; as a counterpoising response to Dylan Thomas's "Do not go gentle into that good night"; as a villanelle that goes where it has to go; as an aubade that goes where it wants to go; and principally as a key poem among Roethke's numerous encounters with fear. "The Waking" is, however, one thing above all: a poem to be read aloud and allowed to do its own affective work in our response to it. That is the "interpretation" of it which I feel sure would please Roethke most: "I think of myself as a poet of love, a poet of praise. And I wish to be read aloud" (*On Poetry and Craft*, 33).

NOTES

1. As Thomas's *Collected Poems* indicates, except toward the very end of his career Thomas regularly headed his poems simply with a quotation of, or from, the opening line rather than with a capitalized independent title. "Do not go gentle into that good night" (128) is no exception.

2. See Julie Kane's and Amanda L. French's entry on the villanelle for an account of its evolution in Anglophone and European poetry (1521–22).

3. See Seager, 76, 84, 85, 93, 94, 100, 103, 104, 112, 117, 118, 125, 136, 157, 159, 164, 172, 218, 222, 237, 241, 246, 248, and 259 and numerous related references to Roethke's insecurity, trepidation, nervousness, agitation, terror, and feelings of guilt. Seager notes that one page in Roethke's notebooks is devoted to just one word, "Frightened" (162).

4. Polyptoton, a rhetorical or poetic device, involves repeating the same word in different forms, such as in Shakespeare's sonnet 146: "And Death once dead, there's no more dying then" (301). Polyptoton is tailor-made for a villanelle, which forges ahead through repetitions with variations.

5. Critics sometimes take "another thing" to be death and "you" to be the reader. George Wolff, for example, argues in his book *Theodore Roethke* that "[t]he other thing that nature has to do to the poet and the reader ('you') is 'other' than the affirmation of life just made in stanza four; it is death" (74). My live-and-let-live reading of stanza 5 is not prescriptive, but I trust will prove worth entertaining.

6. Compare Robert Frost's "Tree at My Window," in which the tree is "taken and tossed" (*Poetry of Robert Frost,* 252). Frost's poem is not an aubade, but an erotic undertone may be heard.

7. In *Eos*, Hatto includes the aubade (from French *aube* = dawn) and related versions of the dawn-song in world love poetry from the thirteenth to the twentieth century. Precise terminological distinctions between the aubade and the alba (from Occitan and Spanish = dawn) dissolve in critical practice, but "aubade" is customarily used (including by the editor of the New Cambridge edition of *Romeo and Juliet*) in the sense that I have used it in. In *The Longman Dictionary of Poetic Terms*, Jack Myers and Michael Simms note that the aubade "is usually considered synonymous with [the] alba" (27). Marisa Galvez in *The Princeton Encyclopedia of Poetry and Poetics* opts solely for "alba" (29–30).

8. An epithalamium (or epithalamion) is a poem which celebrates a wedding, originally meant to be sung outside the bridal chamber which the bride and groom are about to enter, going where they want to go. The most famous example in Anglophone poetry is Edmund Spenser's *Epithalamion* (1595).

9. For an interpretation of the passage along these lines, see Kearful, "Regions of the Self." For another angle on form in the villanelle, including Roethke's "The Waking," see Kearful, "Self-Imposed Fetters."

10. Such a paradoxical unpacking of Roethke's paradox puts "The Waking" in close company with Elizabeth Bishop's villanelle "One Art" in its mastering of fear through writing—in Bishop's case, fear of losing a beloved (1976). Subduing fear is also an underlying theme in "The World and the Child" (1962), James Merrill's villanelle not about waking but staying awake. See Kearful, "'The Child Awake and Wearied Of.'"

Words for the Wind (1958)

27

Love, Selfhood, and Sublimation in "Words for the Wind"

ANDREW DAVID KING

> In fact, [the lover] has knowledge of the Beautiful and his mind is impregnated with the form of his beauty. But because he lacks the essential, in other words, perfect union with the Beautiful, the desire of this main effect that he lacks comes to him.
>
> —Leone Ebreo, *Dialogues of Love* (293)

> What is desire?—
> The impulse to make someone else complete?
>
> —Theodore Roethke, "The Partner," from "Four for Sir John Davies" (*Collected Poems,* 101)

ON FIRST encounter, Roethke's later love poems might recall the lyrics Shakespeare stuffed into the mouths of his most smitten characters. By turns steady and breathless, the poems' speaker—if we can assume a single speaker across them—clamors to expend the resources of lyric expression to articulate his erotic experience. The trouble is that the very resources indispensable to this task also prove insufficient for it, giving rise to jarring, but strangely self-assured, poems.

Regular only in their stanzas, meters, and themes, they alternate between various narratives and surreal, or hyperreal, description; they flirt with rational deliberation but never fully submit to its demands. The love poems are, in this sense, evidence of a failure—a failure of argument, maybe, or of lyrical consistency. But what is a failure in one sense is a success in another, for the speaker alights on insight even as he is too engrossed in the study of his amorphous beloved to fuse the shards of his reports into a coherent picture. His pivots between antitheses, in what Roy Harvey Pearce called an "underground dialectic" (175), resist resolution into a position, view, or even mood. The poems may also succeed as documentation of the speaker's pursuit of his beloved—a pursuit with intrinsic value, one that occasionally stumbles into certainty. The pleasant chaos of "Words for the Wind" (*Collected Poems,* 118–121)—with the speaker's "I," like the forest backdrop, passing in and out of focus—might be read, then, less as a failure of the speaker to say straightforwardly what he means (though it may also be this) than as an enactment of the idea that love, at its strongest, at once requires the self and yet sublimates, even perhaps near-obliterates, it. This sublimated self—radically altered and elevated, in form or in conception—enters into a strange unity: a unity with the beloved, but also with the world of ordinary things, and with the cosmic order that governs that world.

The titular poem of Roethke's 1958 collection shares many of its thematic concerns and much of its formal structure with the other love poems, in which it appears as the third in a sequence of sixteen. Like its counterparts, it takes up the traditional lyric task of addressing a beloved who may or may not love in return, and who may or may not be present to the speaker. Despite the speaker's commitment to his beloved, their relationship is hardly fixed. If anything, one of Roethke's main accomplishments in the poem, and in the sequence, is to distort and confuse the terms of this classic construction. Lover and beloved trade opposing properties, switching from active to passive, hunter to hunted; each grounds the existence of the other and yet calls into question the basic premises and preoccupations of that existence. Love is no pat emotion in these poems, nor is its articulation—or confrontation—a simple matter. Equal parts fear and joy, the speaker reveals, are ingredients in his conception of love. These emotions cycle between lesser and greater intensities, just as the love-saturated self cycles between solid and porous representations of itself, never settling at either end of the spectrum.

The love poems, as Delmore Schwartz noticed, are Shakespearean through and through: rife with lilting, iambic gaits, and as sensitive to the nuances of everyday speech as to the pitfalls of romantic declaration. As Schwartz points out, the exclamations of Roethke's speaker might seem the "uncontrollable and subliminal outcries" of a "primitive lyric poet" when in fact they showcase a sophistication similar to the songs in Shakespeare's plays (203). In "Words for the Wind" (*Collected Poems,* 118–21)—despite its tribulations and lamentations, probably the most triumphant poem in the series—Roethke brings a Shakespearean mastery of the vicissitudes of erotic psychology, and of prosody, to bear on his speaker's song. Roethke himself forces us to consider Shakespeare when the speaker, not far into the second stanza of the first section, declares, "Sweet Phoebe, she's my theme" (1.11). Besides self-consciously suggesting that he has a "theme," and so that he might be purposefully adopting poetic technique rather than merely happening to speak through it, the speaker alludes to a plea made by Silvius to his paramour in *As You Like It:*

> Sweet Phoebe, do not scorn me; do not, Phoebe.
> Say that you love me not, but say not so
> In bitterness. The common executioner,
> Whose heart th'accustomed sight of death makes hard,
> Falls not the axe upon the humbled neck
> But first begs pardon. Will you sterner be
> Than he that dies and lives by bloody drops?
> (56; 3.5.1–7)

Silvius's love, as vocalized here, is so anxious that it prompts him to draw explicit parallels between the "common executioner" and his beloved: both decide the fate of another. On the whole, the speaker of "Words for the Wind" seems joyous, but his joy is also tinged with the curious type of self-doubt that stems from realizing that someone or something else has power over him—a power that he himself has the power to strengthen by accepting it. As Shakespeare weds love and death in Silvius's plea to Phoebe, Roethke weds ecstasy and anguish in his speaker's erotic pursuit, as he does often in the love poems. "Despair and the most transcendental love of God are inseparable," he wrote in his notebooks (*Straw for the Fire,* 186).

This admixture of pain and pleasure may make more sense if understood as a consequence of the view of love propounded in the poem, a view that requires of the lover that he abandon, even destroy, his understanding of himself—what might be called his ego—in order to approach, and attain, his beloved. In one of the poem's less obviously happy moments, the speaker finds himself at once alone and accompanied:

> The shallow stream runs slack;
> The wind creaks slowly by;
> Out of a nestling's beak
> Comes a tremulous cry
> I cannot answer back;
> A shape from deep in the eye—
> That woman I saw in a stone—
> Keeps pace when I walk alone.
>
> (1.25–32)

This passage is not indisputably ominous, but it at least suggests a feeling of weakness in the speaker. He cannot respond to the nestling whose cry reaches him; he remains a recipient, not an initiator, of communication. It also invokes the speaker's sense of being haunted, or even hunted; after all, some woman "[k]eeps pace" (1.32), as a predator or a companion might, when he walks alone. The imagery of the slackening stream and the creaking wind hints at a corresponding diminishment of agency in nature itself; the speaker, unable to converse with his environment ("I cannot answer back" [1.29]), nonetheless finds himself in sync with it. "The movement from the physical to the spiritual" (126), an element that Neal Bowers finds in many of the love poems, is made more apparent by the odd coupling of the natural environment and the unknown, supernatural woman who keeps pace with the speaker, at once affirming and threatening his presence. He spies her, somehow, "in a stone" (1.31); this points to her continuity with nature, but the specifics of this continuity stay beyond the speaker's reach. Given the frequency with which Roethke switches between metaphysical registers, the reverse movement—from the spiritual to the physical—becomes another important feature of the poem's oscillations.

In addition to the speaker's transition from authoring his experience to passively receiving it and back again, he finds his connection with his beloved uncertain. At one point, he correlates his motion with hers (and perhaps, even, his whole existence): "She sways whenever I sway" (1.12). But we are told, further along in the poem, that "[s]he wandered; I did not: / I stayed," evidence that the two have parted, if only spatially (1.20–21). The apparent unease at the end of this first section contrasts with the happy song of its opening, with its spondaic force lilting into balladesque phrasing: "Love, love, a lily's my care, / She's sweeter than a tree" (1.1–2). There, as in many other passages in the poem, naturalistic metaphors clarify the speaker's exultant attitude towards his beloved but also render it—and the conventions by which human love is set apart from events of the natural world—cryptic. Just what is it for the beloved to be "sweeter than a tree"? And what could it mean to say "a lily's my care"?

To seek straight answers to these questions might, I suspect, be to misunderstand the speaker's purpose in using these confrontational, unequivocal metaphors—just as it would be mistaken to assume that the speaker himself has a complete, or completely conscious, grasp on that purpose. Consider the second metaphor. Though there is surely something to be said about the ways in which the speaker's beloved, in her bewildering perfection, can manifest sweetness in a way that nonconscious natural objects like trees cannot, the rhythm of the phrasing—rather than its content or its logic—seems preeminent for Roethke. The whole opening couplet appears more the glossolalia of someone intoxicated with the object of his attachment than fact-like testimony about that object's attributes. In "Words for the Wind," these types of metaphors serve not merely as linguistic ornaments or flights of phrasing, though they are certainly both of these, but as enactments of the poem's philosophical underpinning. This underpinning consists of two separate but related claims, both of which may be a bit counterintuitive. The first, mentioned at the beginning of this essay, is that love at its most intense involves a special form of self-destruction. The second is that, though love is not identical with any part of the nonhuman, or "natural," world, it is—mysteriously—somehow still a participant in that world, and the two can exert influence on each other. Roethke's speaker is not concerned with proving or even arguing about these claims; he expends his energy in song. But these claims govern, and emerge from, that song. The first metaphor ("a lily's my care"), initially opaque, becomes translucent in view of the rest of the poem. Whether we understand the speaker's "care" to be the act of his loving or the object of his love, the fact that this care, this love, is compared with or possibly equated to a lily—even while the variables of this equation are not yet fully revealed to us—suggests that this love and the landscape are somehow inseparable.

The end of the first section, then, makes clear that the speaker is one part of a tenuous whole composed of lover, beloved, and the natural world. The details of this revelation, rescued from triviality by being framed as the essence of the speaker's altered experience, drive the poem's remaining sections. Still, the identity of the "woman [he] saw in a stone"—the woman he first recognizes as a "shape from deep in the eye"—remains unclear (1.30–31). Is she his beloved, or just another shadow? The speaker elaborates upon his relation to his companion in the beginning of the following section, the second of four in this quartet:

> The sun declares the earth;
> The stones leap in the stream;
> On a wide plain, beyond
> The far stretch of a dream,
> A field breaks like the sea;
> The wind's white with her name,
> And I walk with the wind.
>
> (2.1–7)

The scene's components are superficially familiar, but the relations among them are less so. The sun, for one, "declares the earth" (2.1). Does the sun reaffirm or permit the existence of the earth; does the existence of the latter depend on some act by the former? Whatever the case, the tie between the two mirrors the reflexivity of the speaker's quest for his beloved—a quest in which the speaker, struggling to know his beloved, also comes to know himself. And the speaker's claims that the wind is "white with her name" (2.6) and that he walks with the wind suggest an asymmetry between them, one already brought out by her being seen "in a stone" (1.31): the beloved, at this point in the poem, is more a part of nature than he is. She is on the inside; he remains on the outside. But he is linked to nature nonetheless. In his world, the chaotic energy of love modifies even the physical environment, and vice versa. Stones leap in the stream as if they were animals, and a field "breaks like the sea" (2.5). What accounts for these surprising shifts between poles, for land behaving like water, for inanimate objects behaving like sentient beings—beings frenetic, like the speaker, with erotic energy?

Perhaps the explanation can be found in the speaker's assertion that "[p]assion's enough to give / Shape to a random joy" (2.15–16). This enigmatic statement might be understood as the speaker's explanation, or even justification, of his fantasy by appeal to the conviction with which he feels it. The motivating force of the entire paean, the passion of love, imposes order ("shape") on any "random joy" that emerges in the context of this unfolding love, even if the object of that joy is some natural phenomenon as hard and seemingly unalterable as a stone. That the imposition of order in the speaker's world depends partly, if not wholly, on his experience of love (which also depends, in turn, on his beloved) squares with his puzzling statement that he "bear[s], but not alone, / The burden of this joy" (2.27–28). For joy, like love, is for the speaker something to be made sense of with the help of another, comprehended and coped with as much as relished; love, in reconfiguring the world to furnish the speaker with a new kind of knowledge, bears knowledge's attendant, and communal, responsibilities.

At certain moments, the speaker's ecstasy returns again to the more impoverished world that preceded the richer one called into existence by his passion. Consider the last stanza of the third section:

> What time's my heart? I care.
> I cherish what I have
> Had of the temporal:
> I am no longer young
> But the winds and waters are;
> What falls away will fall;
> All things bring me to love.
>
> (3.15–21)

Note how Roethke's enjambment works in the second and third lines of this section. Just as the speaker is claiming in the second line that he cherishes, in the present tense, what he has—that is, currently possesses—of the temporal, the third line modifies the second line's phrasing with "had." This use of the present perfect tense causes the possession that seemed present to revert instantly to the past. And so Roethke's speaker, while cherishing time, reenacts in his song its disappearance from moment to moment. Mysteriously, he also locates himself somewhere outside of time. He has "had" some of the temporal, but presumably has it no longer, though even the grammatical structure of his statement seems to presuppose the existence of time—a time in the past where, confusingly, he "had" time. Here, as in the rest of the poem, colons and semicolons link sentences that might otherwise be severed by periods—another way in which we are prompted to consider each of the poem's objects and utterances, even pieces of the poem's own textual machinery, as flowing into the next.

This discussion of temporality abuts the speaker's own frank, introspective assessment of his age. He takes himself to be older than "the winds and waters"

(3.19), though one might have expected the reverse to be true. He adds a further layer of meaning to this claim—an "upside-down" statement in the style of the Indian ecstatic poet Kabir[1]—when we consider that, as we have learned by this point in the poem, the wind bears a specific symbolic relation to the beloved. He then reminds himself that these natural phenomena, like all things, "bring [him] to love." But the fatalism of "What falls away will fall" that precedes this suggests that, much like the darkness that he and Silvius see as love's companion, loss and anguish do not thwart the search for love. They even aid it, if one interprets the "all" in "All things bring me to love" strongly enough (3.20–21).

The poem closes its fourth and last section with a jubilant celebration of the beloved and an account of the speaker's reunion with her. This reunion is marked by a return to the symmetrical eight-lined stanzas of the first section from the seven-lined stanzas of the more apprehensive middle sections, as if to record formally that the speaker has regained the stable exuberance with which he opened the poem. By now, the gaps between the speaker, his beloved, and the world where she dwells have shrunk; if only for a short while, joy imposes no "burden" but springs into its own pure and effortless existence. Channeling Whitman, Roethke writes: "Being myself, I sing / The soul's immediate joy" (4.9–10). But the speaker's burden has not been entirely banished, for the poem closes with this admission:

> And I dance round and round,
> A fond and foolish man,
> And see and suffer myself
> In another being, at last.
>
> (4.21–24)

It seems fair to ask if the beloved is, for the speaker, any different from the self. Is the beloved human? Randall Stiffler characterizes the beloved of Roethke's love poems as existing on a gradient between human and animal, and writes that the speaker "is most drawn" to the beloved "when she is least human, most animal" (118). At any rate, it is not clear what she is; or, if she is modeled after a living, breathing counterpart, it is not clear that she is fully real for the speaker of the poems, even as she amounts to something to be reckoned with. She may be love personified, or a deity; she may be an actual, embodied lover; or she may be an anthropomorphization of the ideal object of eros, while love itself finds its role expressed in the speaker. What matters is that she serves a constitutive function for the speaker. He finally sees and suffers himself for having found her, and does so "in"—not through, with, or by means of—her. Having undergone what might be called a spiritual transformation as a result of his love, he is a part of her, and she of him.

At this perceptual, intellectual, and somatic union of lover and beloved (and the union of this union with the natural world), the speaker ceases to speak and the poem ends "at last." Left over, of course, are the questions raised by its title. How should we understand its relation to the poem? One might look to Roethke's connection of the beloved with the wind, taking the title to indicate that the poem itself consists of an address ("words") to the beloved ("wind"). A more playful, if cynical, reading would have it that the poem—and by proxy, perhaps, any attempt to chronicle the erotic, to chase after love with language as one's net—consists of "words for the wind" in the sense of Ecclesiastes: testimony that passes away, dust on the breeze, paltry evidence of a passion that poetry can touch but not hold.

NOTE

1. As Linda Hess writes in an appendix to *The Bījak of Kabir*, "[a] particularly intriguing category of Kabir's poems is the type known as *ulaṭbāṃsī*, poems in 'upside-down language.' They intrigue because they are absurd, paradoxical, crazy, impenetrable, and yet they purport to be meaningful. Kabir's upside-down poems are part of a long tradition in India and can be related to similar expressions across the world" (135). Also worth noting is that, while Roethke describes himself as a "fond and foolish man" (4.22) in the poem, Hess maintains that upside-down language is intended to make the reader who takes a merely intellectual approach to *ulaṭbāṃsī* (or one that disregards Indian folklore) "feel like a fool" (135).

28

Moving Circles in "I Knew a Woman"

JAY PARINI

FEW POEMS of Roethke's embrace as many tonalities and modes of poetic being as "I Knew a Woman" (*Collected Poems,* 122), a late poem that considers the nature of love and its possibilities, in lighter and heavier accents, within the course of four six-line stanzas. It's an intensely musical poem of immense playfulness and, finally, a kind of philosophical grandeur that takes the reader somewhat by surprise. Written in the mid-fifties, it shows Roethke at his most formal—he was often in these years mimicking Yeats, Sir John Davies, and other formalists—but there is a lightness of touch in this poem that engages the readers from the outset, giving the lyric its singular aura, its bright momentum, its verbal and emotional power.

One is immediately struck in the first stanza by the deft phrasing. Roethke recalls a woman who is "lovely in her bones" (1). But what does this mean? Does she simply have good bone structure? Is she simply comfortable in her own skin? It's a bit reductive at first glance: this woman seems more physical than metaphysical, and her physicality might lead some to hear a discordant note of sexism in the poem. This was, of course, the fifties, when few writers thought much about sexism. Roethke had, in fact, recently fallen in love with a much younger woman, one of his former students from Bennington. But this woman lives in the past tense of the poem: he knew her once, and seems to have lost her.

Roethke, in fact, writes movingly about women in many of his poems, but he does so within a fairly traditional mode, with the male as voyeur, the female as part of nature, often as Mother Nature's daughter. One thinks of "Elegy for Jane," where the dead girl who was killed after being thrown from a horse is closely associated with a variety of birds and natural creatures: wren, pickerel, sparrow, and so forth. Her hair is "limp and damp as tendrils," and yet with her death, the poet can find no consolation in nature itself: "The sides of wet stones cannot console me," so he tells us (*Collected Poems,* 98). In "Wish for a Young Wife," the beloved is identified with a lizard, called "my lively writher" (*Collected Poems,* 210). In "I Knew a Woman," the poet glides between the physical woman "lovely in her bones" and her metaphysical residue, an afterglow of her material being, which takes the poet beyond nature, into a timeless zone, into eternity itself.

That Roethke associates this woman with the natural world is obvious: "When small birds sighed, she would sigh back at them" (2). Her responsiveness is immediate and primitive, instinctual. Her mind seems of no concern to the poet, but that doesn't feel necessary. This woman simply *is*, not unlike the love object in Robert Frost's "The Silken Tent," where the poem—a single extended sentence drawn through an entire sonnet—is grammatically complete after the first two words: "She is . . . " (*Poetry of Robert Frost,* 331). Roethke's woman in this poem, once known well, now remembered, simply "is." But how can this poet write about her beautiful shapes and their meaning? Roethke plays wittily with his lines now, allowing the rhyme to determine the content:

> Of her choice virtues only gods should speak,
> Or English poets who grew up on Greek
> (I'd have them sing in chorus, cheek to cheek).
>
> (5–7)

The poet seizes the content again in the second stanza, following upon his mention of Greek poets. He refers subtly to the Pindaric ode, with its three parts: *strophe, antistrophe,* and *epode.* These are figured in the references to Turn, Counter-turn, and Stand, of course. But the punning quality of the language ramps up the erotic dimensions as well: a stand is, of course, an erection. There is also a dancing metaphor at work here, as if Roethke has been taught some kind of formal ballroom moves as he strides "cheek to cheek" (7) on the dance floor. The various strains of this poetic waltz come together, giving an amplitude to the second stanza, with a hilarious ending wherein the poet becomes a "rake" (12), itself a pun, coming after her from behind (no doubt referring to copulation) to participate in some "prodigious mowing" (14). Needless to say, "mowing" is a well-known euphemism in English poetry for sexual intercourse.

One could, in fact, profitably compare Roethke's poem to Frost's "Mowing" here, with that famous last line: "My long scythe whispered and left the hay to make" (*Poetry of Robert Frost,* 17).

Moving into the third stanza, Roethke almost flies out of control: "Love likes a gander, and adores a goose." This is loose-tongued writing, and "a goose" is another explicitly sexual joke, a bawdy one. In this complex stanza, Roethke endows the woman with a ferocious erotic drive, "the errant note to seize." She wasn't going to let her man get away as she "played it quick, she played it light and loose" (15–17). What does this actually mean? Is this woman wishing to make hay while the sun shines? Does she get control of the man who covets her, who comes under her powerful sway? She seems in control, at ease, moving from a particular woman in place and time to a more generic one, almost a figure from Marcel Duchamp's 1912 painting *Nude Descending a Staircase,* as Roethke says, "Her several parts could keep a pure repose" (19). One can visualize her body parts moving but in unison, beautifully aligned, graceful, shaking but still. As in each stanza of this poem, Roethke ends with a parenthetical line, and in each case this enclosed line is outside the poem, with the poet commenting on the previous lines in a more general way than would quite be allowed otherwise, without the parenthetical enclosures that allow for a kind of extra-poetical kibitzing. And so we read: "(She moved in circles, and those circles moved)" (21).

What do these many circles suggest? One can think back to Emerson's great essay "Circles," which opens: "The eye is the first circle; the horizon which it forms is the second; and throughout nature this primary picture is repeated without end. It is the highest emblem in the cipher of the world. St. Augustine described the nature of God as a circle whose centre was everywhere and its circumference nowhere" (*Essays and Lectures,* 403). Nature is all circles, a repeating sequence of them; the circle, indeed, represents infinity, and I think Roethke (who found Emerson a continuing inspiration) takes us beyond this particular woman that he once knew, reaching toward some Platonic ideal of Woman. She is the ideal, moving in discrete circles; but this movement plays into the circular movements of the universe, embracing time itself, which is finally a circular movement that suggests endless renewal, as when the sun rises and falls and rises again. The whole universe becomes a sequence of interlocking circles.

By the last stanza, Roethke has opened the door widely to metaphysical speculation. We no longer occupy the realm of this poet's recollection of a single, beautiful woman, somebody with whom he had an erotic connection.

The woman he once knew has drawn the poet up the ladder of creation itself, rising from matter to spirit. We move from physical love to eternal love. The final stanza opens with almost biblical phrasing, with a sweeping rhythm: "Let seed be grass, let grass turn into hay" (22). This is not the same voice we began with. It's the voice of Poetry. Roethke reaches for huge generalization, telling the reader (or telling himself) to let the cycle of life, the circle of creation, complete its business. Seeds, of course, become grass. With the ripe field in full maturity, one "mows" the grass, which ultimately turns to hay. We're in the cycle now of what William Blake calls Generation: the realm of creation. One thinks again of Frost in "Mowing," with that totalizing final image: "My long scythe whispered and left the hay to make" (*Poetry of Robert Frost,* 17). Hay is dead grass, and it bakes in the sun, "making." It is fed to the animals. It becomes seed again in due course, as the wheel of creation turns.

The intriguing next line takes us in a wholly different, confessional direction: "I'm martyr to a motion not my own" (23). The poet steps before us, admitting that he has lost control of the "motion," the animating rhythms of life. He has been completely in thrall to this woman so lovely in her bones. He has lost himself. But he can hardly restrain himself now: the process of creation must continue. The sexual drive is a drive for procreation, for generation. It involves the genitals, from the Latin root meaning people, *gens.* One can't stop oneself from propagation. The cycle of creation pulls us into its sweep and draws us forward. We're all martyrs to a motion not our own.

From here, Roethke moves to a consideration of "freedom." What does it mean to be free when, in fact, one has been martyred to a motion that isn't your own? Freedom is the freedom of formal verse, perhaps: the affirming limits of pentameters that rhyme, of six-line stanzas that adhere to a particular scheme. One looks for freedom within these boundaries, not in free verse. But freedom is a gift, the poet suggests. "What's freedom for?" He answers his own question now: "To know eternity" (24). In another words, it would be impossible to understand freedom without limits. Limits define the possibilities for motion, thought, even action. Without engaging in these formal attachments, without dancing with the other, without being caught up in the great motions of the universe, we could not really know anything about freedom and its function.

The next line has a kinship with other well-known lines in Roethke: "I swear she cast a shadow white as stone" (25). This poet has referred to whiteness before, and to stones. "His look drained the stones," we read in "The Lost Son," referring to the father, whose disparaging glance sucked all erotic life from the adolescent boy. In the same poem we read, "Goodbye, goodbye, old stones, the time-order is going." In that line, the stones represent reality itself, the grit of matter, which dissolves at last in the final apocalyptic dream of the poet. The next line is appropriately masturbatory: "I have married my hands to perpetual agitation" (*Collected Poems,* 53). Sex and death closely align here, *eros* and *thanatos* in a dance of creation and destruction.

The lovely woman in Roethke's poem casts a shadow, although it's not clear whether this represents a good or a bad thing. It's probably a good thing, as the whiteness might be regarded as a symbol of purity here, a vision of love as one ascends the ladder of creation and lingers on the top rung, almost in heaven. But what does this poet think about eternity? He answers this question with a question: "But who would count eternity in days?" (26). That is, you can't measure time in units of twenty-four hours. Clock time finally collapses. In union with the beloved, time dissolves, and one lives in the eternal present. Or one hopes to live in the eternal present.

Roethke ends "I Knew a Woman" on a lighter note, bringing the reader back into the reality of the actual woman he once knew, the lovemaking and the erotic glow: "These old bones live to learn her wanton ways: / (I measure time by how a body sways)" (27–28). Now the poet is the one with the bones, but he isn't "lovely" in his skeletal frame. He has old bones. He doesn't move easily. He wonders if, in fact, he can keep up with her. And how does he measure himself in time? By how a body sways, watching her move in circles, dancing with her cheek to cheek in the eternal time of the poem, which circles back to the beginning at the end, the mythical serpent swallowing its own tail.

It's hard to believe that a poem could embrace so much. "I Knew a Woman" is Roethke at the peak of his wit and craft, drawing on his deep knowledge of traditional verse forms, allowing the formal pattern to evolve in a way that both defines the poem and enlightens its content. The philosophical depth is here, with a numinous aura at times, especially in the magnificent closing stanza; but the poet refuses to move simply from light to heavy verse. He brightens everything at the end, mixing memory and desire. The poem, with its insistent metrical drive, sucks us into a rhythm that takes us beyond ourselves, that absorbs us into the circles themselves, the motions that we can hardly resist.

29

"First Meditation" and Roethke's Career

DON BOGEN

PUBLISHED ORIGINALLY as a single poem titled "Old Woman's Meditation" in the Fall 1955 issue of *Partisan Review,* "First Meditation" (*Collected Poems,* 151–54) became the opening of the five-poem sequence "Meditations of an Old Woman" in Roethke's *Words for the Wind* three years later. Connections in voice and theme to "Old Lady's Winter Words" from 1952 are apparent, but "First Meditation" and the sequence it opens are best seen more as precursors to Roethke's "North American Sequence" in his last book, *The Far Field* (1964), than as extensions of the earlier poem. "First Meditation" shows the poet's first successful engagement with key themes and techniques that reach their culmination in "North American Sequence," including a significant change in style from the work in meter that dominated his poetry of the early 1950s to a distinctive form of lyrical free verse; the transformation of his way of developing themes from what he called the "tensed-up" (*Selected Letters,* 148) dramatic approach of *Praise to the End!* (1951) into something more rich, flexible, and truly meditative; and new insight into his major concerns of memory and the spiritual journey.

Exploration of different possibilities in the poetic sequence is central in Roethke's career, and "Meditations of an Old Woman" is a pivotal work in his development. In writing methods and in the work on the page, it represents the beginning of Roethke's third and final stage of work with sequences: what might be called the "meditational" mode. In the years immediately before his work on

"Meditations" Roethke built two sequences in conventional forms, "Four for Sir John Davies" and "The Dying Man," from work in notebooks made up of largely disconnected lines in iambic pentameter and iambic trimeter. And before that, through much of the 1940s, Roethke undertook his most experimental work with the sequence: the highly charged autobiographical poetry that began with the original four-poem Lost Son sequence in 1948 and was completed in *Praise to the End!* in 1951.

While "Meditations of an Old Woman" is Roethke's first group of poems that qualify as "meditations," the voice behind them is not very plausibly that of "an old woman." As Jay Parini has noted (158), it would be a stretch to define how the old woman differs significantly from the more autobiographical speaker in Roethke's earlier "Lost Son" and *Praise to the End!* sequences. But listening for the voice of an ostensibly fictional character as he worked in his notebooks was central to his development of a new "meditational" mode. As his notebooks changed in the 1950s from collections of individual lines in meter to longer free-verse units anchored in description and memories, we begin to see passages marked with "OL" (for "Old Lady") and systematic attempts to capture specific scenes like the bus ride in part 2 of "First Meditation" (Notebooks, 39-125, 39–133, 40-151, 40-155). What allowed Roethke to gather this material into individual poems and the sequence as a whole was not so much the female perspective per se as his sense that an aging character would naturally ruminate on her past. And since the figure was loosely based on his mother (*On Poetry and Craft,* 32), he could explore his own memories through elements they shared. This focus led him to add observations and clarify key themes as he reread his notebooks, a method he had not employed earlier. He also developed a new kind of line, longer, slower in pacing, and more rhythmically intricate, that could combine extended lyric description with the insights arising from contemplation of the memories he'd written down: a kind of analytical "re-vision" of the past. Both of these elements make their initial appearance in "First Meditation."

The fundamental concern of "First Meditation" and the sequence it opens is made explicit in the first line of the poem's second stanza: "The spirit moves, but not always upward" (1.8). Section 1 of "First Meditation" sets the stage for the poem by noting two key factors that keep the spirit from moving "upward": the essential entropy of nature and, on the human level, the unstoppable process of aging. Both factors reflect the relentlessness of time, which Roethke stresses by presenting the decline in "while" clauses. As the old woman ponders her condition, the natural world is crumbling around her: stones "loosen"; a tree "tilts" and goes "[t]oppling down an embankment" (1.5–7); shale "slides"; and in a line insistently repeating the long *e* sound like a scream of despair, "The bleak wind eats at the weak plateau" (1.10–11). When Roethke turns to the effects of time on the body at the end of the section, entropy is expressed not through another image of falling but through one of cooling and shrinking: "What's left is light as a seed" (1.18). A seed, of course, has potential for new growth; when Roethke announces "I need an old crone's knowing" (1.19) in the last line of section 1, he is playing on a cliché of recompense: that wisdom grows as the body declines. Yet the fact that he presents this as a "need" makes it clear that neither the speaker nor the poet is anywhere near that goal.

The opening section of "First Meditation" basically outlines the spiritual problem, presenting it in short sentences made up of fairly regular lines and stanzas that can feel impacted with images. Section 2 is longer and looser in approach, giving a new sense of openness and calm. Sentences stretch for several lines, with more extended catalogues of images; line lengths vary more; and there is room for details related to specific scenes and memories, in contrast to the more generalized, quasi-allegorical nouns of the first section. Instead of "stones," "animals," or "the sun," we see a bus with individual characters in it, two song sparrows, men working at a particular task in a greenhouse, two horses, and a "great wooden sleigh" (2.35). Physical movement in the section goes beyond the initial entropic sense of everything falling or shrinking, to reflect more of the range of actual experience, including the undulating up-and-down motion of the bus and a vertical perspective that encompasses both the song sparrows near the top of the greenhouse and the men below. Overall, this section doesn't so much respond to the concerns of section 1 as expand beyond them; the movements of "the spirit" and the need for "knowing" are never mentioned.

Allowing himself to go off in a new direction rather than deal with the problem at hand here, Roethke uncovers a key theme in the poem and in his work as a whole: the idea of two interlocking journeys: one physical, moving forward in time and space; and one mental, moving back in time through memory. This is the part of "First Meditation" that, on the thematic level, points most clearly to Roethke's later work in "North American Sequence," specifically "Journey to the Interior." The notebook work shows Roethke struggling to capture the physical part of the journey, the bus ride, at different times over at least a two-year period. A rereading of the notebooks eventually leads him to the insight that engagement with memory is essential to progress in the present: "To go back to go forward— / That is the meaning of journeys" (Notebooks, 39-140). With this Roethke begins to integrate the past with the present spiritual concerns of the poem.

It's important to note that the greenhouse passage in section 2 does not really answer the question of spiritual progress in an entropic world. It sings beautifully, but it presents little the speaker can claim as "knowledge" except for the memory itself. In the last stanza of the section, Roethke deepens the poem's focus by balancing the old woman's sleepy vision of journeys that never happened—"The ticket mislaid or lost, the gate / Inaccessible" (2.30–31)—with a specific journey in memory, but here too there is only an implied sense of how memory might be a response to spiritual inertia. The progress from the first to the second sections of the poem is anchored more in a change in emotional tone than in argument. The bus ride and the memories here show not so much an "old crone's knowing" (1.19) as her calm incorporation of past experience into her present situation.

That calm of section 2 is developed further in the third section of the poem, where, after the integration of past and present, the old woman and Roethke are ready to approach the question of spiritual progress more overtly. One long sentence, section 3 is the part of the poem that points most clearly toward Roethke's style in "North American Sequence," particularly in "Meditation at Oyster River," which is set in a similar watery environment. Its long, varied lines of languid but complex rhythms and intricate specificity alternate with short, fairly abstract statements in a colloquial voice: "So the spirit tries for another life" (3.7); "So, I suppose, the spirit journeys" (3.14). These two statements break the section into two analogies. The first, which compares the spirit to a crab in a pond, suggests a frustrated spiritual journey, including "sliding slowly backward" as part of the search for "another life" (3.6–7). The second, which compares the spirit to a salmon returning to its spawning ground, also involves initial frustrations in the dead ends of the "back-eddy" and "sandy inlet" (3.10) but represents a considerably more secure sense of progress, as, despite the detours, the fish ends up "[s]till swimming forward" (3.13).

Karl Malkoff draws attention to the two analogies here, but his conclusion that the struggles are both "almost unendurably discouraging" (161) disregards key differences between the creatures, their particular movements, and especially the settings in which they are placed. The complementary metaphors of the enclosed pond suggesting spiritual stagnation (hence the need for "another life" [3.7]) and the river suggesting spiritual progress are ones that Roethke used frequently in *Praise to the End!,* but in "First Meditation" they are less allegorical and more embedded in the actual physical context of the creatures' lives, and the longer lines allow the poet to devote more space to describing them. Alternating casual, understated generalizations with fleshed-out examples, section 3 of "First Meditation" represents a new kind of meditational style in Roethke's work, one in which insights and arguments are not juxtaposed dramatically in the manner of *Praise to the End!* and other earlier sequences but rather seem to arise naturally from the context of memory and observation.

Section 4 opens with another motif that points toward the later work: the "waste lonely places" (4.1) of contemporary urban life. "[T]he edge of smoky cities" in the second line of the section will be echoed in "the edge of the raw cities" in "The Longing" at the start of "North American Sequence" (*Collected Poems,* 181). In the first stanza of section 4, the entropic sense of things declining is brought back, now on a more individual level, connected with aging and daily life: dust in hallways, lint, falling hair. The sense of anxiety in part 1 has become something more like despair built from boredom, with the old woman yearning for a prophetic vision, a "riven tree, or lamb dropped by an eagle" (4.9), that would dispel the inertia, though she knows none is forthcoming. Instead, the opening stanza of section 4 is countered by, first, a catalogue of singing birds, a return and expansion of the bird image from the memory in section 2, this time more specific, with the birds' song not a greenhouse memory but recurring in the present; and, second, a more symbolic encounter with a mystical flame that counteracts the "cold wind" and gives the old woman the confidence to make her final assertion: "In such times, lacking a god, / I am still happy" (4.25–26).

This is a thoroughly hedged assertion of joy in the face of old age and mortality in a godless world. Happiness is not seen as a condition of spirit but as a temporary emotional elation at certain "times," and the old woman's use of "still" here reminds us that this is a struggle. To the question of whether her spirit has begun to move "upward" over the course of the poem, we might respond as she herself does in the first line of "I'm Here," the poem that immediately follows in the sequence: "Is it enough?" (*Collected Poems,* 155). After that initial question, the second poem in "Meditations of an Old Woman" goes on to attack or dismiss the motif of bird song that led to her sense of happiness in "First Meditation." The final lines of "First Meditation" are neither conclusive nor terribly persuasive, but they are not meant to be. Despite the ways in which

"Meditations of an Old Woman" looks forward to Roethke's work in *The Far Field,* as sequences both it and "North American Sequence" later retain a fundamental principle of movement dating back to the Lost Son sequence of the 1940s, what Roethke describes in the essay "Open Letter" as a "cyclic" approach: "There is a perpetual slipping-back, then a going-forward; but there is some 'progress'" (*On Poetry and Craft,* 51).

As Richard Allen Blessing notes, it is typical of the poet to "slip back" between the positive conclusion of one poem in a sequence and the opening of the next (127). "First Meditation" itself generally moves forward from the spiritual stagnation of section 1 but "slips back" into different forms of anxiety and despair in each of the sections that follow, from the worries over uncompleted journeys near the end of section 2, to the crab's sliding backward in 3, to the "waste lonely places" (4.1) in 4. But there is genuine "progress" here, anchored in the way the song sparrows of the past in part 2 are integrated into the present and transformed into the cerulean, the phoebe, and the whippoorwill calling recurrently at morning and evening. The tone has changed from anxiety to a level of assurance. If the old woman's conclusion at the end of "First Meditation" is tentative, it nonetheless represents an important stage in her spiritual growth. And the poem as a whole represents a key stage technically and thematically in Roethke's own exploration of emotional and spiritual movement that will culminate in "North American Sequence."

I Am! Says the Lamb (1961)

30

A Few Thousand Words on Theodore Roethke, Children's Poetry, and Three Poems Concerning Two Turtles (One of Whom Is Named Myrtle)

JOSEPH T. THOMAS JR.

IN "THE Teaching Poet," Theodore Roethke gives us a glimpse into his poetic values. These values are as central to this present essay as they are to Roethke's creative project. And yet as central as these values are, the poems that most directly embody them—his children's poems—are consistently neglected by scholars and critics of his work. "The Teaching Poet" is a short pedagogical essay published in *Poetry* magazine in 1952, nine years before the publication of Roethke's first children's book, *I Am! Says the Lamb*. In the essay, Roethke recommends that teachers encourage their students "to play with sound; to work with a particular stanza form; to begin with strongly stressed simple poems, such as nursery rhymes." He continues (and here is the revelation): "This last is hardest but probably best if the group is young and unspoiled" (*On Poetry and Craft*, 103). Notice the pairing of *to play* and *to work*, and notice that the work of play is hardest when it comes to nursery rhymes, those strongly stressed, simple little poems. Moreover, this lesson is *hardest but probably best* if the students are young.

Again and again in Roethke's prose (collected in *On Poetry and Craft* with excerpts from his notebooks), one finds an articulation of his interest in the simple and the small and the young: the short line, the nursery rhyme, the children's nonsense poem ("I'm going to lecture on confusion," he once told his students. "I'm all for it" [87]). In his notebooks (where one finds, apart from his collections of children's poetry, some of his finest writing), Roethke asks his muse to fill his ears with "slang, japes, stale jokes, but lively and funny, and sad at times, with the sadness of animals, moping bears and other things that live by and below the nose" (94). *The sadness of animals. The small things.* Roethke reflects: "a thing may be small but it need not be a cameo; it may be a cinder in the shoe or the mind's eye" (80). He insists: "A small thing well done is better than the pretentious failure" (78). The small, whether child or beast or poem,[1] is so often summoned by Roethke that one wonders why critics and scholars, equally often, ignore this element in his poetry, why they neglect the children's poems that so immediately emerge from his admittedly Romantic concern with the child and the poetry of childhood.[2] "Poetry," he writes, "is the discovery of the legend of one's youth" (76). And how do we discover this legend? Well, in those same notebooks he recalls "an academic precept which says: never listen to the young." To this he responds, "The reverse should be true: Listen, I say, and listen close" (90). Roethke listened. And when he turned his ear to the young he heard the short, accentual lines of nursery rhymes. Consider: "The decasyllable line is fine for someone who wants to meditate—or maunder. Me, I need something to jump in: hence the spins and shifts, the songs, the rants and howls. The shorter line can still serve us: it did when English was young, and when were children" (93). When Roethke listened (and listened close) to the young, he heard the old meters, whose regular accents, so often separated by a pair of unaccented syllables, prefigured that most maligned of accentual-syllabic foot: the anapest, a foot banished from the realm of "serious poetry"—("Maybe, more age upon me, I'll care for the grave and ceremonious. But I doubt it" [89])—a foot unwelcomed in the leather-bound, dusty leaves of the Canon but quite at home between the colorful cardboard covers of Dr. Seuss, in the exuberant poetry of the playground and nursery.[3]

In *Poetry and Childhood* (2010), editors Morag Styles, Louise Joy, and David Whitley argue that children's poetry is the "Cinderella of children's literature" (xv). If even those invested in children's literature neglect children's poetry, then the world of adult poetry neglects it—like a beautiful, if shabby stepchild—doubly so. In the 2015 *Cambridge History of American Poetry*, Angela Sorby explains, "Children's poetry is often seen as a marginal subfield within the already-somewhat-marginal field of poetry. It is barely studied and barely taught" (425). As if to demonstrate Sorby's claim, this thirteen hundred–page tome contains only two chapters treating children's poetry at length, a chapter on nineteenth-century and another on twentieth-century American children's poetry (by Sorby and myself, respectively). Likewise, readers will find not a single chapter on an individual children's poet, and one could read the lone, extended treatment of Theodore Roethke ("'All the Blessings of This Consuming Chance': Robert Lowell, John Berryman, Theodore Roethke, and the Middle-Generation Poets," by David Wojahn) and close the book ignorant of Roethke's forays into children's poetry.

Roethke's fondness for the small—the child, the little animal, the short line, the anapest, and even the limerick—is apparent in a trio of his best children's poems, "Myrtle," "Myrtle's Cousin," and "Goo-Girl" (*Collected Poems,* 173–74), all of which appear, back-to-back, in *I Am! Says the Lamb.* This tercet of poems is unique, as his other children's poems are stand-alone affairs, linked only by form, style, and theme. Although speaking of Roethke's adult poetry, in "Fifty Years of American Poetry" Randall Jarrell suggests the thematic concerns found—undiluted—in *I Am! Says the Lamb.* He writes, "Many poets are sometimes childish; Roethke, uniquely, is sometimes babyish, though he is a powerful Donatello baby who has love affairs, and whose marsh-like unconscious is continually celebrating its marriage with the whole wet dark underside of things" (326). Two days after Roethke's death on August 1, 1963, Robert Lowell wrote a letter to Beatrice, Roethke's grieving widow. In this letter he echoes Jarrell's insights, speaking of the "Rabelaisian energy" in Roethke's poetry (429). Again, while certainly true of his adult work, this praise applies more directly to Roethke's neglected children's poems, which are small, yet undulating with carnivalesque vigor. The first of the three poems I treat here, "Myrtle," is a two-stanza poem: for the first stanza Roethke gives us a formally exact limerick, while for the second he heeds his own advice from "The Teaching Poet" "to work with a particular stanza form" (*On Poetry and Craft,* 103), offering a playful modification of the form. Written from the perspective of the poet, it tells of Myrtle, a turtle who laments the inadequacy of conventional poetry, the second stanza articulating perfectly Roethke's belief that a "small thing well done is better than the pretentious failure" (*On Poetry and Craft,* 78):

> She would sit with a Book on her Knees,—
> *My* Poetry-Book, if you please,—

She'd Rant and She'd Roar:
"This stuff is a Bore!
Why I could do better
With only ONE Letter,—
These Poets, they write like *I* Sneeze!"

(6–12)

The self-effacing contradiction here is evident: although Myrtle praises the small ("I could do better / With only ONE letter"), Roethke finds that it takes him *two* limericks to communicate this idea. Furthermore, the second limerick-like stanza, featuring Myrtle's words, swells from the middle like a snake that has swallowed a mouse. In this case, our limerick has snacked on an additional, dimetrical couplet: excise that pair of short lines and we'd have a perfect limerick. The joke is simple: Roethke, the poet whose book Myrtle critiques, is not up to the task of writing the well-made yet small cinder of a poem he summoned in his notebooks (you'll recall: "a thing may be small but it need not be a cameo; it may be a cinder in the shoe or the mind's eye or a pain in the neck" [80]). Our little turtle (certainly a pain in Roethke's neck) can outmatch him with a single, burning letter (she needs not even a word, unless it be a kind of Whitmanesque *I*, containing multitudes). Indeed, her *sneeze* alone is equal to the work of "[t]hese poets," a crew that includes Roethke, even as the poem that includes Myrtle's critique exemplifies their shortcomings. Of course, Roethke is also the very poet whose book contains the criticism levied against itself. This kind of postmodern intertextuality and puzzling self-reflexivity is unusual for Roethke, and yet here we find it in the seemingly simple nonsense poetry section of his first children's book.

You'll remember Roethke's claim about the short line: "I need something to jump in: hence the spins and shifts, the songs, the rants and howls" (*On Poetry and Craft,* 93). The poetic power of Myrtle's Rabelaisian sneeze—more akin to a howl than a song, summoned here at the end of her "Rant" (and her "Roar")—is a vocalization that, appropriately, does not need even "ONE letter" (11). It returns in "Goo-Girl," the last of this trio of poems (the middle poem, which we'll get to in a moment, is called "Myrtle's Cousin"). However, in "Goo-Girl" this sneeze is transubstantiated into a carnivalesque fart. Aside from the opening two feet (an iamb and an anapest: *Poor Myrtle would sigh*) the speaker of "Goo-Girl" is Myrtle, her language again prefaced by Roethke's own. (Both "Myrtle" and "Goo-Girl" begin with Roethke and end with Myrtle: Roethke leaving her words to stand on their own, unremarked upon. Myrtle always gets the last word.) After Roethke's four-word introduction, Myrtle spends the rest of the sixteen-line poem reflecting on the revolting habits of her cousin (who is also the subject of "Myrtle's Cousin"). Myrtle complains,

> The *Things* you do, Nobody does:
> Putting Egg in your Shoe
> And then making Goo,
> Which, with Slobbers and Snorts,
> You drink up in Quarts;
> And that Gravy and Fat
> All over your Hat,—
> How *Did* you do *That*?
> When you Slurp and go, Poof!
> The Cat runs for a Roof
> Clear under the Chair;
> And your friends,—how they Stare!
>
> (2–13)

Here Roethke revels in the gross-out tradition of playground poetry.[4] The opening, nonverbal "sigh" recalls the "sneeze" found in "Myrtle." And yet—as I suggested above—that selfsame, explosive sneeze returns, although inverted, in the body of "Goo-Girl" (the poem), where Roethke presents for his young reader an uncharacteristically scatological fart (articulated onomatopoetically via the slightly more genteel "Poof"). Within these short lines of chaotically alternating iambic and anapestic feet (with which Roethke "spins and shifts" accentually), the body of the Goo-Girl (the turtle) howls and sneezes and farts: Roethke provides his young reader with a poetry of the flesh, not the spirit. Still, it's a poetry suggestive of a profane reimagining of the etymological roots of *spirit*: the Latin *spirare*, to breathe. Myrtle's cousin—reptilian, hard, clumsy, slow, cold-blooded—slurps, exhales from below (*Poof!*), and frightens the cat—mammalian, soft, agile, mercurial—who "runs for a Roof" (here a sublime bit of nonsense) "Clear under the Chair" (11–12).[5]

Although Myrtle the turtle addresses the eponymous "Goo-Girl" with a disapproving sigh, the poem works, not unlike Shel Silverstein's famous "Sarah Cynthia Sylvia Stout Would Not Take the Garbage Out," by reveling in that which it condemns. In Silverstein's poem the protracted catalogue of

> bacon rinds and chicken bones,
> Drippy ends of ice cream cones,
> Prune pits, peach pits, orange peel,
> Gloppy glumps of cold oatmeal

(etc.) animates the poem, not the ostensible didacticism of "always take the garbage out!" (70–71). Likewise, thirteen years before Silverstein, Roethke delights readers by describing the Goo-Girl's transgressions with a Rabelaisian attention to detail.

This same attention to detail drives the second poem in our triad, "Myrtle's Cousin." Another queer pair of limerick-like stanzas, "Myrtle's Cousin" alone is entirely written in the poet's voice, and thus serves as a nice pivot between the multivoiced poems that precede and follow. As in "Myrtle," the first stanza conforms almost perfectly to the limerick form, while the second plays with it strangely, even as it plays with syntax and line break in disorienting ways:

> She'd Dunk and She'd Gubble:
> She *was* so much Trouble;
> And then without even a Spoon,
> She'd *Muddle* the Whole Afternoon
> What her Friends *Couldn't* Eat at those Lunches!
> (6–10)

The rhyme scheme is peculiar: traditionally limericks end by rhyming the final line with the first (or simply repeating the first line), but here the final line repeats the final word of the first stanza (which ends, "Oh that Cousin! Her Manners! At Lunches!" [5]).

Similarly peculiar are the lines leading to the poem's finish. Appropriately for a poem about a turtle, Roethke performs in this final stanza a formalistic shell game. Traditionally, the third and fourth line of a limerick contain two feet, usually an iamb and an anapest (but sometimes two anapests), as in these lines by Edward Lear:

> She purchased some clogs, [iamb; anapest]
> and some small spotty dogs [anapest; anapest]

or

Two Owls and a Hen, [iamb; anapest]
four Larks and a Wren. [iamb; anapest]

(157)[6]

But the final couplet in "Myrtle's Cousin" has *three* feet per line:

And then [iamb] | without e [anapest] | -ven a Spoon [anapest],

a structure he repeats:

She'd Mudd [iamb] | -le the Whole [anapest] | Afternoon [anapest].

However, Roethke has played a trick on us, a lyrical sleight of hand. After drafting this essay, I discussed it with Michael Heyman, a scholar and writer of literary nonsense. Michael pointed out that the second limerick-stanza in "Myrtle's Cousin" begins, oddly enough, in the middle: the first two lines of the second poem are the dimetrical lines one expects to find in the third and fourth position of a traditional limerick. Again:

She'd Dunk and she'd Gubble;
She *was* so much Trouble.

Thus, one *should* anticipate a trimetrical closer to follow; the second stanza, that is, could be characterized as a headless limerick, with the first two lines of anapestic trimeter surgically removed. Of course, Roethke—in this, the middle poem of his turtle trio—telescopes that final, closing line into *three.* As a master of the shell game, however, he hides the triad with that distracting spoon/afternoon couplet, a formal gambit usually deployed before a final, trimetrical line. Roethke's trimetrical couplet serves as more than a con artist's misdirection. Featuring one two- and two three-syllable feet, it is also a perfect pivot point, leading with flawless rhythm into the rhythmically strange final line of the poem. This final line suggests that Myrtle's Cousin is so rude and irritating that she causes the poet to mar his own otherwise perfectly anapestic conclusion. With one italicized *Couldn't* Roethke shifts from anapestic trimeter into a hiccupping verse of anapest, amphimacer, anapest, concluding, as limericks are wont, with a little unaccented turtle tail of a feminine ending.

The middle poem ends, then, with three lines of three feet, the final line, as I noted earlier, repeating the final word of the first limerick stanza ("Lunches!"). However, it *also* rhymes perfectly with the final line of "Goo-Girl" ("And they'll soon stay away in Great Bunches!" [16]), formally lashing the two poems together, even as "Myrtle" and "Goo-Girl" (the first and third of our trio) echo each other via their more general deployment of voice: *poet speaks*, then *Myrtle speaks*. This sort of metrical and formalistic play, a kind of polyrhythmic dancing, is a master class in both the short line and the short poem, just as it's a classically beautiful illustration of poetic sequence: each poem is perfect on its own, but as a trio, the whole—if you'll excuse the cliché—is greater than the sum of its parts.

These three poems get to the heart of Roethke's playful exuberance, as evident in his essays and notebooks (quoted below from *On Poetry and Craft*) as in his poetry. Roethke writes, "It is the prerogative of old witches to stink: part of their stock and trade as it were" (64). Likewise, it is the prerogative of Roethke to write a Rabelaisian poetry of short lines "shot through with appeals to the unconsciousness, to the fears and desires that go far back into our childhood, into the imagination of the race" (70). It's his stock and trade, as it were, this sort of verse: a poetry within which he can jump, a poetry with verses that spin and shift, that facilitate rant, howl, and song (or sneeze, sigh, and fart). These three poems insist (as does Roethke) "that rhythm is the entire movement, the flow, the recurrence of stress and unstress that is related to the rhythms of the blood, the rhythms of nature" (69). They remind us, yes, that "[t]he shorter line can still serve us: it did when English was young, and when we were children" (93), but they remind us too that Roethke's most unassuming and tiny poems, those that he wrote for the "young and unspoiled" (103), are at the heavy heart of his poetics. His children's poems, like some dark yet massive star, lie at the center of his constellation of poetry, giving it form and structure. And it is there, to that star, that we ought to train our telescopes. For it's a star that has much to teach us.

NOTES

1. And, yes, I understand that the concatenation of *small*, *animal*, and *beast* is a bit distasteful, but I'm reminded of the great Leslie Fiedler, who, in *Freaks: Myths and Images of the Secret Self* (1978), notes of children: "Born unhousebroken and half wild, dabbling in their own feces and popping into their mouths whatever unlikely object they can grab, they remain for a long time unsure . . . whether they are beasts or men: little animals more like their pets than their parents" (28). Although these lines were written fifteen years after Roethke's death, I can't see Roethke disagreeing with the sentiment they express, a sentiment that informs at least two of the three poems I'll be discussing in a moment, and probably all three.

2. In *Midcentury Quartet: Bishop, Lowell, Jarrell, Berryman, and the Making of a Postmodern Aesthetic* (1999), Thomas Travisano argues that Roethke is more Romantic than

the quartet named in his title. While Travisano admits that all four were "preoccupied with . . . the wonder and darkness of childhood," he explains that they "found Roethke's work significantly more romantic" than theirs (17). But if he is Romantic (and he is), then Roethke is darkly so, less interested in the sunshiny innocence of youth than he is interested in "its vagaries, its ambiguous loyalties, its special poignance" (*On Poetry and Craft,* 105). As we see in "Goo-Girl," Roethke summons a childhood less at home skipping across sun-dappled meadows than it is among the "[l]eaf-mold, manure, lime" and "stinks" of the "rank" yet fecund "Root Cellar," in the poem by that title—"dank as a ditch"—his children that lively kind who nonetheless play underground, breathing, along with the dirt, their "small breath" (*Collected Poems,* 36).

3. In *Dr. Seuss: American Icon* (2003), Philip Nel notes that Dr. Seuss's nearly exclusive use of the anapest, forever associated with the limerick, has much to do with "why Seuss is rarely studied as a poet" (20). (Seuss's first *Cat* book came out in 1957, his second the next year. *I Am! Says the Lamb,* Roethke's first collection of children's poetry, was released in 1961, and *Party at the Zoo,* his second, in 1963.) Nel calls the limerick "the punch line of poetic forms," and notes that Seuss's poetry is commonly dismissed as doggerel by virtue of being anapestic (20–21). Surely this tendency to dismiss applies to those who study Roethke, as scholars and critics and biographers hold his limericks at arm's length as an embarrassment hardly worth mentioning.

4. For more on playground poetry, see my essay "Child Poets and the Poetry of the Playground" (2004).

5. The comma after "go" allows for another reading: "When you Slurp and go" could be a colloquial articulation of "When you slurp and *leave,*" the "Poof!" representing that cartoonish puff of smoke left behind, say, by a quickly exiting Road Runner. What we have here is a nice, nonsensical ambiguity: either a genteel fart or the image of conventionally slow turtle moving off stage so quickly that she appears to vanish in a puff of smoke (*Poof!*). Finally, although I'd prefer not to, one could also read "go" in another scatological sense: Myrtle eats and then "goes" (a childish phrasing of "to go to the restroom"). The Goo goes in; the Goo goes out. This last, unsavory interpretation certainly evokes a spectacle worthy of the final line: "And your friends—how they Stare!"

6. Lear's limericks have four lines instead of the conventional five, collapsing the third and fourth lines into a longer third line. The couplets quoted here actually appear as single lines.

The Far Field (1964)

31

"The Longing"

Alienation, Place, and the Desire for Home

KATHARINE BUBEL

> I have long wanted to say,
> just once before I die,
> *I am home.*
>
> —Sam Hamill, "A Lover's Quarrel"

IN SEPTEMBER 1950, near the end of a leave from teaching at the University of Washington, Theodore Roethke was staying with his widowed mother at his childhood home in Saginaw, Michigan. There he purchased a new car "right off the floor" of a dealership (Seager, 172) and drove it to Seattle, where he had been living for the past three years. Afterwards, he wrote in an unsent letter: "Here I don't know just how the material will be resolved but for next or possibly later book will be a happy journey westward—not along the Oregon Trail but on Route 2; in a word, a symbolical journey in my cheap Buick Special toward Alaska and, at least in a spiritual sense toward the east of Russia . . . whence came my own people, the Prussians" (qtd. in Seager, 194). The northernmost cross-continental highway in the United States, Route 2 runs in its western sweep from the Great Lakes and North Woods country, through the

Great Plains and the Rocky Mountains, and into the Pacific Northwest. Roethke had told his mentor Kenneth Burke in the previous year that he was in search of a larger narrative framework for his poetry (*Selected Letters,* 147). This road trip provided him with an expansive possibility. Although he did not develop it right away, the memory unfolded in the "North-West" imagery and quest plot of his "North American Sequence" (Seager, 269).

Composed of six long lyrics published consecutively between 1959 and 1963 and compiled by Roethke just before his death, "North American Sequence" was published posthumously in *The Far Field* (1964).[1] It continues his personal myth, begun in the fourteen-poem Lost Son sequence, "from the vantage point of middle age" (Staples, 190). In "Open Letter" (1950), collected in *On Poetry and Craft,* Roethke describes his Lost Son sequence as a "history of the psyche (or allegorical journey)": "a succession of experiences" of "slipping-back, then a going-forward," of descent into the sub- or unconscious where "agitation and exhaustion" (50–51) is followed by reemergence after some redeeming memory or experience. Likewise, the progress of his aging quest-hero in "North American Sequence" involves a series of retrograde cycles of descent into the past through meditative memory and return to the present.

In its broadest outline, the sequence's circular journey is oriented around the general west-east / east-west axis of a highway. This orientation reflects the cycle of the sun rising in the east and arcing westward across the sky to setting, and so the sequence's journey taps into the atavistic memory of the quest archetype. As Northrop Frye asserts in his 1951 essay "The Archetypes of Literature," the circular quest is the literary analogue of the ritual-myth, in which "a figure who is partly the sun, partly vegetative fertility and partly a god or archetypal human being" undertakes a circular journey.[2] According to Frye, the myth expresses the human desire to synchronize with and "recapture a lost rapport with the natural cycle" (15–16). Analogue of the latent myth's oracular vision, the "dream" of art in Frye's view is "the search of the libido or desiring self for a fulfillment that will deliver it from the anxieties of reality but will still contain that reality" (*Anatomy of Criticism,* 193). A notebook entry Roethke made in the early 1950s chimes with Frye's statement: "A poetry of longing: not for escape, but for a greater reality" (*Straw for the Fire,* 193).

The title of the opening poem of "North American Sequence," "The Longing" (*Collected Poems,* 181–83), denotes the stimulus of the quest: yearning desire. "Longing" also bears root associations with spatial distance and temporal deferral ("long"), as indicated in two other titles in the sequence, "The Long Waters" and "The Far Field," as well as in the opening lines of "Journey to the Interior": "In the long journey out of the self, / There are many detours" (*Collected Poems,* 187). But if desire propels the questing hero on an inner journey afar to his father- and motherland and back, what is its specific object? Drawing on Frye, I propose it is an echo of that mythic longing for rapport with nature. M. H. Abrams shows in *Natural Supernaturalism* (1971) that in their project to reconstitute the Judeo-Christian myth, Roethke's European and British Romantic precursors sought "to announce the certainty, or at least the possibility, of a rebirth in which a renewed mankind will inhabit a renovated earth where he will find himself thoroughly at home" (12). For this task, poets employed the genre of the representative "spiritual autobiography," and Roethke, along with other contemporaries, likewise reclaimed it for his own time and place (*On Poetry and Craft,* 32).

More particularly, I take the object of "The Longing" as the poet-speaker's desire to be home in his Pacific Northwest place.[3] Sam Hamill, in his response poem, "A Lover's Quarrel" (dedicated "after Roethke"), both identifies with and rebukes Roethke's struggle with being there.[4] Indeed, Roethke's biographer Allan Seager reveals that, for various reasons, such as bouts of manic-depressive disorder, feelings of economic insecurity, and physical ailments, including acute arthritis pain exacerbated by the wet climate (251), he "did not feel himself settled" in the Pacific Northwest at the time of his 1950 letter (194). Even after his marriage to his former student Beatrice O'Connell in 1953, he was restless. Through the years of their marriage, the couple changed residence several times in the Seattle region, traveled in Europe, and sojourned in Great Britain.

The *Oxford English Dictionary*'s definition of "home" in its nominal form includes "[a] refuge, a sanctuary; a place or region to which one naturally belongs or where one feels at ease." The word "belong" is cognate with "longing," denoting connection and relationship, ever a primary occupation in Roethke's developing poetic myth: relationships among the self, the father, the beloved, the land or nature, and God. Although all these come into play in "North American Sequence," "The Longing" shows that the quest for home is centered on relationship with the natural environment of his place. The quest-hero seeks to locate within it a "quiet" centre or *axis mundi* in which the eternal intersects with the present, that he might, as in "The Rose," come "upon the true ease of myself" (*Collected Poems,* 199). But as Hamill depicts it, the way is arduous, for the alienated self cannot easily "persuade this battered earth / to let [him] make it home" (15).

"The Longing" inaugurates the quest in three stages. The opening lines of the first section, "On things asleep, no balm: / A kingdom of stinks and sighs" (1.1–2), immediately signal the archetypal quest-myth, which typically opens with the "kingdom" in a state of inertia and decay (as in T. S. Eliot's *The Waste Land* or W.H. Auden's *The Age of Anxiety*). The allusion "no balm" refers to the prophetic lament "Is there no balm in Gilead?" (Jer. 8:22 [KJV]). This "balm," a fragrant resin with medicinal properties, was for the prophet "a symbol for healing and relief from national and spiritual distress," and was taken up into Christian and literary typology (Wauhkonen, 71). With no agent of healing at hand, the wasteland is "one of the modern hells" of alienation and despair described by Roethke in his 1963 lecture "On Identity" (*On Poetry and Craft*, 36). Its "stinks" include "[f]etor of cockroaches, dead fish, petroleum, / Worse than castoreum of mink or weasels" (1.3–4), fuming "slag-heaps," and foul and fowl-scavenged "garbage" (1.15–16). Along with the assonance in "fetor" and "dead," the association by assonance, alliteration, and internal rhyme between "cockroaches," "petroleum," and "castoreum" links what is repulsive to the senses with economic degradation and pollution, the injurious effects of industry.

The juxtaposition of the two kinds of extracted oil signals the continuity of the oil industry with the fur trade, a mixed history on both the national and regional scales. Recalling Roethke's interest in the Oregon Trail, this history includes the fur trade routes–cum–wagon trails, now highways like Route 2, originally the hunting paths of the Native Americans who are mentioned in the conclusion of the poem. Roethke had been researching and making notes for a possible epic poem "dealing with the injustices done to the Indians and based on an automobile journey across the continent where he would pass the site of each tribe's final defeat or betrayal" (Seager, 279). His application for a Ford Foundation grant, awarded in early 1959 as he began to compose "North American Sequence," speaks of "the guilts we Americans feel for our mistakes and misdeeds in history," as well as "our manias, our despairs; our furtive joys" (qtd. in Seager, 257–58). The influence of his research will turn up again in the third section.

At this point in the poem, the historical implications blend with matters more personal in the "sighs" of the following lines.[5] The lines "Saliva dripping from warm microphones" and "Agony of crucifixion on barstools" (1.5–6) may be compared with images from Kenneth Rexroth's elegy for Dylan Thomas, "Thou Shalt Not Kill" (1953), or Allen Ginsberg's Rexroth-influenced "Howl" (1955). Both rail against the modern Moloch, industrial-capitalist society, in which the poet is a prophet without honor in his own country. Indeed, there may be in the following quartet something of an elegy for Roethke's friend Thomas, whose death in 1953 left him shocked (Seager, 220; *On Poetry and Craft,* 157):

> Less and less the illuminated lips,
> Hands active, eyes cherished;
> Happiness left to dogs and children—
> (Matters only a saint mentions!)
>
> (1.7–10)

The reference to "dogs and children" may allude to Thomas's collection of short stories concerning his childhood, entitled *Portrait of the Artist as a Young Dog* (1948). The saint and the Romantic poet agree with the prophet's vision: that "a little child shall lead" in a renewed and peaceable kingdom (Isa. 11:6 [KJV]). For now, though, innocence is lost and "[l]ust fatigues the soul" ("The Longing" 1.11). The speaker asks, "How to transcend this sensual emptiness?" then employs an adverbial variant of the title word as a pun concerning the temporal delay of unfulfilled desire: "(Dreams drain the spirit if we dream too long)" (1.12–13).

In 1957, a difficult year in which the settings for the first two poems of the sequence were conceived, Roethke was distressed over Beatrice's ill health: mild tuberculosis, for which she was committed to care in a sanatorium in the spring (Seager, 241). Just before her release they purchased their first home on Lake Washington, stirring mixed emotions in him, including economic anxiety (Roethke, *Selected Letters,* 214). That summer, prior to a vacation on Orcas Island (in the San Juan Islands) and a trip north to Oyster River, Vancouver Island (Seager, 243–44), they visited the industrial south of Seattle. This is a likely source of the imagery of exhaustion viewed by the alienated speaker at "the edge of the raw cities" (1.15). As Seattle's long winter rainy season brought "draining" physical and psychic pain for Roethke, it was clearly difficult to endure: "In a bleak time, when a week of rain is a year" (1.14). Such details of the poet's struggle underscore the psychological and geographical entwining of place expressed in this section. It concludes with a stanza in which the only movement is retreat, as the spirit "shrinks into a half-life," pictured in those creatures of rainy days,

a slug, a loose worm
Ready for any crevice,
An eyeless starer.

(1.20–23)

With play on the implied homonym of eye/I, as Peter Balakian observes, the speaker is "without [a] center" of self and place (138).

The second section marks the beginning of the hero's quest, whose efforts, by the sequence's end, will be analogous to what Frye calls the myth-ritual's "victory of fertility over the waste land" (*Anatomy of Criticism,* 193). The first two lines enact a sudden shift: "A wretch needs his wretchedness. Yes. / O pride, thou art a plume upon whose head?" Delivered in conventionally formal phrasing at odds with the rest of the poem, they achieve a mocking tone. Still, relinquishment of egoism, and self-pity with it, is a kind of death and purgation. Full "felicity" follows, and sorrow turns to dancing in "[a] body with the motion of a soul." This synergy precipitates the ecstatic movement lacking in the previous section, instigating "a dark dream" with space to "breathe in," a signal of inspiration. Then comes epiphany: "The rose exceeds, the rose exceeds us all" (2.1–6), the repetition underscoring this pivotal image that foretells fulfillment of the sequence's quest-cycle in "The Rose." In Roethke's personal myth, the rose is associated with his father's Michigan hothouses but also, in a long literary tradition, with transcendent love. It stands as his *axis mundi*, analogous to what Evelyn Underhill names "the Secret Rose" of the mystic way, signifying that participation "here and now" in the eternal is the "secret plan of Creation [that] flames out, had we eyes to see, from every department of existence" (447–48).[6] As Dante's river of flame becomes the Empyrean rose in canto 30 of *Paradiso* and Eliot's fire and rose "are one" in "Little Gidding" (*Collected Poems,* 209), so in "The Longing" Roethke entwines his visionary rose with the "great flame" rising out of the depths of the sea, perhaps just after sunset (2.8).

The first-person singular, unused until this moment, along with a play on the homonyms "hear" and "here," announces the call to adventure of the hero: "The light cries out, and I am there to hear" (2.9). It declares *fiat homo* ("let there be man"), for the illumination marks the conception of what Underhill calls "a new and embryonic consciousness" (448), evoked in the shapes of emergent life, "[b]are as a bud, and naked as a worm" (2.11). "Bud" and "worm" are also phallic, contrasting with the earlier "loose worm" and evoking the libido, the life force that unites and enlivens body and spirit, as in the sacramental eros or "epithalamic mysticism" of his love poems (Bowers, 122).[7] The following stanza of antiphonal lines pictures the self as a turgid "stalk" (2.13), reminiscent of the "sticks" whose "urge, wrestle, [and] resurrection" in *The Lost Son* lyric "Cuttings (*later*)" convey the same sense of "beginnings" (*Collected Poems,* 35).

The declaration preceding the stanza, "I'd be beyond; I'd be beyond the moon" (2.10), again recalls Dante, for in the metaphorical cosmological order of *Paradiso* the hero ascends through the spheres above the sublunary earth and "beyond the moon." Indeed, we find Roethke's speaker in the lunar "first heaven of knowing" in "Meditation at Oyster River" (*Collected Poems,* 185). In his earlier poem "The Vigil" (a play on the name of Dante's poet guide, Virgil) Roethke calls on Dante to help him affirm the potential of his desire: "All lovers live by longing, and endure: / Summon a vision and declare it pure" (*Collected Poems,* 103). The great poet of erotic spirituality comes to his aid here, too, as the "other" he seeks to embrace "is nature" (H. Williams, 147).

But if Dante is the predominant influence of the second section, Whitman, joined later by William Carlos Williams, is the guiding presence of the third. There is a shift in the aim of direction from upward to down, for in Roethke's myth, in order to ascend, the hero must first descend in the archetypal *katabasis.* This is not a plunge further into hell, but rather a way out of the modern hell of alienation from place. Roethke, who once identified eros as "embracer of life" (qtd. in Sullivan, 70), engages here, as elsewhere in the sequence, in depicting the Whitmanesque "urge" of what might be called environmental eros, an intense form of "topophilia." Employing two of his favored techniques borrowed from Whitman, the catalogue and participial forms (Roethke, *On Poetry and Craft,* 73), Roethke's speaker recounts an anaphoric litany of natural shapes beginning with "I would" and featuring "-ing" words such as "dancing," "widening," and "growing." His previous elided expression of desire, "I'd be beyond" (2.10), now becomes full-throated, with emphasis on "would" rather than "beyond."

Roethke's hero desires to be with those northern, migrating creatures, "blackening salmon" and "mad lemmings," images of being-toward-death, as much as with "[t]he children dancing, the flowers widening," images of regeneration (3.1–2). Whitman's use of catalogue, as Rosemary Sullivan explains, juxtaposes various "particulars" to emphasize "fluency, candor, unpremeditated attention and assimilation, inclusiveness" (167). With such a technique, the poet-hero wants to purge himself of the effects of "exasperation, all the distortions of malice and hatred" (3.4), all feelings associated with the "kingdom of stinks and sighs" (1.2) that are hindrances to the marriage of spirit and place. "Who sighs from far away?" eschews distancing despondency for embrace (3.3). He "would believe" what his pain has to teach him and "delight in [his] hands." The "excessive bird" balanced by "the branch singing" pictures the integration of the poet. With "eye quiet on the growing rose," the vision that sustains him, he makes the only explicit statement concerning the titular longing: "I long for the imperishable quiet at the heart of form" (3.5–7). In the spirit of Whitman, this desire is grounded in affirmation of the body and nature's processes, a "delighting in the redolent disorder of this mortal life" (3.9). "Redolent" notably implies fragrance opposed to the "stinks" and "fetor" of the wasteland.

"I would be a stream, winding between great striated rocks in late summer" (3.8), with the alliteration of "stream and "striated," suggests effortless movement of the mind's energy in the groove of life's terrain. The image also conjures the flow of time, as the quest-hero is aging. In this light, the stream anticipates the place where river meets the sea, a symbol of life flowing into death, in the sequence's recurring composite Pacific Northwest estuarine setting first introduced in the following "Meditation at Oyster River." Beatrice remembers that Roethke particularly "loved" being on the shoreline of the Salish Sea, "respond[ing] to the beauty" (qtd. in *Remarkable People*) of this liminal region that is the contemplative locus of "the final man," what Frye calls the quest-hero as *penseroso* (*Anatomy of Criticism,* 202). "Meditation at Oyster River" loops back to connect with this third section of "The Longing" by way of the speaker's continued catalogue of coastal biota and his declaration "With these I would be" (*Collected Poems,* 185). The repeated "would" in both poems underscores the longing for "attachment to place by immersion" that will continue to propel the questing hero forward (Sullivan, 150). The water imagery in both poems presents that early stage in the quest of the archetypal night journey sometimes referred to as "the belly of the whale" (Campbell 90)[8] and described by Frye as the passage from death to life (*Anatomy of Criticism,* 192). This is signified in "The Longing" when the conception of the will in section 2 and its birth in section 3 is summarized briefly in the short lines

> This ambush, this silence,
> Where shadow can change into flame,
> And the dark be forgotten,

followed by that pivotal statement, "I have left the body of the whale, but the mouth of the night is still wide" (3.10–13).[9]

Expelled like Jonah onto dry land, the quest-hero heads by memory southeastward in the night, "[o]n the Bullhead, in the Dakotas" (3.14). The "Bullhead" is a return to the 1950 road trip idea, shifting to a more southern highway through the Great Plains instead of Route 2 (Dougherty, 188). In the sequence, the quest-hero must travel to his father- and motherland to recover the lost treasure from childhood, symbolized in the rose, by which he will reconcile with his place. The way lies through a parched interior. The sensory associations of the prairies and steppes contrast starkly with the fluvial bioregion in the Great Lakes watershed, mirror of the Pacific Northwest estuarine. "[T]he Dakotas," home of the Oglala Lakota, are "the country of few lakes," "buffalo grass," and "clay buttes" (3.14–15). Beyond alluding to the mythic antithesis of arid wasteland–fecund paradise that subtends the sequence, the hero's choice to be an "Iroquois" over "Ogalala" (*sic;* 3.21–22) in the enigmatic four-line ending of the poem locates the coming *anagnorisis* in the Great Lakes region of the poet's own origin. The "stench" of decaying dead buffalo and their excrement in "the summer heat" (3.17) recalls the sterile "kingdom of stinks and sighs" (1.2), raising again the specter of alienation from the land entailed in the socioeconomic and environmental "guilts" entangled with the pride of the nation. Such alienation correlates with the wounding injustices against Native Americans in the nation's past that Roethke was considering at the time of the sequence's conception, including the failure to value their intimate knowledge of the land (Barillas, *Midwestern Pastoral,* 134). His quest-hero seeks to rectify the error when he declares, "Old men should be explorers? / I'll be an Indian" (3.19–20). It is a clear rejoinder to Eliot's statement in the final part of "East Coker" (*Four Quartets*): "Old men ought to be explorers / Here and there does not matter" (*Collected Poems,* 189). The implicit argument is that "here or there" does matter to the spiritual explorer. Knowledge of the place in which one wants to be home is not an abstracted affair (Barillas, *Midwestern Pastoral,* 133).

Returning to the unsent letter in which Roethke outlined his plans for the road trip material, it is worth noting that it was likely meant for his mentor William Carlos Williams, with whom he was corresponding at the time (*Selected Letters,* 165). In it he alludes to Eliot's *The Waste Land* by way of eschewing "the boring footnote or the pretentious allusion" (qtd. in Seager, 194). Roethke joined Williams in his grievances over Eliot's perceived abandonment of American culture through "abstraction, elitism, and Eurocentricism" (Barillas, *Midwestern Pastoral,* 114). Williams insisted, "Place is the only reality. . . . [W]e do not have to abandon our familiar and known to achieve distinction" (qtd. in Barillas, *Midwestern Pastoral,* 114). In 1959, as Roethke was working on "North American Sequence," he vowed to take the "Whitmanesque meditative thing," as he describes Eliot's *Four Quartets,* "and use it for other ends, use it as well or better" (*Selected Letters,* 231).

"Better" meant, among other things, embracing his present American place. In the opening of the final poem of the sequence, "The Rose," he states this explicitly:

> There are those to whom place is unimportant,
> But this place, where sea and fresh water meet,
> Is important.
>
> (*Collected Poems,* 196)

Fittingly, then, his quest-hero is reminiscent of the idealized Daniel Boone of Williams's *In the American Grain* (1925), who explores "with primal lust to grow close to [the land], to understand it and to be part of its mysterious movements, like an Indian," in order "to be *himself* in a new world, Indianlike" (136–37). By choosing to be an Iroquois, Roethke's quest-hero wants to find his temporal and spatial present to be, in Williams's phrase, "the land of heart's desire" (139). This longing echoes in the quest-hero's affirmation in "The Rose," after a return journey brings him to his Salish Sea estuary: "Beautiful my desire, and the place of my desire" (*Collected Poems,* 198). His declaration affirms both the object of his longing, a peaceful center embodied in "The Longing" as a "growing rose" (3.5), and the Pacific place he now calls home. Just as in "The Rose" a wild "rose in the sea-wind . . . [s]tays in its true place" (*Collected Poems,* 197), so in "The Longing" a vision of blossoming helps to stay him.

NOTES

1. "The Longing" was published in November 1959, the second and third poems, "Meditation at Oyster River" and "Journey to the Interior," while Roethke was living in England in 1960–61 (Seager, 269, 271). A trip to San Juan Island in the summer of 1961 helped inspire the remaining three poems, "The Long Waters" and "The Far Field," completed and published in 1962, and "The Rose," in 1963 (Seager, 272; Roethke, *Selected Letters,* 246). See Staples's essay for publishing details (189n1). Roethke died of a blood clot to the brain after diving into the pool of his friends, the Bloedels, on August 1, 1963.

2. In keeping with the residual primitive myth at the source of the quest archetype, which features "the mingling of the sun and the hero" (Frye, "Archetypes of Literature," 18), the sequence's temporal setting reflects the circular movement of the sun as the hero meditates from twilight to twilight, or, to use the phrase of "The Abyss," "between dark and dark" (*Collected Poems,* 213). The flame rising from "the sunless sea" in "The Longing" seems to indicate the moment after sunset (2.8), "Meditation at Oyster River" takes place at twilight, "Journey to the Interior" ends at break of morning, "The Long Waters" is set in early morning, "The Far Field" is temporally ambiguous, and "The Rose" begins at sunset but recalls the morning and the rose at noontime.

3. I recognize an informing principle articulated by Lawrence Buell about place: it is not merely space but "a configuration of highly flexible subjective, social, and material dimensions, not reducible to any of these" (60).

4. Sam Hamill, cofounder of Copper Canyon Press, made the Pacific Northwest home after relocating the press from Colorado to Port Townsend, Washington, in 1974. The press has published editions of Roethke's *On Poetry and Craft* and *Straw for the Fire: From the Notebooks of Theodore Roethke* (see Works Cited).

5. "Sighs, sighs, who says they have sequence? / Between the spirit and the flesh,— what war?" is a relevant line from "Elegy" published in *The Far Field* (*Collected Poems,* 215). Seager reports that Roethke was completing this poem, begun after the death of his aunt, when he received news of Dylan Thomas's death (220).

6. Roethke read Underhill's *Mysticism: A Study in the Nature and Development of Man's Spiritual Consciousness* (1911), in which the mystic's apprehension of the Absolute is typified as "a certain spiritual and intangible quest" (3). He outlined in his notebook her five-step pattern of the "mystic way" (Kalaidjian, 17–18).

7. Also see Bowers, 124; Sullivan, 103; and Parini, 142.

8. Roethke's phrasing varies slightly from "the belly of the whale," the title Jungian mythologist Joseph Campbell gives to the stage in the hero's journey that follows his descent across the first threshold into the unknown regions of the archetypal night journey (90). The biblical Jonah's sojourn in and ejection from the whale's belly was taken as a type of the death-rebirth signified in the Christian rite of baptism.

9. It is possible that in the typesetting of this poem an intended space is missing between the section of three short lines and the following long line to emphasize the shift. Sullivan also has noted "discrepancies in the margination of stanzas" between *Collected Poems* and earlier volumes, finding that they affect the "psychic shifts of mood and pace" in certain poems (38n4).

32

Spirit, Self, and Shorebirds

The Pacific Pastoral of "Meditation at Oyster River"

NICHOLAS BRADLEY

"MEDITATION AT Oyster River" (*Collected Poems,* 184–86) is Theodore Roethke's Canadian poem, a contemplative lyric set at the mouth of a river on Vancouver Island that empties into the Strait of Georgia. The location, removed yet not altogether distant from Roethke's home in Washington, was a suitably unfamiliar and evocative site from which to look on the nature of time and place; the solitude discerned in a remote area and the distinctive qualities of the estuarine setting occasioned reflection upon the fluidity of memory and desire. The second poem in the "North American Sequence," the "Meditation" is an expression of Roethke's pastoral vision of the Pacific Northwest, where, in his reckoning, a restless spirit could be calmed and sustained. The coastal locale permits a moment of tranquility in which "the lingo of exasperation" and "the distortions of malice and hatred"—afflictions named in the preceding poem, "The Longing"—are forgotten (*Collected Poems,* 182). What remains is the language of local, living things: the names of gulls, beach grass, "quince-blossom," "morning-glory" (2.6), "beds of kelp" (2.9), sandpiper, kingfisher, and shorebirds. Roethke, by attending carefully to the particulars of the scene, anticipates the powerful proposition that begins "The Rose," the final poem in the "Sequence" and a comparably littoral work:

> There are those to whom place is unimportant,
> But this place, where sea and fresh water meet,
> Is important.
>
> (*Collected Poems,* 196)

The clarity with which the observer in the "Meditation" sees evidence of continual transformation, the change exemplified by the ceaseless motion of wind and water, brings into view the proximity of life and death, and a recognition, perhaps only fleeting, as ethereal as moonlight, that the radiant world's mysteries may surprise and console:

> In the first of the moon,
> All's a scattering,
> A shining.
>
> (4.12–14)

The omnipresence of death leads not to stoic resignation but to an instant of spiritual quiet that is a prelude to the rejoicing that concludes the "Sequence."

In the spring of 1957, Ted and Beatrice Roethke bought a house in Seattle (Seager, 242). While it was being readied for them, they traveled to Orcas Island, north of Puget Sound in the San Juan archipelago, and to "a salmon fishing resort very near Oyster River."[1] The sojourn, according to Allan Seager, Roethke's biographer, was pleasant: "Ted wanted very much to catch a salmon and kept trying. He finally landed a seven-pound one. Beatrice, however, caught the season's biggest on her first day out, sixteen pounds. . . . They fished for crabs and one day there was a school of whales disporting themselves not far from the shore" (Seager, 244).[2] The "Meditation" emerged from the brief time that Roethke spent on Vancouver Island, but the poem is not solely rooted in biography. It also takes up recurring themes and draws upon the fecund literary past. The presence of T. S. Eliot's *Four Quartets* is felt throughout the "North American Sequence," not least because of the unmistakable allusion to "East Coker" that ends "The Longing,"[3] and Wordsworthian intimations of immortality may be detected in the "Meditation."

A descriptive phrase hints at a correspondence between "Meditation at Oyster River" and a poem by Wallace Stevens, whose writing vexed and enchanted Roethke.[4] In "The Man on the Dump," a puzzling examination of poetic meaning, Stevens's singer of tales surveys his unlikely surroundings and makes a peculiar, diminished music: "One sits and beats an old tin can, lard pail. / One beats and beats for that which one believes."[5] Stevens's realm of rejectamenta is an accumulation of outworn figures: "The dump is full / Of images." The poem has little use for "the floweriest of flowers dewed with the dewiest dew," and even more vivid "azaleas, trilliums, / Myrtle, viburnums, daffodils, blue phlox" seem powerless to prick the imagination. The poet's creative force, however, allows things to be seen anew. "One rejects / The trash," and the world becomes its strange self again: "Everything is shed; and the moon comes up as the moon." Yet even when confronted with such revelations, Stevens trades in images and invention: "One looks at the elephant-colorings of tires" (201–2). Imagination, language, and material things, the self and the world, are not easily disentangled.

In the first lines of "Meditation at Oyster River" a similar phrase describes oncoming waves: "Over the low, barnacled, elephant-colored rocks, / Come the first tide-ripples, moving, almost without sound, toward me" (1.1–2). The resemblance of "elephant-colored rocks" to "the elephant-colorings of tires" could bespeak coincidence, but Roethke's poem has a Stevensian dimension. The "Meditation" is not solely or indubitably a response to "The Man on the Dump."[6] The setting of Stevens's poem is allegorical, while that of the "Meditation" is tethered to an actual place, and Roethke's unadorned utterances do not share Stevens's rococo style. But both poems are concerned with the possibility of seeing things as they are. In Roethke's animate world other beings serve an illuminating, explanatory function. "And things throw light on things, / And all the stones have wings," he wrote in "The Small," a delicate but resonant lyric (*Collected Poems,* 142).[7] "Meditation at Oyster River" portrays the desire for immersion in things themselves: nearness to natural beauty rejuvenates the observer and assuages existential dread. But Roethke's view of nature is not naïve, although it is romantic; the idyll leads his speaker not to unthinking reverence but to self-scrutiny instead. Roethke's poetry does not revel in the linguistic artifice that distinguishes Stevens's writing, yet the "Meditation," like "The Man on the Dump," examines the mutual constitution of world and self, and the artist's capacity to figure that relation. Roethke's poem seeks an escape from the dump of images through precise attention and perception, which bring the observer closer to selflessness.

Despite the title, "Meditation at Oyster River" is in fact a poem of three waterways and two locations: Vancouver Island and Michigan's Lower Peninsula in the speaker's memory. *Insula* (island) and faraway *paeninsula* are fused by the associative imagination. The name "Oyster River" was a donnée of geography, but "oyster" denotes the mollusk's grayish color, which bears considerable importance. Although only the "elephant-colored rocks" (1.1) are identified by their hue, other images summon to mind the color between the light of day and the dark of night: "dead clam shells" (1.3), "brackish foam" (1.15), "salt-soaked wood" (1.21), "ridges of stone" (2.11). Oyster River as the night falls is an intermediate place, a pause. An unnamed "Michigan brook" (3.7) and the Tittabawassee River are described in the third section. The Tittabawassee is a tributary of the Saginaw River, which flows through the city of Saginaw, Roethke's childhood hometown, and then to Lake Huron.[8] The speaker's memories of the brook and the river introduce depictions of diurnal and seasonal change. The sudden, violent thawing of the Tittabawassee suggests the turbulence of an earlier time of life, and stands in contrast to the gradual transformations of the estuary. A poem of the Northwest and the Midwest alike, the "Meditation" yokes together present and past, perception and recollection, motion and stasis. The crucial image of ebbing and flowing water illustrates the view that life and spirit are configured by reversals and countercurrents. "Water's my will, and my way," Roethke's speaker contends (4.7). The estuary is a *locus amoenus,* a pastoral site of repose and seclusion. What Thomas G. Rosenmeyer calls the green cabinet of pastoral convention—*cabinet* in the sense of a private room (vii)—is in the coastal poem a domain of blue and gray.[9] Roethke's shore is less "the habitat of Pan" the piper (Rosenmeyer, vii) than the habitat of *Calidris* the sandpiper, but it is a pleasance nonetheless. In the opening stanza, "the first tide-ripples" draw near (1.2). The speaker tests the waters—"I dabble my toes in the brackish foam sliding forward" (1.15)—and retreats to a higher point, from which he apprehends the prospect in flux. A host of participles creates the impression of movement: "moving," "[r]unning," "creeping," "climbing," "deepening," "[s]lapping," "sliding," "fanning," "catching" (1.2–23). The landscape is crescent and waning; the world's cycles are embodied by the microcosmic place. Contradictions resolve into peace: "No sound from the bay. No violence" (1.6).

As the title indicates, the poem is a spiritual, even devotional, exercise, an attempt to fathom matters of significance and mystery, which in Roethke's case involve the relation, characterized by simultaneous proximity and distance, of the spirit to the world.[10] The poem evokes patterns of thought that follow from attention to place. Its four parts—an Eliotian quartet—chart the riverine course of the speaker's cogitation.[11] He first observes the progress of the tide, the apparent stillness of evening, and the teeming landscape that is "[a]live with tiny striped fish, and young crabs" (1.5). He and his vantage are mirrored by the fish raven on its perch (1.22); the human presence is not intrusive, but the vital world plunges the speaker into memory even as it pulls him to the present.[12] The second part of the poem begins with an abstract, oblique assertion: "The self persists like a dying star, / In sleep, afraid" (2.1–2). "With these I would be" (2.7), the speaker later says of "the shy beasts" (2.3). But neither he nor the poet can escape the human world to join other kingdoms; the longing can be sung but not satisfied. The third section turns to remembrance, and especially to memories of Michigan. "I long for the blast of dynamite," the speaker avers, that marks the beginning of the Tittabawassee's spring motion (3.17). But his yearning is quelled by the peaceful spell at the ocean's edge. As the day ends, the speaker, in the final section, is graced by calm: "In the cradle of all that is, / I'm lulled into half-sleep" (4.3–4). He suggests again the cyclical patterns by which he and his environs are governed. "Now, in this waning of light, / I rock with the motion of morning" (4.1–2): the passage suggests childhood, but Roethke's peace, neither an escape from consciousness nor a return to infancy, is only a reprieve from the usual course of life. Dawn approaches; time continues.[13]

The themes and impulses of "Meditation at Oyster River" have been duly perceived by commentators on Roethke's works. In his appreciative review of *The Far Field,* X. J. Kennedy wrote that the poetry registers a desire for union with other beings: "not content merely to look, Roethke keeps striving to quit his body and enter into leaf, bird and stream" (BR5). In a more severe account of the same volume, W. D. Snodgrass cited a passage from the "Meditation" as evidence of Roethke's longing "to escape *all* form and shape, to lose all awareness of otherness, not through entrance to woman as lover, but rather through reentrance into eternity conceived as womb, into water as woman, into earth as goddess-mother" (6). And in "Roethke's Last Poems," his review of *The Far Field,* Ralph J. Mills Jr. noted the Whitmanesque dimension of the "North American Sequence" and used lines from the "Meditation" to illustrate the concerns of the "Sequence" as a whole, including "the desire to escape from self and its attachments" (124).[14] The dimming light, slackening wind, and incoming tide inevitably connote last things, but the "Meditation" is not simply the author's anticipation of his own demise. It is instead a rumination upon the constant presence of death in life. The late light and the gathering waters are reminders of mortality, but the same light reveals the beauty of living things, which Roethke captures with lovely music:

Death's face rises afresh,
Among the shy beasts, the deer at the salt-lick,
The doe with its sloped shoulders loping across the highway,
The young snake, poised in green leaves, waiting for its fly,
The hummingbird, whirring from quince-blossom to morning-glory—
With these I would be.

(2.2–7)

The observer considers not death by water, but life and death, and land and sea, together. He wishes not to die but impossibly to be selfless in nature. The "shy beasts," like the "intrepid shorebirds" of the poem's close, show human visitors how to face eternity and the Pacific: "How graceful the small before danger!" (4.10–11). Their observer cannot remain in place; Ted and Beatrice had to return to Seattle. Yet the poem's sober study of coastal life leads to the celebration that concludes "The Rose" and thus the "Sequence." "And I rejoiced in being what I was," Roethke's speaker announces in "The Rose" (*Collected Poems,* 199); he thrills as well to plants, creatures, and change. The contemplation of twilight precedes the resolution of the "Sequence," and the equanimous encounter with silence in the "Meditation" ushers in the incantatory speech of "The Rose." In a book review titled "Meditations of a Sensitive Man" (1946), Roethke expressed a hope that "the poetry of the future" would be "sensuous but not simple-minded; above all, rooted deeply in life; passionate and perhaps even suffused, on occasion, with wisdom and light" (221). "Meditation at Oyster River" fulfills this aspiration. The poem is a song as well as a meditation, a praiseful offering to a meaningful place.[15]

NOTES

1. Oyster River is the name of the small settlement near the estuary as well as the name of the river itself. Campbell River, to the north, is the nearest major town and a celebrated center of commercial and recreational fishing.

2. In *The Glass House,* Roethke's biography and the source of this information, the island's name is misspelled ("Orchis") (Seager, 243–44). Hugh B. Staples suggests that the "Meditation" is set in "the Puget Sound area" (196); the specificity of the title aside, the poem describes a landscape that could plausibly be located in the state of Washington. Peter Balakian likewise identifies Puget Sound as the poem's setting (140). An Oyster Creek runs through Washington's Skagit and Whatcom Counties. Even so, the biographical evidence indicates that the poem is tied to the province of British Columbia.

3. The allusion occurs in the last stanza of "The Longing": "Old men should be explorers? / I'll be an Indian" (*Collected Poems,* 183). Bernard W. Quetchenbach has proposed (163n8) that the beginning of the "Meditation" is reminiscent of T. S. Eliot's "Marina": "What seas what shores what grey rocks and what islands / What water lapping the bow" (*Collected Poems,* 105). Roethke's knowledge of Eliot's works and his occasional borrowings are beyond dispute; aspects of "The Dry Salvages," for instance, resound in the "Meditation."

4. In 1958 Roethke wrote in a letter to James Wright that he had "[b]een reading [Robert] Graves and Stevens lately, and damned if I don't think both are over-rated. I get so tired of Stevens' doodling with a subject-matter—the same subject-matter" (*Selected Letters,* 218); but the next year Roethke mentioned in a letter to Roy Harvey Pearce that "A Rouse for Stevens," a jesting tribute, "*was* written out of love" (228). Indeed, the "Rouse" suggests, albeit satirically, that Stevens's parental influence on contemporary poets was inescapable: "Wallace Stevens—are we *for* him? / Brother, he's our father!" (*Collected Poems,* 258).

5. "The Man on the Dump" was included in Stevens's *Parts of a World* (1942), a volume published a year after Roethke's first book, *Open House* (1941). The chronological separation between the two poets, who were born in 1879 and 1908, respectively, is not absolute.

6. Other lexical parallels may be observed. Both poems use forms of the verb "to creep": "Day creeps down. The moon is creeping up" (W. Stevens, 184); "Then a runnel behind me, creeping closer" (Roethke, 1.4); "The tongues of water, creeping in, quietly" (2.12). Roethke's "Meditation" contains an image—"The dew revives on the beach-grass" (1.20)—that employs the very word ("dew") that is repeated to comic effect in Stevens's poem. The third section of Roethke's poem contains an image of refuse: "the culvert loosens its debris of branches and sticks, / Welter of tin cans, pails, old bird nests, a child's shoe riding a log" (3.18–19).

7. An exclamation in the "Meditation"—"How graceful the small before danger!" (4.11)—echoes "The Small" and another poem from *Words for the Wind,* "A Walk in Late Summer": "The small! The small! I hear them singing clear / On the long banks, in the soft summer air" (*Collected Poems,* 143). Roethke's affinity for "the small" is reiterated in "In Evening Air," the second poem in the "Sequence, Sometimes Metaphysical": "Ye littles, lie more close!" (232).

8. In the poem the river's name is misspelled: "Tittebawasee" (3.12). William Barillas has noted that the juxtaposition of places links the six poems in the "Sequence": "Even in the 'North American Sequence,' his most 'northwestern' work, Roethke returns to Michigan in every poem" (*Midwestern Pastoral,* 136).

9. The verdurous phrase is that of Edmund Spenser, who adopted it from Clément Marot (Rosenmeyer, vii).

10. The title links the "Meditation" to poems by Roethke with similar titles, namely the five poems in "Meditations of an Old Woman," from *Words for the Wind,* and "Meditation in Hydrotherapy," from *The Collected Poems of Theodore Roethke.* "Meditations of a Sensitive Man," Roethke's review of Roy Fuller's *A Lost Season,* appeared in the journal *Poetry* in 1946. The title's resemblance to those of later poems is incidental: Fuller, not Roethke, was the "sensitive man."

11. Eliot's *Four Quartets* are composed of five parts each; the title is not a simple description of structure but instead a musical metaphor. The extended form of the poems in the "North American Sequence" is nonetheless comparable to that of the *Four Quartets.*

12. Roethke's admirable ecological attentiveness did not preclude occasional errors or obscurities. "[F]ish raven" (1.22) is an uncommon and in all likelihood erroneous term. Perhaps he meant "fish hawk" (an osprey) or "fish crow," although *Corvus ossifragus* is not found in the Pacific Northwest. The common raven (*Corvus corax*) exists throughout the region. The seemingly related term "sea raven" offers no help: it refers to a fish, *Hemitripterus americanus.*

13. A differing view is supplied by Rosemary Sullivan, who suggests that the "Meditation" depicts the beginning of "the long process of mergence with elemental waters through a lapsing of rational consciousness" (151).

14. Mills had already identified, in "Roethke's Garden," a review (1964) of Roethke's *I Am! Says the Lamb* (1961), traces in the "Meditation" of Whitman, Wordsworth, and John Clare (58).

15. The constituent poems in the "North American Sequence," closely linked by theme, style, and setting, were first published separately. "Meditation at Oyster River" appeared in *The New Yorker* in 1960 and in *The London Magazine* in 1961. It was printed in *The London Magazine* with minor variations in spelling ("elephant-coloured rocks," "Their child-wimpering" [34]). The Faber edition of *The Far Field* (1965) retained the American orthography—"elephant-colored rocks" (16)—of the Doubleday edition of 1964.

The poem assumed its place in the "Sequence" in *The Far Field*, published posthumously in the United States in 1964 and in England in 1965, and it was later gathered in *The Collected Poems of Theodore Roethke* (1966; expanded 1975). The poem is presented identically in both editions of *The Far Field.* The magazine versions tend to forgo hyphens: "tide ripples," "Blue black," "beach grass," and "salt lick" are in Roethke's books "tide-ripples," "Blue-black," "beach-grass," and "salt-lick" (1.2, 1.12, 1.20, 2.3). Some compounds that appear as single words in the magazines ("clamshells," "sandbars") are split in the books ("clam shells," "sand-bars"), while certain nominal phrases in the magazines ("river mouth," "shore birds") are combined in the books ("rivermouth," "shorebirds") (1.22, 4.10). A noun in the fourth part of the "Meditation" was altered: "the lapping of waves" in the magazines became "the lapping of water" in the books (4.5).

The poem was emended after its initial publication. Certain changes suggest Roethke's desire for economy and directness. "The cries of the sandpiper" in the magazine versions, for instance, became "Cries of the sandpiper" in Roethke's books (4.6). But while the version of "Meditation" in *The New Yorker* includes the phrase "a double rainbow in early morning" (54), the equivalent phrase in *The London Magazine* contains a rare extraneous word: "a double rainbow in the early morning" (35). The *London* version gives "And the wrist-thick cascade" (35) instead of "And that wrist-thick cascade," the phrase found elsewhere (3.9); the demonstrative adjective is more forceful than the definite article, although the difference is undoubtedly slight. Another phrase exists in three forms: "old bird's nests" in *The New Yorker* (54), "old birds' nests" in *The London Magazine* (36), and "old bird nests" in *The Far Field* (18) and subsequent volumes (3.19). The hyphenated "rain-bow" (3.10) in the *Collected Poems* is more likely a misprint than a deliberate archaism or idiosyncrasy. The *Selected Poems* of 2005 retains the hyphenated form (88).

Such minutiae do not greatly affect the shape and sense of the "Meditation," yet they are editorial matters that have not been settled. "Meditation at Oyster River," no less than Roethke's other works, awaits a meticulous editor who will serve author and readers faithfully.

33

"Journey to the Interior," "The Longing," and the Search for a Definitive Text

NEAL BOWERS

IN THE event of an author's sudden death, manuscripts are sometimes left incomplete or in disarray, and we have to accept flawed texts or none at all. When Theodore Roethke died of a heart attack in 1963, he had worked on the manuscript of *The Far Field* since the late 1950s, so there's reason to assume he had a mostly complete book in progress. But manuscripts tend to be palimpsests of erasures and textual variants, never ready for print until the publisher sends them to the printer; it's not uncommon, even at that late stage, for authors to attempt changes. Regrettably, Roethke never had the chance to produce a truly final version of *The Far Field* or to drive his publisher mad with last-minute revisions.

In a note that prefaces *The Collected Poems of Theodore Roethke,* Beatrice Roethke states that "North American Sequence" and "Sequence Sometimes Metaphysical" "are, in content and order, as arranged by Theodore Roethke in the original manuscript" of *The Far Field,* but then notes that "other sections in that book were altered slightly." Specifically, she explains that "[t]wo of the pub songs, 'The Saginaw Song' and 'Gob Music'—pieces that did not seem appropriate in a last book of poems"—were withheld "for later publication," evidently in *Collected Poems* (xv). She also acknowledges adding "Wish for a Young Wife" and "The Tranced." Unfortunately, she doesn't reveal precisely how the "Love

Poems" and "Mixed Sequence" sections of the book were altered to accommodate those two poems.

While the kinds of changes Beatrice Roethke says she made are understandable, they represent the intrusions of a sensibility other than the poet's. No matter how well intentioned, such alterations result in a kind of collaborative text that the poet never intended and also introduce the possibility that other changes were made without acknowledgment. Curiously, the note about the changes Roethke's widow made was not included in the first edition of *The Far Field,* where it logically belonged. Also missing is a description of the manuscript's condition and the kinds of decisions the editors were obliged to make. In the absence of such a useful preface, those who care about a definitive text—the author's best and final version—are left to wonder if such a thing exists for many of Roethke's final poems.

Some of the problems that arise from this omission are evident in "The Longing" (*Collected Poems,* 181–83) and "Journey to the Interior" (187–89). Like the other four poems in the "North American Sequence," they appeared individually in journals before their publication in *The Far Field.* Clearly, Roethke felt each poem could stand on its own, without reference to the others, and he later found it necessary to revise several of the poems to make them fit better into the sequence. Even if his changes were provisional rather than final, they were fixed in place by his death and the rapid publication of *The Far Field.*

"The Longing" was the poem that came first to Roethke as he set about working on an idea he proposed to the Ford Foundation in 1959: "a sequence of serious poems beginning with a long dirge which will express through suggestive and highly charged symbolical language the guilts we Americans feel as a people for our mistakes and misdeeds in history and in time" (qtd. in Seager, 257). Of course, Roethke had no intention of delving into the American psyche, but he wanted the grant money and the time to write whatever poems came to him. To his credit, "The Longing" carries a tinge of the proposal idea in its first section, where it describes a "sensual emptiness" that seems cultural as well as individual. And the poem also essays an American exploration that is made specific in personal terms in "Journey to the Interior."

When it appeared in the June 24, 1961, issue of *Saturday Review,* "The Longing" had no third section. In that configuration, its two sections counterpoint the physical world of lust and garbage with the spiritual world of rose and moon, and they also represent the movement between depression and mania that characterized Roethke's bipolar disorder. During revisions, Roethke must have hoped a third section would set up the rest of the poems in the sequence by acting as a kind of overture.

But tying together poems not specifically written to blend can be risky, and in this case the process makes explicit what was more elegantly implied in the original version, which has a compressed power the revision lacks. With only two sections, the poem moves from despair to joy and arrives at the central paradox of life—everything originates from nothing—an existential truth that resonates beyond the end of the original version but is muted in the revision.

In the third part of "The Longing," added for the sequence, the language lumbers prosaically: "the lingo of exasperation, all the distortions of malice and hatred" (3.4), and "I have left the body of the whale, but the mouth of the night is still wide" (3.13). Equally cumbersome are the final nine lines of the section, with their reference to the Dakotas and "buffalo grass," "buttes" and "buffalo chips" (3.15–18). Obviously meant to prepare the way for "Journey to the Interior," with its trip across the plains, these lines serve mostly a transitional purpose and contribute little to the poem they conclude. But most gratuitous are the Native American options at the very end: "Ogalala? / Iroquois" (3.21–22).

The oddity of this question/answer rhetoric is increased by the misspelling of Oglala and by the fact that "Ogalala" does not appear in the first edition of *The Far Field,* where the lines move more fluidly:

> Old men should be explorers.
> I'll be an Indian.
> Iroquois.
>
> (15)

"Ogalala" appears only in *The Collected Poems,* presumably inserted by someone who found it in one of Roethke's drafts. Of course, it may have been accidentally omitted in *The Far Field* by a typist or typesetter and then restored in *The Collected Poems,* which reduces the problem to nothing more than poor copyediting. Possibly, an examination of Roethke's manuscripts in the University of Washington's collection would clarify things, assuming a clear, final version of the poem exists in manuscript form.

The discovery of this kind of discrepancy raises doubts about the reliability of the rest of the texts published after Roethke's death. Even minor changes (whether made by editors or poor typesetters) become troubling—for example, stanza breaks that occur at lines 1.18 and 2.11 in the *Collected Poems* version of "The Longing" but are absent in the *Saturday Review* version of the poem. Such matters may seem minor, but poets worry over them because they represent the way the poet sees and hears his own work.

If Roethke wasn't finished with the "North American Sequence," then his addition to "The Longing" may have been preparation for a realignment of the poems in the sequence, with the expanded opening poem flowing directly into "Journey to the Interior." As things stand, "Meditation at Oyster River" disrupts the continuity and makes the added section seem like a graft that didn't take hold.

In "Journey to the Interior," the third poem in the "North American Sequence," lines were deleted and rearranged rather than added. First published in the January 7, 1961, issue of *The New Yorker,* the poem's third section began with these lines:

> Between the rising and the falling,
> Between the lifting and the relinquishing,
> Between the swung rope of the bell
> And the full peal of sound across the field over the broad valley,
> Between the first trembling of the wren's throat and the burst of song from
>   the hedgerow.
>
> (27)

Roethke deleted this passage when preparing the poem for the "North American Sequence," possibly because it echoes too loudly the phrasing of a familiar section near the end of T. S. Eliot's "The Hollow Men":

> Between the idea
> And the reality
> Between the motion
> And the act.
>
> (*Collected Poems,* 81–82)

Through his deliberate allusion to Eliot's work throughout the "North American Sequence," Roethke offers an ecstatic route to illumination as a counterpoint to Eliot's considered, intellectual deliberations. Sometimes, however, the allusions seem more like appropriations, and Roethke must have worried that drawing too near to Eliot might cast a shadow on his own work and particularly on his originality.

In further changes to the third section of "Journey to the Interior," Roethke relocated the seven lines beginning with "In the moment of time when the small drop forms, but does not fall" (3.7), which followed the deleted passage, to just after "And the waves flattening out when the fishermen drag their nets over the stones" (3.6). The revised version moves directly from the hypnotic power of the highway at the end of the first section to a perception of "the flower of all water" (3.1).

Together, the deletion and relocation abbreviate the speaker's experience of the "long moment" (1.30), which is both finite and infinite, causing the transcendent vision in the poem to arrive more quickly and with less sensory impact. Roethke may have undertaken these changes to avoid dissipating the impact of the overall sequence as it moves toward that final flower, "The Rose." But he also reduced the tonal power of the poem and its potential effect on the reader by eliminating the lulling repetitions.

Because Roethke was working with lyric rather than narrative poetry (his cross-country trip in "Journey to the Interior" notwithstanding), finding a way to build a coherent unit of smaller parts required him to subordinate those parts to a whole they couldn't possibly sustain. In both "The Longing" and "Journey to the Interior," the process resulted in poems that are arguably weaker than the originals and in a final sequence that coheres not because of the poet's revisions but as an expression of his manic urgency.

It's interesting that Roethke made no substantial changes to the rest of the poems in the "North American Sequence." Perhaps he had plans to modify them as well, though it's possible that he realized it was better to let them justify their place in the sequence on organic rather than programmatic terms. Maybe he simply ran out of time.

Once these kinds of speculation begin, there's no end to them. Did Roethke alter the long, complex second sentence in *The New Yorker* version of "Journey to the Interior" in favor of fragments, or did someone else make that change? Whose proofreading and copyediting repeatedly changed parentheses to dashes and failed to notice the article "the" missing from the first line of section 3 in "The Long Waters," thereby changing the sense of the line from a seasonal reference to a clumsy prepositional phrase? How could an astute editor not see that the original second stanza of section 2 in "The Long Waters," where the whole stanza functions as a question, is fundamentally changed when only the first line is an interrogative sentence and the pronoun "Who" is left without an antecedent?

These seemingly small matters have a big impact on the poems and contribute to a larger uncertainty concerning the finished nature of the "North American Sequence" and the rest of the poems in *The Far Field.* There's no reason to imagine that anyone associated with the publication of *The Far Field* and *Collected Poems* did anything in bad faith, but even the best editors can get things wrong, especially when manuscripts are rushed into publication, as both volumes seem to have been. *The Far Field* came out less than a year after Roethke's death and the first edition of *Collected Poems* a year after that. Considering the massive amount of material Roethke left behind, perhaps a slower pace to publishing would have allowed time for a fuller evaluation of variant texts.

Definitely, the readers of Roethke's last poems deserve an updated edition of *The Far Field* as it appears in *Collected Poems,* if only one that corrects the obvious editorial failures of the original. But no matter how much care is taken with that posthumous book, it will never represent Roethke at his best, simply because he never truly finished it. Still, we have the journal publications for every poem in the volume, and readers would do well to find and savor them individually, especially the poems in the "North American Sequence."

34

Mnetha in "The Long Waters"

JOHN J. MCKENNA

THEODORE ROETHKE'S poetry is not learned in the sense of Eliot's or Pound's. Nor is it academic in the way of Richard Wilbur's verse. Even an allusion to the work of another writer is rare in Roethke's poetry—an occasional tip of the hat to Yeats, Whitman, or another modern poet.[1] It is surprising, then, to find a line in "The Long Waters" (*Collected Poems,* 190–92), the fourth poem in the six-poem "North American Sequence," which reads "Mnetha, Mother of Har, protect me" (2.1). Mnetha is a figure in William Blake's *Tiriel* (ca. 1789), one of his unfinished prophetic poems. Roethke's allusion to Blake's Tiriel is significant because there are important parallels between the figures in Blake's poem and the psychological and philosophical locus of the speaker in "The Long Waters" that help clarify a central theme in Roethke's poetry: a resolution to the problem of mortality.

As the "greenhouse" poems show early on, Roethke is acutely aware that humans are physical creatures in a physical universe. Walter Kalaidjian observes that in "'The Long Waters' each instant of life shares in a moment of death, and vice versa, decay is creation" (146). To be physical is to be mutable, and to be mutable is to be mortal. Roethke yearns to transcend this mortality, especially when it is characterized by a spiritual emptiness. He believes an individual can achieve transcendence by becoming a part of the eternal other, the natural context, out of which all life comes and to which it returns. The natural world with its recurrent cycle represents continuance, the thing which abides. In Roethke's cosmology, the natural world, viewed as an ethereal mother and often symbolized by water, both creates by giving life and destroys by subsuming the individual back into the ethereal context. Roethke's speaker in "The Long Waters" knows he can "lose and find [him]self in the long water" (5.17). The speaker continually wrestles with the following paradox: in order to find a way to see the limited self as immortal, it is necessary to lose one's self in the all-consuming, but endless, context.

Because he fears the thing he must embrace (i.e., the contextual other, the natural world), the speaker of "The Long Waters" asks for protection from Blake's Mnetha:

> Mnetha, Mother of Har, protect me
> From the worm's advance and retreat, from the butterfly's havoc,
> From the slow sinking of the island peninsula, the coral efflorescence,
> The dubious sea-change, the heaving sands, and my tentacled sea-cousins.
> (2.1–4)

The worm's advance and retreat represents the slow motion of Darwinian evolution. The sinking of the peninsula reveals the slow changes that affect even land masses. And the coral efflorescence combines the idea of change in animate and inanimate objects. Coral is alive, but once dead its limestone excretion hardens into the reefs that eventually create land. The efflorescence is an indication of life but a rather ghostly one at that. The speaker's kinship with other life forms is necessary for transcendence but nonetheless frightening, as are the mutable sands. The "dubious sea-change," with its echo of Shakespeare's *The Tempest,* underscores the uncertain nature of this momentous journey which the speaker is undertaking. As Karl Malkoff observes, the speaker is "calling upon nature to teach him to accept the natural processes and he is calling upon intuition to deliver him from the purely rational" (182–83).

For the speaker of the "The Long Waters," Mnetha represents protection from the loss of self in the presence of the enchanting but awe-inspiring natural world. Aged but vital, Mnetha is reminiscent of the three crones in Roethke's "Frau Bauman, Frau Schmidt, and Frau Schwartze." These three wise ladies provide an image of care and tenderness, not only for the greenhouse plants they tend but also for the speaker's youthful self.

> Now, when I'm alone and cold in my bed,
> They still hover over me,
> These ancient leathery crones,
> With their bandannas stiffened with sweat,
> And their thorn-bitten wrists,
> And their snuff-laden breath blowing lightly over me in my first sleep.
> (*Collected Poems,* 42)

The mixture of positive images (blowing lightly, first sleep) and negative images (alone, cold, leathery, thorn-bitten wrists, snuff-laden breath) catches the bittersweet flavor of a young child's going off to bed and eventually to sleep. The journey that the speaker makes in "The Long Waters" is similar in its mottled psychological texture. This journey is a little disquieting, for it is, after all, the journey toward death, where the individual resides namelessly in the contextual all.

The anxiety of Roethke's speaker, then, is understandable, as is his desire for protection from the unknown consequences of this frightening journey. Little wonder that he beseeches Mnetha for succor. In *Tiriel,* Mnetha protects Har and his female companion, Heva. Har and Heva "ran weeping like frighted infants for refuge in Mnethas [*sic*] arms" (Blake, 277). Roethke uses the frightened Har as an analog to the frightening spiritual decadence of the speaker of "The Long Waters." Like Har, Roethke's speaker seeks a mother's assurances and protection. Similarly, the speaker in the poem seeks refuge in a spiritual embrace of the phenomenal world: "I am gathered together once more; / I embrace the world" (5.18–19). These final lines to "The Long Waters" show the speaker's transcendence from his original state of anxiety.[2] The phenomenal world is, for Roethke, the ultimate "mother," the primordial ether, the source of all life.

In *Tiriel,* Mnetha not only protects Heva and Har; she also gives comfort to Tiriel. Like the speaker of "The Long Waters," Tiriel is a wanderer. Mnetha says to him, "[C]ome in aged wanderer[,] tell us thy name[.] / Why shouldest thou conceal thyself from those of thine own flesh[?]" (278). Come in, come in to the protection of your own flesh; come in, she entreats, to the context which gives you birth, self, identity. Ironically, as the self struggles toward the protection it receives from identifying with a larger context like kinship, the self also loses its individual identity. It merges into the context. An individual has to give up some parts of the self in order to be a member of a larger context. This is exactly what Roethke's speaker faces: the need for contextual support and the fear that identifying with the context will mean the death of the self.

In addition, Mnetha protests that the blind Tiriel "must not go to wander dark alone." Instead, she wishes that he "dwell with us & let us be to thee instead of eyes / And I will bring thee food old man till death shall call thee hence" (279). She is, therefore, the agent who proposes to protect, give contextual succor, provide sight, bring sustenance, and generally ease Tiriel's life right up to the point of his death. All of her proffered offices will make his approach to death easier to bear.

Roethke's speaker desires the same assurances and protection, the same ease as death approaches. Like Tiriel, the speaker has wandered a dark journey. The latter's hegira has been what Roethke, in "Journey to the Interior," calls a "long journey out of the self" (*Collected Poems,* 187). He is striving toward a contextual succor psychologically, at least, very much like that which Mnetha offers to provide for Tiriel. As we have seen, the speaker's context is not human society, as it is for Tiriel, but is an identification with the natural world. A long, or cosmic, view of nature provides insight into a yin/yang duality composed of an individual but mortal self and an immortal but indeterminate context. As Roethke writes in "The Longing," the first poem in the "North American Sequence," "I would with the fish, the blackening salmon, and the mad lemmings, / The children dancing, the flowers widening" (*Collected Poems,* 182). There the speaker would like to be identified with the contextual world, especially other life forms, whether they be dying or dancing. Rosemary Sullivan says the speaker "rejects the appeal of a fixed and final order and the desire for absolutes" (158). The images of the blackening salmon after their spawning runs and the lemmings madly plunging to collective deaths invoke death. The children dancing and the flowers widening bespeak exuberant life. The speaker is attracted to both: yin and yang, life and death, the world of the self and the world of the context. Like Mnetha, who can be Tiriel's eyes, the natural world, the "mother" for Roethke's speaker, has the potential to provide enlightenment to him.

Mnetha is, then, an allusion of considerable significance for the speaker of "The Long Waters," for she is a figure of succor who offers Tiriel relief from his sightless and lonely travels, and in this she is an analog to the natural world in Roethke's cosmology. The "North American Sequence" depicts a journey that begins in longing and ends in affirmation. "The Long Waters" is a poem central to the theme and drama of this sequence. It is located near the center of the sequence, and on this fulcrum the speaker is enabled to move forward with affirmation even in the face of death. Mnetha is a refuge for Har. Har's fears and Tiriel's lonely wandering have their parallels in the psychological fears and hopes and in the philosophical angst of the speaker of "The Long Waters." Like Har, Roethke's speaker is frightened. He fears the momentous journey; he sees that the context will enfold him again and erase his individual self; he, like Har, calls out to Mnetha for protection: "Mnetha, Mother of Har, protect me" (2.1). "Protect us all," he might have said. For we all make the speaker's momentous journey. We all feel its attractions and repulsion, its hopes and its fears. We all cry out, "Mother, protect me."

NOTES

1. "I take this cadence from a man named Yeats; / I take it, and I give it back again" from Roethke's "Four for Sir John Davies," part 1, "The Dance" (*Collected Poems,* 101); "Be with me, Whitman, maker of catalogues," from "The Abyss" (*Collected Poems,* 212).

2. Thomas Gardner partially disagrees. He calls the progression made up by the final lines of "The Long Waters" a "strikingly pat presentation [that] contrasts noticeably with the painstaking advance and retreat" of the speaker's previously traversed psychic landscape (189).

35

The Ecological Vision of "The Far Field"

BERNARD QUETCHENBACH

"I DREAM of journeys repeatedly" (1.1), Theodore Roethke's "The Far Field" begins (*Collected Poems* 193–95), echoing the opening of "Journey to the Interior," placed earlier in the six-poem "North American Sequence." The first lines of both poems include a form of the word *journey,* both first sections end with something growing dark, and both feature an initial turn from the first line's beckoning possibilities into a claustrophobic, isolated narrowness, so constrained in "The Far Field" as to press in even on a bat. James McMichael has characterized the section's final image, a car with a failing battery stalled in a snowdrift, as "even more final in its bleakness" than that of the corresponding section of "Journey to the Interior" (92). In both poems, the journey seems to be ending even as it begins.

The second section of "The Far Field," however, finds the speaker abruptly and inexplicably transported to the titular field, a childhood corner of forgotten machinery, vibrant birds, and discarded flowers. While its solidity counters the dream imagery of section 1, the place "[a]t the field's edge, in the corner missed by the mower" (2.1), represents, in one important respect, a continuation of rather than a departure from the previous section. Like the snowdrift, the drop-off into the culvert marks an impasse, necessitating a self-conscious shift with only a break followed by "—Or" (2.26) for transition. The passage set at the field's edge is logically isolated from what precedes it and what follows it. A defining characteristic of the sequence's development, such sudden scene changes are associative rather than conventionally narrative, the culvert leading imagistically to "the silted shallows of a slow river" (2.27).

In his prose, Roethke speaks of the tentative, halting motion of his own search for both an authentic poetic voice and something like mystical illumination, a dynamic McMichael describes as the soul's tension between "falling back" and "moving forward" (87). In a brief self-portrait written for Stanley Kunitz's *Twentieth Century Authors: First Supplement* (1955), Roethke talks about his decision to dedicate himself to writing as "the end (really the beginning) of a trail" (*On Poetry and Craft,* 28). In "An American Poet Introduces Himself and His Poems," he elaborates on the progression of the "spiritual man," who "must go back in order to go forward. The way is circuitous, and sometimes lost, but invariably returned to" (*On Poetry and Craft,* 25). By reverting to the landscape of childhood, the speaker in "The Far Field" "goes back" to find a still point where close empathetic attention reveals "the way forward."

The far field is meticulously delineated; it is clearly important that it be seen as an actual place. The setting is familiar and literal, its life both miraculous—the spellbinding appearance of the warblers—and daily. The field incorporates both childhood and death, represented by the decomposing rat and the cat dispatched by the night watchman. And the field's edge is "[n]ot too far away from the ever-changing flower-dump" (2.4), establishing that death's transformation is mundane as well as transcendent. That the last stanza in section 2 vaults so completely into the mystical imagery of the turning wheel and "the windy cliffs of forever" (2.39) serves to ground even the extremes of spiritual experience in the ordinary. At the most basic level, the "windy cliff" is nothing more than the sloping border between field and culvert.

Throughout his work, Roethke demonstrates a descriptive empathy with the commonplace that Camille Paglia characterizes as his "microscopic attention to and compassion for the tiniest twigs and pebbles of the American landscape" ("Dance of the Senses," 242). Marianne Boruch, too, recognizes Roethke's writing as "passionately accurate about detail, especially natural detail" ("Three Spirits," 11). Applied on a vast scale in the "North American Sequence," Roethke's perceptual and emotional attentiveness results, according to Cary Nelson, in "precise though kaleidoscopic descriptions of nature." Though Nelson distinguishes the descriptive catalogues from the "periods of emotionally-charged self-exploration," he concludes that "the willed rhythm of movement between inside and outside, between the self and the world," is a means to "propel poet and reader into the final vision" (39). Time and place are fluid to the freely associating self, but, as the title implies, "North American Sequence" is firmly rooted in the physical world; the continent's landscapes and creatures are carefully, even lovingly, observed.

The sequence's catalogues have often been attributed to the influence of Walt Whitman. As is true of his nineteenth-century predecessor, Roethke's journeying traces a course through the American land, traversed in the sequence by automobile, the characteristic twentieth-century mode of negotiating the United States's real distances. In "The Far Field," the listing of New World warbler species—"Cape May, Blackburnian, Cerulean" (2.18)—reminds the alert reader of the sequence's geography and scope, birds and speaker joined in continental-scale migrations. James Dougherty finds the extension of Roethke's mystical quest beyond the confines of the individual self to be the sequence's signal accomplishment. That the "poems are grounded in encounters with specific places and things to an extent that was unprecedented in his poetry," according to Dougherty, arises from Roethke's discovery of "a spiritual being who did not emerge from the depths of the self but was present in what is other than the self" (177).

Dougherty considers the discovery of this "being" in, among other places, "the landscapes of the American West and Northwest" (177) a late development in Roethke's poetry, but the autobiographical speaker in "The Far Field" first comes into contact with such a presence, or presences, as a child at the field's edge. Any apparent contradiction, however, is resolved by the agency of memory. The field is "far" not only in its geographical situation, but also as a regression into the distant past. William Barillas points out that "'field' in Roethke's vocabulary . . . signifies the embodiment of eternity in the physical world" (*Midwestern Pastoral,* 112). Eternity obviates distinctions of time and, in effect, place. At the beginning of the fourth section of "The Far Field," for example, the "lost self" (4.1) is figured as a "sea-shape turning around" (4.3). This protean transformation flashes forward to the homely retrospective of the old man by the fire, and prepares the reader for the imagistic conclusiveness of "The Rose."

"The Rose," which follows "The Far Field" and closes the "North American Sequence," begins with an assertion that "this place . . . / Is important" (*Collected Poems,* 196). "The Far Field," however, makes a point of questioning the significance, at least as generally understood, of its out-of-the-way settings. The dead-end peninsula leads to the neglected field, the culvert, and, in section 3, "to a still, but not a deep center, / A point outside the glittering current" (3.16–17). In the familiar but obscure landscapes of "The Far Field," the speaker comes to see daily, lived reality as the habitat in which both physical and spiritual transformations occur. Even death, though apparently disjunctive, is as ordinary and transitory as "a dying garden in September" (3.23). But such universality does not entail insignificance. Figured in the deceptively comforting guise of an old man at the fireside, the lost self is "faced with his own immensity" (4.6). Dressed "[i]n robes of green, in garments of adieu" (4.5), vestments embracing both life and death, he becomes "the final man" to whom "[a]ll finite things reveal infinitude" (4.12–13). Nature is transcendence; the individual is the cosmic. "A ripple widening from a single stone" (4.21) is connected to, of a substance with, all "the waters of the world" (4.22).

The transition introduced by "—Or" is a key point in the sequence as well as in the individual poem; the culvert-turned-river bounds the flower-strewn field with sluggish yet moving water, thus linking "Meditation at Oyster River" and "The Long Waters" to the seashore in "The Rose." Surrounded by water imagery, the childhood field is a kind of stable island in the flow. Expanding on an idea advanced previously by Nelson, Dougherty considers "the actuality of childhood landscapes" in the sequence an advance from the "archetypal, dreamlike generalizations" of childhood in the poet's previous work (185). The field's "actuality" anchors "The Far Field," which, in turn, provides the metaphorical and structural soil from which the sequence's conclusion, and perhaps in retrospect its beginning, spring.

"The Far Field" brings the speaker to a destination both deeply personal and geographically central, a point of origin from which the sequence's other named places and rendered landscapes emanate mostly westward. The return in "The Rose" to Pacific Coast imagery reminiscent of "Meditation at Oyster River" completes a pivoting movement, the rediscovery of the far field restoring the speaker to surroundings from both earlier in the sequence and later in the poet's life. The link between the ensuing "rose in the sea-wind" (*Collected Poems,* 199) and the Michigan greenhouse is clear and explicit, and it is perhaps not unreasonable to see the rose, despite its ocean environs, as rising transformed from the flower dump by the far field's edge.

Though freighted with religious connotations, the figure of the single rose is accompanied by a rejection of a separate transcendent realm: "What need for heaven, then," Roethke's speaker asks (*Collected Poems,* 197). Perhaps "The Rose" is nothing more than a final apotheosis of a realization that emerges in "The Far Field": "What I love is near at hand, / Always, in earth and air" (3.25–26). In "The Divine Abyss: Theodore Roethke's Mysticism," William Heyen establishes Roethke's debt to Evelyn Underhill's outline of the stages of mystical development, and McMichael proposes a hierarchy of natural elements leading the speaker out of the self toward higher orders of awareness and being. But progression in "North American Sequence" can also be understood as a quest for holistic integration of aspects of the self's lived experience. Whereas the mystic's quest has traditionally been imagined as a vertical ascent into a realm of pure spirit, Roethke's ecological mysticism emphasizes horizontal movement across liminal zones where matter and spirit intersect and communicate. It is at such edges that the soul is most fully aware of its multifarious nature, leading Roethke, in another late poem, "In a Dark Time," to the discovery that "[t]he edge is what I have" (*Collected Poems,* 231). Barillas compares such edges in Roethke's work to ecotones, the ecological borderlands in which one environment, one place, becomes another (*Midwestern Pastoral,* 112). The physical space occupied by an ecotone may shift somewhat over time, but unlike stages in a teleological progression toward the divine, the liminal zone is fluid and permeable. An ecotone defines the convergence of worlds, and a traveler could cross between environments in either direction.

At what may be the sequence's most important ecotone transition, the "—Or" in "The Far Field" introduces an imagistic passage that follows the path of water across the boundary between sections 2 and 3 of the poem. "The river turns on itself" (3.1), the speaker asserts at the beginning of section 3, reiterating the earlier reversal of the "wheel turning away from itself" (2.41) and projecting ahead to the "sea-shape" in section 4. The river imagery continues its retrograde motion from "The sprawl of the wave, / The on-coming water" (2.42–43), that closes section 2 up to a more inland, younger stage in the hydrologic cycle where streams gather from glaciers and "the mountainy upland" (3.7), once more "descending to the alluvial plain" (3.10). The flow linking midcontinent to sea is not sequential; all parts of the cycle occur simultaneously. Though embedded in time and circumstance, taken as a whole nature's systems are synchronous. Nature abides in immediate particulars integrated into a holistic, enduring net of relationships; like the path of the "spiritual man," the hydrologic course is "circuitous" but inevitable.

Roethke's valorization of the immediate and particular recalls not only Blake's "To see a World in a Grain of Sand" (490), alluded to specifically, perhaps, in the suspended droplet image that occurs elsewhere in the "North American Sequence," but also the Zen proverb that one should "chop wood, carry water" after, as well as before, enlightenment. In his 2012 interview with Andrew De Haan, Heyen attributes a parallel insight to one of Roethke's significant sources: "Even today, outside splitting wood, I reminded myself of what Evelyn Underhill tells us, that for the mystics eternity is now." The self's situation may be unchanged, but spiritual growth opens perception to the multidimensional web in which the individual joins family and national history—Roethke's immigrant father in "The Far Field," the slaughtered buffalo in "The Longing"—in an intimate and cosmic ecology. Even at the expansive conclusion of "The Far Field," the speaker stops to honor the particular details of the natural world, the "[o]dor of basswood on a mountain slope, / A scent beloved of bees" (4.17–18). This aside could be seen as one more distraction or regression, but the appearance of the basswood and bees just a few lines from the end of "The Far Field" suggests that the advancing self does not abandon the material world, an interpretation bolstered by the speaker's fascinated focus on an ecological relationship in which he is not directly involved. As the basswood remains "beloved of bees," it appears that both, and the interaction binding them, are beloved of the speaker. It is especially telling that the poem's final descriptive catalogue draws on the physiological connections linking the olfactory, the emotions, and "[t]he pure serene of memory in one man" (4.20). Like the associative shifts that characterize the poem's narrative development and the hydrologic networks that knit the continent's geography, memory unites the perceptual, emotional, and intellectual interchanges comprising the self's lived experience.

Roethke's speaker defends his empathetic response to nature's ordinary losses, asserting that

> [m]y grief was not excessive.
> For to come upon warblers in early May
> Was to forget time and death.
>
> (2.13–15)

The "to be" verb "was" establishes identity, marking Roethke's view of transcendence as implicated and ecological, rather than esoteric or gnostic. Even in these late poems, Roethke remains committed to the vision expressed in his student essay "Some Self-Analysis," in which he links nature and memory ("A perception of nature—no matter how delicate, how subtle, how evanescent,—remains with me forever"), and proclaims his loyalty to American nature writers "Muir and Thoreau and Burroughs" (*On Poetry and Craft,* 18). When the speaker asserts that at the field's edge "[o]ne learned of the eternal" (2.6), the shift to third person may seem peculiarly distant or evasive, but it echoes John Muir's insight regarding ecological interconnectedness: any one thing, presumably including an individual consciousness, proves to be "hitched to everything else in the Universe" (211).

Roethke's ecological perspective functions as a counterpoint to the mystic's indirect but basically linear or vertical progression from material nature toward a transcendent communion with the divine. Roethke maintains the dignity of the commonplace by expanding the net of connections in all directions, the sequence's disjunctive image shifts enacting a more synthetic, less ordered form of illumination. If, as Paglia claims, Roethke "has integrated the standard mystic vision of ecstatic unity with the cosmos with a darker, mustier, more realistic organicism" ("Dance of the Senses"), the result is that, in a poem like "The Far Field," the soul's potential is reached not by overcoming the limitations of the physical world but by discovering the depths of its entanglement; the self's goal is to come into the presence of the multifarious beings and rhythms of its necessary context. There is no heaven beyond, and no need for one. By finding the eternal in the natural, and by declaring "love" for what is "near at hand," the journeying self in "The Far Field" emerges into a vision of comprehensive ecological connectedness, prepared to participate in the grandeur and fulfillment of "The Rose," as the reader is equipped for the resolution of the "North American Sequence" as a whole.

36

Nature Mysticism in "The Rose"

EDWARD MORIN

"THE ROSE" (*Collected Poems,* 196–99) is the sixth and final long poem in the "North American Sequence," which the poet wrote with relative ease and confidence during the last four years of his life (Seager, 252). No longer searching for his identity as a man and poet through recovery of the imagined lost Eden of his dead father's vanished greenhouses, Roethke now seems concerned about his failing health, mortality, and the endurance of his well-established literary reputation. One commentator purports that the entire sequence, including "The Rose," reveals the poet seeking "to transcend the sensual" and achieve union with "the Absolute" (Bowers, 159, 170). Another says that "'The Rose'. . . embodies Roethke's most complete presentation of the mystical Way of Illumination" (Parini, 168). Acknowledging the experiences recounted in the poem as the poet's quest for spiritual illumination, we can delineate the qualities of enlightenment he seeks and seems to achieve in the course of the poem. The poet aspires to transcend the limitations of his physical existence through mystical union with something other than an absolute being. Structured as a meditation in the mystical tradition, "The Rose" presents an ordered sequence of sensory perceptions and recollections that draws its author away from lifelong insecurities and inner conflict and inspires a sustained mystical union with the varied, beautiful forms of life surrounding him.

In his essay "Some Self-Analysis," Roethke explains how the outdoors affected him: "Ever since I could walk, I have spent as much time as I could in the open. . . . When I get alone under an open sky where man isn't too evident,—then I'm tremendously exalted and a thousand vivid ideas and sweet visions flood my consciousness" (*On Poetry and Craft,* 18). Mammals, birds, trees, plants, and insects were things he cared about most. He accompanied his father on hunting and fishing expeditions and spent many hours alone in a nearby woods that the family owned. This love of solitude in remote natural surroundings prevailed throughout the poet's life. His protégé and close friend, the poet David Wagoner, who used to drive him on excursions to the countryside around Seattle, describes how Roethke dealt with nature in the 1950s, when he wrote the "North American Sequence":

> As far as I know he never walked more than one hundred yards, if he could help it. . . . He would go to woodsy places and then he would sit. That was it. Sit as soon as possible. And think and watch and listen. Be involved in the landscape around him. No, he was not a hiker or a climber. . . . I don't think he liked the wild either. . . . You could drive for an hour in any direction except under water and be where there was no trace of man. (95–96)

Roethke's large, ungainly frame made walking difficult; his deteriorating health also may have impeded him with circulatory and foot problems. Wagoner's observations, however, also document Roethke's preference for a contemplative rather than an active life, a tendency that intensified with age. The final line in a poem of this period, "The Abyss," asserts Roethke's contemplative leanings: "Being, not doing, is my first joy" (*Collected Poems,* 214).

Roethke's contemplative disposition may have roots in his youthful involvement with institutional religion. Through his parents, young Theodore attended a Christian church in his hometown of Saginaw and at age fifteen was awarded a certificate by the Presbyterian Training Conference at Alma, Michigan, for "having completed the required class work in Bible Study—Stewardship, Home Missions, Essential Christian Doctrine" (qtd. in Seager, 43–44). Although he probably had no further affiliation with any religious organization, Roethke's notebooks show his interest in the Christian contemplatives Meister Eckhart, St. Theresa of Avila, and St. Francis of Assisi (Seager, 164): "Everything will be found to hinge finally on the idea of meditation. This idea has suffered a steady decline in the Occident, along with the transcendent view of life in general . . . yet it is not certain that religion itself can survive unless men retain some sense of wisdom which may be won by sitting in quiet meditation" (qtd. in Parini, 155–56). Roethke's notes focus mainly on "the Western (specifically Catholic) mystics" (Bowers, 22), who assume a separateness of body and soul, a dichotomy between physical and spiritual existence. Although such abstractions intrigued Roethke, he harbored no abiding interest in the neo-Platonic body-soul conflict that has preoccupied Christianity and poets such as T. S. Eliot and William Butler Yeats. Instead, Roethke strove to merge emotion and sensory experience into what he calls in the poem "I Cry, Love! Love!" "[t]hat anguish of concreteness" (*Collected Poems,* 88).

The rose, this poem's central image, had paramount importance for the poet. His father had specialized in growing and hybridizing roses, and young Ted had delivered bouquets to homes on holidays (Seager, 21). He learned about their emblematic significance in Western culture, as shown by this notebook entry: "The rose: emblem of human love becoming divine" (qtd. in Bowers, 168). Roethke's remark corresponds to Dante's Christian ideal of beauty and love in the physical world leading humanity to a merging with the Absolute. By contrast, the secular courtly love tradition, exemplified in Guillaume de Lorris's medieval allegory of sensual love, *The Romance of the Rose,* makes the rose a symbol of the beloved as well as of human love itself. Roethke could have encountered these ideas in Denis de Rougemont's *Love in the Western World,* which he "read and made copious notes on" (Bowers, 122). Integrating youthful experience and mature gallantry into his amours and social life, Roethke customarily showed courtesy to women, young or old, by giving them roses (Seager, 264).

"The Rose" is structured in a way that resembles religious meditation practiced in Europe, as delineated by Louis L. Martz in *The Poetry of Meditation: A Study in English Religious Literature of the Seventeenth Century* (1954). Martz connects devotional treatises to the rhetorical strategies of Donne, Herbert, Crashaw, and other metaphysical poets. Between 1522 and 1524 St. Ignatius of Loyola synthesized the traditional format into the age's most popular and widely disseminated meditation guide, *The Spiritual Exercises.* Martz discusses seventeenth-century poets whom Roethke studied and emulated; affinities exist between their rhetorical strategies and the organization of "The Rose." St. Ignatius's procedure, as Martz explains, has three parts: (1) composition of place; (2) examination of points; and (3) colloquies. In "composition of place" the meditator uses "the image-forming faculty to provide a concrete and vivid setting for a meditation on invisible things" (28). "Examination of points" is the division of a subject into parts, or imagined action into a sequence, all perceived in sensory detail, as a preparation for communicating intimately with God. Finally, in a "colloquy" the soul directly expresses "affections, resolutions, thanksgivings, and petitions" (Martz, *Poetry of Meditation,* 27). These three functions are distributed sequentially through the four parts of "The Rose," but the speaker's relationship is with something other than a personal God.

Part 1 begins by disclaiming T. S. Eliot's assertion in "East Coker" that place or "[h]ere and there does not matter" (*Collected Poems,* 189). Eliot, who valued time and eternity much more than locality, transplanted himself from America to England, and in *Four Quartets* treated the rose mainly as an emblem of Christian divine love; Roethke implicitly discards this religious symbolism as a model for his own poem (Dougherty, 195–96, 198; Barillas, *Midwestern Pastoral,* 132–33). "There are those to whom place is unimportant," Roethke asserts, "[b]ut this place, where sea and fresh water meet, / Is important" (1.1–3). These opening lines of "The Rose" visually "compose" a scene somewhere on Puget Sound near where Roethke lived, or out on the Olympic Peninsula. Except for the speaker, no human beings are present, only birds and plants, and faint traces of sheep and rabbits. Graceful free verse of widely varying line length describes active birds—hawks, eagles, herons, towhees, finches—moving or calling, as the tide rises, waves "lessen," and the speaker imagines himself swaying "outside [him]self / Into the darkening currents" (22–23).

Verbal vignettes begin the second step of meditation, an "examination of points"—not analytical observations but pictorial expressions of the poet's feelings toward the wild creatures he loves. Nine of the ten named bird species have a range spanning the U.S., but one, the scoter, is a sea duck, dark with bright orange on its bill, common only in the Pacific Northwest. Scoters fly as a flock strung in long wavy lines, settling on the water in a formation called a "raft" (Udvardy, 368). This may be the species Roethke speaks of when he asks,

> Was it here I wore a crown of birds for a moment
> While on a far point of the rocks
> The light heightened . . . ?
>
> (1.26–28)

The "crown of birds" could be an ironic parallel to Christ's "crown of thorns" on Calvary. Light is a common image in Roethke's poems, symbolizing spiritual illumination and happiness; that it is "heightened" suggests brilliant light the poet may be recalling from a prior manic hallucination.

Part 2 continues the "examination of points" with an elaborate Homeric simile comparing the gentle motion of the water to a ship among waves and finally to a child's boat dipping in a pond; by watching the water long enough we ourselves appear to be moving and "[o]ur motion continues" (2.8). The speaker notices a rosebush tangled in matted underbrush:

> But this rose, this rose in the sea-wind,
> Stays,
> Stays in its true place,
> Flowering out of the dark,
> Widening at high noon, face upward,
> A single wild rose, struggling out of the white embrace of the morning-glory.
>
> (2.9–14)

The word "rose" can denote a whole rosebush or a single rose blossom; while the poet may be using both designations interchangeably, he likely sees a wild rosebush which has produced just one blossom. Crowded by aggressively competing plants, the rose barely holds on, a fixed point in an unstable setting of rocks, briars, and grass. The poet is fascinated by the shrub's feat of primitive survival, "[f]lowering out of the dark" (2.12). Perhaps he recognizes a correspondence between its situation and his own as he emerged from the darkness of depression in periods of low self-esteem—a plain, clumsy kid from Saginaw suffering from bipolar disorder.

A wild rose is usually flat and pale pink, not layered and deep in color and spherical in shape like a prize-winning hybrid rose. Yet this wild rose prompts him to recall the apparition of roses in an archetypal moment of his life:

> And I think of roses, roses,
> White and red, in the wide six-hundred-foot greenhouses,
> And my father standing astride the cement benches,
> Lifting me high over the four-foot stems, the Mrs. Russells, and his own elaborate hybrids,
> And how those flowerheads seemed to flow toward me, to beckon me, only a child, out of myself.
>
> (2.21–25)

The child's view of the massive greenhouse in full color amplifies the scene's magnitude. This paradisiacal experience, of which Roethke speaks in *On Poetry and Craft* (21–23), lifts him ecstatically (from Greek, *ek-stasis*) out of his own body, an act physically prompted by his father's lifting, which repeats the sensation of mystical levitation suggested in line 1.22: "I sway outside myself." That "flowerheads . . . flow toward" the speaker suggests the dynamic effect of water approaching in waves, as water does elsewhere in the poem. Rosemary Sullivan calls the rose scene between Roethke and his father "an experience of primitive atonement with nature . . . shattering the sense of isolation and separateness which has haunted the poet. . . . For one of the few times in Roethke's poetry, the father is recovered in an intimate and personalized memory of reconciliation and love" (163). This event seems to Roethke the closest he has ever come to transcendence toward an absolute, a beatific vision with his father in the place of God. The following two lines support this interpretation: "What need for heaven, then, / With that man and those roses?" (2.26–27). These are no offhand, throwaway lines, but a deeply sincere statement. Roethke revealed his hero worship of his father in a college essay written three years after Otto Roethke's death: Otto, he wrote, was "a truly great man. I have never found anyone remotely like him in life or literature" (qtd. in Seager, 41).

Part 3 expands the examination of points toward the third step of formal meditation, the colloquy, but instead of portraying a traditional Christian colloquy between a human speaker and the Absolute, Roethke asks, "What do they tell us, sound and silence?" He answers with auditory images: "I think of American sounds in this silence" (3.1–2). The first twenty mainly end-stopped lines in part 3 catalogue the sounds associated with places and animals, much in the style of Walt Whitman. Several consecutive lines beginning with "The" and "And" are characteristic of Whitmanian catalogues, with repeated words at the beginnings of lines, the first letter of each line being capitalized.

These sounds in places across America are subtly allusive. For example, "wind-harps having their say" on "the banks of the Tombstone" (3.3) are Aeolian harps: box-shaped stringed instruments that make delicate sounds when blown by the wind. "Tombstone" refers to either the Babocomari River near Tombstone, Arizona, or the nearby San Pedro River flowing north out of Mexico. A symphony of auditory images includes the onomatopoetic "ticking of snow around oil drums in the Dakotas," the "thin whine of telephone wires in the wind of a Michigan winter" (3.11–12), bird calls, a bulldozer, sandblaster, and honking car horns. These end in diminuendo with

> that single sound
> When the mind remembers all,
> And gently the light enters the sleeping soul,
> A sound so thin it could not woo a bird.
>
> (3.17–20)

Although light has no sound in the real world, this light (a symbol of happiness) is accompanied by the faintest of sounds in the poet's consciousness. The next line is spaced for emphasis apart from the preceding lines, but is part of the sentence they form: "Beautiful my desire, and the place of my desire" (3.21). It suggests a new context beyond enjoyment of the preceding music. Here the speaker expresses satisfaction with present and past desire and with the place where it is manifested. Part 3 ends with pleasant recollections mainly of natural images. Throughout part 3, the poet has listened to nature's objects telling who and what they are, and he has begun telling who he is. In this passage the poet has delivered his version of a colloquy.

In part 4, Roethke says he lives with rocks, weeds, sea slime, and the salmon that "ease their way into the kelp beds" (4.8). Within a grove of "wind-warped madronas" (exotic-looking red-barked evergreen trees of the Pacific Northwest), he celebrates "this rose" which has occasioned his finding "the true ease of myself" (4.10–11), echoing Whitman's diction in "Song of Myself." He restates his Whitmanian ideal seven lines later: "And I rejoiced in being what I am." Dusk approaches "[i]n the lilac change" as a bird flies and a dolphin rises "from the darkening waves" (4.18–22). Symbolically, the light of spiritual illumination has prevailed over darkness, depression, and death. The speaker has shed his fear of death.

In the last four lines of the poem, and of the entire sequence, the poet triumphantly announces that "this rose in the sea-wind" keeps

> the whole of light,
> Gathering to itself sound and silence—
> Mine and the sea-wind's.
>
> (4.23–26)

By gathering "the whole of light" (symbolizing truth, beauty, happiness, and perhaps "the One" or absolute being) to itself, the rose as a fixed, stable entity has laid claim to perpetuity, but the poet is silent about such entitlements for himself. The main value of transcendence for Roethke seems to be the experience of getting out of himself, out of his own ego and fear—"[a]s if another man appeared out of the depths of my being, / And I stood outside myself" (4.12–13)—and appreciating the presence of something greater than himself.

Roethke avoids grappling with abstract ideas of what that something is. To say, as Jay Parini has, that "substituting the word 'rose' for" the neo-Platonic philosopher Plotinus's idea of "The One" yields "a fair paraphrase of the last part of Roethke's meditative poem" (171) invites mistaken expectations of what the poem is about and what its author believes. The poem has tracked what Christian mystics call the "Illuminative Way" of spiritual enlightenment, but it stops short of their final step, the "Unitive Way," whereby the devout person becomes intimately united to God by means of spiritual love. Roethke expresses no desire for divine reward, but is content with the terrestrial denouement of his meditation. James Applewhite accurately states Roethke's alternative course: "Having fled from abstraction to childhood and the particular, he must assert his ultimate values through symbols rather than concepts," and his symbols tend to reside in "lowly organic life" (206–7). Roethke's profound attachment to plant, insect, and animal species throughout the corpus of his poetry helps him feel at home in the cosmos. He portrays various species playfully in poems that entertain children. In his poems for mature readers, these species fulfill his human need for belonging similar to what primitive people experience when they attribute a soul or a spirit to familiar "lowly" organisms.

Let's consider Roethke's mystical or transcendental beliefs. In a well-known speech from the last year of his life, Roethke candidly espoused animism (from Latin "anima," soul):

> If the dead can come to our aid in a quest for identity, so can the living—and I mean *all* living things, including the subhuman. This is not so much a naïve as a primitive attitude: animistic, maybe. Why not? Everything that lives is holy: I call upon these holy forms of life. . . .
>
> For there *is* a God, and He's here, immediate, accessible. . . . [I]n the lowest forms of life, He moves and has His being. Nobody has killed off the snails. Is this a new thought? Hardly. But it needs some practicing in Western society. Could Reinhold Niebuhr love a worm? I doubt it. But I—we—can. (*On Poetry and Craft*, 40, 42)

These words concluding the essay "On 'Identity'" are Roethke's clearest comprehensive statement about human beings' relationship to the cosmos. He defends animism, a belief that every living thing has a soul, against assumed opposition from Reinhold Niebuhr, the most prominent Protestant theologian of the day. Roethke seems aware of a traditional antagonism between animism and Christianity that scientist Lynn White Jr. explained in 1967: "By destroying pagan animism, Christianity made it possible to exploit nature in a mood of indifference to the feelings of natural objects. . . . The spirits *in* natural objects, which formerly had protected nature from man, evaporated" (10). Without the anthropomorphisms of Greek or other mythologies, animism survives in our era as *panpsychism,* which claims that "all things have a mind, or a mind-like quality" (Skrbina, 16). Roethke's version of panpsychism resembles what distinguished philosophers Henri Bergson, Alfred North Whitehead, and Teilhard du Chardin offer as an alternative to empiricism's mechanistic worldview (Skrbina, 157–84). Their perspective finds adherents among scientists, Buddhists, and environmentalists. Its prominence in Roethke's works throws considerable light on interpretations of "The Rose" and other poems of his. It contextualizes his thinking as an up-to-date postmodern poet.

37

"The Abyss"

Finding the Next Life in This One

TRENTON HICKMAN

ON FEBRUARY 9, 1963, Theodore Roethke appeared on a panel at Northwestern University titled "A Spectrum of Perspectives," with British historian Arnold Toynbee and linguist and semanticist S. I. Hayakawa, among others. Designed to offer "perspectives on personal identity, perspectives on attaining knowledge," and "the challenge of global perspectives," the panel afforded Roethke a chance to address how the writing of poetry aided in approaching the divine (Seager, 282). In the final sentences of his statement at the panel, Roethke argues that

> there *is* a God, and He's here, immediate, accessible. I don't hold with those thinkers who believe in this time He is farther away—that in the Middle Ages, for instance, He was closer. He is equally accessible now, not only in works of art or in the glories of a particular religious service, or in the light, the aftermath that follows the dark night of the soul, but in the lowest forms of life, He moves and has His being. Nobody has killed off the snails. Is this a new thought? Hardly. But it needs some practicing in Western society. (*On Poetry and Craft,* 42)

Nowhere can we find these views about Roethke's perceived relationship between God and "the lowest forms of life" more compellingly framed than in his poem "The Abyss" (*Collected Poems,* 211–14), first published in *Encounter*

(October 1962) and subsequently in Roethke's posthumous collection *The Far Field* (1964). While the poem is, as William Heyen notably argues in "The Divine Abyss: Theodore Roethke's Mysticism" (1969), assuredly a depiction of a speaker's mystical journey towards the divine, "The Abyss" finds God not in a renunciation of the world but in a fuller, more complete embrace of it, a fullness following "the dark night of the soul." What finally bridges the abyss between this life and the next, the poem suggests, are the ways in which we can finally perceive the ways in which God inhabits the small but not insignificant manifestations of life that have always been around us.

The poem's first canto begins, as Heyen points out, in the middle of a spiritual crisis ("Divine Abyss," 1054). We find the poem's speaker on a staircase, caught between a symbolic step up into "nowhere" (1.4) or a "step down the stair" into the "abyss," which, as an unidentified voice points out, "you can't miss" because "[i]t's right where you are" (1.6–7). Readers don't know how the speaker arrived at this place, only that he is caught there midflight, in all that entails. Indeed, images similarly caught in the middle of incompletion fill the remaining lines of the canto: a "[n]oon of failure," "[p]art of a house," and an indeterminate place "in the middle of" and "around a cloud" where "on top" there is "a thistle" (1.11–15). Thus readers find themselves trapped with the speaker in a similar dilemma: Where to go? How to get there? and more importantly, Why to try? In these lines, readers may be reminded of the original sense of the word "abyss," before its association with the hell of Judeo-Christian eschatology, as a site of primordial chaos: a terrain of formlessness, to be sure, but also the location of creation in its first moments, a void paradoxically full of promise.

But what will be created in this abyss, and who will shape its chaotic void? In the second canto, the speaker finds himself almost as incomplete as the images that he has seen emerging into his field of vision; he is one who has "been spoken to variously / But heard little" (2.1–2) and who has

> taken, too often, the dangerous path,
> The vague, the arid,
> Neither in nor out of this life.
>
> (2.5–7)

It isn't that the poem's speaker hasn't heard explanations that might make sense of the abyss for him—apparently, many people "have declared themselves" to him (2.11)—but he doesn't know which, among all these voices, "is holy," and he must decide which "speech" he has heard is that which "abides" (2.8–9) or remains valid in deciphering the nondescript, abysmal staircase where he finds himself.

One voice the speaker clearly seeks is that of Walt Whitman, here invoked as the "maker of catalogues." When the "world invades" the speaker with its "tongues" that renew their "babbling" and its "hunger for objects" (2.13–16), the speaker's only respite comes in the form of a "furred caterpillar" (2.19) on the string of a window blind, presumably of the window in the "[p]art of the house" (1.12) hinted at in the first canto. Like the blade of grass turned "uniform hieroglyphic" for Walt Whitman (31), Roethke's caterpillar emerges in this poem as the speaker's own "symbol," one earned as he "moved closer to death, lived with death" (2.20–21), and one perfectly suited to a speaker who finds himself caught in the middle of something he doesn't yet understand. The caterpillar is itself a transitional creature—not an egg, but not yet the butterfly it will become, mirroring the indeterminate position in which the speaker finds himself but pointing also to the eventual transformation through which the speaker will pass before the poem's end. Soon the speaker chooses other animal symbols, which like the caterpillar capture aspects of his precarious, contingent position. The speaker is "a mole" and "a night-fishing otter" (2.26–27), two animals which, like the caterpillar, which must cocoon itself before emerging again anew, go either into the earth or under the water before surfacing into new light. In these lines, the speaker finds, Whitman-like, that the key to a holiness that abides (and, apparently, that keeps the "sly surly attendant" (2.22) of death at bay at least for a while) can be found in the natural world that Roethke has so often chronicled and catalogued in his own poems.

The challenge of finding holiness infused in the particular images of the natural world, the third canto would suggest, is that the apprehension of all these images in their richness overwhelms the sensorium of the speaker. "Too much reality," the lines argue, "can be a dazzle, a surfeit." The danger of finding oneself in "too close immediacy" of all these features of the natural world is "exhaustion," not unlike the experience of entering "a florist's storeroom" and having all the odors of the many flowers overwhelm the nose and throat with "a rush of smells," forcing a retreat to warmer, simpler airs in the "heat of August" outdoors (3.1–5). In other words, these lines suggest that in considering the world of the caterpillar, the mole, and the otter, the speaker finds himself facing a problem opposite to the one he encountered in the half-finished images in the poem's first canto. How might the sheer onslaught of multitudinous specific sights and smells in the natural world confuse the speaker as much as would a world full of shifting vagueness? For the abyss, in its "slippery cold heights" and its "blinding misery" (3.8–9), offers the possibility of both bewildering vagueness and maddening particularity in its "terrible violence of creation" (3.12) as its primordial chaos churns through many possible futures.

What the third canto of "The Abyss" suggests, however, is that the speaker's own ability to "wait, unafraid, beyond the fearful instant" (3.14) has everything to do with the shape and form that the abyss eventually assumes for him, and that the "sunlit silence" (3.17), the "calm" (4.21), and the "luminous stillness" (4.24) that follow the initial churn of the abyss might mediate for the speaker either the shapelessness or the surfeit of specifics that he encounters in the world around him. In fact, the speaker's fearless waiting starts to feel like a sort of faith as he asks, "How can I dream except beyond this life?" and "Can I outleap the sea— / The edge of all the land, the final sea?" (4.1–3). The stillness of the speaker's waiting allows the speaker, finally, to begin his metamorphosis, caterpillar-like, into someone different, as he moves from someone preoccupied with "[k]nowing" into someone slowed into a state of "non-knowing" (4.9–10), lulled by the ocean and the stream which he sees into a cocoon-like condition "between dark and dark" (4.18), finally ready to "embrace" the "quiet under the small leaves" (4.21–22). He finally finds himself ready to change.

When he does change, the speaker joins the divinity that infuses the natural world which surrounds him. His question, "Do we move toward God, or merely another condition?" (4.15), sounds increasingly like a false binary, as the speaker moves toward God precisely by entering another condition in which the animals, the "forest pool," the "rings of water" (3.15–16), and the "tendrils" in their "eyeless seeking" teach him a simplicity of seeing that has been with him all along. The speaker must, like the child who reaches his hand into "the coiled smilax," learn that to "obey the wind" at his "back" (4.4–6) is to fill himself with the not-knowing of omnipresent nature. This, too, is a Whitmanian sort of truth, where the frantic catalogues give way to a sense of the divine in the long list of what has been seen and witnessed. Finally, the speaker of "The Abyss" is ready to understand what the mysterious voice of the first canto meant when it said that the abyss "is right where you are": the primordial chaos only takes shape for the speaker once he is ready to apprehend and comprehend that the most important stillness in nature, the one that will allow him to see God and reach beyond this life, is the one found inside himself. Once full of the not-knowing of the natural truths all around him, the speaker hears the same mysterious voice from the opening lines of the poem, now identified as the "shade" who "speaks slowly" at the end of the fourth canto:

> "Adore and draw near.
> Who knows this—
> Knows all."
>
> (4.25–28)

The antecedent for "this" in the shade's speech is the speaker's hard-earned "embrace" of the "luminous stillness," a quiet that now pervades the speaker's soul as well as the landscape in which he has finally found himself.

In the final canto of "The Abyss," we find the poem's speaker emerged from his cocoon of self-transformation into a world where he is able to see how "joy" (5.13) grows out of living "merged" with "the bright air" (5.11), having "receive[d]" and "been received" by the nature around him. The speaker, who now hears "the flowers drinking in their light" and takes "counsel of the crab and the sea-urchin" (5.2–4), finds himself "most immoderately married" to a landscape where the abyss has settled into a creation full of life, of cascading waters, "mossy logs," and the beauties of "irregular sand" (5.6–7). At the poem's end, we see the full metamorphosis from the fearful, half-formed speaker of the first two cantos, a person characterized by confusion and an unsatisfied "terrible hunger" (2.16), into a person whom "[t]he Lord God" has unburdened of all of this previous discontent and "heaviness" (5.10). The speaker now no longer concerns himself with "doing," like the endless climbing of the staircase in the earlier part of the poem, but with "being," called here his "first joy" (5.13). He is no longer concerned with human action that would set him apart from the contemplative holiness of nature. Rather, he seeks to inhabit a happiness that unites him with the nature against which he previously struggled.

In the poem's last line, it would be tempting to discuss the speaker's transformation almost entirely in terms of what Jay Parini calls "the Oriental concept of the empty mind" (173), especially because of the reference in the poem's penultimate line to "the place by the bo-tree" (5.12), the tree under which Buddha achieved enlightenment. But the speaker's change isn't the renunciation of desire, as Buddha taught, or a weaning of one's heart away from the things of the world and toward the features of some nonterrestrial plane, but the achievement of peace and an internal quiet that is connected to and deeply rooted in the riotous beauty of the natural world. One is reminded in the closing lines of "The Abyss" of the closing lines of Roethke's "Journey to the Interior," a poem from the first section of *The Far Field,* where a similar change in the speaker's perspective leads not to Buddhist renunciation but to a "breath[ing] with the birds," a way of divine knowledge that is similarly silent but also "[u]nperplexed, in a place leading nowhere" (*Collected Poems,* 189). In "The Abyss," Roethke's speaker hasn't found God by giving up the world and its nature, but by refusing any longer to hold himself separate from it in his spiritual quest.

"The spirit or soul," says Roethke in the text of his 1963 panel at Northwestern, "this I was keeping 'spare'" in my desire for the essential. But the spirit need not be spare: it can grow gracefully and beautifully like a tendril, like a flower" (*On Poetry and Craft,* 37). In "The Abyss," we as readers watch this process unfold firsthand as the poem's speaker frees himself from the terrible constraints of the vague staircase early in the poem to find contentment in the immoderate marriage between self, nature, and the divine at the poem's conclusion. As Roethke himself asserted, "The Abyss" displays a world where God and the Creation are not separate from the smilax but deeply rooted in it, in that place where being, not doing, is the most sacred expression of happiness.

38

"Otto"

An Insight into Roethke's Poetic Vision

JEFF VANDE ZANDE

AS I write this, I'm sitting in the enclosed second-floor porch of Theodore Roethke's boyhood home at 1805 Gratiot Avenue in Saginaw, Michigan. The room's floors and walls are hardwood, with casement windows that look out over Roethke Court, a subdivision of houses where the Roethke greenhouses once stood. It's not the first time I've had the pleasure of writing in Roethke's home. When I was working on my novel *American Poet* (2012), the Friends of Theodore Roethke offered me the opportunity to spend a night in the house to write. *American Poet* is the fictional coming-of-age story of a young man, Denver Hoptner, who returns to Saginaw after graduating from the University of Michigan with a bachelor of fine arts in poetry. With no acceptances from graduate schools and no job, Denver moves into the basement of his estranged father's house. Uncertain of his identity and what it means to be a poet, he finds an unlikely calling in a quest to save the Roethke House from being condemned. Hearing of my novel, the board members of the Friends of Theodore Roethke took an immediate interest and did what they could to support me in the writing of it.

According to their website, the mission of the Friends of Theodore Roethke is to "promote, preserve, and protect the literary legacy of Theodore Roethke by restoring his family residences in Saginaw, Michigan, for cultural and educational opportunities." Because of them, I can hear Roethke reading his poetry aloud in his boyhood bedroom as I write. They have a recording of him on a continuous loop. Without them and their efforts, I likely would not have the opportunity to write on this porch.

The porch and this house are significant in Roethke's literary legacy. He didn't just grow up in this house and then move away. The house and his florist father's greenhouses behind it haunted Roethke throughout his life. Memories of growing up here became the source material for much of his poetry. His boyhood provided not only visual texture to his work, but also a way of looking at the world. Roethke often returned to the house to write. Many of the poems in his groundbreaking second book, *The Lost Son and Other Poems* (1948), were written in the Gratiot Avenue house. According to Annie Ransford, president of the Friends of Theodore Roethke, the second-floor porch was one of Roethke's favorite places to write. In 1946, having won a Guggenheim fellowship, Roethke returned to Saginaw to work on his now-famous greenhouse poems. Allan Seager, Roethke's biographer, notes that "[u]sually Guggenheim fellows travel abroad," but Roethke "stayed in Saginaw" (149). He seemed to know that the poems were not to be found in Europe, but instead had to be cultivated where his father, Otto Roethke, had cultivated and experimented with flowers in the greenhouses.

The second-floor porch was also a favorite spot for Roethke's father. According to Seager, when Otto was dying of cancer, "he would be taken to the back porch on sunny days in a chair and sit there looking out toward the greenhouse" (42). It is fitting that both men were drawn to the porch. In his last days, Otto wanted to look out at his life's work. Similarly, finding his own voice in poetry, Theodore Roethke looked out over his father's world at the beginning of what would be his life's work. It was his father's world that gave Roethke something unique to say. It was his father's early death that kept the man a mystery—a force of nature to be studied in the same way he would study the natural images and memories of his childhood. "Had the relationship of father and son been able to take its course," Rosemary Sullivan writes, "understanding and reconciliation would have been gradual" (7). Had this reconciliation happened, one wonders if we would have Roethke the poet as we know him. Otto's work as a florist, his confounding personality, and his early death seem to have allowed Roethke to blossom poetically.

Published in his final, posthumous book, *The Far Field* (1963), the poem "Otto" (*Collected Poems,* 216–17) is Roethke's tribute to his father. Older than his father at the time of his death, Roethke reflects on the man whose world and temperament gave him so much to write about. Among scholars who have written about the poem, Karl Malkoff notes how the poem's formalism is appropriate to the poet's formal Prussian father (200). Jenijoy La Belle comments similarly on the rhyme and meter of the poem and contrasts it with the free verse approach of poems like "Elegy," which is also a reflection on an adult remembered from childhood, Roethke's Aunt Tilly (*Echoing Wood,* 148). Examining the poem from a psychological perspective, Sullivan writes that Otto "presented an exterior of authoritarian order and discipline, and, from Roethke's perspective, little angered him more than the 'effeminate' sensibility of his only son." She looks at "Otto" as a poem in which Roethke "seems to reconcile in his mind his father's harshness and his underlying sensitivity, the violence and the deeper gentleness of the man." Like other critics, Sullivan explores the idea that "from the consequent sense of his own inadequacy Roethke seems to have acquired the burden of fears and guilts which haunted him all his life" (6–7). "Otto" then becomes Roethke's attempt to come to terms with his late father.

Beyond its poetic style or its psychological ramifications, "Otto" also offers a way to understand Roethke's poetic vision. Walter Kalaidjian writes that "'Otto' is another filial poem that ruminates on the shaping influence Roethke's father exerted over the poet's career" (168). This influence is not limited to guilt or inadequacy. The best poets offer a way to see the world—a way in which we haven't seen it before. For most children, there comes a point when they begin to see their fathers not as godlike, but as human. For Roethke, Otto died as a god, or at least as a phenomenon of nature. Gone too soon, he left to Roethke the business of studying the man from what he could recall. In much of his poetry, Roethke seeks to understand his father and his inherent contradictions.

In "Otto," Roethke considers a man who could be violent enough to shoot cats for getting near his pheasant runs, even coldly returning one of the dead cats to a neighbor "by the tail" (3.8). In the same stanza, he acknowledges of his father that "[t]he Indians loved him, and the Polish poor" (3.11). Roethke doesn't explore what charity or kindness engendered this love, but it was there. He also notes that his father's slender hand could "fit into a woman's glove" (2.1), but that same hand could slap with masculine impunity the faces of two poachers on his land. Even reflecting on his father's seemingly gentle work as a florist, Roethke recalls his father potting plants "as if he hated them" (1.9). Regardless of this perceived hostility, Roethke writes, "[w]hen flowers grew, their bloom extended him" (1.11). Beauty blooms from exasperated toil—another contradiction.

Awareness of contradictions became a way for Roethke to see the world and to explore it in his poetry. In "Root Cellar," he finds splendor in a place where others might only see dank ugliness. In "Weed Puller," he explores the idea that behind much beauty is the unseen toil of someone who suffers for that beauty. In "Child on Top of a Greenhouse," he explores the danger that comes with curious innocence. Where others might romanticize the child who climbs on top of a greenhouse to get a better look at the world, Roethke explores the scene's contradictions. Roethke's most anthologized poem, "My Papa's Waltz," is not only a depiction of his father, but also an examination of contradictions. The poem exhibits tension and relaxation, joy and frustration, love and longing—an uneasy waltzing, to be certain. So much of Roethke's poetry is an exploration of contradictions, of seeing and then seeing again. Subconsciously reflecting on Otto throughout his life, the poet reflected upon the world with that same vision. His father in his mystery and contradictions became a gift for Roethke as a poet. "Otto" stands as an acknowledgment of that gift.

Contradictory in its own way, the last stanza of the poem feels very different from the rest. Whereas the first three stanzas characterize Otto, the last stanza steps back to take a broader view of his greenhouse world. In the apostrophe of the last line, Roethke laments, "O world so far away! O my lost world!" (4.11). La Belle suggests that in the poem "the death of the father is conceived of as a loss of the whole world of childhood and innocence" (149). Nowhere in the poem, however, does Roethke mention Otto's death. Instead, the ending feels like a nostalgic lamentation for a world to which Roethke can never return, except in his mind, as he does in the first three stanzas. He can only see that world "[i]n [his] mind's eye" (4.1). Writing of Roethke's mother's death, Seager notes, "Ted, in Seattle, broke down in tears at the news but he did not go to the funeral. With his father and mother gone, the greenhouse gone, the proofs of his old life had dwindled but it still lay vividly, ineradicably in his memory" (221).

Maybe the last stanza of "Otto" is Roethke's recognition that, Guggenheim fellowship or no, he could never physically return to his father's world. Too much of what was important to him was gone, the greenhouses having been razed sometime between 1936 and 1948, according to Tom Trombley, deputy director of the Castle Museum of Saginaw County History. Recalling his father so truthfully made Roethke long for that lost world out of which he'd always been able to write. "Otto" sets out to be a poem of tribute and yet can't help but be a poem that recognizes that there's no separating the father from the world he represented. Despite a partial reconciliation between son and deceased father, Otto remains the god of the greenhouses.

From my point of view, Roethke's world is not completely lost. The Friends of Theodore Roethke have done an outstanding job of preserving the home. Until they purchased the house, it had only been lived in by Roethkes, and so had never been broken up into apartments, like so many of the large, older homes of Saginaw. Much of the Roethke family furniture is still here. The piano that Roethke practiced on as a child is still here. Obviously, the kitchen of "My Papa's Waltz" is still here. The bed that Roethke stands on in the last stanza of "Otto" is still in his bedroom, as is the window out of which he viewed "the waking" of his father's greenhouse world. The porch, too—the porch on which so many Roethke's poems were written—is still here. I spent a wonderful day on the porch working on this essay while my good friend Josh Maday worked on his novel. The spirit of Roethke fueled our writing, and so this house remains very much a sanctuary for writers. For Roethke, it was a lost world, but for me, this house has been a world found—giving me time and inspiration to work on my novel, and now to work on this essay. How fitting that even his house is both lost and found, still a place ripe with contradictions.

39

"The Meadow Mouse"

A Poem of Compassion

NORMAN CHANEY

IN AN essay he wrote for a rhetoric class when he was an undergraduate at the University of Michigan, Theodore Roethke said, "I have a genuine love of nature. . . . A perception of nature—no matter how delicate, how subtle, how evanescent—remains with me forever" (*On Poetry and Craft,* 17–18). From early to late in his literary career Roethke exhibited a deep love of the world of nature. In a poem titled "The Small" he writes,

I live
To woo the fearful small;
What moves in grass I love.

(*Collected Poems,* 142)

A captivating expression of his poetic wooing of the "small" is a poem titled "The Meadow Mouse" (*Collected Poems,* 219). It illuminates Roethke's love of nature as tendered toward nature's creatures. The poem is reminiscent of two other notable poems in English literature on the subject of the mouse. In Robert Burns's "To a Mouse," the speaker tells that while he was plowing he turned up the nest of a mouse. He reflects on the creature as an "earth-born companion / An' *fellow-mortal*" (72). In John Clare's "Mouse's Nest," the speaker tells that while walking in a hay field he poked a clump of grass, out of which "an old mouse bolted . . . / With all her young ones hanging at her teats" (154). In the poems of Burns and Clare, as in Roethke's "The Meadow Mouse," the discovery of a mouse represents a surprised eruption in the speakers' immediate consciousness of life.

In "An Evening with Theodore Roethke," the text of a 1967 memorial event featuring Roethke's biographer Allan Seager and friends Stanley Kunitz and John Ciardi, Seager states that "The Meadow Mouse" grew out of an actual experience: "Ted once went out into the field near his house. He went out and found a field mouse and brought it into the house exactly as he tells in the poem" (242). Roethke refined his experience of finding the mouse into a poem that consists of thirty lines of free verse divided into two main parts, numbered in the text as 1 and 2. Part 1—the first three stanzas—tells a story; part 2—the last two stanzas—is a meditative extension of that story.

The poem artfully effects a conversation, as though the speaker might be telling his story to a bystander. But no bystander is mentioned in the poem. The reader is privy to a stream of thought in which the speaker is talking to himself without sounding the words. The first two lines, in the present tense, tell of the baby mouse the speaker has found in the meadow and placed in a shoebox. The mouse lies sleeping, "stuffed in an old nylon stocking" (1). The entire first stanza is a single sentence, a fluidity of eighty-four words that link phrase-to-phrase, image-to-image. The speaker is fascinated at the mouse's anatomical features. Its feet are "like small leaves," and also like "little lizard feet" (8–9). It has the "absurd whiskers of a "cartoon mouse," something Walt Disney might draw. It is full of life, "[w]riggling like a min[u]scule puppy" (11).

In this mixing of disparate images as the speaker describes the mouse to himself ("leaves," "lizard," "cartoon mouse," "puppy"), we witness an identifying trait of Roethke both as a lover and as a poet of nature. That trait, as Roethke himself pinpointed it, is the feeling that in seeing one thing in nature, such as a mouse, "one is on the edge of many things: that there are many worlds from which we are separated by only a film: that a flick of the wrist, a turn of the body another way will bring us to a new world" (*Straw for the Fire,* 143). The world of nature is kaleidoscopic. Turn slightly the tube of the kaleidoscope and the image you have seen becomes something else. The feeling this trait of Roethke's poetry produces—its mixing of disparate images—is that individual entities in the world of nature wondrously blend into one another within a *oneness* that is nature itself.

A note of pity enters the first stanza. The speaker recalls the mouse's fear when he first picked it up by its tail: "A little quaker, the whole body of him trembling" (6). As the story continues, in the second stanza, the speaker tells that he has fed the mouse a careful selection of "three kinds of cheese" and provided it with a "[b]ottle-cap watering-trough." As a result of this care, the mouse appears contented:

> So much he just lies in one corner,
> His tail curled under him, his belly big
> As his head.

Is this small creature not something like a human infant? In the third stanza, the doting speaker imagines that the sleeping mouse, its "bat-like ears / Twitching, tilting toward the least sound," is blissfully attuned to it protective human surroundings:

> Do I imagine he no longer trembles
> When I come close to him?
> He seems no longer to tremble.
>
> (12–19)

The pity the speaker feels for the mouse is an index to the speaker's personality. A number of terms might serve to characterize him: sensitive, considerate, empathetic, loving, kind, all of which might be gathered under the umbrella term *compassionate,* signifying a personality capable of deep awareness of the mouse's fear and of desire to relieve it.

In part 2 of the poem, the first two lines tell in the present tense of something that has happened in the recent past. The speaker has gone "this morning" to "the shoe-box house on the back porch" only to find the box empty. His disappointment registers in a question: "Where has he gone, my meadow mouse[?]" (2.2). Indeed, where has the mouse gone? It has gone

> [t]o run under the hawk's wing,
> Under the eye of the great owl watching from the elm-tree,
> To live by courtesy of the shrike, the snake, the tom-cat.
>
> (2.2–6)

But implied in that question of *where* the mouse has gone is an unspoken question of *why.* Why should the mouse leave the care of the human who has "nuzzled" it in the palm of his hand and nurtured it as though it were a "child" (2.3)? The question of *why* goes unanswered in the poem itself, but the very lack of an answer leaves a gap for the reader to bridge.

Within the great world of nature is a vital force that drives every living thing toward individual self-fulfillment. The self-fulfillment of the acorn is the oak tree. The self-fulfillment of the baby mouse is the adult mouse. The baby mouse in its escape is on its way to becoming what nature drives it to be. *Why* has the mouse escaped? Because its *where* is not in a shoebox, but in a meadow that nature has given as the mouse's rightful habitat of self-fulfillment.

In the last four lines of the poem, the mouse story proper serves as a backdrop for a meditation that draws parallels between the mouse's life and the lives of other creatures, including humans:

> I think of the nestling fallen into the deep grass,
> The turtle gasping in the dusty rubble of the highway,
> The paralytic stunned in the tub, and the water rising,—
> All things innocent, hapless, forsaken.
>
> (2.7–10)

Roethke, for all the love of nature he expresses in his poetry, was acutely aware of nature's dark underside. No metaphysical theory satisfactorily accounts for why life is accompanied by predation, suffering, and death. It is a world in which the mouse lives "under the hawk's wing" (2.4), in which the paralytic lies "stunned in the tub, the water rising" (2.9). A feeling of melancholy hangs over the last four lines of "The Meadow Mouse." But that melancholy is tempered in part 1 of the poem by the speaker's compassion: his feeling-into the conditions of a form of life not his own. To many people, perhaps most, the mouse is a pesky rodent to be killed. To the speaker of "The Meadow Mouse," the mouse is a creature to be admired, nurtured, coddled, and kept. The mouse has escaped; it has its own natural destiny to fulfill. Nonetheless, the speaker of the poem in his compassion has given the mouse a chance for life—life, like the speaker's own, that is susceptible to all the contingencies that nature heaps upon it.

John Felstiner, in a book titled *Can Poetry Save the Earth?* (2009), advocates for poetry as a way to awaken people to the environmental perils of our day. In a chapter that affectionately ranges over Roethke's work, Felstiner speaks of Roethke "revering every kind of lowlife" (218). In my reading of Roethke's "The Meadow Mouse" and of numerous other poems in which he singles out nonhuman creatures as subjects, I am reminded of the humanist philosopher Albert Schweitzer. Schweitzer tells in his autobiography *Out of My Life and Thought* (1933) of an insight that flashed upon him one evening at sunset while he was traveling up an African river that was populated by a herd of hippopotami. Out of that experience he coined the phrase "Reverence for Life" (155), which became his guiding principle for conduct. He went on to express the meaning of the phrase in behavioral terms: "A man is ethical only when life as such is sacred to him—the life of plants and animals as well as that of his fellow men—and when he devotes himself to helping all life that is in need of help" (157–58). Schweitzer's principle of reverence for life was prompted by his insight that life is life, whether in a hippopotamus or a human being. He acknowledged life in all its given forms and conditions, and asked how within his orbit a human being he could be a positive rather than a negative influence within life's ongoing processes.

Roethke was a poet, not a humanist philosopher. Yet in his poetic expressiveness is an overtone of what Schweitzer calls the "ethical." A memorable title of a poem by Richard Wilbur is "Love Calls Us to the Things of This World" (307). Roethke's love of nature, as rendered in "The Meadow Mouse," calls us in our capacity as human beings to be attentive to forms of life that share the earth with us and to be compassionate to all life that is in need of help.

40

The Zoopoetics of "The Pike"

AARON M. MOE

IN THE early months of 2011, I discovered the phrase "Kafka's vast zoopoetics" from Jacques Derrida's *The Animal That Therefore I Am,* and I staggered (6). The multifaceted theories surrounding "ecopoetics" had already impacted studies of poetry, opening up new ways of seeing what it means to dwell in language and on the earth. Derrida, though, does not define nor delve into the potential for zoopoetics to open up new ways of engaging poetry. To define the term, I draw on its etymology: animals (*zoion*) and the making of poetry (*poiesis*). Zoopoetics is the "process of discovering innovative breakthroughs in form through an attentiveness to another species' bodily *poiesis*" (Moe, 10)—that is, another species' gestures, vocalizations, ways of being, or, more technically, their material semiotics. Form is crucial. We already know that animals abound in the content of stories and poems. Zoopoetics foregrounds the animal presences in the *gestures* of a poem, of a making.

Donna Haraway provides a way of seeing human-animal interactions in the "ecotone" (or ecological transition zone) of play. When two species meet and play, both parties undergo what she calls an "ontological and semiotic invention" in the material makings of their signs (232). She cites many examples, such as Barbara Smuts, who learned a new way of being in order to gain entrance into the "social semiotics" of baboons (24), and a donkey and a dog who learned to "reinvent their own repertoires through affective semiotic intra-action" (234).

They turned away from former ways of relating (prey-predator) and learned new ways to gesture, relate, and play. I extend Haraway's insight to the poetic tradition. When a poet meets another species, the inventive play involves words on a page. Zoopoetics explores the animal presences in the *gestures* of a poem—and not simply its content. The energy of animal gestures, vocalizations, movements, and lurkings contributes to the energy of the material motions of the words/lines/stanzas on a page.

Zoopoetics ought not to be limited to the human sphere. Other species, too, achieve breakthroughs in their makings through innovatively imitating other ways of being. My work discusses the elephant Koshik, who places his trunk in his mouth to vocalize five Korean words, as well as the beluga whale, who manipulates his vestibular sacs to reach the lower frequencies necessary to imitate human speech patterns (121; 91–92). More examples abound, and the fact that nonhuman animals possess the agency to innovatively imitate the *poiesis* of other species has far-reaching implications for who counts as poetic makers.

Here, though, I am interested in the animal presences in Theodore Roethke's work, specifically in "The Pike" (*Collected Poems,* 225). A zoopoetic perspective foregrounds the ways the poem *gestures* in response to an attentive engagement with another species. To enrich the reading of the poem, I will first contextualize it within zoopoetic statements by several poets across the long twentieth century, and then zoopoetic statements in Roethke's larger body of work.

As I have argued, many writers in the Euro-American tradition have made statements that point toward the zoopoetic dynamic. Emerson, for instance, calls for a poem to have an "architecture" that moves "like the spirit of a plant or an animal" (450); Whitman argues that he and other animals share "the same old law" of, I infer, a bodily poetics (199); Dickinson's process of making poems involves, as she has it in poem 333, "stir[ring]" the ways of being of other species into the materiality of her makings (149); Wallace Stevens recognizes that a "blackbird is involved" in the "noble accents" and "lucid, inescapable rhythms" of poetry (94); William Carlos Williams suggests a poem should be "made of" the stuff of flowers and animals, of "gentians" and "wasps" (*Collected Poems,* 2:74)—and he wrote the famous poem that gestures like the cat descending into the flowerpot (*Collected Poems,* 1:352); Brenda Hillman writes that "[i]f bees can detect ultraviolet rays, there are surely more possibilities in language & government" (33), thereby suggesting that breakthroughs occur when a writer attentively engages the ways of being of other species; Gary Snyder sees a poem as having "the trails and tracks . . . living beings leave in each other" (114); and E. E. Cummings suggests his animal poems are a "collection of . . . *a number of ways of being alive*" (174). What might be called zoopoems gesture and play with the gestures of other species.

A brief survey of Roethke's aphorisms, quoted below from *Straw for the Fire: From the Notebooks of Theodore Roethke, 1943–63* (originally published in 1972), demonstrates that he, too, made similar statements. Like Emerson, he sees the form of a poem as having the potential to be plant or animal-like: "when I looked for form, / I found a leaf, and on the leaf a worm" (89). Two other aphorisms, which appear back to back, further suggest how a poem could, Proteus-like, take on the form of another way of being: "And shall we leap the trees as light as birds?" and "I leap to the wind" (24). He gives a soul the flesh of another species: "The course hunger of a raw soul: a fish loose in the grass, slopping and slipping" (210). Through the onomatopoetic *s*'s and the rhythmic "slopping and slipping" of the frantic body, a fish's way of being emerges in the materiality of the language, illustrating a subtle zoopoetic dynamic. Roethke emphasizes that a "poet's rhythmical energy is . . . the index to his psychic energy" (192). What happens, though, when nonhuman animals permeate a poet's psyche? Gail F. Melson has traced the overwhelming presence of animals in the lives of children. What about adults? She draws upon Edward O. Wilson's biophilia hypothesis—"the innate tendency to focus on life and lifelike processes" (Wilson, 1)—to argue that "human brains are wired to vibrate to animals" (Melson, 188). Roethke might say, as he does in the poem "Night Crow," that "tremendous bird[s]"—as well as innumerable other animals—fly, creep, slither, crawl, leap, and pounce "[d]eep, in the brain, far back" (*Collected Poems,* 47).

One longer statement from *Straw for the Fire* further suggests the zoopoetic dynamic in Roethke's process of making poetry. In the section "The Plain Speech of a Crow," Roethke includes a description of a pond similar to that found in "The Pike." It begins with the tantalizing suggestion of a simile: "Like the minnow nudging the edge of the water, / Picking the bug-laden surface." As the aphorism continues, Roethke describes the ecology of this "world of the skimming dragon-fly" in which the minnow participates and that includes reeds, grass, "black-backed small gold-fish," carp, black fish, and scum (95). Provocatively, he never tells the reader *what,* exactly, is *like the minnow.* A zoopoetic reading suggests that his aphorisms are "like the minnow" as they "nudge the edge" of silence and epiphany. Roethke's attentiveness to the minnow, coupled with the suggestive simile, helps direct the reader's imagination to see how these aphorisms behave, what they do, and what they accomplish. The animal radicalism helps readers make breakthroughs in how we understand the work of reading. It is as if *Straw for the Fire* is a collection of innumerable minnows, darting this way and that. Later in "The Plain Speech of a Crow," Roethke makes this work explicit: "To tell the droll farewell, the final sense / Of what earth is," is a "place for heavy work" (98).

In "The Pike," Roethke undergoes the "heavy work" of telling a story of an encounter with another species. The speaker of the poem is, above all, *attentive. Attentiveness* is a crucial term in the definition of zoopoetics. The Latin roots suggest a physical gesture: *ad* and *tendere,* a *stretching toward* (Moe, 24–26). The speaker *stretches toward* "a furred, a rocky pool, / A bottom of water" (3–4): "And I lean, almost into the water . . . I lean and love these manifold shapes" (11, 13). The "shapes" include "crabs [that] tilt," "small fish," "weeds," "bottom-stones [that] shimmer back their irregular striations," and a "half-sunken branch [that] bends away" (5–9). In the context of Roethke's overall gravitation toward the forms of leaves and worms, the phrases "manifold shapes" and "irregular striations" take on greater significance. The poem becomes an irregular shape, with an irregular symmetry, as the first and last stanzas are both one sentence though they differ in their number of lines.

A zoopoetic perspective exposes how the form of this poem emerges from an attentive engagement with another species. There is no other poem like this one. It is wholly unique. It has been shaped in accordance with an attentive, stretching, leaning disposition of the speaker. For instance, the subtle musicality in many lines carries the reader across the turn in each line, accentuating the leaning energy of the poem: the *r*'s in *furred* carry across to *rocky;* the *ahh* and *uhh* in *bottom* leans into the *uhh* and *ahh* in *of* and *water* respectively; the *b* in *branch* leans into *bend*; the *l* in *lean* leans into *almost;* the *l* in lean also carries over to *love* and *manifold.* Such innovative musicality further compliments the leaning posture of the speaker/reader.

The zoopoetic dynamic emerges with full force through the innovative form of the overall progression of the pike's strike. Neal Bowers observes that the pike, perhaps, attacks the speaker: "Although it is never made explicit that the speaker is attacked by the pike, the poem certainly suggests it. And even if we say the pike strikes one of the small fish in the water, the speaker's sense of identification with these creatures is so strong that he feels the pike's violence himself" (181).

Indeed, Roethke withholds the subject and verb until the last two words, suggesting that the fury of the moment overrides a conscious, left-brained naming of what just happened. The strike happens so quickly, the speaker has no time to respond. Zoopoetics deepens this discussion. The pike's attack begins almost imperceptibly through "one sinuous ripple" that suddenly becomes a "rush, / A thrashing-up of the whole pool" (16–17). The *r* from *ripple* leans into *rush*, and the *sh* of *rush* carries across the line break to *thrashing*. The onomatopoetic sounds of *shh* and *thrr* allow the reader to hear the thrashing of the pool, while the language carries a sense of the fish's muscularity and movement through the water. Another way to put it: the pike *thrashes up* the pool of language.

The power of the strike culminates in the final two words: "pike strikes" (18). After beginning with the speaker in calm waters; after leaning with the speaker through seven lines of a compound/complex sentence; after leaning across lines and line breaks; after sensing the tension mount through an increased internal alliteration and a suspense generated by a sublime obscurity, the reader arrives at the strength and violence of a spondaic, internal rhyme. The rhyme reinforces the power of the last line and expresses the power of the fish's sudden strike.

As "The Pike" recreates the moment when species meet, it also achieves breakthroughs regarding what is possible in the form of a poem. The final stanza takes on a pike way of being. This is serious play on the part of Roethke, but it is in the act of playing with language that such breakthroughs occur. This poem, to echo Cummings, exhibits *one way of being alive.* It manifests a pike way of being in the mode of a strike, and it suggests that pike, along with night crows and minnows, have found their way "[d]eep, in the brain, far back" (*Collected Poems,* 47), from where they contribute to breakthroughs in poetic form.

41

Roethke's Dark Society

Revisiting "In a Dark Time"

WALTER KALAIDJIAN

A POPULAR poet in his own lifetime, Theodore Roethke became something of an American icon following his death in 1963. Roethke's national stature was brought home to me when I was invited to serve as a consultant for the U.S. Postal Service in designing the 2012 Theodore Roethke commemorative stamp. Along with the other modern American poets in the USPS series, Roethke now abides as a perennial favorite in the high school and university classroom.[1] Among his several touchstones—"My Papa's Waltz," "The Waking," "I Knew a Woman," and "Elegy for Jane"—no poem in Roethke's canon is more frequently anthologized than "In a Dark Time" (*Collected Poems,* 231). As a signature piece, it provided the title for David Myers's 1964 McGraw-Hill art-house film, an elegiac tribute documenting Roethke's late career. Critics' fascination with "In a Dark Time" was further driven, in part, by Roethke's commentary on the poem responding to a symposium including Babette Deutsch, John Crowe Ransom, and Stanley Kunitz published in Anthony Ostroff's anthology *The Contemporary Poet as Artist and Critic* (1964).

For several decades thereafter, critics interpreted the poem's governing themes, tropes, and symbols in terms of what Roethke himself characterized in his essay "On 'In a Dark Time'" as "part of a hunt, a drive toward God" (49). They noted Roethke's fascination with existential theologians such as Paul

Tillich and Reinhold Niebuhr, whom Roethke had met while teaching at Bennington College (Seager, 202). Indeed, in his 1964 reading of "In a Dark Time," Roethke's friend, colleague, and commentator Stanley Kunitz suggested a line from Tillich as the definitive epigraph for the poem: "The self-affirmation of a being is the stronger the more non-being it can take into itself" (48). Not unlike Hamlet's famous soliloquy "To be, or not to be? That is the question," Roethke's "In a Dark Time" bears the imprint of Tillich's existential conviction that "to be"—one's sense of being-in-the-world—depends, paradoxically enough, on a sense of what it is "not to be." Being is bound up with the "shock of nonbeing" (Tillich, 186): contingency, finitude, boredom, and ultimately what Martin Heidegger theorized as one's authentic "being-toward-death" (249).

Some five years earlier before composing "In a Dark Time," Roethke had already explored the paradoxical and salutary relation between being and nonbeing in "The Waking," his masterful villanelle and title piece for his Pulitzer Prize–winning fourth volume of verse. The poetic formalism of "The Waking" made it a natural companion piece to Roethke's use of pentameter sestets rhyming *abbacc* of "In a Dark Time." Critics such as Wyatt Prunty linked the two poems not just in terms of their "speechlike qualities" and "songlike intensity" but also in the tensions both strike between formal unity and "personal vulnerability" (96). In the vein of carpe diem poetics, Roethke famously mused in "The Waking" that

> Great Nature has another thing to do
> To you and me; so take the lively air,
> And lovely, learn by going where to go.

In "The Waking," the poet's authentic "being-in-the-world" is achieved by an empathic attentiveness to the presence of other beings, where, as Roethke has it,

> We think by feeling. What is there to know?
> I hear my being dance from ear to ear.
> I wake to sleep, and take my waking slow.
>
> (*Collected Poems,* 104)

Thus, in approaching "In a Dark Time," critics recalled Roethke's reliance on paradox and contradiction in "The Waking": the interplay of waking and sleep, thinking and feeling, the lowly worm's ascent of the winding stair, and so on. Such ironies similarly structure the various binaries of "In a Dark Time" as the poem toggles between light and darkness, hill and den, cave and path, nobility of soul and madness, broad day and midnight, soul and fly, the fallen and the free. The tendency in Roethke criticism was to acknowledge both the biographical context of the poet's vulnerable struggle with "non-being"—alcoholism and recurring episodes of manic depression—that, paradoxically enough, gave him insight not just into a fuller appreciation of "being-in-the world" but, more importantly, into the soul's journey toward spiritual transcendence. Thus, "[t]o embrace this knowledge," Stanley Kunitz concluded, "is to overcome the dread of non-being, is to be redeemed or, so to speak, reborn" (47).

This kind of spiritual supersession was further underscored in Roethke's reception insofar as "In a Dark Time" appeared as the lead poem in his late volume *Sequence, Sometimes Metaphysical* (1963). The soul's metaphysical journey toward transcendence was something, critics argued, that Roethke was familiar with from his reading in the mystical literature of key figures recorded in his 1942 notebook entries: Meister Eckhart, St. Theresa of Avila, St. John of the Cross, and St. Francis of Assisi (Seager, 164). Edith Underhill's influential study *Mysticism* (1911) was a further influence on Roethke's thinking and set the pattern of spiritual fits and starts that shape Roethke's late canon. In 1946, as Jay Parini observes, Roethke recorded Underhill's stages of mystical union virtually verbatim into his notebooks:

> 1. Awakening—to a sense of divine reality.
> 2. Purgation of self, when it realizes its own (unprojecting) divine.
> 3. An enhanced return to the sense of the divine order, after the Self has achieved detachment from the world.
> 4. Dark night of the Soul.
>
> Sacramental perception.
>
> *Singleness:* Discovery of the self is the same as discovery of God in oneself. (Qtd. in Parini, 135–36)

Several of the key tropes and memorable phrasings in "In a Dark Time" resonate with the account of St. John's poem "La noche oscura del alma," or "Dark Night of the Soul," which Roethke read in Underhill. There, Roethke witnesses to what Underhill describes as a "Divine Wisdom, which is not only night and darkness to the soul, but pain and torment too" (399; cited in Bowers, 174). Roethke's rendering of an ultimate release, in which the "day is on fire" (8) and "one is One," finally "free in the tearing wind" (24), recapitulates the rhetoric of Underhill's account of "mystical death": "It is the last painful break with the life of illusion, the tearing away of the self from that World of Becoming in which all its natural affections and desires are rooted, to which its intellect and senses correspond; and the thrusting of it into that World of Being where at first, weak and blinded, it can but find a wilderness, a 'dark.' No transmutation without fire, say the alchemists" (401; cited in Parini, 178).

But in addition to Roethke's leanings toward the *noche oscura* of metaphysical spirituality, he also possessed a more modern, psychoanalytic understanding of the role of unconscious intuition in his creative process. Indeed, as someone who suffered from recurring episodes of mania and depression, Roethke had a necessary commitment to contemporary psychoanalysis, free association, and the talking cure. As is well known, Roethke was first hospitalized for mental illness in 1935; a second incident occurred a decade later, and they became more frequent thereafter. In July 1958, in the week after Roethke wrote "In a Dark Time," he sent Marianne Moore a copy of the poem and reported that "I'm in 'deep therapy'—see the doctor six times a week, and really scraping bedrock. . . . I *am,* at long last, getting to the causes of the damned neurosis with someone who is careful and whom I respect" (*Selected Letters,* 218–19). Similarly, at the end of the summer he recounted his psychological treatment in a letter to William Carlos Williams: "I see a head-shrinker five times a week—was seeing him six. . . . It's tough going, but I'll make it, I daresay. This guy is careful, conscientious, and bright" (*Selected Letters,* 221). Thus, Roethke's explicit characterization of "madness" in the poem as a "nobility of soul" grounds metaphysical transcendence in the more worldly and biographical vicissitudes of treatment for recurrent mental illness. In this vein, Roethke pursued the psychoanalytic cure as both a therapeutic and a creative resource, identifying the unconscious with the poet's muse. "Good poets," he wrote, "wait for the muse, the unconscious to spring something loose, to temper and test the promptings of the intuition with the pressures of craftsmanship: they can think while they sing" (*On Poetry and Craft,* 139).

Thus, "In a Dark Time" begins, as Roethke describes it in his commentary on the poem, with an invocation of the muse as "my shadow, my double, my Other" ("On 'In a Dark Time,'" 50). Roethke's framing of the shadow as a kind of psychic doppelgänger resonates with Carl Jung's description of the shadow as a figure for what the ego represses as an unconscious Other: "Everyone carries a shadow," Jung writes in *Psychology and Religion* (1938), "and the less it is embodied in the individual's conscious life, the blacker and denser it is. . . . At all events, it forms an unconscious snag, blocking the most well-meant attempts" (93). Similarly, in a 1948 letter to Babette Deutsch, Roethke quoted from Jung's "Psychology and Literature" (1930) to underscore his belief that the poet's sources of creativity lie precisely outside one's conscious, authorial intent: "The truth is that poets are human beings, and that what a poet has to say about his work is often far from being the most illuminating word on the subject" (*Selected Letters,* 139). On the one hand, Roethke gave credence to this psychoanalytic notion that a poem's "truth" lies in the shadow of an author's conscious intent—that "what the poet has to say about his work is often far from being the most illuminating word on the subject." On the other hand, Roethke's own conscious interpretation of "In a Dark Time" as a drama of "the dark night of the soul" and the subsequent critical reception of the poem as primarily a metaphysical tour de force have nevertheless acted out a deeply unconscious foreclosure: one that is blind to the trope of "the dark" less as a signpost of spiritual than of social and, more precisely, racial otherness.

Teaching "In a Dark Time" over the years has shifted my own appreciation of the poem, in part responding to my students' changing experience of its governing tropes. Increasingly in the decades after 9/11, my students have read the poem's title "In a Dark Time" not just as a metaphysical, existential, or psychological state of personal despair but more as a symptom of the social, cultural, and political traumas of contemporary life. Certainly, there is ample evidence that Roethke understood his poetry, and "In a Dark Time" in particular, to have pertinence to contemporary society. Indeed, in his own commentary on the lines "What's madness but nobility of soul / At odds with circumstance?" (7–8) Roethke writes that "'[m]adness' is a sociological term, a good deal of the time: what is madness in the Northwest is normal conduct in Italy, and a hero's privilege in western Ireland" ("On 'In a Dark Time,'" 51). Moreover, in Roethke's voice-over for Myers's 1964 film *In a Dark Time,* he explicitly addresses the relationship between modern poetry and society:

> A public poet like Auden when he says "we must love one another or die" said in a very few words the very central thing in our civilization. The best modern poetry is characterized by a kind of terrible honesty of imagination as one of the things that we inherit from Blake. Poetry makes

> in a sense a profound and terrible demand; it says "change your life," and I think that that's why the general public backs away from poets like Bogan or Kunitz. They don't want their lives to change; they don't want to enter some other consciousness; they are in a sense . . . unconsciously or consciously afraid.

Pressing a bit further on poetry's social relation to the "general public" and its resistance to change, I would suggest that Roethke's own tendency to inscribe states of fear, anxiety, melancholy, and desire in tropes of Blackness encodes poems such as "In a Dark Time" with social determinants of race that are uniquely American. In the wake of such field-changing readings as *Playing in the Dark: Whiteness and the Literary Imagination* (1992), Toni Morrison's study of classic American literature, today's students are particularly alert to the deep history of the Middle Passage, African American slavery, and the Civil Rights struggle as they are encrypted in literary tropes of darkness projected by the founding fathers of the American Renaissance up through canonical modernists such as Ernest Hemingway. Nowhere that I am aware of, however, does the critical reception account for an African American presence encountered in the shadows of Roethke's imaginary. Such critical silence surrounding Roethke and race is even more pronounced given the charged context of desegregation in which he wrote "In a Dark Time."

Consider the troubled times defining race relations in the United States of the 1950s, the decade in which Roethke composed his lament to darkness. In 1954, the governors of twelve Southern states caucused in Richmond, Virginia, in resistance to the Supreme Court's decision in *Brown v. Board of Education* ruling segregation in public education to be unconstitutional. The following year witnessed a series of racial murders of voting rights activists, culminating in an all-white jury's acquittal of Roy Bryant and J. W. Milam in the brutal murder of a fourteen-year-old Black teenager, Emmett Till, a crime they later confessed to in a 1956 *Look Magazine* exposé. That same year, following Supreme Court rulings outlawing racial segregation in public recreational facilities and interstate transportation, Rosa Parks was arrested for violating Alabama's state laws mandating racial segregation on buses. The years leading up to Roethke's "In a Dark Time" witnessed, among other events, the bombing of Martin Luther King's home, rioting over the desegregation of the University of Alabama, the Montgomery bus boycott, as well as numerous other boycotts and home and church bombings. Nineteen fifty-seven and fifty-eight, when Roethke composed "In a Dark Time," became known as the "lost year" in reference to Governor Orval Faubus's challenge to the federal mandate to desegregate Little Rock's public schools. In fact, just days before Roethke composed "In a Dark Time," newspapers carried accounts of the bombing of Rev. Fred Shuttlesworth's Bethel Street Church in Birmingham for the second time in two years. Some six decades on from Rosa Parks's defiance of the color line, racial violence persists as an oppressive everyday reality, as witnessed in the racially charged killings by whites and police of Black Americans such as George Floyd, Breonna Taylor, Ahmaud Arbery, Trayvon Martin, Michael Brown, Freddie Gray, and Tamir Rice, as well as in Dylann Storm Roof's racial murder of state senator Clementa C. Pinckney and eight other Black parishioners worshipping at the historic Emanuel African Methodist Episcopal Church in Charleston, South Carolina.

In this racially fraught historical context, Roethke's rhetorical question "What's madness but nobility of soul / At odds with circumstance" takes on an arresting social pertinence. Similarly, however intended as a metaphor for mania, Roethke's exclamation "The day's on fire!" (7–8) witnesses, albeit unconsciously perhaps, to the literal scenes of bombings, burnings, and alarm everywhere erupting in the poem's contemporaneous public sphere. Indeed, the madness of what Morrison characterizes as "an American Africanism—a fabricated brew of darkness, otherness, alarm, and desire" (38) is particularly resonant with Roethke's tropes of psychic extremity and their cumulative tone of urgency and panic. For his part, Roethke regarded his poem as a heuristic statement: one that would inaugurate rather than fix its interpretative possibilities. "It is important to remember," he commented in "On 'In a Dark Time,'" "that the eye only begins to see: this is only a stage in a long process" (50). Remaining attentive to what W. E. B. Du Bois characterized as the "second-sight" afforded by the "veil" of "double-consciousness" (3), the contemporary reader can perhaps begin to glimpse the traces of a latent "American Africanism" inscribed between the lines of Roethke's "In a Dark Time." Witnessed in such figures as the "shadow in the deepening shade" (2), a "night flowing with birds, a ragged moon, / And in broad day the midnight come again!" (14–15), the poet undergoes "[d]eath of the self in a long, tearless night" (17) and reiterates with uncanny insistence a telling trope for libidinal currents that cross the color line: "Dark, dark my light, and darker," he avows, "my desire" (19). Beset in his own moment by a national imaginary torn apart by racial strife and division, Roethke's courage to query "[w]hich I is I?" (21) leads to a utopian social vision where "one is One, free in the tearing wind" (24). Today, the challenge to "change your life" lies, I would suggest, in what could not be consciously imagined in the poet's own moment: a racial reconciliation where American national identity is One, paradoxically enough, with the Other of Roethke's dark society.

NOTE

1. The ten poets honored in 2012 with commemorative stamps are Elizabeth Bishop, Joseph Brodsky, Gwendolyn Brooks, E. E. Cummings, Robert Hayden, Denise Levertov, Sylvia Plath, Theodore Roethke, Wallace Stevens, and William Carlos Williams.

42

"I Am Not Yet Undone"

Navigating the Journey from Life to Death in "Infirmity"

LAURA GILL

THEODORE ROETHKE'S poem "Infirmity" (*Collected Poems,* 236) was first published in 1963, in the October 19 issue of *The New Yorker,* shortly after Roethke's premature death at the age of fifty-five. A year later it was incorporated into "Sequence, Sometimes Metaphysical," the final section of the posthumous collection *The Far Field* (1964). With a history of illnesses of different kinds, Roethke may, as Ralph J. Mills Jr. states in his introduction to *The Selected Letters of Theodore Roethke,* have had a "prophetic insight" that his own demise was looming when he wrote "Infirmity" (xvii), but the poem can be read without further recourse to the poet's personal struggles.

In "Infirmity" Roethke tackles humans' unique awareness of their own mortality as well as the irrational belief that coexists with this knowledge that somehow this fact cannot—must not—apply to oneself. "Infirmity" addresses this paradox, which for Roethke means not only depicting the painful process of watching one's own body slowly disintegrate, but also juxtaposing physical decay with the alert mind that initially refuses to accept what it knows cannot be changed. Roethke is rooted in the Christian tradition, but "Infirmity" more specifically exemplifies his belief in mystical insight, with the poem depicting the way towards a moment of profound discernment.

In discussing "Infirmity," it would be easy to neglect the title of the poem, for which Roethke uses a rather unassuming unqualified noun. Although most of the poem titles in *The Far Field* contain nouns, "Infirmity" stands out as the only one-word title that is not a proper name ("Otto") or a designation for a poetic form ("Elegy," "Song"). In her study of poem titles, Anne Ferry points out that a "noun by itself in the title space is inherently the least expressive grammatical form for a presentation. In what it purports to do it comes closest to a label stating what is in a container or to a sign on a door saying what is in the space beyond it. It seems to invite no interpretation, claiming only to identify by naming. It has no voice and implicates no performer other than someone anonymous who sticks on the label or sign." For Ferry, an impersonal term can only be powerful through its very inexpressiveness (192), and indeed, "Infirmity" is effective as a title because of its simplicity. According to Kenneth Burke, Roethke usually "goes as far as humanly possible in quest of a speech wholly devoid of abstractions," eschewing terms ending in '-ness' or '-ity' ("Vegetal Radicalism," 73). In this case, however, his choice of just such a term appears strikingly appropriate. Forgoing a verb/participle construction that would convey a sense of action, Roethke emphasizes the state of helplessness that the poem addresses. In the second stanza Roethke modifies the term, with the speaker now referring to "my infirmity" (7); by providing an insight into his personal confrontation with the end of life, he thus lifts the term from the realm of the abstract. At the same time, omitting the pronoun from the title indicates that what the poem discusses transcends individual experience.

The poem consists of six stanzas, each containing six lines with an unobtrusive iambic pentameter. The rhyme scheme is *ababcc cdcdcc bedcff gdgdhh ijijkk lbmcnn*. Thus, the first, second, fourth, and fifth stanzas feature four lines of (not always perfect) alternate rhymes followed by a heroic couplet, whereas the third and sixth rhyme only in the final couplet. The heroic couplet serves as a conclusion to the issue or idea presented in the first four lines of the respective stanza, turning each section into a self-contained unit. Apart from the expression that forms the title, Roethke hardly uses words with more than two syllables. The great majority of rhymes are even made up of one-syllable words; consequently, the rhymes are all masculine.[1] The resulting impression is one of clarity and directness.

Right at the outset the speaker addresses the fundamental human inability to accept that death makes no exceptions. There is an impersonal pronoun "one" in the first line, but the perspective immediately shifts to a more specific and more intimate "I," which is heard throughout the rest of the poem. Roethke also introduces the image of the eye and of sight here. The main trope, a "shimmer[ing]" reflection of the speaker's image in an abyss-like "deepening pool" (2–3), is an obvious reference to the Greek mythical figure Narcissus, who fell in love with his own reflection and died because he found himself unable to leave the object of his affection. For the speaker of this poem the presence of his mirrored image makes it at once impossible to deny that his appearance is changing and at the same time unimaginable that the image and thus he, the individual behind the reflection, could cease to exist.

The changes that the speaker perceives leave more than a sensory impression; they affect the "inner eye," a term that implies the notion that the mind has to process aging and its effects as well. The tone of the first stanza is, as Richard Allen Blessing has said, "gently self-mocking" (208). The last two lines, "I love myself: that's my one constancy. / Oh, to be something else, yet still to be!" (5–6),[2] are also refreshingly straightforward in the way they encapsulate "[t]he universal dream . . . to have a fresh start, to reach a higher state, without letting go of what one has and is" (Blessing, 209). Roethke poignantly captures the fact that for the speaker he himself is the single most important person in the world, and his indignation is evident when he realizes that he cannot continue to "tell [him]self [his] image cannot die" (4).[3]

The second stanza begins with an apostrophe to Jesus that displays an accepting humility: "Sweet Christ, rejoice in my infirmity; / There's little left I care to call my own" (7–8); yet what follows is not a concern with heaven or the afterlife, but a description of the prosaic reality of aging and sickness: "Today they drained the fluid from a knee / And pumped a shoulder full of cortisone" (9–10). The speaker expresses a much more resigned stance than in the first stanza, observing others handle a body that does not seem to be his own anymore and feeling removed from the material world. As Neal Bowers remarks, Roethke acknowledges in line 12 that "[d]ying is a natural process, like the decaying of a tree" (192).

It is in the third stanza that Roethke deals in greater detail with the religious dimension of impending death. The line "The instant ages on the living eye" (13) implies that for the speaker time has slowed down, as he now has an increased awareness of its passing. He enters a state of heightened sensibility, which becomes evident in his reference in line 14 to the engulfing presence of light. Roethke here stresses the exceptional quality of the experience by repeating the word "extreme" from line 14 as "extremity" in line 16.

In the penultimate line of this stanza Roethke modifies Matthew 5:5 from the Bible, "Blessed be the meek, for they shall inherit the earth," and turns it into the assertive "Blessed the meek; they shall inherit wrath; / I'm son and father of my only death" (17–18). In these lines Rosemary Sullivan finds a "solitary ecstasy and dread," with "the spirit rag[ing] to consume the dying body in a willful suicide" (187). The speaker does not count himself among the meek; instead he claims control by being not only subject ("son") to, but also creator ("father") of his own death. One can even go so far as to see Roethke establishing a trinity by declaring in the last line of the poem that "we are pure spirit at the end" (36). Thus he draws on Christian symbols, but challenges their conventional meaning.

Stanza 4 moves the persona even closer to death, as Bowers notes, citing line 19: "Recognizing that stubborn resistance is the wrong stance, the speaker declares, 'a mind too active is no mind at all,' thereby proclaiming the primacy of intuition over analysis, the God-loving soul over the self-loving ego. Instead of fighting approaching death, he decides to yield to it" (192). The "inner eye" and the "living eye" from previous lines are no more; the "deep eye" now "sees the shimmer on the stone" (20). In contrast to the first stanza there is, encouragingly, something for the eye to discern, and indeed a synthesis takes place between the eternal and the temporal, darkness and light. The speaker receives a glimpse of the hereafter in the now. Moving "beyond the reach of wind and fire" (24), the speaker finds reassurance in this moment of illumination, this "brief vision of Eternity" (Blessing 209).[4]

The fifth stanza brings a sense of renewed defiance, with the speaker claiming that he is still aware of "the greens of summer" (25), the vibrancy of nature. Roethke now supplants visual with aural perception. Perched like the bird, he hears singing, as "[t]he great day balances upon the leaves" (27). The great day is the day of his death, but as long as he can still hear the bird's life-affirming song reverberating in his soul, all is not lost. "I am not yet undone" (30), the speaker asserts; he still possesses awareness of his existence and of the unity of his body and soul.

In his notes Roethke identifies "constant antithesis, word against word, phrase against phrase" as one of the devices that he believes "[heighten] the intensity" of a poem (qtd. in Blessing, 159), and "Infirmity" is undeniably full of opposites, as has been shown in this analysis: life and death, body and soul, darkness and light, the self and the outside world. In the last stanza there is another synthesis: "Things without hands take hands: there is no choice," Roethke writes (31). Heretofore clearly defined senses become interchangeable: "I teach my eyes to hear, my ears to see" (34). In the end, body and spirit will become disunited, with only spirit remaining (35–36). Through this final separation the tension is resolved.[5]

Looking at the formal aspects in this second half of the poem makes it clear that the sixth stanza, just as the fourth and fifth, introduces new rhymes, but departs from the clear structure found there in its use of two ending sounds that have appeared before, yet do not rhyme with each other: "by" (32) and "see" (34). The last stanza thus displays an irregularity that is reminiscent of that in stanza three. These asymmetries are particularly stirring because the loosening of the rhyme scheme corresponds to the separation of body and soul from each other: in the two stanzas there is a direct confrontation with "death" (18) and "the end" (36) in the speaker's thoughts. Moreover, these terms each conclude a segment, the latter phrase even the whole poem. Thus their position in the text becomes an implicit comment on the finite nature of life. The fact that the final couplets in stanzas 3 and 6 ("wrath"/"death," 17–18; "unwind / end," 35–36), as well as in stanza 4 ("dear"/"fire," 23–24), are characterized by slant rhyme, such that the lines forming the couplet do not fit together seamlessly, further reinforces the impression of separation, the parting of the spiritual from the corporeal.

These bits of imperfect harmony in an otherwise clear structure indicate both the patterns and the flux of nature. On the one hand Roethke had a mystical sense of the cohesion of the physical world, overwhelming in its perfection and full of transcendental truth and beauty; on the other hand he saw its unsettling transience. The movement from "I" to "we" in the last line reminds the reader of the universality of the experience of dying, a fact that is at once distressing and comforting.

Christianity, which is alluded to throughout the poem, does not provide any easy answers. "Infirmity" shows the speaker of the poem clinging to life: in approaching death, he wants to take as much control as he can. At the same time he is able to enter a contemplative, introspective state that allows the mind to perceive the eternal and thus to achieve a deeper understanding of what is to come.

NOTES

1. Blessing notes that "any fledgling poet might benefit from comparing the effect of the Latinate diction of Roethke's apprenticeship with that of the rugged Anglo-Saxon of, say, 'The Song' or 'Infirmity'" (160).

2. As this line clearly stands out, it has frequently been commented on. Stephen Spender, for example, writes, "If this is moving, it is because one sympathizes with the poet, tragic in his concern with his own tragedy" (10). Having discussed a selection of Roethke's poems, Denis Donoghue comments that "it might seem that Roethke was concerned with only one thing—himself. And this is true. . . . The saving grace in Roethke, as in Whitman, is the assumption that he is a representative instance, no more if no less. When Roethke searches for value and meaning he assumes that this is interesting insofar as it is representative and not at all interesting when it ceases to be so" ("Theodore Roethke," 51).

3. Bowers observes that "The Motion," the poem that precedes "Infirmity" in *The Far Field,* concludes with a "vision of transcendent love," an idea which is notably absent here. It is "replaced in the opening stanza of 'Infirmity' . . . by a cynical view of self-love" (192).

4. Parini comes to the same conclusion: "Still, in the midst of physical decay, he takes comfort in the eternal presence" (181).

5. Given the aforementioned syntheses, the last few lines of the poem can be seen as "the ultimate reconciliation of . . . opposites in death and union" (Bowers, 193), a union of the spirit with God. Since in these closing lines Roethke emphasizes the fact that body and spirit lose their connection to each other, I interpret the final image as one of separation. For a similar reading, see Parini (6).

43

Symbolism and the Mystic's Way in "The Tree, the Bird"

CHRISTOPHER GIROUX

IN HIS 1969 article "The Divine Abyss: Theodore Roethke's Mysticism," William Heyen references Evelyn Underhill's *Mysticism: A Study of Man's Spiritual Consciousness* (1911), reminding readers that the traditional path of the mystic involves "The Awakening of Self, The Purification of Self, Illumination, The Dark Night of the Soul, [and] Union" (1053). Throughout these stages, the mystic moves between such polarities, or "contraries," as light and dark (1060) and joy and pain; constant negotiations involving being, becoming, and doing, as well as separation, belonging, the self, and the Other, also occur. As Heyen notes (1068), these aspects of the mystic's way are similarly apparent in "The Tree, the Bird" (*Collected Poems,* 240), which is situated in the second half of "Sequence, Sometimes Metaphysical," the closing section of *The Far Field.* "The Tree, the Bird" is of interest though, not only for its mysticism, but also because of the religious symbolism embedded within this "text that dramatizes the duality of the sensory and the spiritual" (Goldberg, 35).

As a poem concerned with spirituality, "The Tree, the Bird" moves between dark and light, night and day. The opening stanza evokes the presence of the moon and the poem's events as part of a "midnight scene" (8), with the idea of darkness reiterated in the second stanza through reference to the speaker's "midnight eyes" (16). The poem, however, ends as expected with mention of "the rising day" (19). The isolation and separation associated with the mystic and felt by the speaker of the "The Tree, the Bird" are even more obvious than the pull between light and dark. Although he describes himself in the first stanza as "[a]t ease with joy" (6), the speaker's joy is short-lived. The next line begins with the conjunction "[y]et," and the speaker is left standing "outside [his] life" (7). Smallness and fragmentation define his condition too: only a "small" voice calls to him (4), he is merely "a finger pointing at the moon" (5), and he remains separated in the last stanza by "[t]he white sea widening on a farther shore" (20). Even his description of the tree points to separation. Rather than fully identify with the willow, the unspecified bird it houses, or the larger world that surrounds tree and bird, the poem's speaker remains separated: standing outside his own life, he identifies himself as merely a leaf—and one unchanged by the scene that presents itself to him—rather than the stately willow and the others of its kind with which he could identify. Moreover, the speaker cannot "bear" the bird's song (14). In fact, the bird reinforces the speaker's sense of difference: the bird's trill is compared to the rain and described in negative terms, as "bleak." Its song, because it is merely "[k]in to the wind" (12), does not fully belong either.

In addition to this focus on alienation felt by the spiritual pilgrim, Heyen quotes Underhill, who identifies "[o]ptical disturbance, auditions, and the sense of levitation" as experiences linked to the first stages of the mystic's way ("Divine Abyss," 1053; Underhill, 186). These aspects are likewise found in the first stanza of "The Tree, the Bird." Unlike "The Abyss," which opens indoors, "The Tree, the Bird" is grounded in nature, and the opening lines convey both a sense of levitation and an optical disturbance with the rising stones of the field and the snails that bow in reverence to the speaker of the poem. The "small voice calling from a distant cloud" (4) serves as the auditory experience described by Underhill, as does the call of the bird: "a double sound, / Kin to the wind, and the bleak whistling rain" (11–12) and "[t]he lonely buzz behind . . . midnight eyes" (16).

"The Tree, the Bird" undoubtedly sheds light on Roethke's interest in mysticism, but the poem is also unique in its specific imagery. Although the voice calling from a distant cloud may allude to Jesus's baptism in Matthew 3:17, Heyen asserts that Roethke's "choice was not traditional Christianity or atheism, but a reliance upon the mystic perceptions of his own imagination" ("Divine Abyss," 1052). Roethke biographer Allan Seager similarly reminds us that Roethke "was a religious man but he was not concerned with sin as might have been expected from his Presbyterian upbringing nor was he much interested in being his brother's keeper, although he performed many spontaneous kindnesses. Rather, he was troubled about the nature of God, not necessarily a Christian God, his own relation to Him, and his relationship to what he believed to be God's primary creation, nature" (225). Perhaps it is because of this interest in spirituality rather than strictly in a Christian God, that Roethke relies on images in "The Tree, the Bird" from different cultural traditions, including Christianity, as a way of advancing his individualized view of mysticism. References in the poem that have greater spiritual significance include the bird, snail, moon, and willow.

Although Roethke was typically specific when naming the flora and fauna appearing in his poetry (in materials it provides to area teachers who visit Roethke's birthplace, the Friends of Theodore Roethke note more than thirty individual types of plants or flowers in his writings), the bird in this poem remains unidentified by species. Nevertheless, it still can be seen as functioning as a traditional literary symbol for the spirit. Roethke's bird with its "beating" (15, 21) and "extending" (21) wings connects to the Christian concept of the trinity, in that the flapping wings are linked to air, breath, and wind—to movement. Roethke's bird not only "shifts" the air, but the bird, its song, and the tree are also connected to the wind and thus present change and progress, or at least their potential. Progress, however, is actually lacking in this case; as Heyen notes in "The Divine Abyss," "[i]n Roethke's poetry a slowing or shifting wind is often ominous" (1055), and indeed in "The Tree, the Bird," the leaf to which the speaker of the poem compares himself remains "unaltered" (8) and "[p]art of a tree, still dark, still, deathly still" (9). Indeed, in the second stanza he is so disconnected from the bird and tree that he remains unable to "bear [the bird's] song" (14). Given that bird imagery, like that voice descending from a cloud, is also linked to Jesus's baptism in Matthew, these two details allude to the suffering and joy to be experienced by the Christian savior in the crucifixion and resurrection, foreshadowing the emotions typically encountered by the mystic on his pilgrimage.

The snail also speaks to issues of spirituality and morality. Though often associated with slowness and thus, in Christianity, with sloth and the seven deadly sins (Werness, 376), the snail has positive significance in other traditions and cultures. A nocturnal creature, the snail is often tied to the moon and the spirit world. Among the Aztecs, for example, snails were specifically linked to the lunar god, Tecciztecatl, or "He from the Sea Snail" (Vaillant, 189). For the Greeks, the snail, born in springtime, was linked to the life cycle: Hesiod claimed that snails appearing on wheat were a sign to begin harvesting (87). As a creature that bears its home on its back and grows its own home, in the form of a spiral, the snail conveys a sense of safety, progress, wholeness, and self-actualization, all of which are goals of the mystic. Because of these ties to maturation and growth, the snails that appear early in the poem and bow to the text's speaker emphasize the speaker's higher status. Additionally, as an animal that can survive on land and in water, the snail has particular relevance in a poem about bridging the gap between worlds, in this case those of the human and the divine. The snail's spiraled shell particularly highlights the religious pilgrim's ongoing search for spiritual elevation and unity, states that do not occur once and then are forever attained. Like the mazes found in many a meditation garden or cathedral floor that meander and curve back upon themselves, spiritual growth is slow and circular in nature. Communion with the divine, particularly as described by Underhill, involves circuitous moments between light and dark. The reference to the spiral in "The Tree, the Bird" thus foreshadows that the speaker of "Sequence, Sometimes Metaphysical" will most likely move between a sense of connection with the natural world and one of alienation.

The willow in "The Tree, the Bird" is another object tied to matters of spirituality, religion, the emotions, and healing. To begin with the obvious, the willow, like the snail, is linked to water and thus connected to the moon. Additionally, Fred Hageneder reminds us that the wood of the willow was known for its flexibility and healing properties—qualities and conditions sought by the devout—and as such, the tree has also been linked to creative energy and psychic potential. In fact, Hageneder relates that the willow held special meaning for poets in Greece (*Spirit,* 125–26) and that according to creationist stories in the Druidic tradition, the leaves of a willow tree held an embryonic sun and moon (*Meaning,* 181).

The connection between life, death, and harvesttime, a period of liminality when plants are destroyed in preparation for future growth, also applies to the willow just as it did, per Hesiod, to snails. As described in Leviticus, the branches of the willow were used as part of the Jewish Feast of Sukkot (23:40), sometimes called the Feast of the Tabernacles, Booths, or Ingathering. An autumnal feast of the full moon and "*the* holiday of the biblical period" (Strassfeld, 126), the Feast of Sukkot commemorates Solomon's consecration of the temple (126) and, as such, is a feast of joy. However, as a harvest celebration, the Feast of Sukkot, which involves the erection of temporary shelters, or *sukkot,* is also a reminder of the Israelites' past suffering: branches of willows, among other plants, are used on this holiday to commemorate the Jews' need for protection during their forty years of wandering in the desert, as well as their creation of temporary shelters to facilitate the reaping of the harvest. As part of the feast, willow branches may also be beaten against a lectern to acknowledge humanity's frailty (Gaster, 95) and need to turn from sinful ways (Strassfeld, 135), as well as the tensions between fertility and famine, bounty and drought (131). These reminders of joy and suffering, of closeness to and separation from God, and of the precarious balance between a fruitful harvest and good weather (as well as between a present reaping and future well-being) all mimic the spiritual tension felt by a mystic and the speaker of Roethke's poem. As Theodor H. Gaster notes in discussing the Jewish Feast of Sukkot, "The essential point about the festival, alike in its seasonal and historical aspect, is that what it celebrates is not an achievement but a prospect, not something finally accomplished but something which has been but begun and the consummation of which lies in the future" (91). In fact, these ideas parallel the search for spiritual oneness sought by the speaker of "The Tree, the Bird," for whom "[t]he present falls, the present falls away" (18) while he awaits "[t]he dire dimension of a final thing" (23).

As Heyen notes, such critics as M. L. Rosenthal, David Ferry, and Denis Donoghue argue that the ecstasy felt by the spiritual speaker who narrates Roethke's poetry is too easily won ("Divine Abyss," 1062), but "The Tree, the Bird" throws that assertion into question, for the happiness that the speaker of the poem describes actually remains largely out of reach. Granted, the last couplet specifically uses the word "joy," but this is a joy that is to be "endure[d]" (22)—to be suffered and borne rather than celebrated. Perhaps the point that these critics are missing, especially given that "The Tree, the Bird" is part of a larger sequence wherein the speaker moves between light and dark both literally and figuratively, is that the joy and transcendence reached by the mystic are almost always *temporarily* won. Union is the mystic's goal, but what Roethke most effectively and specifically captures in "The Tree, the Bird" and the larger sequence in which it is embedded (as well as much of Roethke's work as a whole) is the back-and-forth tension between joy, pain, sacrifice, and humiliation that the mystic experiences. As Gaster notes in his discussion of the Feast of Sukkot, "the transcendental theme of the Feast of Booths is the persistent hope and confidence without which all such trials are insupportable, all such achievements impossible, and all such obligations unacceptable" (97). In the case of "The

Tree, the Bird," the long dark night of the soul is not the opening movement in the mystic's journey, but just one stage of the larger search for mystical union, one section of the believer's path. Roethke's references to moon, bird, snail, and willow highlight, through images with Christian and non-Christian ties, that for his spiritual pilgrim, belief precedes, follows, and continues to be marked by the long dark night of the soul.

44

"Once More, the Round"

Roethke's Last Word

WILLIAM BARILLAS

CERTAIN POEMS by Theodore Roethke bear consideration as pivotal statements in the author's *Collected Poems* (1966, 1975). In addition to their intrinsic qualities, they offer keys to this poet's body of work, opening doors to what he called, at the beginning of his career, the "open house" of his continuously developing spirituality and sense of self. Some appear as the first or last poems in books, like "Open House," the curiously hermetic and cautious first and title poem of his inaugural volume of 1941, and "Night Journey," the closing poem in that book, which emphasizes the quest motif that became central in Roethke's vision. "The Waking," the last poem in the Pulitzer Prize–winning 1953 volume by that same title, is the essential self-reflexive *ars poetica* by the poet from Saginaw. As Frank J. Kearful avers in his essay on the poem for this book, "[i]t is as if all of Roethke's poetry thus far, the prior work selectively represented and the new poems culminating in 'The Waking,' had been a learning process leading to the title poem on the last printed page" (179).

The same may be said of "Once More, the Round" (*Collected Poems,* 243), the last poem in Roethke's last book, *The Far Field* (1964), published shortly after the poet's death in 1963.[1] In this short, loosely metered, and mostly slant-rhymed poem, as in other late verses, Roethke seems to know that his remaining days are few; it reads like a last poem. Touching on motifs, themes, and literary influences familiar to his readers, he alludes to his psychological and spiritual struggles, the subject of major poems like "The Lost Son" and "In a Dark Time." He speaks affectionately of flora and fauna, the simultaneously literal and figurative fellow beings that provide so much of the imagery in his best work, from the greenhouse poems of *The Lost Son and Other Poems* (1948) to the expansive "North American Sequence," which opens *The Far Field.* Moving through a landscape at once inner and outer, Roethke in this final poem takes his leave of the reader and of the world, yielding himself to a joyful and mystical union with all creation, a symbolic dance referred to in the poem's title and suggested by the repetition in the last line, Roethke's last words as a poet.

The spiritual quest in "Once More, the Round" is of course consistent with Roethke's Romantic perspective. Roethke saw himself as working in the main line of English-language Romanticism from Blake to Yeats, with Emerson and Whitman being especially influential on his thinking about nature and the numinous, eternal reality beyond and within the physical world. Emerson's *Nature* (1836) was for Roethke a guide, even a sacred text, emphasizing as it does the Platonic doctrine of correspondence, by which everything in the material world stands for an abstract, ideal, and eternal reality. "Nature is the symbol of spirit" (20), Emerson famously wrote in that essay, and like other American poets since Whitman, Roethke strove to identify and develop a symbolic language suited to the particularities of his own experience. Roethke's major symbols, as Jay Parini notes in his classic study of Roethke's Romanticism, consist of the father, the greenhouse, and the field. "These images," Parini asserts, "became the signposts of his secret planet, and we can know Roethke best by knowing his entire work, by following his personal development from unrealized potential to self-discovery and, ultimately, self-transcendence" (4). Other symbols are also crucial; Parini mentions the wind, the stone, and the tree, a list to which may be added the nouns in "Once More, the Round" that Roethke capitalized so as to identify them as archetypes—Pebble, Pond, Hill, Bird, Leaf, Fish, Snail, and Eye—along with the abstractions Unknown, Love, and One, and the overarching motifs of the circle and the dance. By means of these figures, familiar from poems throughout his body of work, Roethke recapitulates and extends his poetic and spiritual journey in "Once More, the Round."

The poem's title introduces the archetypal "round," whose eternal, universal persistence, as well as previous development in Roethke's poetry, is communicated by the adverbial phrase "Once More." A number of meanings inhere, including forms of song and dance in which the speaker and his fellow beings may be said to be participating in unison. In regard to song, the round is an arrangement of multiple voices singing the same melody, with each voice beginning at a different point. ("Row, Row, Row Your Boat" is perhaps the most familiar round, easy to teach to schoolchildren because it features only one chord.) Two types of dances are referred to as "round dance," the simplest involving many dancers holding hands in a circle. "Round dancing" otherwise refers to many dancing partners following the steps called out by a leader. The reader may imagine any or all of these song and dance forms being enacted in the poem. Roethke is both singing and dancing with the myriad elements of nature, which in his world have selfhood and voice, as in the poem "Unfold! Unfold!" when he exhorts his fellow beings:

> Sing, sing, you symbols! All simple creatures,
> All small shapes, willow-shy,
> In the obscure haze, sing!
>
> (*Collected Poems,* 86)

Perhaps the round dancing specified at the end of "Once More, the Round" begins as partnered, with Roethke taking a turn with William Blake, his mentor in mysticism and poetry, before the poets join all living things in a circle in which "everything comes to One" (11).

In the poem's first line the alliteration of Pebble and Pond places them in parity as aspects of nature and consciousness, as does the rhetorical nature of Roethke's question as to which is "greater." Neither is greater or more significant; the speaker honors each equally as an emblem of self—not ego, bound by desire, fear, memory, and hope, but the universal self of which Emerson speaks in *Nature* when he declares himself "part or particle of God" (10). Roethke's Pebble and Pond recall the first lines of the poem that Emerson places as an epigraph at the beginning of *Nature*: "A subtle chain of countless rings / The next unto the farther brings." Although the absence of concrete nouns makes the scenario implicit rather than explicit, Emerson is evoking the ripples that extend in every direction when a stone is tossed into a body of water. This image serves as the first illustration in *Nature* of Platonic correspondence, by which (as the third line in Emerson's poem has it) the "eye reads omens where it goes" (5). Roethke employs the same image at the end of "The Far Field," where a "ripple widening from a single stone / Winding around the waters of the world" concludes a catalogue of natural images illustrating the transcendentalist assertion that "[a]ll finite things reveal infinitude" (*Collected Poems,* 195). The image also appears in "Praise to the

End!": "The rings have gone from the pond. / The river's alone with its water" (81). Later in that poem, Roethke says, "I lost my identity to a pebble" (84), a statement that illustrates Parini's assertion that for Roethke "the stone [is] associated with transcendental experiences" (4). Selfhood is imagined not as separate but as relational, represented by an image (a pebble being thrown into water) that suggests consciousness, bodily gesture, motion through space, immersion in a greater whole, and persistent effect on the world at large. "What falls away is always," Roethke assures us in "The Waking" (*Collected Poems,* 104), a phrase that in this context supports a reading of "Once More, the Round" as an *ars poetica.* "Throw a stone into the stream," Emerson writes in chapter 4 of *Nature,* "and the circles that propagate themselves are the beautiful type of all influence" (21).[2] The pebble in this regard stands for Roethke's immortality in verse, with the pond representing the world and eternity.

The two questions that open "Once More, the Round" strike Neal Bowers as being "very much like riddles or koans. . . . To the first question there is no answer, and the answer to the second is vintage Roethke and standard mystical doctrine" (198). The second question, "What can be known?" reminds us of another line from "The Waking": "We think by feeling. What is there to know?" (*Collected Poems,* 104). Roethke suspends that question in "The Waking," having stressed the primacy of emotion and intuition over rational thought. In the second line of "Once More, the Round," however, he supplies an answer: "The Unknown" (2). Alluding to "The Waking," Bowers contends that "[b]y abandoning his attempts to know, the speaker [of 'Once More, the Round'] learns by going, and as he progresses, the Absolute he seeks becomes more visible" (199).

Spiritual insight and perspective come in lines 3 and 4, in which the speaker's "true self" (as opposed to the false self of his fearful and possessive ego) "runs toward a Hill" (3). The hill reprises the experience of "prospects" in eighteenth-century English topographical poetry, which the Romantics, Wordsworth in particular, later sublimated into mountaintop epiphanies in which emotional and aesthetic ecstasies supersede mere description. "A prospect," as John Wilson Foster defines it, "is a view into the distance (space); it is also a view into the future (distance in time), often with the suggestion of opportunity or expectation: in each case, a prospect is a view of something beyond, yet to be achieved or satisfying merely in the spectacle" (238). In Roethke's poem, that "something beyond," the Unknown, includes life, death, love, and eternity. For Richard Allen Blessing, the hill "is, perhaps, both the elevation leading upward to God and the grave"; he implies that Roethke's speaker does not attain the hilltop with its prospect of time and space, at least within the poem itself (218). We are free, however, to imagine that he does, that the anapest in the last foot of line 3 ("toward a Hill") conveys his ecstatic momentum toward the height.[3] That rising rhythm and the hard stresses that begin line 4 ("More! O More!) imply the widening of his view; that he takes in a full prospect of the landscape is also suggested by how the last word in the line (and in the stanza) reverses the previous line's final metrical foot. The dactylic "Visible," with a heavy stress followed by two unstressed syllables, reinforced by an end stop and the expanse of a stanza break, acts as a falling away and an auditory manifestation of the speaker's elevated view of the circling horizon and the landscape around and below him.

The second stanza begins by hinting at the shadow of memory as well as the daylight of the soul's illumination. By saying "*Now* I adore my life" (5; emphasis added) the speaker implies that he has not always so felt. He may have reached the top of a hill but the summit recalls its antithesis, the valley of despair traversed in "The Lost Son" and "In a Dark Time." The word "now" resonates with what Christopher Giroux identifies as a "tension between spiritual unity and spiritual despair" in "Once More, the Round," an emotional oscillation in which "the joy of unification with the One is tempered" by darker feelings (45). Reading the litany that follows ("I adore my life / with the Bird, the abiding Leaf, / With the Fish, the questing Snail" [5–7]), one remembers that in earlier poems these and other totemic beings sometimes failed to answer the poet's calls for spiritual succor. The first stanza of "The Lost Son," for example, concludes with the speaker summoning three familiar presences:

> Snail, snail, glister me forward,
> Bird, soft-sigh me home,
> Worm, be with me.
> This is my hard time.

The subsequent stanza break conveys the silence that follows his requests. Snail, bird, and worm do not speak, sing, or even approach. In the next stanza, the refusal continues:

> Fished in an old wound,
> The soft pond of repose;
> Nothing nibbled my line,
> Not even the minnows came.
>
> (*Collected Poems,* 50)

Closed in by grief and mental illness, the isolated speaker finds himself unable to communicate with his fellow beings, to access those aspects of his soul that would help him advance in his quest. "The Lost Son" then proceeds with Roethke's most harrowing and memorable evocation of mania and despair, an experience that he portrays as a spiritual crisis as much as a psychological one.

The Lost Son's descent, however, makes possible the ascent in those poems in which Roethke moves toward joy and affirmation. In an oft-quoted passage from his essay "Open Letter," Roethke emphasizes how in the soul's quest, "the method is cyclic. I believe that to go forward as a spiritual man it is necessary first to go back. . . . There is a perpetual slipping-back, then a going-forward; but there is *some* 'progress'" (*On Poetry and Craft,* 51). Regression and progression are represented in Roethke's poetry as plants and small creatures either retreating from or advancing towards a heightened state of consciousness. In "The Longing," for example,

> the spirit fails to move forward,
> But shrinks into a half-life, less than itself,
> Falls back, a slug, a loose worm
> Ready for any crevice,
> An eyeless starer.
>
> (*Collected Poems,* 181)

By contrast, in "A Light Breather,"

> The spirit moves,
> Yet stays:
> . . . .
> Moves, like the snail,
> Still inward,
> Taking and embracing its surroundings,
> Never wishing itself away,
> Unafraid of what it is,
> A music in a hood,
> A small thing,
> Singing.
>
> (*Collected Poems,* 97)

Forward movement may convey one towards apotheosis, always and necessarily accompanied by the fellow beings that Roethke collectively identifies, in the titles of two poems, as "The Minimal" and "The Small." In such wise the speaker of "The Longing" presents his response to alienation in modern industrial society:

> I would with the fish, the blackening salmon, and the mad lemmings,
> The children dancing, the flowers widening.
> . . . .
> A leaf, I would love the leaves, delighting in the redolent disorder of this mortal life.
>
> (*Collected Poems,* 182)

This primary motif in Roethke's work—the "lovely diminutives" of nature (*Collected Poems,* 60)—can be understood in relation to Taoist philosophy. "*Tao,*" as Julian F. Pas defines it, "is the eternal reality beyond, but also within, the visible universe." It is "deepest mystery; it cannot be grasped by the rational mind only, but intuitively, if the mind is still and desires are controlled" (308–9). Sometimes visualized as the great river of existence, the Tao is both creator and creation, the universe itself and something beyond and within all forms. Roethke's affinity with Taoism may be gauged by the first sentence of *Tao Te Ching,* the ancient classic attributed to the legendary Lao-Tzu: "The Tao that can be told / is not the eternal Tao" (Mitchell, *Tao Te Ching,* 3). Roethke echoes that fundamental truth in "Once More, the Round" when he invokes the knowable Unknown. His primary way of telling the Tao, however, was to speak of the virtue and power of the infinite multitude of forms referred to in Chinese tradition as the "ten thousand things," which appear in Roethke's poetry as small elements of nature: mineral, vegetable, or animal. Perhaps more than any Anglo American poet, Roethke was a poet of *Te,* the second word in the title *Tao Te Ching.* Pas's definition of *Te* is particularly apt in relation to Roethke's imagery of nature: "If Tao is the overarching reality and cosmic energy, *Te* is what all beings receive from Tao; it is their own nature, with its specific talents and potentials, that enables them to act in their own way as if by their inner compulsion. . . . *Te* is the power of Tao, individualized, as for example, in a seed, which has the inner potential and unfailing power to sprout and grow into a preprogrammed plant or tree" (332). Roethke's greenhouse poems in *The Lost Son and Other Poems* illustrate precisely that principle, although when it came to propagation, Roethke favored images of cuttings and bulbs over seeds. Whether implicitly or explicitly, he always linked what we may call the *Te* of plants to the transcendent life force he hoped to sustain in himself. "I can hear, underground, that sucking and sobbing," he wrote in "Cuttings (*later*)" of the horticultural starts in his father's forcing house. "In my veins, in my bones I feel it" (*Collected Poems,* 35).

That same identification with small organisms recurs in the litany of "Once More, the Round," with the verb "adore" resembling Christian-derived diction in "Cuttings (*later*)," in which the "resurrection of dry sticks" figures as more miraculous than any events recounted in the Bible: "What saint strained so much?" (*Collected Poems,* 35). Using "adore" in the sense of worship and prayer, Roethke praises and expresses gratitude for his life and all life. Boundaries between himself and the ten thousand things dissolve, as the parallelisms of lines 5 through 10 (noun phrases and clauses beginning in "with," "and," and "for") configure selfhood as situated, mutual, and participatory. The Bird, traditionally an archetype of the soul's freedom and joy,[4] also invokes the actual birds of Roethke's life and poetry: heron, crow, sparrow, wren, lark, phoebe, killdeer, and many others, mostly species native to Michigan, Roethke's home state, and the Pacific Northwest, where he lived the last decade and a half of his life. The "abiding Leaf" (6) stands for all plant life, bringing to mind the orchids, roses, cyclamen, and carnations of the greenhouse poems; it also echoes Whitman's *Leaves of Grass* (1855–92), in which the single leaf, simultaneously distinctive and part of a greater whole, represents the self as organic, democratic, and immortal. The "Fish" (7) embodies what Carl Jung, in *The Archetypes and the Collective Unconscious* (1959), calls a "'nourishing' influence of unconscious contents, which maintain the vitality of consciousness by a continual influx of energy" (142). Consistent with his borrowing of Christian terms to express his decidedly non-Christian spirituality, Roethke declares in "Unfold! Unfold!" that his "mission became the salvation of minnows" (*Collected Poems,* 86). Named in Roethke's poems more than any other fish, the diminutive minnow complements the horticultural starts of the "Cuttings" poems as an emblem of Te, the power and grace inherent even (and, for Roethke, especially) in small beings. In "Cuttings," "[o]ne nub of growth / Nudges a sand crumb loose" (*Collected Poems,* 35). Similarly, in "The Sequel," the poet evokes how "a minnow nudged its stone" (*Collected Poems,* 233). The subtle actions of plant and animal in these passages involve interaction with and alteration of their environments. Growth and creativity presuppose purposeful movement, whether so subtle as nudging or as active as the running and dancing in "Once More, the Round." Like the pebble falling into the pond, these natural images represent Te as individual, bodied selves participating joyfully in Tao, the sacred mysteries of life.

The last figure, "the questing Snail" (7), draws on traditional associations of snails with patience, sensitivity, fertility, healing, androgyny, self-reliance, and change. It also hearkens back to "The Waking," in which "the lowly worm climbs up a winding stair" (*Collected Poems,* 104). The snail, in Roethke's iconography, resembles a worm that carries its own winding stair in the form of its shell, which spirals outward and around itself as it grows. The quests of both creatures involve a steady ascent to a higher state of consciousness. "[T]he unfolding life-cycle is well conceived as a spiral staircase," Anthony Stevens observes in *Archetype: An Updated Natural History of the Self* (2002), "each stage of the cycle being a landing or 'secure base' which, once reached, provides a temporary resting place before yet another rite of passage moves one onwards and upwards to the next" (196). By such means, analogous to the adaptations that occur in biological evolution, the worm, the snail, the poet, and every other being may fulfill more exalted destinies.

Roethke's image of the worm and the staircase builds on literary precedent. Kearful cites William Butler Yeats's "A Dialogue of Self and Soul" (*A Field Guide to the Poetry of Theodore Roethke,* 320); Roethke was undoubtedly familiar with "the winding ancient stair" (234) to which Yeats summons his soul at the beginning of that poem and which provided the title of his 1933 volume *The Winding Stair and Other Poems*. The "winding stair" in "The Waking" almost certainly alludes to that poem and book. Yet intertextuality is also evident with the poem that introduces Emerson's *Nature*. After the concentric waves, the eye reading omens, and the rose that "speaks all languages" (surely a motif to inspire the greenhouse keeper's son), Emerson concludes with a final archetypal image: "[S]triving to be man, the worm / Mounts through all the spires of form" (5). The affinity of those lines with Roethke's "lowly worm" that "climbs up a winding stair" reflects repeated readings of *Nature,* with its initial poem whose motifs so closely parallel Roethke's. This resemblance is a wave washing up on the shore of "The Waking," propagated by Emerson's essay hitting the water a century earlier.

Roethke, however, would never have said that the worm strives "to be man." Such anthropocentrism is inconsistent with Roethke's pantheistic, panpsychic, or panentheist faith, in which all beings have their own identities and evolutionary paths. In his essay "On Identity," Roethke stresses that he regards humble creatures like the worm and the questing snail not only as signposts on his own journey toward self-identity, but also as conscious, intrinsically valuable selves with their own relationship to the eternal: "If the dead can come to our aid in a quest for identity, so can the living—and I mean *all* living things. . . . This is not so much a naïve as a primitive attitude: animistic, maybe. Why not? Everything that lives is holy: I call upon these holy forms of life. . . . Therefore, in calling upon the snail, I am calling, in a sense, upon God" (*On Poetry and Craft,* 40). An uncredited citation of Blake appears here: "[E]very thing that lives is holy" (*Complete Poetry and Prose,* 45) is the last line in *The Marriage of Heaven and Hell* (1790–1793), a text of Blake's that profoundly influenced Roethke's poetry, both in its aphoristic and archetypal style and in its prophetic mysticism. When it comes to the allusion to Blake in line 8 of "Once More, the Round" and Roethke's outright naming of the English poet in line 9, it is important to keep in mind that he "dance[s] with William Blake" as a fellow poet and earthly being, not as a mere acolyte.[5] In regard to writing what he called "the referential poem," Roethke advised taking "what you will with authority and see[ing] that you give it another, or even better life, in the new context" (*On Poetry and Craft,* 56). Just as he adapted Emerson's worm mounting the spire to become human into the more biocentric symbol of the worm climbing up a winding stair, so too with his Blakean references Roethke emphasizes what is congenial to his own idiosyncratic vision of nature and spirit.[6]

The "Eye altering all" in line 8 comes from Blake's esoteric poem "The Mental Traveller" (ca. 1801), which "describes the whole of the fallen time-world where innocence and experience shade into one another [and e]verything travels around the wheel of existence (Adams, 77). The poem's mythic narrative involves the mutual tormenting of a boy and an old woman, whose malevolent spell causes the boy to grow rapidly through manhood and old age and her to become young, before he does the same to her and the cycle starts again, apparently to repeat endlessly. The sixteenth quatrain reads as follows:

> The Guests are scatterd [*sic*] thro' the land
> For the Eye altering alters all
> The Senses roll themselves in fear
> And the flat Earth becomes a Ball.
>
> (*Complete Poetry and Prose,* 485)

Jesse S. Cohn sees the altering eye as "the pivot for the revolving whole" envisioned by Blake, who "regards the consequences of empirical philosophy as a kind of materialistically legitimized selfishness; the infinite cruelty of this universe Blake describes is a consequence of the narrowing of the senses" (131–32). In asserting the superiority of imagination over reason, Blake rejected eighteenth-century rationalism, which he characterizes in terms of "Single vision & Newtons [*sic*] sleep," as opposed to his own double and even "fourfold vision" of a material world charged with spiritual energy and significance (722).[7] As he wrote in "There Is No Natural Religion" (1788), "If it were not for the Poetic or Prophetic character the Philosophical & Experimental would soon be at the ratio of all things, & stand still, unable to do other than repeat the same dull round over again" (*Complete Poetry and Prose,* 3). That soul-deadening round is the world of "The Mental Traveller," in which "Single vision," rationalist, materialist, and unimaginative, reduces all of creation, including human beings, to the status of objects with merely instrumental value. Only through the imagination's "mental travelling" may humanity perceive the world as bright rather than dull, ecstatically alive rather than spiritually dead.

Roethke, in keeping with his theory of giving poetic borrowings "another, or even better life," reverses the action of Blake's altering eye so that imagination revitalizes the world. His is not the "dull round" of Blake's nightmarish allegory, but a reciprocal cycle in which Roethke's own poetic and prophetic character dances with all beings, including "William Blake / For love, for Love's sake" (9–10). Emerson, alluded to earlier in the poem, also joins the dance, though he goes unnamed: the line "The eye altering, alters all" appears in his writings more often than any other passage from Blake (O'Keefe, 28). Clare Elliott, who points out that Emerson started reading Blake in the early 1840s, argues that "this "crucial passage . . . summarizes both writers' obsessions with the relationship between the 'eye' and the 'I.'" Like Blake before him and Roethke after, Emerson found the homophony of "Eye" and "I" instructive, collapsing as it does vision and the self, so that the world is only properly seen with the imaginative faculty, which can alter all for the better as well as for the worse. "Vision," Elliott continues, "for Blake, is imaginative, not merely ocular, and this is the instruction which Emerson gleans from his reading of Blake's poetry" (81). So too with Roethke, whose gleanings from both Blake and Emerson are on self-conscious display in "Once More, the Round." The "love" which he names twice in line 10 is synonymous with imaginative vision, which, as lines 3 and 4 have it, makes "More! O More! Visible" to his I/Eye, his "true self."[8]

The poem's concluding couplet should be read with the entire poem in mind, particularly the foregoing pairs of complementary motifs and ideas: Pebble/Pond, Known/Unknown, Self/Hill, Past/Present, Human/Animal, Roethke/

Blake, and Everything/One. The dualities culminate in that ultimate pairing in line 11, which expresses the speaker's mystical perception of unity: "everything comes to One." Roethke's monism reflects his readings in Asian literature, Neoplatonism, Yeats, and scholars of mysticism like Evelyn Underhill (Parini, 135). His primary models, however, were Blake and Emerson, both of whom, as Richard A. O'Keefe observes, "thought dialectically—that is, contraries for them were generative or creative. Dualism, polarity, dichotomy—these modes of perceiving and organizing human experience not only appear throughout the major literary productions of both writers, but they also seem to produce those works, both poems and prose" (6–7). As Blake wrote in *The Marriage of Heaven and Hell* (the title of which is notably dialectic), "[w]ithout Contraries is no Progression." The progression of which Blake speaks is from materialism to idealism, from a world that is fallen because it is *seen* as fallen, to a world in which "Energy is Eternal Delight" (*Complete Poetry and Prose,* 34). Emerson, for his part, asserts in "The Over-Soul" (1841) that "[w]e live in succession, in division, in parts, in particles. Meantime within man is the soul of the whole; the wise silence; the universal beauty, to which every part and particle is equally related; the eternal ONE" (*Essays and Lectures,* 386).[9] Such a formulation, echoed by Roethke in line 11 of his poem, may seem to devalue the physical world of nature in all its multiplicity. But Roethke forestalls that misreading: none is greater, Pebble or Pond, Te or Tao, particular or universal, material or ideal. Roethke's "One" should be understood in light of the valorization of the Earth and its denizens that permeates his poetry. "God bless the Ground!" he declares in "The Waking" (*Collected Poems,* 104). Even more to the point is his exclamation in "A Field of Light," which emphasizes the sacredness of nature's discrete minimals: "I saw the separateness of all things!" (*Collected Poems,* 60).

In the last line Roethke, Blake, and their fellow beings "dance on, dance on, dance on" (12). Blessing describes this as "an ending that does not end. The dance goes on and on, like a musical round, like a spiraling gyre, like the evolutionary process" (218). Audrey T. Rodgers, in her study of the dance motif in the work of Roethke and other modern poets, identifies this final moment as "a resolution of the vexations of the spirit and the affirmation of a truth he had struggled a lifetime to accept: the unity of all things in nature and in man. Perceiving the cyclic pattern of life in Papa's greenhouse, he knows himself to be one with leaf, bird, fish, and snail" (133). Don Bogen, who has done the most thorough investigation to date of Roethke's working methods as evidenced in the poet's papers, tells us that "Roethke considered *Dance On, Dance On, Dance On* as a title for his last volume," a fact that "shows how central this affirmative vision was for him" (168). It is fitting to cite so many scholars of Roethke in concluding this essay and this book; they too have their part in the dance, their turn in the round. Roethke's last poem, his last word, along with of all his work, still commands the admiration of readers and the attention of scholars, its impact continuing like that of a "ripple widening from a single stone / Winding around the waters of the world" (*Collected Poems,* 195).

NOTES

1. Roethke and his wife Beatrice sent "Once More, the Round" to friends as their Christmas greeting for 1961. The poem had its first journal publication in *Encounter* 18, no. 5 (May 1962): 45, and subsequently appeared in the January 1963 issue of *Harper's Bazaar* (117).

2. The image of concentric waves emanating from a center appears elsewhere in Emerson's writing, as in "Circles" (1841): "The life of man is a self-evolving circle, which, from a ring imperceptibly small, rushes on all sides outward to new and larger circles, and that without end" (403).

3. Pronunciation of "toward" varies according to dialect, including whether it is spoken with one syllable or two, and if two, whether the stress should go on the second syllable or the first. In most of the United States, including Roethke's (and my) native Michigan, "toward" is monosyllabic. I scan "My true self runs toward a Hill" as iambic trimeter with an anapestic substitution in the last foot: U/ U/ UU/.

Those who take "toward" to be a two-syllable word may scan line 3 as either iambic tetrameter or iambic tetrameter with a trochee in the third foot. In any case, the line ends with a rising rhythm, like nine out of twelve lines in the poem. My point about the speaker's topographical and spiritual elevation being reflected in the meter stands regardless.

4. In her study of bird symbolism, Beryl Rowland writes that the "idea of the soul as a winged creature is not new. . . . It is a widespread and extremely ancient belief that the soul assumes the form of a bird, or, put more extremely, that all birds are human souls" (xiii).

5. Compare the dancing with Blake in "Once More, the Round" to these lines from Roethke's poem "The Dance": "I take this cadence from a man named Yeats; / I take it, and I give it back again" (*Collected Poems,* 101). Each reference honors its subject by viewing poetic tradition as an exchange, a cycle, a rhythm, a song, or a dance.

6. See, for example, Roethke's poem "The Slug," which begins with the exclamation "How I loved one like you when I was little!" and ends with the poet asking that "most odious" creature "Would Blake call you holy?" (*Collected Poems,* 145). Roethke thus expresses uncertainty about the extent to which Blake would have agreed with his animistic creed. The question calls to mind the line of criticism that sees the Platonic idealism of the Romantics as fundamentally human-centered and potentially antiecological.

Both Emerson and Blake have been characterized by some critics as concerned with the human relation to the supernatural at the expense of the natural world. Fredrik Chr. Brøgger, for example, asserts that Transcendentalism "proves to be a very shaky ground for the interpretation of natural phenomena. It tends to cater to an anthropomorphic and even anthropocentric inclination that is hazardous to the health of the language used to describe the natural environment, and perhaps, ultimately, to the health of that environment itself" (31).

Recent ecocriticism, however, has argued for a green Romanticism. Acknowledging that "it has been customary to categorize [Blake] as a 'gnostic' visionary who treated the natural or 'vegetative' world with contempt," Lawrence Coupe reminds us that "we must bear in mind that it was the dead universe of Newton's physics that he was rejecting; what he believed in, by contrast, was nature as a mode of revelation" (13). Kevin Hutchings makes a persuasive case for a "distinctively Blakean view of the relationship between humanity and nature, a view that productively challenges the traditional Western notion that humans should exercise a hierarchical and narrowly anthropocentric 'dominion' over the entire non-human portion of creation" (3). Also see works by Mark S. Lussier and James C. McKusick, listed in Works Cited. Ecocritical reassessment of Roethke needs to consider conclusions drawn in such studies of his Romantic precursors.

7. A passage in the untitled poem Blake sent to Thomas Butts on November 22, 1802, is indicated:

> For double the vision my Eyes do see
> And a double vision is always with me
> With my inward Eye 'tis an old Man grey
> With my outward a Thistle across my way.
>
> (721–22)

8. Emerson approvingly quotes Blake in his essay "Poetry and Imagination" (1883): "He who does not imagine in stronger and better light than his perishing mortal eye can see, does not imagine at all. . . . I assert for myself that I do not behold the outward creation, and that to me it would be a hindrance, and not action. I question not my corporeal eye any more than I would question a window concerning sight. I look through it, and not with it" (qtd. in Elliott, 80). Elliott compares Blake's statement to the famous "transparent eyeball" passage in Emerson's *Nature.*

9. This is the Eleatic One of Parmenides, subsequently discussed and developed by Greek philosophers from Plato to Plotinus.

Works Cited

Abrams, M. H. *Natural Supernaturalism: Tradition and Revolution in Romantic Literature.* New York: W. W. Norton, 1971.

Adams, Hazard. *William Blake: A Reading of the Shorter Poems.* Seattle: University of Washington Press, 1963.

Alkalay-Gut, Karen. "The Birth of the Poet's Mind: A Study of Theodore Roethke's 'Where Knock Is Open Wide.'" *Contemporary Poetry* 5, no. 2 (1983): 17–40.

Applewhite, James. "Death and Rebirth in a Modern Landscape." 1985. In Bloom, *Theodore Roethke,* 195–209.

Auden, W. H. "September 1, 1939." 1939. In *Selected Poems: Expanded Edition,* edited by Edward Mendelson, 95–97. New York: Vintage, 2007.

Bachelard, Gaston. *The Poetics of Space.* Boston: Beacon Press, 1969.

Bacon, Sir Francis. *The Essayes or Counsels, Civill and Morall.* 1625. Edited by Michael Kiernan. Oxford: Oxford University Press, 1985.

Balakian, Peter. *Theodore Roethke's Far Fields: The Evolution of His Poetry.* Baton Rouge: Louisiana State University Press, 1989.

Barillas, William. *The Midwestern Pastoral: Place and Landscape in Literature of the American Heartland.* Athens: Ohio University Press, 2006.

———. "Re: More on 'Frau Bauman.'" Message to Marcia Noe, 20 November 2014. Email.

Barthes, Roland. *A Lover's Discourse.* Translated by Richard Howard. New York: Hill and Wang, 1978.

Bearss, Linda, and Ronald Primeau, eds. "Being a Collection of Essays on Theodore Roethke." Special issue, *Midwestern Miscellany* 36 (Spring/Fall 2008).

Benoit, Raymond. "'Moss-Picking': An Undergraduate Theme of Theodore Roethke." *English Language Notes* 33, no. 3 (March 1996): 47–51.

Blake, William. *The Complete Poetry and Prose of William Blake.* Edited by David V. Erdman. Rev. ed. Berkeley: University of California Press, 1982.

Blessing, Richard Allen. *Theodore Roethke's Dynamic Vision.* Bloomington: Indiana University Press, 1974.

Bloom, Harold. *The Anxiety of Influence: A Theory of Poetry.* New York: Oxford University Press, 1973.

———, ed. *Theodore Roethke.* Modern Critical Views. New York: Chelsea House, 1988.

Bogan, Louise. *What the Woman Lived: Selected Letters of Louise Bogan.* Edited by Ruth Limmer. New York: Harcourt Brace Jovanovich, 1973.

Bogen, Don. *A Necessary Order: Theodore Roethke and the Writing Process.* Athens: Ohio University Press, 1991.

Boruch, Marianne. "A Conversation with Marianne Boruch." Interview by Brooke Horvath. *Denver Quarterly* 28, no. 2 (1993): 105–21.

———. "Three Spirits." *Field* 53 (1995): 7–40.

Bottigheimer, Ruth B., ed. *Fairy Tales and Society: Illusion, Allusion, and Paradigm.* Philadelphia: University of Pennsylvania Press, 1986.

Bowers, Neal. *Theodore Roethke: The Journey from I to Otherwise.* Columbia: University of Missouri Press, 1982.

Boyd, John D. "Texture and Form in Theodore Roethke's Greenhouse Poems." *Modern Language Quarterly* 32, no. 4 (December 1971): 409–24.

Boyers, Robert. "Imagine Wrestling with an Angel: An Interview with Stanley Kunitz." *Salmagundi* 22/23 (Spring/Summer 1973): 71–83.

Brewer, James, and Gail A. McPeek. *The Atlas of Breeding Birds of Michigan.* East Lansing: Michigan State University Press, 1991.

Brøgger, Fredrik Chr. "Anthropocentric Nature Lover: Annie Dillard and the Transcendentalist Tradition in American Nature Writing." *American Studies in Scandinavia* 39, no. 2 (2007): 29–40.

Brown, Dennis E. "Theodore Roethke's 'Self-World' and the Modernist Position." *Journal of Modern Literature* 3, no. 5 (July 1974): 1239–54.

Buell, Lawrence. *Writing for an Endangered World: Literature, Culture, and Environment in the U.S. and Beyond.* Cambridge, MA: Belknap Press, 2001.

Burke, Kenneth. "The Cult of the Breakthrough." *New Republic,* September 21, 1968, 25–26.

———. "The Vegetal Radicalism of Theodore Roethke." *The Sewanee Review* 58, no. 1 (January–March 1950): 68–108.

Burklund, Carl Edwin, ed. *New Michigan Verse.* Ann Arbor: University of Michigan Press, 1940.

Burns, Robert. *Selected Poems and Songs.* Edited by Robert P. Irvine. Oxford: Oxford University Press, 2013.

Campbell, Joseph. *The Hero with a Thousand Faces.* 1949. Princeton: Princeton University Press, 1973.

Cixous, Hélène. "The Laugh of the Medusa." 1975. In *New French Feminisms,* edited by Elaine Marks and Isabelle de Courtivron, 245–64. New York: Schocken Books, 1981.

Clare, John. *Selected Poetry and Prose.* Edited by Merryn Williams and Raymond Williams. London: Methuen, 1986.

Cohn, Jesse S. "Blake's 'The Mental Traveller.'" *The Explicator* 58, no. 3 (Spring 2000): 130–33.

Coupe, Laurence. *The Green Studies Reader: From Romanticism to Ecocriticism.* London: Routledge, 2000.

Cummings, E. E. *A Miscellany Revised.* Edited by George J. Firmage. New York: October House, 1965.

Dante Alighieri. *The Divine Comedy of Dante Alighieri: Paradiso.* Translated by Allen Mandelbaum. 1982. New York: Bantam, 1986.

Derrida, Jacques. *The Animal That Therefore I Am.* Edited by Marie-Louise Mallet. Translated by David Wills. New York: Fordham University Press, 2008.

Dickey, James. "The Greatest American Poet: Roethke." 1968. In *Sorties,* 214–24.

———. *Sorties.* Garden City, NY: Doubleday, 1971.

———. "Theodore Roethke." 1961. In *Babel to Byzantium: Poets and Poetry Now*, 147–52. New York: Farrar, Straus and Giroux, 1968.

Dickinson, Emily. *The Poems of Emily Dickinson*. Reading edition. Edited by Ralph William Franklin. Cambridge, MA: Belknap Press, 1999.

Donoghue, Denis. "Theodore Roethke." 1964. In Bloom, *Theodore Roethke*, 37–59.

Dougherty, James. "Theodore Roethke's 'North American Sequence': Religious Awakening in the West." *Literature and Belief* 21, no. 1 (2001): 177–203.

Du Bois, W. E. B. *The Souls of Black Folk*. Chicago: A. C. McClurg, 1903.

Ebreo, Leone. *Dialogues of Love*. 1535. Edited by Rossella Pescatori. Translated by Damian Bacich and Rossella Pescatori. Toronto: University of Toronto Press, 2009.

Eliot, T. S. *Collected Poems, 1909–1962*. San Diego: Harcourt Brace Jovanovich, 1970.

———. "Tradition and the Individual Talent." 1919. In *Selected Essays 1917–1932*, 3–11. New York: Houghton Mifflin Harcourt, 2014.

Elliott, Clare. "'A Backward Glance O'er' the (Dis)United States: William Blake, Ralph Waldo Emerson and the 'Authentic American Religion.'" *The European Journal for American Culture* 28, no. 1 (2009): 9–25.

Emerson, Ralph Waldo. *Essays and Lectures*. New York: Library of America, 1983.

Emig, Rainer. *W. H. Auden: Towards a Postmodern Poetics*. London: Macmillan, 2000.

Evernden, Neil. *The Social Creation of Nature*. Baltimore: John Hopkins University Press, 1992.

Felstiner, John. *Can Poetry Save the Earth? A Field Guide to Nature Poems*. New Haven: Yale University Press, 2009.

Ferry, Anne. *The Title to the Poem*. Stanford: Stanford University Press, 1996.

Fiedler, Leslie. *Freaks: Myths and Images of the Secret Self*. New York: Simon and Schuster, 1978.

Floyd-Wilson, Mary. "Poetic Empathy: Theodore Roethke's Conception of Woman in the Love Poems." *South Atlantic Review* 56, no. 1 (January 1991): 61–78.

Foster, Ann T. *Theodore Roethke's Meditative Sequences: Contemplation and the Creative Process*. Lewiston, NY: Edwin Mellen Press, 1985.

Foster, John Wilson. "The Measure of Paradise: Topography in Eighteenth-Century Poetry." *Eighteenth-Century Studies* 9, no. 2 (Winter 1975–76): 232–56.

Frost, Robert. *The Poetry of Robert Frost*. New York: Holt, Rinehart and Winston, 1969.

Foucault, Michel. "What Is an Author?" 1969. In *The Foucault Reader*, edited by Paul Rabinow, translated by Josué Harari, 101–20. New York: Pantheon Books, 1984.

Frye, Northrop. *Anatomy of Criticism: Four Essays*. 1957. Princeton: Princeton University Press, 1990.

———. "The Archetypes of Literature." In *Fables of Identity: Studies in Poetic Mythology*, 7–20. New York: Harcourt, Brace and World, 1963.

Galvez, Marisa. "Alba." In *The Princeton Encyclopedia of Poetry and Poetics*, 4th ed., edited by Roland Greene, 29–30. Princeton: Princeton University Press, 2012.

Galvin, Brendan. "Kenneth Burke and Theodore Roethke's 'Lost Son' Poems." 1971. In Bloom, *Theodore Roethke*, 85–112.

Gardner, Thomas. "'North American Sequence': Theodore Roethke and the Contemporary American Long Poem." 1984. In Bloom, *Theodore Roethke*, 177–94.

"A Garland for Theodore Roethke." *The Michigan Quarterly Review* 6, no. 4 (Fall 1967): 252–75.

Gaster, Theodor H. *Festivals of the Jewish Year: A Modern Interpretation and Guide*. New York: William Sloane Associates, 1952.

Giroux, Christopher. "Once More, the Despair: Revisiting Roethke's 'Once More, the Round.'" *The Explicator* 74, no. 1 (January–March 2016): 44–46.

Glotfelty, Cheryll, and Harold Fromm, eds. *The Ecocriticism Reader: Landmarks in Literary Ecology*. Athens: University of Georgia Press, 1996.

Goldberg, Beckian Fritz. "The Case of 'The Tree, the Bird.'" *Field* 53 (1995): 32–40.

Gould, Joan. *Spinning Straw into Gold: What Fairy Tales Reveal about the Transformations in a Woman's Life*. New York: Random House, 2005.

Hageneder, Fred. *The Meaning of Trees: Botany, History, Meaning, Lore*. San Francisco: Chronicle Books, 2005.

———. *The Spirit of Trees: Science, Symbolism, and Inspiration*. New York: Continuum, 2000.

Hamill, Sam. "A Lover's Quarrel." In *The Nootka Rose: Poems by Sam Hamill*, 12–15. Portland: Breitenbush Books, 1987.

Haralson, Eric, ed. *Reading the Middle Generation Anew: Culture, Community, and Form in Twentieth-Century American Poetry*. Iowa City: University of Iowa Press, 2006.

Haraway, Donna. *When Species Meet*. Minneapolis: University of Minnesota Press, 2008.

Hatto, Arthur T., ed. *Eos: An Enquiry into the Theme of Lovers' Meetings and Partings at Dawn in Poetry*. The Hague: Mouton, 1965.

Hawthorne, Nathaniel. "Wakefield." In *Hawthorne's Short Stories*, 1946, edited by Newton Arvin, 63–71. New York: Vintage, 2011.

Heaney, Seamus. "Canticles to the Earth." In *Preoccupations*, 191–92. London: Faber and Faber, 1980.

———. "Digging." In *Death of a Naturalist*, 13–14. London: Faber and Faber, 1966.

Heidegger, Martin. *Being and Time*. Translated by Joan Stambaugh. Albany: SUNY Press, 2010.

Herbert, George. *The Complete English Poems*. Edited by John Tobin. London: Penguin Books, 1991.

Herrick, Robert. "To the Virgins, to Make Much of Time." In *Selected Poems*, edited by David Jesson-Dibley, 72–73. New York: Routledge, 2003.

Hesiod. *The Works and Days; Theogony; The Shield of Herakles*. 1959. Translated by Richmond Lattimore. Ann Arbor: University of Michigan Press, 1991.

Hess, Linda. "Appendix A: Upside-Down Language." In *The Bījak of Kabir*, translated by Linda Hess and Shukdev Singh, 135–61. San Francisco: North Point Press, 1983.

Heyen, William. "Andrew De Haan Interviews William Heyen." *Through the Third Eye*, October 2012. Web, 25 August 2014.

———. "The Divine Abyss: Theodore Roethke's Mysticism." *Texas Studies in Literature and Language* 11, no. 2 (1969): 1051–68.

———. "The Yeats Influence: Roethke's Formal Lyrics of the Fifties." *John Berryman Studies* 3, no. 4 (1977): 17–63.

Hickman, Trenton. "Theodore Roethke and the Poetics of Place." In Haralson, *Reading the Middle Generation Anew*, 183–202.

Hillman, Brenda. *Practical Water*. Middletown, CT: Wesleyan University Press, 2009.

Hirsch, Edward. Introduction to Roethke, *Selected Poems,* xiii–xxv.

Hobsbaum, Philip. *Metre, Rhythm and Verse Form*. London: Routledge, 1996.

Hoffman, Daniel. "Poetry: After Modernism." In *Harvard Guide to Contemporary American Writing,* 439–95. Cambridge, MA: Belknap Press, 1979.

Holderness, Graham. "'Dressing Old Words New': Shakespeare, Science, and Appropriation." *Borrowers and Lenders* 1, no. 2 (Fall/Winter 2005): n.p. Web, 1 September 2015.

Hugo, Richard. "Stray Thoughts on Roethke and Teaching." *The American Poetry Review* 3, no. 1 (January/February 1974): 50–51.

Hutcheon, Linda, with Siobhan O'Flynn. *A Theory of Adaptation*. 2nd ed. New York: Routledge, 2013.

Hutchings, Kevin. *Imagining Nature: Blake's Environmental Poetics*. Montreal: McGill–Queen's University Press, 2003.

In a Dark Time. Directed by David Myers. McGraw-Hill Films, 1964.

James, Clive. "'Break, Blow, Burn': Well Versed." Review of *Break, Blow, Burn,* by Camille Paglia. *The New York Times Sunday Book Review,* 27 March 2005. Web.

Jarrell, Randall. "Fifty Years of American Poetry." In *The Third Book of Criticism,* 295–334. New York: Farrar, Straus and Giroux, 1969.

Jung, Carl. *The Archetypes and the Collective Unconscious*. Edited by Herbert Read, Michael Fordham, and Gerhard Adler. Translated by R. F. C. Hull. Vol. 9, pt. 1, of *The Collected Works of C. G. Jung*. 2nd ed. Princeton: Princeton University Press, 2014.

———. *Psychology and Religion*. New Haven, CT: Yale University Press, 1938.

Kalaidjian, Walter B. *Understanding Theodore Roethke*. Columbia: University of South Carolina Press, 1987.

Kane, Julie, and Amanda L. French. "Villanelle." In *The Princeton Encyclopedia of Poetry and Poetics,* edited by Roland Greene, 1551–22. 4th ed. Princeton: Princeton University Press, 2012.

Kearful, Frank J. "'The Child Awake and Wearied Of': James Merrill's Art of the Villanelle."In *Zum Begriff der Imagination in Dichtung und Dichtungstheorie,* edited by Manfred Beyer, 271–88. Trier, Germany: Wissenschaftlicher Verlag Trier, 1998.

———. "Regions of the Self: Theodore Roethke's North American Sequence." In *Regional Images and Regional Realities,* edited by Lothar Hönnighausen, 249–69. Tübingen, Germany: Stauffenburg Verlag, 2000. Web. maps-legacy.org.

———. "Self-Imposed Fetters in Four Golden Age Villanelles." *Connotations* 28 (November 2019): 163–91.

Kennedy, X. J. "Joys, Griefs and 'All Things Innocent, Hapless, Forsaken.'" Review of, *inter alia, The Far Field,* by Theodore Roethke. *The New York Times,* 23 August 1964, BR5.

Kinnell, Galway. "To the Roots: An Interview with Galway Kinnell." Interview by James J. McKenzie. *Salmagundi* 22/23 (Spring–Summer 1973): 206–21.

Kirsch, Adam. "Primal Fear: Roethke, Wright, and the Cult of Authenticity." *The New Yorker* August 8–15, 2005, 89–92.

Knoeller, Christian. *Reimagining Environmental History: Ecological Memory in the Wake of Landscape Change*. Reno: University of Nevada Press, 2017.

Kostelanetz, Richard. "How to Be a Difficult Poet." *The New York Times,* 23 May 1976, SM5.

Kunitz, Stanley. "On Theodore Roethke's 'In a Dark Time.'" In Ostroff, *Contemporary Poet,* 41–48.

Kusch, Robert. *"My Toughest Mentor": Theodore Roethke and William Carlos Williams (1940–1948).* Cranbury, NJ: Associated University Presses, 1999.

La Belle, Jenijoy. *The Echoing Wood of Theodore Roethke.* Princeton: Princeton University Press, 1976.

———. "Theodore Roethke's 'The Lost Son': From Archetypes to Literary History." *Modern Language Quarterly* 37, no. 2 (June 1976): 179–95.

Lane, Gary. *A Concordance to the Poems of Theodore Roethke.* Metuchen, NJ: Scarecrow Press, 1972.

Lear, Edward. *Edward Lear: The Complete Verse and Other Nonsense.* Edited by Vivien Noakes. New York: Penguin Books, 2002.

Lecourt, Jean-Philippe. "Theodore Roethke: The Inner Wilderness and the Barrier of Ideology." In *Myth and Ideology in American Literature,* edited by Régis Durand, 43–62. Lille, France: Centre d'Etudes et de Recherches Nord-Américaines et Canadiennes, Université de Lille, 1976.

Lee, Charlotte I. "Roethke Writes about Women." *Literature and Performance* 1, no. 1 (November 1980): 23–32.

Lenz, Frederick Phillip. "The Evolution of Matter and Spirit in the Poetry of Theodore Roethke." Ph.D. diss., State University of New York at Stony Brook, 1978.

Lincoln, Kenneth. *Sing with the Heart of a Bear: Fusions of Native and American Poetry, 1890–1999.* Berkeley: University of California Press, 2000.

Lowell, Robert. *The Letters of Robert Lowell.* Edited by Saskia Hamilton. New York: Farrar, Straus and Giroux, 2005.

Lowenthal, David. *George Perkins Marsh: Prophet of Conservation.* Seattle: University of Washington Press, 2000.

Lussier, Mark S. "Blake's Deep Ecology." *Studies in Romanticism* 35, no. 3 (Fall 1996): 393–408.

Maguire, Sarah, ed. *Flora Poetica: The Chatto Book of Botanical Verse.* London: Chatto and Windus, 2001.

Maki, Jacqueline R. "The Dance: Roethke's Legacy from Yeats." *Kentucky Philological Association Bulletin* (1981): 1–23.

Malkoff, Karl. *Theodore Roethke: An Introduction to the Poetry.* New York: Columbia University Press, 1966.

Mariani, Paul. *William Carlos Williams: A New World Naked.* New York: McGraw-Hill, 1981.

Marsden, Jean I., ed. *The Appropriation of Shakespeare: Post-Renaissance Reconstructions of the Works and the Myth.* London: Harvester Wheatsheaf, 1991.

Martz, Louis L. "A Greenhouse Eden." In Stein, *Theodore Roethke,* 14–35.

———. *The Poetry of Meditation: A Study in English Religious Literature of the Seventeenth Century.* New Haven, CT: Yale University Press, 1962.

McGowan, Kat. "How Plants Secretly Talk to Each Other." *Wired,* 20 December 2013. Web, 13 September 2014.

McKusick, James C. *Green Writing: Romanticism and Ecology*. New York: St. Martin's Press, 2000.

McMichael, James. "The Poetry of Theodore Roethke." In *Profile of Theodore Roethke,* edited by William Heyen, 78–95. Columbus, OH: Merrill, 1971.

Melson, Gail F. *Why the Wild Things Are: Animals in the Lives of Children*. Cambridge, MA: Harvard University Press, 2001.

Mill, John Stuart. "Thoughts on Poetry and Its Varieties." *The Crayon* 7, no. 4 (April 1860): 93–97.

Mills, James Cooke. *History of Saginaw County, Michigan: Historical, Commercial, Biographical.* Vol. 2. Saginaw, MI: Seemann and Peters, 1918.

Mills, Ralph J., Jr. Introduction to Roethke, *Selected Letters,* xi–xx.

———. "Roethke's Garden." Review of *I Am! Says the Lamb,* by Theodore Roethke. *Poetry* 100, no. 1 (April 1962): 54–59.

———. "Roethke's Last Poems." Review of *The Far Field,* by Theodore Roethke. *Poetry* 105, no. 2 (November 1964): 122–24.

———. *Theodore Roethke*. Minneapolis: University of Minnesota Press, 1963.

Milton, John. *The Complete Poetry of John Milton*. Edited by John T. Shawcross. New York: Anchor Books, 1971.

Mitchell, Stephen, ed. *The Enlightened Heart: An Anthology of Sacred Poetry.* New York: Harper and Row, 1989.

———. *Tao Te Ching.* New York: Harper and Row, 1988.

Moe, Aaron. *Zoopoetics: Animals and the Making of Poetry*. Lanham, MD: Lexington Books, 2014.

Morrison, Toni. *Playing in the Dark: Whiteness and the Literary Imagination*. Cambridge, MA: Harvard University Press, 1992.

Muir, John. *My First Summer in the Sierra*. Boston: Houghton Mifflin, 1911.

Mulvey, Laura. *Fetishism and Curiosity*. Bloomington: Indiana University Press, 1996.

Myers, Jack, and Michael Simms. *The Longman Dictionary of Poetic Terms.* New York: Longman, 1989.

Nel, Philip. *Dr. Seuss: American Icon*. New York: Continuum Books, 2003.

Nelson, Cary. "The Field Where Water Flowers: An Essay on Theodore Roethke's 'North American Sequence.'" In *Our Last First Poets: Vision and History in Contemporary American Poetry,* 31–61. Urbana: University of Illinois Press, 1981.

Northcott, Michael. "The Desire for Speed and the Rhythm of the Earth." In *The Ethics of Mobilities: Rethinking Place, Exclusion, Freedom and Environment,* edited by Sigurd Bergman and Tore Sager, 215–32. Aldershot, UK: Ashgate, 2008.

O'Keefe, Richard R. *Mythic Archetypes in Ralph Waldo Emerson: A Blakean Reading.* Kent, OH: Kent State University Press, 1995.

Onion, Rebecca. "Theodore Roethke." In *Modern American Environmentalists: A Biographical Encyclopedia,* edited by George A. Cevasco and Richard P. Harmon, 421–26. Baltimore: Johns Hopkins University Press, 2009.

Opie, Peter, and Iona Opie, eds. *The Classic Fairy Tales*. London: Oxford University Press, 1974.

"Orchid Flower Meaning & Symbolism." Teleflora. Web, 11 May 2015.

"Orchid Poems." PoetrySoup. Web, 11 May 2015.

Ostroff, Anthony, ed. *The Contemporary Poet as Artist and Critic: Eight Symposia*. Boston: Little, Brown, 1964.

O'Sullivan, Michael. "'Bare Life' and the Garden Politics of Roethke and Heaney." *Mosaic: A Journal for the Interdisciplinary Study of Literature* 38, no. 4 (2005): 17–34.

Padma, P. Hannah. *The Poetry of Theodore Roethke: Poetics of Response.* Delhi, India: Prestig, 1996.

Paglia, Camille. *Break, Blow, Burn: Camille Paglia Reads Forty-three of the World's Best Poems.* New York: Vintage, 2006.

———. "Dance of the Senses: Natural Vision and Psychotic Mysticism in Theodore Roethke's Poetry." In *Provocations: Collected Essays on Art, Feminism, Politics, Sex, and Education,* 240–54. New York: Pantheon, 2018.

Parini, Jay. *Theodore Roethke: An American Romantic.* Amherst: University of Massachusetts Press, 1979.

Pas, Julian F. *The A to Z of Taoism.* Lanham, MD: Scarecrow Press, 1998.

Pearce, Roy Harvey. "Theodore Roethke: The Power of Sympathy." In Stein, *Theodore Roethke,* 167–99.

Pence, Janet. Letter to Carrie Duke, 28 August 2014.

Prunty, Wyatt. *"Fallen from the Symboled World": Precedents for the New Formalism.* New York: Oxford University Press, 1990.

Quetchenbach, Bernard W. *Back from the Far Field: American Nature Poetry in the Late Twentieth Century.* Charlottesville: University Press of Virginia, 2000.

Ramsey, Jarold. "Roethke in the Greenhouse." *Western Humanities Review* 26, no. 1 (Winter 1972): 35–47.

Ransford, Annie. "Re: Question about Otto." Email message to Jeff Vande Zande, 3 May 2014.

Remarkable People: Theodore Roethke. Directed by Jean Walkinshaw. Seattle Channel. Web, 4 June 2014.

Rodgers, Audrey T. *The Universal Drum: Dance Imagery in the Poetry of Eliot, Crane, Roethke.* University Park: Pennsylvania State University Press, 1979.

Roethke, Theodore. *The Collected Poems of Theodore Roethke.* Garden City, NY: Anchor Books, 1975.

———. *The Far Field.* Garden City, NY: Doubleday, 1964.

———. "Journey to the Interior." *The New Yorker,* 7 January 1961, 27.

———. "The Longing." *Saturday Review,* 24 June 1961, 46.

———. "Meditation at Oyster River." *The London Magazine* 1, no. 2 (May 1961): 34–36.

———. "Meditation at Oyster River." *The New Yorker,* 19 November 1960, 54.

———. "Meditations of a Sensitive Man." Review of *A Lost Season,* by Roy Fuller. *Poetry* 67, no. 4 (January 1946): 218–21.

———. Notebooks in the Theodore Roethke Papers. Special Collections, University of Washington Libraries.

———. "On 'In a Dark Time.'" In Ostroff, *Contemporary Poet,* 49–53.

———. *On Poetry and Craft: Selected Prose of Theodore Roethke.* Port Townsend, WA: Copper Canyon Press, 2001.

———. "Once More, the Round." *Encounter* 18, no. 5 (May 1962): 45.

———. "Once More, the Round." *Harper's Bazaar,* January 1963, 117.

———. *Selected Letters of Theodore Roethke.* Edited by Ralph J. Mills Jr. Seattle: University of Washington Press, 1968.

———. *Straw for the Fire: From the Notebooks of Theodore Roethke, 1943–63.* 1972. Edited by David Wagoner. Port Townsend, WA: Copper Canyon Press, 2006.

———. *Selected Poems.* Edited by Edward Hirsch. New York: Library of America, 2005.

Rohrkemper, John. "'When the Mind Remembers All': Dream and Memory in Theodore Roethke's North American Sequence." *The Journal of the Midwest Modern Language Association* 21, no. 1 (Spring 1988): 28–37.

Rosenmeyer, Thomas G. *The Green Cabinet: Theocritus and the European Pastoral Lyric.* Berkeley: University of California Press, 1969.

Ross-Bryant, Lynn. *Theodore Roethke: Poetry of the Earth . . . Poet of the Spirit . . .* Port Washington, NY: Kennikat Press, 1981.

Rowe, Karen E. "To Spin a Yarn: The Female Voice in Folklore and Fairy Tale." In Bottigheimer, *Fairy Tales and Society,* 53–74.

Rowland, Beryl. *Birds with Human Souls: A Guide to Bird Symbolism.* Knoxville: University of Tennessee Press, 1978.

Rueckert, William. "Literature and Ecology: An Experiment in Ecocriticism." 1978. In Glotfelty and Fromm, *Ecocriticism Reader,* 105–23.

Schwartz, Delmore. "The Cunning and the Craft of the Unconscious and the Preconscious: *Words for the Wind* by Theodore Roethke." *Poetry* 94, no. 3 (June 1959): 203–5.

Schweitzer, Albert. *Out of My Life and Thought.* 1933. Translated by Antje Bultmann Lemke. New York: Henry Holt, 1990.

Scoble, Gretchen, and Anne Field. *The Meaning of Flowers: Myth, Language and Lore.* San Francisco: Chronicle Books, 1998.

Seager, Allan. *The Glass House: The Life of Theodore Roethke.* 1968. Ann Arbor: University of Michigan Press, 1991.

Seager, Allan, Stanley Kunitz, and John Ciardi. "An Evening with Ted Roethke." *Michigan Quarterly Review* 6, no. 4 (Fall 1967): 227–45.

Shakespeare, William. *As You Like It.* Edited by Leah S. Marcus. New York: W. W. Norton, 2012.

———. *Romeo and Juliet.* Updated ed. Edited by G. Blakemore Evans. Cambridge: Cambridge University Press, 2003.

———. Sonnet 146. In *Shakespeare's Sonnets,* 301. New York: Washington Square Press, 2011.

Sharpe, Peter. *The Ground of Our Beseeching: Metaphor and the Poetics of Meditation.* Selingsgrove, PA: Susquehanna University Press, 2004.

Shelley, Percy Bysshe. *Prometheus Unbound.* 1820. In *Poetical Works,* edited by Thomas Hutchinson, 204–70. New ed., corrected by G. M. Matthews. Oxford: Oxford University Press, 1970.

Shepard, Glenn H. "Specters of a Civilization." Review of *The Lost Tribes of Tierra del Fuego,* by Martin Gusinde, edited by Christine Barthe and Xavier Barral. *The New York Review of Books Daily,* 8 August 2015. Web.

Shklovsky, Victor. "Art as Technique." 1917. In *Russian Formalist Criticism: Four Essays,* translated and edited by Lee T. Lemon and Marion J. Reis, 5–24. Lincoln: University of Nebraska Press, 1965.

Silverstein, Shel. *Where the Sidewalk Ends*. New York: HarperCollins, 1974.

Simpson, Louis. "Walt Whitman at Bear Mountain." In *At the End of the Open Road,* 64–65. Middletown, CT: Wesleyan University Press, 1963.

Singh, Mina Surjit. *Theodore Roethke: A Body with the Motion of a Soul.* Delhi, India: Sterling, 1991.

Skelton, Robin. "A Note on the Texts Used." In *Poetry of the Thirties,* edited by Robin Skelton, 39–41. London: Penguin Books, 1964.

Skrbina, David. *Panpsychism in the West.* Cambridge, MA: MIT Press, 2005.

Smart, Christopher. *Selected Poems.* Edited by Marcus Walsh. Manchester, UK: Carcanet, 1979.

Snyder, Gary. *Turtle Island.* New York: New Directions, 1974.

Snodgrass, W. D. "The Last Poems of Theodore Roethke." Review of *The Far Field* and *Sequence, Sometimes Metaphysical,* by Theodore Roethke. *The New York Review of Books,* 8 October 1964, 5–6.

Sorby, Angela. "Disciplined Play: American Children's Poetry to 1920." In *The Cambridge History of American Poetry,* edited by Alfred Bendixen and Stephen Burt, 425–44. New York: Cambridge University Press, 2014.

Soron, Dennis. "Driven to Drive: Cars and the Problem of 'Compulsory Consumption.'" In *Car Troubles: Critical Studies of Automobility and Auto-Mobility,* edited by Jim Conley and Arlene Tigar McLaren, 181–96. London: Routledge, 2009.

Spender, Stephen. "The Objective Ego." In Stein, *Theodore Roethke,* 3–13.

Staples, Hugh B. "The Rose in the Sea-Wind: A Reading of Theodore Roethke's 'North American Sequence.'" *American Literature* 36, no. 2 (May 1964): 189–203.

Stein, Arnold, ed. *Theodore Roethke: Essays on the Poetry.* Seattle: University of Washington Press, 1965.

Stevens, Anthony. *Archetype: An Updated Natural History of the Self.* London: Brunner-Routledge, 2002.

Stevens, Wallace. *The Collected Poems.* New York: Vintage Books, 1982.

Stiffler, Randall. *Theodore Roethke: The Poet and His Critics.* Chicago: American Library Association, 1986.

Stone, Kay F. "Feminist Approaches to Interpretation." In Bottigheimer, *Fairy Tales and Society,* 229–36.

Strassfeld, Michael. *The Jewish Holidays: A Guide and Commentary.* New York: Harper and Row, 1985.

Styles, Morag, Louise Joy, and David Whitley, eds. *Poetry and Childhood.* Stoke on Trent, UK: Trentham Books, 2010.

Sullivan, Rosemary. *Theodore Roethke: The Garden Master.* Seattle: University of Washington Press, 1975.

Theodore Roethke Museum. Friends of Theodore Roethke, n.d. Web, 5 May 2014.

Thomas, Dylan. *Collected Poems.* Augmented ed. New York: New Directions, 1957.

Thomas, Joseph. "Child Poets and the Poetry of the Playground." *Children's Literature* 32 (2004): 152–77.

Tillich, Paul. *Systematic Theology*. Vol. 1. Chicago: University of Chicago Press, 1951.
Travisano, Thomas. *Midcentury Quartet: Bishop, Lowell, Jarrell, Berryman, and the Making of a Postmodern Aesthetic*. Charlottesville: University Press of Virginia, 1999.
Trombley, Tom. "Re: Greenhouse Demolition." Email message to Jeff Vande Zande, 5 May 2014.
Underhill, Evelyn. *Mysticism: A Study in the Nature and Development of Man's Spiritual Consciousness*. 1911. 12th ed. New York: E. P. Dutton, 1930.
Udvardy, Miklos D. F. *The Audubon Society Field Guide to North American Birds: Western Region*. New York: Alfred A. Knopf, 1977.
Vaillant, George C. *Aztecs of Mexico: Origin, Rise, and Fall of the Aztec Nation*. 1941. New York: Penguin Books, 1978.
Wagoner, David. "In a Class with Poets: An Interview with Poet David Wagoner about His Teacher Theodore Roethke." Interview with Michael Kleven. *Cirque: A Literary Journal for the North Pacific Rim* 2, no. 2 (Summer Solstice 2011): 91–96.
Wauhkonen, Rhonda L. "Balm of Gilead." In *A Dictionary of Biblical Tradition in English Literature,* gen. ed. Lyle Jeffrey, 71–73. Grand Rapids: William B. Eerdmans, 1992.
Werness, Hope B. *The Continuum Encyclopedia of Animal Symbolism in World Art.* New York: Continuum, 2006.
White, Lynn, Jr. "The Historical Roots of Our Ecologic Crisis." 1967. In Glotfelty and Fromm, *Ecocriticism Reader,* 3–14.
Whitman, Walt. *Poetry and Prose.* New York: Library of America, 1982.
Wilbur, Richard. *Collected Poems, 1943–2004.* Orlando: Harcourt, 2004.
Williams, Harry. *"The Edge Is What I Have": Theodore Roethke and After*. Lewisburg, PA: Bucknell University Press; London: Associated University Presses, 1977.
Williams, William Carlos. *The Collected Poems of William Carlos Williams*. Edited by A. Walton Litz and Christopher MacGowan. 2 vols. New York: New Directions, 1988.
———. *In the American Grain.* 1925. New York: New Directions, 1956.
Wilson, Edward O. *Biophilia.* Cambridge, MA: Harvard University Press, 1984.
Wolff, George. "Syntactical and Imagistic Distortion in Roethke's Greenhouse Poems." *Language and Style* 6 (1973): 281–88.
———. *Theodore Roethke.* Boston: Twayne, 1981.
Wordsworth, William. "I Wandered Lonely as a Cloud." 1807. In *Selected Poems,* edited by John O. Hayden, 207. London: Penguin Books, 1994.
———. "Preface." 1800. In *Lyrical Ballads 1789 and 1800,* by Samuel Taylor Coleridge and William Wordsworth, edited by Michael Gamer and Dahlia Porter, 171–87. Toronto: Broadview, 2008.
Wright, James. Letter to Dr. Arnold Stein, 8 April 1964. In *A Wild Perfection: The Selected Letters of James Wright,* edited by Anne Wright and Saundra Rose Maley, 296–97. Middletown, CT: Wesleyan University Press, 2005.
Yeats, W. B. *The Collected Works of W. B. Yeats.* Vol. 1, *The Poems.* 2nd ed. Edited by Richard J. Finneran. New York: Scribner, 1997.
Young, David. "Theodore Roethke: A *Field* Symposium." *Field* 53 (Fall 1995): 7–9.

ABOUT THE EDITOR

WILLIAM BARILLAS is the author of *The Midwestern Pastoral: Place and Landscape in Literature of the American Heartland* (2006), which includes a chapter on Roethke, and a recipient of the MidAmerica Award for Distinguished Contributions to the Study of Midwestern Literature.

CONTRIBUTORS

BORJA AGUILÓ OBRADOR teaches at Arxiduc Lluis Salvador High School in Palma de Mallorca, Spain. In 2014, he earned his PhD at the University of Salamanca with a dissertation on Roethke. His essay "Imagery and Vision in Theodore Roethke's 'Greenhouse Poems'" appeared in *Current Trends in Anglophone Studies: Cultural, Linguistic and Literary Research* (2011), edited by Javier Ruano García et al. He also coedited and translated into Spanish a selection of First World War poets, *Tengo una cita con la muerte* (2011), and translated Mark Twain's *A Family Sketch*, published as *Un bosquejo de familia* (2018).

PETER BALAKIAN is the author of *Ozone Journal*, winner of the 2016 Pulitzer Prize for poetry. His other books include *June-tree: New and Selected Poems* (2001); *Black Dog of Fate: A Memoir* (1997); *The Burning Tigris: The Armenian Genocide and America's Response* (2003); and *Theodore Roethke's Far Fields: The Evolution of His Poetry* (1989). "Theodore Roethke's Lost Son and the Confessional Era" appears in his book of essays *Vise and Shadow* (2015). He is the Donald M. and Constance H. Rebar Professor of the Humanities in the Department of English and director of creative writing at Colgate University.

DON BOGEN has published five books of poetry, most recently *Immediate Song* (2019), as well as the critical study *A Necessary Order: Theodore Roethke and the Writing Process* (1991). He is Nathaniel Ropes Professor of English and Comparative Literature Emeritus at the University of Cincinnati and editor-at-large of *The Cincinnati Review*.

NEAL BOWERS is the author of several books of poetry, including *Out of the South* (2002), as well as novels, memoirs, and *Theodore Roethke: The Journey from I to Otherwise* (1982). He retired from Iowa State University in 2008 with the rank of Distinguished Professor.

NICHOLAS BRADLEY is an associate professor in the Department of English at the University of Victoria. His research focuses on Canadian literature and American literature, and he is the author of a book of poetry, *Rain Shadow* (2018). He has contributed two essays on Roethke to *Notes and Queries*.

LUKE BREKKE has published poems in various journals including *The Missouri Review*, *Denver Quarterly*, and *New England Review*, where he also served as a member of the editorial panel. He holds an MFA from Warren Wilson College. He is Director of Operations for Wonderstate Coffee in Viroqua, Wisconsin.

RUSSELL BRICKEY has poetry collections from Spuyten Duyvil Press, Wild Leaf Press, and Kelsay Books, and he is the lead editor of a composition text from McFarland. His reader's guide *Understanding Sharon Olds* was published in 2016. Currently a full-time lecturer in English at Youngstown State University, he holds a BA from the University of Oregon, and an MFA and PhD from Purdue University.

KATHARINE BUBEL is Assistant Professor in the Department of English and Creative Writing at Trinity Western University. Her research has focused on representations of sacred nature in the work of five poets of the North American west coast: Robinson Jeffers, Theodore Roethke, Robert Hass, Denise Levertov, and Jan Zwicky. She especially attends to the relations between place, spiritual practices, and aesthetics of relinquishment and affirmation.

NORMAN CHANEY (1935–2020) was Professor of English at Otterbein University for over fifty years and the author of *Theodore Roethke: The Poetics of Wonder* (1981). His research interests included nature writing, environmental studies, literature and religion, and Shakespeare.

JEFFREY CLAPP is Associate Professor, and Head, of the Department of Literature and Cultural Studies at the Education University of Hong Kong. He writes about American literature, particularly poetry. His work has appeared in such publications as *Texas Studies in Literature and Language* and *College Literature*, and he is the coeditor of the volume *Security and Hospitality in Literature and Culture* (2016). He is the director of the large-scale community reading project 我城我書 / One City One Book Hong Kong.

LYN COFFIN has had over thirty of her books published by Doubleday, Ithaca House, and other presses. Her novella *Tinder* was published by Serotonin Press, and her novel *The Aftermath* by Adelaide Books, both in 2020.

KRISTIN M. DISTEL is a doctoral candidate of English literature at Ohio University, where she is researching eighteenth-century gender, shame, and the rise of the novel. She has published articles and chapters on such authors as Toni Morrison and Kate Chopin, and coedited a reissue of Sherwood Anderson's *The Triumph of the Egg*. She is editor-in-chief of *Parlour: A Journal of Literary Criticism and Analysis* and holds editorial positions at other academic periodicals.

CARRIE DUKE is an assistant professor of English at Indiana Institute of Technology. Her scholarship focuses on how literary representations of gardens remind readers of the healing aspects of nature and plants. Her essay "Recovering John Muir's Wild Gardens" appeared in *Writing the Environment in Nineteenth-Century American Literature* (2015), edited by Steven Petersheim and Madison Jones IV.

LAURA DUNCAN is a PhD candidate in English Literature at Louisiana State University writing a dissertation on the portrayal of immigration in twenty-first-century magical realist literature. She coauthored an essay with Marcia Noe on dark fairy tale elements in the fiction of Bonnie Jo Campbell, published in *Midwestern Miscellany* 42. Her research interests include global Anglophone literature, works in translation, and global mythologies, folktales, fairy tales, and legends.

LAURA GILL received her MA in English at Mainz University, Germany. She is a foreign language coordinator at Darmstadt University of Applied Sciences, Germany.

PATRICK GILL is a senior lecturer in English Literature at Mainz University, with research interests in poetry and poetics, and contemporary fiction. His monograph *Origins and Effects of Poetic Ambiguity* was published in 2014, and he is the coeditor of *Constructing Coherence in the British Short Story Cycle* (2018).

CHRISTOPHER GIROUX is an associate professor of English at Saginaw Valley State University and codirector of the university's Center for Community Writing. His 2013 dissertation at Wayne State University focuses on twentieth-century African American playwrights, exploring the relationship between trauma and drama. "Once More, the Despair: Revisiting Roethke's 'Once More, The Round'" appeared in the January/March 2016 issue of *The Explicator*. A poet and a resident of Saginaw, he draws inspiration from Roethke, his writings, and his haunts.

WILLIAM HEYEN has won Guggenheim, NEA, American Academy of Arts and Letters, and other awards for his many books, which include *Shoah Train* (Finalist for the 2004 National Book Award), three 2012 collections: *The Football Corporations*, *Straight's Suite for Craig Cotter & Frank O'Hara*, and *Hiroshima Suite*; *The Candle: Poems of Our 20th Century Holocausts* (2016); and *Yawp: Heyen's Whitman* (2019). His 1967 dissertation was one of the first on Roethke, and he edited *A Profile of Theodore Roethke* (1971).

TRENTON HICKMAN is Associate Professor of English at Brigham Young University, where he specializes in twentieth-century American literature and Latinx literature. His essay "Theodore Roethke and the Poetics of Place" appears in *Reading the Middle Generation Anew: Culture, Community, and Form in Twentieth-Century American Poetry* (2006), edited by Eric Haralson.

MICHAEL HINDS is Associate Professor in the School of English at Dublin City University. His publications include *Johnny Cash International: How and Why the World Loves the Man in Black* (with Jonathan Silverman, 2020), *Rebound: The American Poetry Book* (edited with Stephen Matterson, 2006), and the Roethke entry in *Encyclopedia of American Poetry: The Twentieth Century* (2001), edited by Eric Haralson.

EDWARD HIRSCH is the author of ten books of poetry, most recently *Stranger by Night* (2020), and five books of prose, including *How to Read a Poem and Fall in Love with Poetry* (1999). He has also edited many books and written articles for *American Poetry Review*, *The New York Times Book Review*, *The Washington*

Post Book World, and other publications. His many honors include the National Book Critics Circle Award, the American Academy of Arts and Letters Award for Literature, and a MacArthur Foundation "Genius Grant." President of the John Simon Guggenheim Memorial Foundation and a former Chancellor of the Academy of American Poets, he edited and wrote the introduction for Theodore Roethke's *Selected Poems* (2005).

BROOKE HORVATH is Professor Emeritus at Kent State University. The author of four books of poetry, most recently *At Times: New and Selected Poems* (2020), his poems and essays on poetry have appeared in *American Literature, American Poetry Review, Poetry, Sewanee Review*, and elsewhere. His scholarship includes *Understanding Nelson Algren* (2005) and, as coeditor with Dan Simon, *"Entrapment" and Other Writings* (2009), a selection of Algren's previously unpublished and uncollected work.

MARCEL INHOFF is completing a doctoral dissertation on midcentury American poetry, autobiography, and religion at Bonn University (Germany). He has written and published essays on Derek Walcott, Theodore Roethke, Tracy K. Smith, Robert Lowell, Hunter S. Thompson, and Elizabeth Bishop. His publications also include a volume of poetry (*Prosopopeia*, 2015) and a chapbook (*Our Church is Here*, 2018), as well as individually published poems in both English and German.

WALTER KALAIDJIAN is Professor of English and former Department Chair at Emory University and the author of four books on twentieth-century American literature, including *Understanding Theodore Roethke* (1987). His research and teaching focus on transnational modern and contemporary literature and culture, with special concern for poetics, critical theory, and psychoanalysis.

FRANK J. KEARFUL is Professor Emeritus of English at the University of Bonn. His diverse publications on modern American poetry include the profile of Roethke in *The American Midwest: An Interpretive Encyclopedia* (2006), edited by Richard Sisson, Christian Zachler, and Andrew Clayton, "Regions of the Self: Theodore Roethke's 'North American Sequence'" in *Regional Images and Regional Realities* (2000), edited by Lothar Hönnighausen, and "Self-Imposed Fetters in Four Golden Age Villanelles" in *Connotations* 28 (2019), which relates Roethke's "The Waking" to other twentieth-century villanelles.

ANDREW DAVID KING holds an MFA from the Iowa Writers' Workshop, where he was a Teaching-Writing Fellow, and a Graduate Certificate from the University of Iowa Center for the Book. He is currently Provost's Postgraduate Visiting Writer and Visiting Assistant Professor in the Department of English at the University of Iowa and Research Assistant for the Walt Whitman Archive. The author of several articles on creative writing pedagogy and the artist's chapbook *Fire Sonnets* (2018), he has published poems and prose in *ZYZZYVA*, *Poetry*, *The Kenyon Review*, *Crab Orchard Review*, and other journals.

MARC MALANDRA is Professor of English at Biola University, where his specializations include nineteenth and twentieth-century American literature, especially poetry. In addition to scholarly articles, he has published poems in journals such as *Puerto del Sol* and *Poetry Northwest*.

JOHN J. MCKENNA is Professor Emeritus of English at the University of Nebraska Omaha. In addition to scholarly articles on American and British literature, he has published poetry in journals and in his book *Wind and Water* (2010). His essay "Roethke's Revisions and the Tone of 'My Papa's Waltz'" appeared in *ANQ: A Quarterly Journal of Short Articles, Notes, and Reviews* in 1998.

AARON M. MOE has published several articles on animals, ecology, and poetry. His book *Zoopoetics: Animals and the Making of Poetry* appeared in 2014, followed by *Ecocriticism and the Poiesis of Form: Holding on to Proteus*, which appeared in 2019. He is an independent scholar living in Colorado with his family.

SARAH KATHRYN MOORE has received both an MFA in Poetry and a PhD in English Literature from the University of Washington. Her poems have been published, most recently, in *Poetry Northwest*, *Cutbank*, and *Pacifica Literary Review*.

EDWARD MORIN is author of four poetry collections including *Labor Day at Walden Pond* (1997) and *The Bold News of Birdcalls* (forthcoming). His cotranslations of Chinese and Arabic poems have appeared in *Prairie Schooner*, *Banipal*, and his anthology *The Red Azalea: Chinese Poetry Since the Cultural Revolution* (1990). As editor of the Poetry Society of Michigan's journal, *Peninsula Poets*, he coedited *Water Music: The Great Lakes State Poetry Anthology* (2016).

MARCIA NOE is Professor of English and Director of Women's Studies at the University of Tennessee at Chattanooga. Editor of the journal *MidAmerica* and 2003 recipient of the MidAmerica Award for Distinguished Contributions to the Study of Midwestern Literature, she is the author of *Susan Glaspell: Voice from the Heartland* (1993) and many scholarly articles.

CAMILLE PAGLIA is the author of *Sexual Personae: Art and Decadence from Nefertiti to Emily Dickinson* (1990) and other books on art, literature, and popular culture. *Break, Blow, Burn: Camille Paglia Reads Forty-three of the World's Best Poems* (2005) includes explications of three poems by Roethke. Her keynote lecture at a Roethke centennial event held at the University of Michigan in 2008 was published as "Dance of the Senses: Natural Vision and Psychotic Mysticism in Theodore Roethke's Poetry" in the Winter 2009 issue of *Michigan Quarterly Review*. She is University Professor of Humanities and Media Studies at the University of the Arts in Philadelphia.

JAY PARINI is a poet, novelist, biographer, and critic whose books include *Theodore Roethke: An American Romantic* (1979), *The Last Station* (1990), *Robert Frost: A Life* (2000), *New and Collected Poems: 1975–2015* (2016), and *Borges and Me: An Encounter* (2020). A frequent contributor to such publications as *The New York Times* and websites like Salon.com, he is Axinn Professor of English at Middlebury College.

ROD PHILLIPS is Professor Emeritus of Humanities, Culture & Writing at Michigan State University's James Madison College. His books include *"Forest Beatniks" and "Urban Thoreaus": Jack Kerouac, Gary Snyder, Lew Welch, and Michael McClure* (2001). His poetry has appeared in many journals and in his chapbooks *Bullheading on the Looking Glass* (2002) and *The Ledge* (2009). "Five Poems for Theodore Roethke" appeared in *Midwestern Miscellany* 36 (Spring/Fall 2008).

RONALD PRIMEAU is Professor Emeritus of English at Central Michigan University. As author, his books include *Romance of the Road: The Literature of the American Highway* (1996) and *Herbert Woodward Martin and the African American Tradition in Poetry* (2004); he is the editor of *American Road Literature* (2013), *Midwestern Literature* (2013), and other scholarly volumes.

ADAM PUTZ is the author of *The Celtic Revival in Shakespeare's Wake: Appropriation and Cultural Politics in Ireland, 1867–1922* (2013). He is currently an analyst with private markets data provider PitchBook, where his research centers on investment trends in venture capital and private equity as well as emerging technology.

BERNARD QUETCHENBACH is the author of *Back from the Far Field: American Nature Poetry in the Late Twentieth Century* (2000). His recent publications include *Accidental Gravity* (2017), an essay collection, and *The Hermit's Place* (2010), a volume of poems. He edited *The Bunch Grass Motel* (2017), a posthumous collected poems of Randall Gloege, who studied with Theodore Roethke at the University of Washington, and coedited *Poetics for the More-than-Human World: An Anthology of Poetry and Commentary* (2020). He is a professor of English at Montana State University Billings.

DAVID RADAVICH is a poet and playwright, as well as a scholar specializing in drama and Midwestern literature. He has published two epics, *America Bound* (2007) and *America Abroad* (2019), along with six lyric collections. He is Professor Emeritus of English at Eastern Illinois University.

JOHN ROHRKEMPER is the author of *John Dos Passos: A Reference Guide* (1980), many scholarly articles about American and modern literature, including "'When the Mind Remembers All': Dream and Memory in Theodore Roethke's 'North American Sequence'" in the *Journal of the Midwest Modern Language Association* 21.1 (Spring 1988), and more than thirty works for the theater. He teaches at Elizabethtown College where he is Director of the Program in Creative Writing.

BRANDON RUSHTON has had poems appear in *The Southern Review, Denver Quarterly, Pleiades, Bennington Review, Passages North,* and *World Literature Today*. In 2016, he was awarded prizes from *Gulf Coast* and *Ninth Letter*. After earning his MFA from the University of South Carolina, he joined the writing faculty at the College of Charleston. He is currently a Visiting Assistant Professor at Grand Valley State University.

JOSEPH T. THOMAS JR. is Professor of English and Comparative Literature at San Diego State University and Director of the National Center for the Study of Children's Literature. He is also author of *Poetry's Playground: The Culture of Contemporary American Children's Poetry* (2007) and *Strong Measures* (2007), and he coedited *Prizing Children's Literature: The Cultural Politics of Children's Book Awards* (2016).

JEFF VANDE ZANDE teaches screenwriting, fiction writing, and literature at Delta College in Saginaw, Michigan. His novel *American Poet* (2012) won the Stuart and Vernice Gross Award for Excellence in Writing by a Michigan Author and a Michigan Notable Book Award from the Library of Michigan. He published the collection *The Neighborhood Division and Other Stories* in 2020, and his essay "The Soul of Time: Theodore Roethke's Boyhood Home" appeared in the Spring/Summer 2013 issue of *Great River Review*.

DAVID WOJAHN is the author most recently of *From the Valley of Making: Essays on Contemporary Poetry* (2015) and *For the Scribe* (2017), a collection of poetry. His essay "'All the Blessings of This Consuming Chance': Robert Lowell, John Berryman, Theodore Roethke, and the Middle-Generation Poets" appeared in *The Cambridge History of American Poetry* (2015), edited by Alfred Bendixen and Stephen Burt. He teaches at Virginia Commonwealth University and in the MFA in Writing Program of Vermont College of Fine Arts.

Index